# Catherine and Tilly

# Porchey Carnarvon's Two Duped Wives

*The Tragic Tales of the Sixth Countesses of Carnarvon*

# The Prologue
## I
## Porchey Carnarvon

## 'Hunting, Shooting and Flirting'

*Henry George Alfred Marius Victor Herbert*

Names are deceptive. Take the Sixth Earl of Carnarvon: his full baptismal names were *Henry George Alfred Marius Victor Francis Herbert* but he was better known as just 'Porchey' Carnarvon. The name Porchey was a nickname derived from his courtesy title of 'Lord Porchester'.[1]

Informally, family and friends addressed Henry as Porchey *before and after* 1923. This was the year when on 5th April ( at the age of twenty-four) he became the Sixth Earl of Carnarvon, succeeding his infamous predecessor George (the Fifth Earl) who was the Lord Carnarvon who discovered the priceless Tomb of Tutankhamun in Egypt's Valley of the Kings.

The Fifth Earl had used the same nickname of Porchey before he succeeded his father, Henry, the Fourth Earl.[2]   No doubt it continues for the Carnarvon heir-in-waiting who is currently the eldest son of George, ( Geordie ) the present Eighth Earl of Carnarvon.

The Carnarvons are a cadet branch of the Herbert family which is headed by the Earls of Pembroke and Montgomery and whose seat is at Wilton House, Salisbury, Wiltshire.   The Carnarvon earldom was created in 1793, and with this thrown into the marriage wheeling and dealing came a large house and country estate at Highclere Castle, Hampshire.[3] Highclere is the backdrop to  British television's period-piece drama *Downton Abbey* which is allegedly a product of HM Queen Elizabeth II commanding  the screenwriter (Julian Fellowes, famed for his Oscar-winning script *Gosford Park* [4]  which is set in a stately home), to write something similar to raise the revenues at Highclere,  for her godson,  Geordie , Eighth Earl of Carnarvon). [5]   The rest is history, as they say! And thank you, Ma'am!

The Carnarvons' other past family seats were at Pixton Park, Devonshire and Bretby Park, Derbyshire. Pixton remains in the possession of a branch of the Herbert family but Bretby was sold-off by the Fifth Earl and his wife Almina (the Fifth Countess) to help make ends meet during the Great War.

Besides names, appearances are deceptive.   The Sixth Earl of Carnarvon was small, thick-set and a bright and breezy sort.  But this jovial persona hid a less adorable feature:  he was a born philanderer. One observer records that he was "a most uncompromisingly direct ladies' man"[6] whilst another describes his life as one spent largely hunting, shooting and flirting.[7]

He was tagged by his fellows as 'Lusty Carnarvon' or 'Randy Carnarvon', especially in the all-male Gentlemen's Clubs such as *Whites* in London. This was probably out of envy because his scatter-gun approach to the fairer sex meant (amidst many knock backs) that he occasionally 'got lucky'.  He was by most standards a nuisance around women and one who, being titled, was rarely brought into line.

Among the women Porchey pursued two were unfortunate enough to be cajoled into marriage. First, in 1922, he wooed an American-born beauty named Catherine Wendell and second, in 1939, he persuaded the well-known Austrian dancer Tilly Losch, if not to the altar, then at least to the Registry Office at the famous Caxton Hall in London. [8]

When they married Porchey both women were vulnerable and penniless. Their marital capitulation into the chore of being Porchey's bedmate was nothing to do with his looks or magnetic sex appeal or of being wonderfully romanced: it was instead all down to a personal/familial requirement to acquire a husband who was better off than they were financially.

Socially both women had a public profile and had made an impact on many suitors. Whilst Porchey made reasonable husband material on the grounds of title, money and property, neither relationship was a love-match and, to some extent, both women were duped by their family and friends into risking the holy state of matrimony.

# II
## Porchey's Two Duped Wives

*Anne Catherine Tredick Wendell*

5

# Marriage to Catherine

Porchey was aged twenty-three in 1922 when he married the twenty-two-year-old American-born refugee Anne Catherine Tredick Wendell (almost always known as 'Catherine').

Famous for her good looks, Catherine left America in 1911, homeless at the age of ten. She was brought to Britain by her widowed mother, Marian Fendall Wendell, who was living in much reduced circumstances after her husband's death. Catherine was accompanied by her three siblings, two older brothers and a younger sister.

As Catherine grew up in Britain, marriage to a well-off titled man was a primary goal set by her pushy American mother, a talented matchmaker, who was the chief architect in arranging altogether three up-market marital pairings for her offspring. Firstly, Catherine's match with Porchey, then secondly, Marian successfully arranged that her eldest son Jac (Jacob) was married off to a wealthy stockbroker's daughter, Eileen Victoria Carr. Finally her second daughter Philippa, (a darker beauty), married a British peer, Randolph Stewart, the Twelfth Earl of Galloway.

Both before and after marriage to Catherine, Porchey was incapable of being faithful to one woman. Catherine was infuriated by Porchey's behaviour but she persevered in the abusive and at times violent relationship where she was the victim. She bore Porchey two children but the fringe benefits of the marriage came at a heavy price in terms of her physical health and mental well-being which at times imperilled her life. Indeed, at her most depressed Catherine harboured thoughts of suicide and at least once aimed to kill herself.

Despite her inner conflict Catherine held on patiently in her coupling with Porchey for thirteen years before she took the decision to divorce a selfish, brutal, womanising spouse, by issuing two High Court writs between 1935 and 1936.

She ditched her title of Countess and remarried twice, weathering the tragedy of losing a second husband in the Second World War. Her third husband survived her by a number of years and proved the most steadfast of all three.

Catherine's children, a son Henry, (Lord Porchester, later Seventh Earl of Carnarvon) and a daughter, Lady Penelope Herbert, were her greatest and proudest triumphs. Sadly, in later years Catherine's mental state and alcohol dependency affected her relationship with her children and therefore she was never a part of the royal circle at Windsor Castle (and other Royal palaces) in which her son especially then moved; this made Catherine drink even more because she thought Porchester was ashamed of her. But he worried about her constantly, moreover it must have been a source of great sorrow when in 1956 he married without his mother being in attendance. This was in New York, albeit Porchey, Catherine's erstwhile rascal of a husband, was present.

Leaving aside Catherine's alcoholism (brought on in the main by Porchey's excesses, but there were tragedies, too, that didn't help) she was a knowledgeable woman, a worthy chatelaine of Highclere for thirteen years, liked by Highclere staff, had a real flair for entertaining and even as she grew older, a beauty and style that hardly ever tarnished.

## Marriage to Tilly Losch

*Ottilie Ethel Leopoldine Losch*

In 1939, to the surprise of many, the forty-one-year-old Porchey Carnarvon began an infatuation with, and married, Ottilie Ethel Leopoldine Losch (known as 'Tilly'), "a very pretty Jewess".[9] Almost certainly an Austrian by birth, she was a very successful ballet dancer in Europe but later changed her dancing style to attract a wider following, starring on the popular stage and in film. She was closely associated in England and America with the Austrian director Max Reinhardt[10] and the British impresario Charles B Cochran[11]. She was a divorcee, having been married for a couple of years to the eccentric artist Edward James[12] who greatly preferred men and boys to women. Tilly was famous for her hand ballets and twirling fingers;[13] she also painted and was the star of stage shows written by Noel Coward. She "took London by storm in the 1928 revue *This Year of Grace*, dancing to all unexpected things as a figurine from a stained-glass window to 'Air on a G String' by Bach." [14]

In London in the late 1920s and early 1930s and in Hollywood of the 1930s and 1940s Tilly oozed glamour, climbing the rankings with her considerable dancing charm and gaining exposure on the silver screen with a variety of bizarre characterisations for directors Sidney Franklin, Herbert Wilcox and King Vidor.[15] Through Tilly's stage and movieland contacts Porchey cunningly romped his way through a chorus line of actresses in Britain and America, trying his luck with leading ladies of the era including Jessie Matthews, Deana Durbin and Rita Hayworth. Tilly was also Porchey's meal ticket for many years in Hollywood, where he appeared at parties, sat on film sets, and was even tested once or twice for the movies. He also boasted of playing golf with Bing Crosby and on being on first name terms with film legends such as Humphrey Bogart.

Tilly (described as "pretty as a kitten, with a shrewd eye for this world's goods"[16]) hesitated over marrying Porchey in England in 1939. She didn't love him but he offered money, a safe home base and a title. However, even this did not answer her growing concern about her possible fate; as the Nazi jackboot began to stomp around Europe her Jewish blood would certainly have put her in grave danger were Germany to invade England. In the end she opted for her portly aristocratic Lothario and a civil wedding took place at Caxton Hall,

London, a few hours before war was declared. Porchey's mother Almina and his sister Lady Evelyn Beauchamp stood in as witnesses.

The arrangement of Porchey conquering Austria was short lived. Tilly put up with his attentions but when he was with a woman the Earl's own pleasure always came first. This was the price she had to pay for the title but since she had an ageing mother living in America (whom she doted on and genuinely missed) and a film career at the point where she was still being offered parts in Hollywood, Porchey could not be allowed to stand in her way.

Thus after only ten weeks at Highclere (which had been converted to accommodate evacuee children from war-torn London) Tilly escaped to America. In July 1940 there was a brief reunion centred on Porchey feigning a near-death plea; he was only ill with a minor ailment but Tilly heard the sound of the cash register and travelled to Genoa where Porchey met her ship. A year after marrying they finally enjoyed a honeymoon at the *Hotel de Paris* in Monte Carlo and spent time together in Paris (only weeks before the Germans entered the city) and finally in London before Tilly hightailed it back to America; whether to avoid further advances from the Germans or from Porchey one can never be sure.

The rest of Porchey's brief and tangled second marriage was interrupted by the events of the Second World War, as he went back into uniform in a dull, but safe administrative post. Porchey wanted as always to have his cake and eat it, quickly installing one of his mistresses, the actress Jeanne Stuart, [17] at Highclere almost as soon as Tilly landed in the USA on board the *Empress of Britain*.[18] Jeanne, briefly married to the businessman Sir Bernard Docker, [19]was one of Porchey's persistent old flames. The complete matrimonial farce, with countless secrets and lies on both sides of the Atlantic, was finally ended by a divorce in 1947 which had been preceded by a failed Court action by Porchey a few years earlier on the grounds that Tilly had in effect deserted him in July 1940.

Later Tilly found a role for herself in America, whilst travelling backwards and forwards to a little flat she rented in London. Unlike Catherine she clung to her title of "Countess of Carnarvon", despite famously declaring:

"My role of ballerina comes first. Second is my work as a choreographer. My acting comes third, my painting fourth, I rate my role as Lady Carnarvon fifth in importance simply because I can't think of anything interesting to put after painting...." [20]

Catherine died in Switzerland in 1977, Tilly died in America on Christmas Eve of 1975.

Porchey outlived both wives. After the divorces he still tried to charm them and deceive them; he was neither easy to live with as their husband nor to fob off as an ex- husband.

Porchey's attitude to women was like Toad of Toad Hall's attitude to cars in *The Wind in the Willows:* if he saw one he had to have it, *Poop! Poop!* Both of Porchey's wives, though worldly wise, were shocked by his serial infidelities. As this book will show, Porchey's demons came from a childhood largely devoid of affection. However a Freudian explanation for behaviour that meant notches were added to the bedpost of his four poster, whether he was nominally married at the time or not, may be a little simplistic. It is certainly true that all this extra-marital activity at times left both wives humiliated. They were, however, as hinted at, not complete paragons of virtue themselves.

## III
## American Beauties or Dollar Wives

Going back to Catherine Wendell, the American immigrant, Porchey was not the only British nobleman who sought a sale wife from American shores.

In the mid-1920s in London a photographer loosed a storm over England by declaring, tactlessly, that "the only really beautiful English women were – Americans". [21]

"If England today has many more strikingly handsome women than it had in Victorian times, it is only because so many American beauties have married Englishmen of title." [22]

works down), was an impressive red brick confection with the kind of colonnaded porch that made its intentions perfectly clear. This was a house not to be taken lightly. However, it was on stepping inside the house that one became aware that here was the home of a serious collector.

Despite the musty half-light of some of the formal reception rooms it was easy to detect the presence on the walls of great portraits and landscapes from the brushes of some of Europe's finest artists. Delicate porcelain adorned marbled Adams fireplaces, each room more splendid than the last.

Then there was the library which was on such a scale that its reading would have taken 'many a lifetime' (or so the under-footman at *Sandridgebury* would have it). In any event it was clear that being a senior partner in *Deloitte, Dever, Griffiths and Co* enabled Percy to earn rather more than a crust. There was only one thing missing in Percy and, more particularly, Gertrude's life: the patter of tiny feet echoing down the long *Sandridgebury* corridors and stunning wooden staircase.

During the Wendell's stay Catherine's cousin who she referred to as 'Aunt Gertrude' (on account of the age gap between them and whose pet name was 'Aunt Bunny'[36]) was quickly won over by the outwardly pretty, well-mannered child. She festooned Catherine with lacey-dressed dollies, candy- stripe parasols and all the kind of frippery that many a little girl would have given their eye teeth for.

Unbeknown to Gertrude, Catherine was at heart a bit of a tomboy. Back home in America, she played rough games with her brothers during long summer holidays in the peaceful open countryside around Kittery[37] in the US State of Maine where the Wendells kept a beautiful summer house. It was not uncommon to see Catherine stripped to her undies, encouraging her brothers as they fished ambitiously for 'Old Stonewall', an enormous (possibly mythical) catfish that supposedly inhabited the lake at the bottom of the Wendell's garden.

However indulgent Aunt Gertrude was towards Catherine the little girl longed for her less formal life back home and, to her relief, the Wendell family's time in Britain finally ended on 18 June 1904 when they returned to New York from Liverpool on the White Star's trans-Atlantic steamer, *Cretic*.[38]

As Catherine looked back from the top deck of the *Cretic* as the grey rainswept shores of Britain receded, she was not to know that seven years later, in the aftermath of a great family tragedy, she would return to spend her formative years as a teenage girl, growing-up at *Sandridgebury* under the Griffiths family's roof, and that she was destined to marry a certain English lord, Henry, Lord Porchester, the heir to the Earldom of Carnarvon.

Where does one begin to tell Catherine's story? Perhaps with her own parents Jacob Jnr. and Marian's marriage.

## The Wedding of the Parents of Catherine Wendell in 1895 Marian Fendall and Jacob Wendell Jnr.

*St John's Church, Washington DC*

One commentator described the wedding as "a gorgeous affair." [39] This in part was down to the setting: St John's Church, Lafayette Square, Washington DC couldn't have been more redolent of east coast charm and elegance. The bride was Miss Marian Fendall, an attractive, fair-haired, twenty-five-year-old from Baltimore. The groom (also aged twenty-five) was a handsome, urbane, dark-haired New Yorker, Mr Jacob Wendell Jnr.

At the door under her veil, Marion gazed ahead at the nave of the Church, with the chancel beautifully decorated with an abundance of palms and Easter lilies - no expense had been spared. She took a deep breath, recalling with pride when she had been a bridesmaid for friends and family, including an earlier occasion at this very same church of St John's[40]

### Wendell—Fendall.

WASHINGTON, D. C., April 16.—Miss Marian Fendall, daughter of the late Major Philip R. Fendall, United States Marine Corps, and Jacob Wendell, Jr., of New-York, were married at noon to-day at St. John's Church.

The chancel was beautifully decorated with palms and Easter lilies. The bride, escorted by her uncle, Titus Salter Tredick, of Portsmouth, N. H., was preceded to the altar by the ushers, Messrs. Lloyd McKim Garrison, Rufus McDuffie, Charles D. Wetmore, Morton C. Nichols, and George Blagden, Jr., all of New-York. Matthew Luce, Jr., of Boston, and Walter D. Davidge, of Washington, and the bridesmaids, Miss Gertrude Tredick, and Miss Mary Fendall, cousins of the bride; Miss Louise Kellogg, of Williamstown, Mass., Miss Kittie Taylor, of New-York, Miss Mary Magruder of Annapolis, and Miss Maud Davidge of this city.

The groom, with his best man, Evert Jansen Wendell, of New-York, his brother, awaited them at the chancel steps, where the marriage service was performed by the Rev. Dr. Mackey-Smith, the rector of St. John's. The ceremony was finished by the Rev. Mr. Southgate of Annapolis.

The bride wore a rich gown of white satin, the high bodice trimmed with point lace and a garland of orange blossoms reaching over the shoulders. The veil of tulle was held in place by two mercury wings of diamonds, the gift of the groom. The bridal bouquet was of lilies of the valley and white violets.

*New York Times reports on the marriage of Catherine's parents*

At twelve noon precisely, to a triumphant peal of bells (the great bell at St Johns had been cast by Joseph the son of Paul Revere at his foundry

17

in Boston), the bride accompanied by her uncle Titus Tredick (standing in for her late father), glided as if in a dream down the aisle, surrounded by most of the Washington elite along with kinfolk from nearby Philadelphia, New York and Boston. Her cousin who'd come up from Baltimore gave her one of his winks and she began to relax. It was then, for the first time, that she became aware of her Jacob at the front of the church, waiting quietly for the service to begin: if he was nervous his bearing did little to betray the fact.

Jacob's calm demeanour was, in large part, due to the presence at his side of his best man, older brother Evert Jansen Wendell and his ushers. These were all Harvard men decked out in crimson waistcoats, high collars and bow ties which varied in hue from the tasteful to the distinctly bilious. Jacob however only had eyes for his blushing bride.

As she neared the altar there was an audible intake of breath in appreciation. Marian had never felt more special adorned as she was in "a rich gown of heavy white satin, the high bodice trimmed with chiffon edged with a ruffle of point lace and a garland of orange blossoms reaching over her shoulders. The veil of tulle was held in place by a diamond tiara formed by two mercury wings, fastened to a gold band, the gift of the groom." [41]

She carried a beautiful bouquet of lilies of the valley and white violets. The six bridesmaids, two dressed in pink, two in green and two in yellow offered a mass of colour contrasts. One of these girls acting as maid of honour was a cousin, Gertrude Bailey Tredick (daughter of Titus). Later, as Gertrude Griffiths, she would play a crucial role in providing a home (in England) for her prematurely widowed cousin, Marian. But that is fast forwarding the story perhaps too far, just yet, for today was a happy day.

Both the Fendall and Wendell families coming together in holy wedlock (blessed by St John's own resident pastor, Reverend Dr Alexander Mackay-Smith, and assisted by Rev Mr Southgate of Annapolis) had long-standing links with Kittery and Portsmouth on the coastal State of New England.

Marian, for her part, was marrying into a noteworthy family of merchants whose honest trade spanned several generations. The

Wendells (the family was originally of Dutch origin[42]) were hard-working and straightforward people, the cornerstone on which the United States of America was built.

*Philip Fendell*        *Mrs J Wendell*        *Jacob Wendell*
*Some Antecedents of Catherine Wendell[43]*

Jacob was marrying into a distinguished family of lawyers, military and naval men who had played no little part in the forging of a new self-confident country and bowed to no-one save perhaps their wives.[44] The west may have been won but the family home was a completely different matter.

Jacob's new wife had been born at Portsmouth in 1870,[45] the same town as had Jacob and his siblings (Barrett, Gordon and Evert) prior to his father (a wealthy merchant, Jacob Wendell II) moving his family to Boston and then to New York where he himself had been born in 1869, a year prior to Marian.

Sadly, Marian's father, Major Philip R Fendall [46] of the US Marine Corps, died in 1879 when she was only nine. Her Fendall grandparents were also deceased. Her grandfather was Philip Richard Fendall, a well-known Washington lawyer and a cousin of the famous US Confederate General, Robert E Lee.[47] Marian's mother, Anne Catherine Tredick,[48] had also passed on ten years later, in 1889, leaving Marian, at the age of nineteen, an only child still dependant on her parent's families for guardianship and support; in particular from her mother's Tredick relations who were well- respected mariners in Portsmouth. A few years later Marian went to live in Baltimore.

Gertrude, like Marian's other maids including a second maid of honour (her Fendall cousin, Mary), were all charming in their "large hats of white straw, trimmed with white ostrich plumes and flowers to match their gown." [49]

The newlyweds now standing under the magnificent portico of St John's, lost in each other, had enjoyed a leisurely courtship. They had first met when Jacob spent a summer in Portsmouth at the same that Marian was there (from Baltimore ) visiting her relations. Later they saw each other at a dance at Harvard and fell in love.

During Jacob's student days he was the sporty type (although it was his brother Evert who was the more accomplished athlete, holding a host of American sports records). [50] But Jacob had other talents: he was a notable figure in the Harvard Club as well as a member of the University's dramatics group, the 'Hasty Pudding Club', where he acted and wrote his own plays to star and perform in. This love of the theatre was one he and Marian shared and today the happy couple shared centre stage, "Standing in a bower of green arranged in a bay window in which under an arch the couple received the congratulations of the company on which hung a curtain of asparagus, looped back with bunches of Easter lilies. In the centre was a wedding bell of white blossoms, with a lining of jonquils and a clapper of violets." [51]

Marian's aunt (Cousin Gertrude's mother) Sarah Bailey Tredick acted as co-hostess for her beloved niece on this, the most important day of her life. Marian's paternal aunt Mary Lee Fendall (her late father's sister[52]) successfully shared the nuptial tasks with Sarah Tredick staging a wonderful reception after the wedding ceremony. The decorations were superb, everything was perfect.

The wedding breakfast was sumptuous in every way. "The bridesmaids' cake was a pretty feature of the refreshment table and had in it a ring, a coin and a thimble", [53] all symbolising good luck and prosperity.

The bride and groom were a popular couple, as indicated by the vast array of presents (250 items for the bride alone) including expensive silver, cut glass, jewellery, pieces of inlaid and antique furniture and pictures.

During the afternoon, to a band playing and large scale cheering, the newly-weds left for New York to begin a life together. Later, on 4 May 1895, they sailed off to Spain to start a honeymoon full of fun, leisure and travel. Jacob was a seasoned traveller; he had already been backwards and forward to Europe twice during his bachelor days.

## Jacob and Marian's Early Years Raising a Family in New York

Following an exciting summer travelling through several countries, Jacob and Marian Wendell, the parents of the future Sixth Countess of Carnarvon, set up home together back in New York.

The newlyweds wanted a large family, and in quick succession two fine, healthy sons, Jacob (Jac) and Reginald (Reggie) were born in 1896 and in 1898 respectively. [54]

The two boys were followed by the arrival of two lovely daughters. The first girl, Anne Catherine Tredick Wendell (known to all as Catherine), was born in Kittery on 20 November 1900 and the second daughter named Philippa Fendall Wendell was born in New York on 24 June, 1905. Like her older sister, Philippa too was destined to become the wife of a British Earl - Randolph Stewart, the Twelfth Earl of Galloway.

To the Wendell children life must have seemed like one endless summer living a privileged idyllic life in and around Portsmouth New Hampshire; even the fall each year brought delight in the changing colours of the landscape. This country idyll was interspersed with more frenetic period at the family's well-situated town house in New York. The family's lifestyle was underpinned by a substantial trading empire founded by Jacob's own father, Jacob Wendell II. [55]

## Jacob Wendell II: Catherine's wealthy grandfather

The death of Jacob Jnr's father, Jacob II in 1898 (Catherine's grandfather) would eventually bring about something of a sea change in the family's financial affairs. Certain provisions had been made in

Jacob senior's last Will and Testament; a house, (albeit with strings attached[56]), and a retinue of servants.

Jacob's brother Gordon was a neighbour on East Thirty Fifth Street, New York, and the family enjoyed the good times. However the well left by his father soon began to dry up due to the fact that his sons seemed to have inherited little of their father's sharp business acumen. There was in fact prescience in the strict and unbendable terms of the family trust arrangement made by Jacob Wendell II and despite various cajoling and maneuvering Jacob Jnr. was unable to extract further sums from his co-trustees.

To understand the reasons for such caution one needs to appreciate that Jacob II was something of an autocrat; he had known hard times when his own father's financial world collapsed.[57] His sons were obliged to show reverence to the old man's authority.

When Jacob Jnr. was a student at Harvard University he had cause to write to his father to explain about being apprehended for a misdemeanor. Diana Fitzpatrick (who has studied the Wendell papers in the Portsmouth Athenæum on the author's behalf) reflects on this incident with her own emphasis on the nature of their father-son relationship.

"What struck me was how lovingly affectionate he [Jacob Jnr] was in those letters to his father, constantly thanking him for his support and for being such a wonderful father to him and giving him so much. And apologizing profusely when his frat house was raided and it was discovered there was liquor and wine there and then he and three others had to go to court and pay fines of $35 each and yet at the same time Jacob Jnr expressed disdain and abhorrence that such goings on what had come to pass (meaning frat use of wine and liquor etc) all this to his father who he evidently loved very much and would never do anything to dishonor him in any way."[58]

So it was that within a few years of his father death Jacob Jnr. was forced to secretly re-mortgage the family home, borrow money from his siblings and resort to taking out high-interest loans owing to the fact that, in a final precaution against the follies of youth, old Jacob had stipulated in his Will that the principal sums would only be paid out when his sons each reached the age of forty-five, or earlier distribution only with the agreement of the trustees.

## Wendell History

In times of adversity the Wendells took pride in their distant European origins. The first Wendells were Dutch traders who hailed from the Delft region and later from Emden in Holland. The first Wendell emigrant, Evert Jansen, settled in New York with Evert's sons later heading to Portsmouth and Albany. They had business, trade and commerce embedded in their bloodstream.

Charles W Wendell, a present-day member of the family advises:

"My branch of the family is parallel to the Portsmouth Wendells descended from Johannes through his eldest son Abraham (of New York); mine is through Johannes's younger brother Philip (ever in Albany)…. Johannes and Philip's father, Evert Jansen arrived in Nieuw Amsterdam [New York] in 1639 without a last name. To secure safe delivery of money and goods from home (Emden) his brother-in law suggested that Evert use as a last name Wendel, "after your beloved grandmother." [59]

In the next few generations the Wendells became a highly successful dynasty.

*Mary Bertodi Barrett Wendell, Catherine's Grandmother* [60]

Like his ancestors, Jacob Wendell II knew there was always a risk in trade and business so he instilled in the hearts and minds of his four sons (who were all brought up in affluent respectability[61]) traditional family values, a strong belief in education and in scholarship.[62] Coupled with this came an expectation of his sons to buckle down and fashion out a successful career, preferably in business. Jacob II was well supported in this by the woman chosen for his wife, Mary Bertodi Barrett Wendell.[63] How far these expectations were met by Jacob's sons makes interesting reading.

# Two Wendell sons break the mould, two others falter

*Barrett Wendell*

Barrett Wendell,[64] Jacob II's eldest son, was a family man but he broke the mould of Wendells going into business and commerce. Barrett became a highly respected literary figure, a published author who taught English at Harvard University.

But Barrett's health was erratic; he was "never strong"[65]. In 1872, at the early age of seventeen, he suffered "a hysterical paralysis"[66], a condition that dogged his life. Barrett's biographer writes "Jacob Wendell [II] was a successful commanding personality and [Barrett] never felt he had matched his father's expectations."[67] For such a distinguished literary scholar as Barrett Wendell to feel inadequate in this way provides an indication of the long shadow that Jacob II cast over his family.

Perhaps in another effort to avoid comparisons with his forbears another of Jacob II's sons turned his back on business. Evert, Jacob's third son, chose other national arenas in which to make a name for himself: in athletics and philanthropy as well as excelling in track and field and serving his country on the US Olympic Committee. Evert steeped himself in charitable youth work.

*Evert Jansen Wendell*

Like Baden-Powell in Britain (founder of the Boy Scout movement) Evert established a similar type of National Boys Camp, he was also a pioneering social worker, resettling young vagrants from the streets of New York, encouraging them into working on farms, with adopted families or accommodated in Boy's Homes. [68] Although it is clear that his path was not one his father would have chosen Evert found fulfillment in his chosen fields. He was also, like Jacob Jnr., an actor.

The two other sons of Mary and Jacob II were Gordon and Jacob Jnr, the latter (Catherine's father) being the youngest. Neither literature nor philanthropy were their bag, nor for that matter were the harsh disciplines of managing the family business for profit and so the dependence placed upon him by his father (and later also by his widowed mother) appeared to weigh heavily on Gordon.

Jacob Jnr, although described as "an experienced man of business", [69] had his heart set on another kind of life. However, like several of the Wendell boys he was highly strung. In fact Barrett, Gordon and Jacob

Jnr all shared "a nervous disability...attributed to a genetic inheritance from three generations in [their] father's family." [70]

*Jacob Wendell Jnr. : Catherine's Father*

With such sensibilities and pressures it is little wonder that Jacob's sons presided over the decline of his once evergreen business. Trade, agency commissions and property wheeling and dealing, built up over sixty years, all gradually began to slip into the past, broken up to pay off taxes or sold to more eager and energetic entrepreneurs.

To give him his due Gordon, against the odds, was a major figure in the world of New York merchant business and real estate.

Following an injury received at football Gordon was forced to leave Harvard in his year as a freshman (1882). After he'd recovered his health he worked for his father and records in 1906 that he is "a member of the firm of Jacob Wendell & Co, wholesale dry-goods merchants in New York [living] at 126 East 35th Street." [71]

He comments (somewhat prophetically): "I have been in the same business, and leading an eventful life." [72]

Gordon strove manfully for years trying to hold onto the power and control of the family firm. There were complications, however; as a designated partner in his father's firm (with large scale options on advances and borrowing) he loaned sums to his brother Jacob Jnr. unbeknown to the other trustees.

He had little time for other pastimes but was a keen yachtsman and old Jacob left him his handsome sailing boat in his last Will and Testament.

**TRIAL STOPPED ON ACCOUNT OF ILLNESS**

Evert Jansen Wendell, the ancestor of the family, was born in 1615 in Embden, Friesland, came to New Amsterdam in 1640 in the service of the Dutch West India Company, moved to Fort Orange, married Susanna Du Trieux and died 1709. Their son Johannes was born 1649, married Elizabeth Staats, and died 1691. Their son Abraham was born 1678, married Catrina De Kay, and died 1734. John of the next generation was born 1703, married Elizabeth Quincy, and died 1762. John, Jr., was born 1731, married Dorothy Sherburne, and died 1808. Their son Jacob was born 1788, married Mehitabel Rindge Rogers, and died 1865. Jacob, Jr., was born 1826, married Mary Bertodi Barrett, and died 1898, and they were the parents of Gordon Wendell.

*'The Morse Case' and Gordon's Pedigree*[73]

Tragedy struck during 1908-9 when Gordon fell seriously ill, suffering a nervous breakdown after taking part as a jury member in a high profile fraud case (The Morse Case[74]). This resulted in the trial being initially stopped, to glaring newspaper headlines and personal protection for Gordon by the secret service. It was all too much; Gordon died a year afterwards, from heart failure. He left a widow, Fannie and one daughter, Frances[75]

# Jacob Jnr's head is turned by the allure of the Stage

Once the good times in the prosperous years after Jacob II's death began to recede the parents of Catherine Wendell, who later became Sixth Countess of Carnarvon, sometimes had difficulty in meeting regular bills, and Jacob Jnr. often had his head high in the clouds.

Jacob Jnr. had always had a passion for the stage. He had been interested in the theatre all his life; this is aptly evidenced from his days as a student at Harvard University where the plays he wrote and performed were acclaimed by critics. But the pay of an actor was not large enough to support Marian and the children.

In the early years of his marriage to Marian, in order to please his father (and his equally demanding mother, Mary, who survived her husband Jacob II until 1912[76]) and to guarantee a steady flow of income to provide for Marian and the four growing children, Jacob knuckled down to work in earnest, But he was far from happy sitting in a dull office or climbing ladders in a cold warehouse. All the tedium of merchandising, and laying railway cables broke his spirit and Jacob Jnr. felt all along that his destiny was a career on the stage.

*Jacob Wendell Jnr. ( far right) ( as a 'Dog' ) in 'The Blue Bird'*

# An Actor's Life For Me

At Harvard University Jacob Jnr. had initially shown some prowess as an athlete but had abandoned hope of winning a 'Varsity H' (the famous large letter 'H' embroidered on Harvard sports shirts, possessed by his three brothers, who had all been basketball players). Instead, Jacob spent his spare time as a member of the University's privileged sect in the dramatic group, the "Hasty Pudding Club". [77] He graduated in 1891, the same year in which he was dubbed "the best amateur actor in the country"[78] Later he appeared in New York at the Strollers and Comedy Clubs and soon became a regular face in the Players Company at the New Theatre in New York.

In 1905, (a year after Jacob and Marian had taken their family to Europe and where the three-year-old Catherine saw London and the British countryside around St Albans for the first time), Jacob is listed in "The Financial Red Book of America" as a "Capitalist" based at 26 Cortlandt Street, New York where he was working in a business called Wendell & McDuffie. This firm appears in trade directories as a general merchant supplier with government orders, one being for the supply of "one thousand two hundred feet of 2A inch cotton fire hose for the sum of $ 864"[79]. This an example of the humdrum life of business that drove Jacob ultimately into a state, first of boredom, then depression and finally to despair. [80]

Jacob's partner, Rufus Leighton McDuffie, was also his best friend. When Rufus married (also in 1895) Jacob was his best man[81] and when the partnership ceased in 1909 Rufus continued the business successfully.[82] References in a book on Catherine Wendell by Highclere's ghost writers[83] fail to source a reference made to Jacob Wendell Jnr's alleged bankruptcy in 1909.[84]

Jacob's wife Marian was a strong, forceful woman who had a more pragmatic approach to business matters, which she tried to foster in the sensitive artistic Jacob. As well as bringing up the children day by day she enhanced her husband's commercial dealings by fraternizing with her fellow business wives, drawing upon the impressive list of social and political contacts she had spread across New York's parlours.

Although always one to put her family first and last, during her marriage Marian became an accomplished hostess. She was "one of New York's matrons",[85] who entertained in her town house at 106 East Thirty Fifth Street, New York and a country home ( that Marian had inherited from her parents ) at *Willowbank*, Kittery.

Jacob's career continued to falter; he really was hopeless in business and without telling Marian he borrowed more money to make things look better than they really were. His real ambitions and skills were still set more on exploring artistic pursuits. He dreamed of the limelight, secretly hoping that one of his plays would be an overnight success (which never happened).

Against advice, and no longer prepared to slog away in the business world he detested as a commission agent and on railway investment projects, Jacob took to treading the boards as an actor, full time. In 1910 one observer records:

"Mr Wendell …is an amateur actor, last year he finally passed over to the professional stage when he became a member of the company at the New Theatre. Until that time, Mr Wendell's amateur engagement took up almost as much time as his duties subsequently did on the professional boards." [86]

In her youth in Portsmouth Marian had also acted, just for fun, but now as a full-time wife and mother she had little time for such pursuits. However, one commentator records that she "rarely missed an evening when her husband appeared at the New Theatre [New York] last winter." [87]

With Jacob's switch of profession, and all the inheritance from Jacob II either already spent or earmarked for regular expenses, money was often extremely tight but the education of the four Wendell offspring was provided for through trust funds from family legacies in Jacob Wendell II's last Will and Testament. Generally every effort was made to ensure the children had an uninterrupted life and the very best opportunities to thrive; they received private tuition and the boys were enrolled in a good preparatory school with a view to them entering Harvard later on.

Despite the grimness of their financial affairs, home life was cheerful. Notwithstanding Jacob's restlessness, in the children's developmental years each of the Wendell parents contributed an equal measure of thought to improve their four children's upbringing, ensuring the great English and American literary classics from Dickens to Mark Twain were known to them. They understood a tolerance towards other races and religions, which enhanced their general wellbeing and welfare as they emerged as individuals and US citizens.

Catherine Wendell took centre stage on one occasion when, at the age of nine, she was one of the two little flower girls in the bridal procession for a Society wedding in New York. [88] She also played a part (with her little five-year- old sister Philippa) when Marian hosted a coming-out party for one of her Wendell nieces (the daughter of Jacob's deceased brother, Gordon).

There were some exciting days out away from their schoolwork for the children, usually orchestrated by Catherine's grandmother, Mary (the only grandparent she knew, as the others had died before she was born) involving trips to the theatre to see Jacob perform.

## A Terrible Blow Falls on the Wendell Family

### JACOB WENDELL, JR., IS DEAD.

Actor and Harvard Graduate Dies of Pneumonia—Acted in "The Blue Bird."

Jacob Wendell, Jr., a Harvard graduate and actor, who was to have appeared in the leading rôle in "What the Doctor Ordered" at the Astor Theatre Friday night, died yesterday at his home, 186 East Thirty-fifth Street of pneumonia. The attack which caused Mr. Wendell's collapse on the stage at Trenton, N. J., last Wednesday, followed a nervous breakdown and a long period of ill-health. He was brought from Trenton in a private car and grew rapidly worse until his death, his physicians at no time holding out hope for his recovery. He was 42 years old.

The career of the young actor at Harvard and afterward in professional life was a remarkable one in many ways. He …

*Jacob Wendell Jnr. and Death Notice*

32

Sadly, as fate would have it, a great disaster was looming for this close knit, loving family just as Jacob was approaching his height as an actor: playing a starring role. In 1911 he was due to appear in the leading part in a play (ironically called) "What the Doctor Ordered" at the Astor Theatre, New York, and advance tickets were much sought after by the public.

The career of the young actor at Harvard and afterward in professional life was a remarkable one in many ways. He first attracted attention as an amateur athlete and then as an actor in Harvard's Hasty Pudding Club, having forsaken his hopes to win a 'Varsity "H," possessed by three of his brothers, to attempt a histrionic career. Many critics of undergraduate drama declared that "Jake" Wendell was the best amateur actor in the country. Coming to New York after graduating in 1891, he appeared in amateur efforts of The Strollers and the Comedy Club. He played all kinds of rôles in a way to win admirers, and the result was that with the opening of The New Theatre stock company there was a demand that he join. His opening performance with the company was in "Antony and Cleopatra." His second rôle, that of the dog in Maeterlinck's "The Blue Bird," brought him instant success. He considered that the dog was not meant to be any particular kind of dog, but just a plain dog, and a dog soul at that. He sought to avoid "animalizing" the rôle too much, and achieved a happy result that brought him general recognition.

*Jacob Wendell Jr with a snapshot of his acting career*

The play was on a pre-New York tour, with two performances due at Trenton, New Jersey. But the preparation and excitement proved too much for Jacob's genetic nervous disposition. Before going on stage, he suffered "a complete breakdown". [89] He was brought home to New York in a private car but grew rapidly worse, with his doctors holding out no hope (to Marian and the children) for a recovery. He was forty-two-years-old. The official cause of death on 22 April, 1911 was given as "pneumonia".[90] The grief resulting from hearing about Jacob's plight proved fatal to one other member of Marian's family, her aunt Mary Lee Fendall (who had co-hosted her wedding reception in 1895). Mary died very suddenly in Washington on 29 March 1911; what small estate she had was left to her last surviving sister, Florence. [91]

The widowed Marian was the same age as Jacob; at forty-two-years old she had to face the prospect of bringing up her four young children on her own. Jac had just turned fifteen, Reggie thirteen, Catherine ten and Philippa was only five.

## The Aftermath of Jacob's Death

*Calvary Church, New York*
*The Wendell Family Place of Worship*

It was a gigantic shock for everyone, but in the aftermath of Jacob's death and an impressive public funeral with family, business folk, New York actors and members of the Harvard Club streaming out in force for the service at the Wendell family's regular place of worship (Calvary Church on 21st Street and 4th Avenue[92]) there came the stark revelation that Jacob had been neglectful in his past business affairs over several years. Matters were made worse when it emerged that, despite previous funds from legacies being available, there were several large debts of tens of thousands of dollars owing to creditors, including his mother and brothers.

Although Marian was in a state of bereavement this was no time for sentiment. A solution had to be found to avoid the spectre of possible complete financial ruin. Notwithstanding Jacob's debts, Marian's income from the Wendell coffers was uncertain. Besides, Marian was too proud to try to maintain her position coping with any greatly reduced cirmstances.

Jacob's two surviving brothers, Barrett and Evert, were mortified at the news but help and advice was scanty. It became clear to Marian that there was no scope for a long term, secure plan from the wider Wendell family which could provide sufficiently for her and her children's future. Jacob's eldest brother Barrett, the distinguished, writer and teacher at Harvard University, was the head of the family. But Barrett was not good with money matters; "his own son [also named Barrett[93]] had to handle the financial affairs because of his [father's] extreme nervousness". Barrett Jnr gave his aunt Marian some immediate support in his father's absence, since at the time of Jacob's death Barrett Snr was travelling in the Far East in Shanghai, China and only heard of Jacob's death by telegram from Evert and a letter from Barrett Jnr.

In a letter Barrett Snr writes:

"Poor old Jac is with me all the time, not unkindly, or troublously, but tenderly. He was really simply affectionate, I think – a boy at heart to the end," but adding "I am glad that chance put me so far away at the sad moment...for I could have done nothing, so far as I can see, which cannot be as well done by others." [94]

Back in his daughter Mary's[95] house in Shanghai, (Mary's husband was a businessman in China) Barrett studied a letter from his son recording the event including giving support to Marian in her hour of need. He found some inner calm from his son's actions: "[the] Dear old chap ...did [things} more tactfully and more firmly than I could", adding "as for the children... they are dear little things......I shall be better able to advise and to help in time to come".[96]

The next of Jacob Jnr's brothers, Evert, a bachelor, had commitments with his charity work with his various trusts and bodies for keeping wayward youths, including the City of New York's army of vagrant newsboys, housed, better employed or out of jail.

One other possible avenue for Marian and her family was to move in with Jacob's mother, the widowed Mary, who was living nearby with her son Evert. However Marian's mother-in-law, an infirm lady approaching eighty, was against this plan, as was Evert. [97]

Jacob II's widow Mary only survived her son Jacob Jnr. by a year and a half. Her last Will and Testament spelt out the extent to which the Wendell family fortune had diminished in the period of fourteen years after old Jacob's death, and despite the sums owed by her son, Jacob Jnr, thankfully there was a small legacy for her grandchildren which included Catherine and her siblings. [98]

## A Moonlight Flit

What could Marian now do to save herself and the four young fatherless children from destitution or at least humiliation? The best solution did not come from the Wendell clan but from Marian's Tredick cousin, Gertrude Bailey Griffths, who was married to an Englishman and living at Sandridge, near St Albans, England, Marian must leave America, with the children, and emigrate across the Atlantic Ocean. Jacob's creditors would be unlikely to pursue Marian in England at once and this move, tantamount to a moonlight flit, would give her time to manage repayment of the unpaid accounts and loans in the years that followed.

# Chapter 2

## 1911 – 1921

## Escape To England

Marian's flight to England took place in the summer of 1911. Gertrude Griffiths had agreed to take care of her and the four young Wendell children, provide a roof over their heads and help with the children's upbringing.

*Sandridgebury, Sandridge, Near St Albans, England c1905*

Ronan Donohoe of the Portsmouth Athenaeum, New England, who was responsible for staging an exhibition to Catherine Wendell in Portsmouth during 2012-13, [99] explains:

"Marian went to *Sandridgebury* near St Albans to live with her first cousin Gertrude Tredick Griffiths [who had] a huge house……….
Gertrude was a childhood chum in Portsmouth." [100]

# Griffiths Generosity Stretched

The move to Britain had to be sanctioned by Gertrude's husband, Percy. Percival (Percy) Davis Griffiths had had the good fortune to be born into a prosperous family of Welsh and French origin who were involved in the lucrative early twentieth century world of international accountancy. Along with his older brother John[101] Percy was a rising star in the London-based firm of accountants *Deloitte, Dever, Griffiths & Co.* and worked in London. *Deloittes'* client base encompassed the wealthy families of London, allowing Percy a prized opportunity to mix and flirt with the upper social classes. He cut a dapper figure; he had something of an eye for the ladies and also kept himself busy on the sports field and riding to hounds.

*Deloittes* had fingers in several American pies including the emerging cable industry and the railways, and the world markets opened up before them. Rising stars like Percy were expected to serve time in an American office and tackle clients' needs. It was during one assignment (he was a member of the British colony on Staten Island for some years) that Percy's raffish charms came to the attention of a certain Miss Gertrude Bailey Tredick, of Portsmouth, New Hampshire, a writer of both crime and romantic fiction.[102]

Living on Staten Island, Percy enjoyed and fully exploited his membership of the local Polo Club. His prowess on horseback was a special draw for the young Gertrude Tredick. She was an only child, who wrote stories of "adventures of exotic feats in the deserts of Arabia",[103] and she dreamed of a gallant knight in shining armour coming to carry her off to his turreted castle in another land, which is exactly what happened! Percy proposed marriage and Gertrude accepted. Percy's secondment soon ended but it was the Home Counties of England, not the Arabian sands, which beckoned. So it was that after the wedding in Portsmouth, on 19 October 1898, Percy and Gertrude went to live in England. Somewhat quaintly the *New York Times* continued to mark their wedding anniversary in their columns with congratulations.

There are parallels in the way Percy Davis Griffiths helped to settle and meet the demands of the widow, Marian Fendall Wendell, his wife's poor relation from the USA, to the actions taken by Baron Alfred de Rothschild in supporting and bankrolling Almina, the Fifth Countess of Carnarvon's mother, Marie Boyer. On the death of Marie's husband, Frederick Wombwell, in 1889 Alfred was quick to go to his friend's aid and assumed the role of Almina's guardian and sponsor. Marie knew too much about Alfred's darker side as a predatory homosexual so his ready-made family of Marie and her two children (Almina and her brother Frederick) was a perfect cover for normality.[104]

*Percy Davies Griffiths*

Although not in Rothschild's super-rich league, Percy Griffiths was comfortably-off. The Griffiths' had no children. Their sprawling home near St Albans called *Sandridgebury* was full of antiques because Percy was an avid collector of old furniture, paintings and silver, a veritable hoarder (again like Alfred de Rothschild). He also had a London town house (again stacked to the brim with antiques) with a full staff including butler, cook, servants, chauffeur and gardeners. Percy had his own relations too; the clutch of Griffiths' nieces and nephews were jealous and suspicious of their cousins and regarded them as vulgar, new world interlopers railroading their way into the lives of their ageing and well-off uncle and aunt.

*Staff at Sandridgebury*[105]

What's more, they already had one American living in the Griffiths household, even if the old girl in question posed little threat to any future inheritance.

For Marian, however, this other inhabitant at *Sandridgebury* provided a sentimental reminder of home. In 1898 Gertrude and her husband had paid for a holiday trip to England for Gertrude's ageing parents, Titus Salter Tredick (who had given Marian away at her wedding in 1895) and his wife, Sarah Bailey, from Portsmouth. However Titus died in 1899, at Tunbridge Wells, whilst taking a health break away from London. So instead of returning home to America the widowed Sarah stayed on in the Griffiths household in London and at their mansion of *Sandridgebury* until she finally passed away in 1916.[106]   As Sarah had been Marian's chief provider after the death of her mother (Sarah's sister in law, Anne Tredick) these years with old aunt Sarah (who perked up in overseeing Marian's children growing up in England) proved to be a happy time; they were an escape and a relief from how the future had looked for the widowed Marian in 1911.

## Marian's Letter to Barrett Wendell in USA[107]

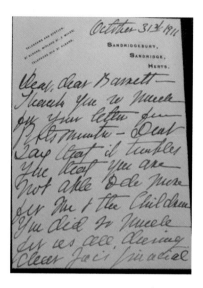

Writing on 31 October 1911 (which establishes a date for Marian's elopement to England) on headed paper from *Sandridgebury* to her brother-in- law *"Dear, dear Barrett"* in the USA, Marian begins by saying she fully understood that she ought not to take the money ( in the Wendell coffers) intended for the education of her sons to use instead to pay off her dead husbands debts, including those to his family. Besides this she acknowledges that Barrett's help would have to be limited but that he was already helping with "advice and approval". But she was unable to resist a dig at Barrett, adding aside that "....Dare I say that it troubles you that you are not able to do more for me and the children?" She also leaves him to contemplate (underlining the words in her letter) that if Jacob had been the one that was alive to help Barrett's family if they were in similar trouble: "if he [Jacob] could, he would do the same for you, and you know it!" [108]

Marian later went to law to establish her own best position.

When Justice Lehman signed an order Monday permitting Mrs. Marian Wendell to spend each year without reserve the combined incomes of herself and her four children, he shortened the list of American expatriates by five.

Mrs. Wendell and her two girls and two boys have been living in Sandbridgebury, England, since the death of Jacob Wendell, Jr., her husband, in April, 1911. The mother, too proud to stay in America and attempt to maintain the social position of her family on an income of $8,000 a year, an amount she knew to be inadequate, closed the town house at 106 East Thirty-fifth street, New York.

Living in a modest way in the English home, Mrs. Wendell has been able to approximate her former condition, but she says in her petition, she has been anxious to return to America because of the children, who belong here. Money from the estate of her father-in-law now has brought the income of her children to $13,000 a year, and Mrs. Wendell has schemed out a way to put the two boys, Jacob Wendell, 17 years old, and Reginald, 15, through preparatory school and send them to Harvard, where the men of the Wendell family for several generations have been educated.

Dr. Barrett Wendell, the children's uncle, is a professor in Harvard.

*Marian Goes to Court in USA*[109]

## Marian establishes herself in London

Marian Wendell frequently accompanied Gertrude to London, where the Griffiths' rented town houses at 11 and 73 Grosvenor Street, Grosvenor Square, and later at 30 Bruton Street, for the Season's events during the years before the Great War.

Marian's children were usually left behind at *Sandridgebury* with their nanny and the Griffiths' family servants. In 1911, the Wendell's elderly nursemaid Nellie Hurley (always called Nana[110]) from another Portsmouth connection also came over from New York so the children had a familiar face and voice to guide them in the absence of their mother's otherwise devoted attentions.

In Mayfair circles (dominated by the idle and rich British aristocracy) Marian became a friend of Lord Leigh[111] whose American wife Frances Helene Forbes hailed originally from New York and was known there by Marian. Lady Leigh had died in 1909. The sprightly Lord Leigh, despite having broken his neck in a hunting accident as a young man, often invited Marian to the theatre in London and dined with her at the *Ritz* or *Savoy* hotels and at his London house in Grosvenor Square. However Leigh was wooing several other women (he was a very wealthy catch, especially from the large legacy of his deceased wife's money) and marriage to Marian was not thought to be on the cards; he enjoyed her company but he later married another American, Marie Campbell, in 1923.

For her part Marian put her own personal happiness aside or at least on hold in favour of seeing her four children settled in marriage.

## The Wendell Children at Home: Life in Sandridge

*Catherine Wendell as a Young Girl*

No one pined for New York. Marian's four children took well to growing up in the quiet Hertfordshire countryside.

The Griffiths home of *Sandridgebury* (which was gaslit, electricity not being installed until 1932[112]) was described as "a low creeper-covered house, off the road that passes through the little village of Sandridge, past St Albans, and is on the borders of a stretch of common so wide that it is called 'No Man's Land'". [113]   Whilst the older two boys continued their education away from home, at Eton College and Repton, the younger children, Catherine and Philippa, came to know the other village children and were taken into St Albans or brought up to London for treats. A later portrait of Philippa's own family mentions the delight of being driven up to town by the Griffiths chauffeur, Mr French, for shopping excursions, visits to the zoo and for sightseeing. [114]

The Wendell children learned quickly that Percy was very set in his ways. He spent long periods alone in his study after meals and could never be disturbed, particularly on Saturdays mornings after coming back from his office in London because he always had business to conduct on the telephone.   Percy sometimes slept in the afternoons and the children were obliged to keep the noise levels down for he was sharp with them if his nap was disturbed.

Gertrude, on the other hand, was always sweetness and light. She loved nothing better than reading one of her adventure stories to Marian's two girls.  Outside the house were many different flowers, plants and trees; these were a haven in summertime for birds and wildlife generally and where the children played games or enjoyed a picnic or garden party, especially when Jac and Reggie came home for the holidays, Jac from Repton and Reggie from Eton College.

Village life was slow and tranquil. Garden fetes were a central theme. It was Church on Sundays and the little school in Sandridge for Catherine and Philippa during weekdays.

# The Great War

A Red Cross "Tank" on Canteen Service in London

When the Great War came Marian Wendell was one of the early volunteers for war work. She was a VAD in a nursing home in 1914-15. She also waited on tables at NY Headquarters Canteen in Belgrave Mansions, a military refuge established in response to request from American officers concerned about food scarcities and rationing whilst stationed in London. Most of the ground floor and basement of the main headquarters building of the US army in the Belgrave Mansions Hotel, Victoria, was allotted for the purpose of providing support, with four large dining rooms and kitchens.[115] Alongside Gertrude Griffiths, Marian also supported the American Women's War Relief Fund whose object was the care of wounded officers. [116]

Gertrude was an assiduous social climber who never missed an opportunity to shine in the eyes of the British Royal Family. When Queen Mary was expected to attend a matinee show at the New Theatre to raise funds for soldiers and sailors charities, Gertrude volunteered to supply the china and silver from her own family pieces at Grosvenor Square. On marrying Percy these ancestral treasures had come over with her from America; they had had a chequered history including being buried deep beneath a Tredick family estate in Virginia[117] during the four bloody years of the American Civil War.

## Marian's two sons, Jac and Reggie, go to English Public Schools

Some money had been found and wired across from the trust funds within the Wendell Estate in the USA to provide for the education in England of Marian's two sons, Jac and Reggie at English public schools. Of the two boys, Jac expressed a hope of following the established Wendell tradition of going to Harvard. He later gave up the notion of residing in the USA, but there were a few trips to New York and Boston in the years that followed to catch up with old school friends and the family of his uncle Barrett Wendell. Percy also promised his wife's cousin Marian that he would offer the Wendell boys some opportunity to enter the world of accountancy, but it seems that this plan was not pushed very far.

## The Wendell Boys in the Ambulance Corps followed by University

*American Ambulances in France*

The Wendell brothers served with the French Army of 1917 with the Norton-a-Harjes Ambulance Corps[118] attached to the American Red Cross. Jac was wounded and was later decorated with the *Croix de Guerre*. He later went on to Cambridge University.

Reggie, who was first a cadet in the Household Brigade in October 1918, enrolled at Balliol College, Oxford, where he studied from 1919-20[119] and made a name for himself as an Oxford University rower.

## Jacob's Old Debts Paid Off

*Evert Jansen Wendell*[120]

The sudden death in France during 1917 (whilst doing war work) of Marian's brother in law, Jacob Jnr's brother, Evert Jansen Wendell, brought at last the financial relief needed by Marian from carrying the burden of Jacob Wendell Jnr's debts. Evert's last Will and Testament (with a substantial estate in the USA, which had previously been tied up) made specific provisions for the discharge of several of his late brother's outstanding accounts. It had been a tough journey for Marian but now, at long last, one of the Wendells had honoured some age-old family debts and she could breathe a little easier.

## Catherine Wendell a pretty bridesmaid

Marian's pride and joy, her seventeen-year-old daughter Catherine Wendell, was the pretty bridesmaid at a wedding in St Albans in June 1917.[121] Catherine was a couple of years older than her sister Philippa. With a determined mother-hen of a coach and marriage broker, who could determine the lineage and bank balance of a prospective suitor from fifty paces, the odds on Catherine being advantageously placed in marriage were shortened considerably. In fact, a few years later Marion's aggressive matchmaking skills were commented upon as 'dazzling' in her success at marrying Catherine, Jac and Phillipa into elite British families.[122] Marian was easily marked as the "Most Brilliant Match-Maker of the Season". [123]

*How the American Press saw the match making skills of Catherine's mother, Marian Fendall Wendell*

## Catherine Arrives on the London Scene

Catherine made one of her early appearances on the social scene in November 1919 when her 'arrival' is recorded in the *Court Circular* of 15 November:

"Mr and Mrs Percival Griffiths, Mrs Wendell, and Miss Wendell have arrived at 37 Portman Square for the winter." [124]

So it was that the caterpillar took to flight in all her butterfly finery, flitting around some of London's smartest addresses. The nineteen-year-old Catherine had arrived; she soon became one of *the* faces to watch around the Capital.

## Hon.Lois Sturt: A Friend of Catherine

*Hon. Lois Sturt and Prince George*

Following in the family's theatrical tradition, in 1919 Catherine appeared on stage with the attractive, round-faced flapper the Hon. Lois Sturt,[125] an exact contemporary and another of the era's young, captivating women. Lois was an aspiring actress, art studio proprietoress, painter and one of the original 'Chelsea chicks'. Lois, it seemed, also made time in her schedule to be the lover of several of the Royal Princes, notably the bisexual Prince George, the best looking son of King George V and Queen Mary. George himself didn't let the grass grow under his feet, being on what might be called bedroom terms with Lois's bisexual brother Napier (Naps) Sturt (from 1921 the third Lord Alington of Crichel, Dorset).[126]

Lois went on to star in feature films with Lady Diana Manners including *A Glorious Adventure.* In her private life she enjoyed a long affair with the married and much older Reginald Herbert, 15th Earl of Pembroke and Montgomery, [127]who was a cousin of Porchey Carnarvon; indeed, of all the Herberts of Highclere.

## State Balls and Debutantes

The Great War, apart from costing countless lives, had brought an inconvenient hiatus in State Balls and of young ladies (debutantes) being presented at Court. Normal service wasn't resumed until July 1921. However, when you have two such formidable 'corner men' as Marian Wendell and Gertrude Griffiths rooting for you and you are a beauty like Catherine it came as no surprise that her appearance on 14 April 1920 at the Devonshire House Ball (apparently "a magnificent spectacle"[128]) was followed by a scrum of fawning young men (many fresh from the privations of war) vying for her attention. Subsequently the invitations that Marian had prayed for arrived in droves. In Highclere's account[129] of Catherine life it is suggested that she received fourteen proposals of marriage prior to that of Henry, Viscount Porchester.

## Catherine's engagement to Francis Collingwood Drake

Her first ardent suitor was not in fact from a landed or titled family on the London scene. She was romanced by a local man from St Albans, close to Sandridge, where she had grown up as the young emigrant from New York. Her pursuer was Francis Collingwood Drake of the 10th Hussars, a war hero, who had won the Military Cross. He still had good enough credentials to please Marian and Gertrude for he was the son of Mr J Ramsey Drake, JP, the High Sheriff of Hertfordshire. The Drake's large home was at *Batchwood Hall* near St Albans.

The announcement of an engagement followed in *The Times* of 17 August 1920:

### MR F C DRAKE AND MISS WENDELL

"An engagement is announced between Francis Collingwood Drake, MC, late 10th Hussars, son of Mr J Ramsey Drake, JP, High Sheriff of Hertfordshire, and Mrs J Ramsey Drake, of Batchwood Hall near St Albans, Hertfordshire, and Miss Catherine Wendell, daughter of the late Jacob Wendell of New York, and Mrs Wendell, of Sandridgebury, Sandridge, Hertfordshire."

Francis was born in 1897 and attended Eton College at about the same time as Porchey Carnarvon. Both went on to join Sandhurst Military Academy and were attached to the Hussars, Francis to the 10th Royal Hussars, Porchey to the 7th Queen's Own Hussars.[130] They are bound to have known each other during their school years and military training period and it is also highly likely that the years Reggie Wendell spent at Eton (he was the same age as Porchey) coincided in part with Porchey and Francis's schooldays.

Sadly, marriage plans collapsed between Francis Drake and Catherine. The facts are at variance on exactly what happened to end Catherine's romance with Drake and his well-placed St Albans family[131] but in October 1921 Drake announced he was to marry Daphne Joyce Wolton of *Kibworth Hall*. Leicester. Their wedding took place in London on 31 December 1921, and they almost immediately removed themselves to New York. [132]

Unknown to Catherine but not to the eagle-eyed Marian and Gertrude (as much a pair of conspirators as Lear's daughters Goneril and Regan), several young heirs offered a much better titled prospect than Drake. One of these men was Henry, Viscount Porchester (better known to his friends as Porchey), who was the heir to the Earldom of Carnarvon.

Who exactly was Porchey and how did he come to meet Catherine?

*Porchey Carnarvon as A Young Man*[133]

# Chapter 3

## Porchey Carnarvon's Background

## Conception[134]

*Fifth Earl, Prince Victor Duleep Singh and Almina*

Porchey Carnarvon was conceived in Egypt in 1898 when his mother Almina was impregnated at the request of the Fifth Earl and with Almina's consent ( or else by her own plot ) and the collaboration of the Earl's pre-eminent and intimate friend, Prince Victor Duleep Singh,[135] the eldest son of the deceased Maharajah of Lahore.[136] This remarkable act of surrogacy was practised solely to secure the creation of a Carnarvon heir. Victor stood in 'on race day' due to the fact his Lordship was not in the best physical condition and therefore was something of a non-starter in the heir production stakes.

Victor's altruism in stepping up to the plate for his friend eventually became known in Society circles long before Almina's history exploded in 2011 with two books[137] including the author's *The Life and Secrets of Almina Carnarvon*. One well-placed correspondent (who mixed in Royal chambers), commenting on the aforementioned book, also adds: "In your book ...you disclose paternity by a certain Prince – it's the first time I've ever seen this in print, though lots of people knew!"[138]

Additionally a present-day member of the Carnarvon family *personally* told the author that when the book was reviewed by a feature in the British newspaper *The Daily Telegraph*, "they suffered cardiac arrest at Highclere." [139]

In the public domain Highclere continues to avoid the truth. Besides the hypocrisy there is a greater issue because the *real* Earl of Carnarvon (in a blood line from Henry, the Fourth Earl) is a shy schoolteacher who lives in Taunton, North Somerset.[140]

Going back to Porchey's origins of 1898 at the time of the proposed conception, Victor and his wife, Lady Anne Coventry, were seen by contemporaries as a curious couple living in a celibate marriage, never consummated (on the orders of Queen Victoria[141]) but which state suited them both).

*Lord Carnarvon and Prince Victor Duleep Singh*

The parties, Carnarvon and Duleep Singh and spouses, were both dubbed 'odd couples'.[142] They had also chosen an odd setting for Victor to do the honours for the House of Herbert, since the Duleep Singhs were on their honeymoon in Egypt. The Carnarvons made a short stopover in Paris, enjoyed some merriment playing the gaming tables at Monte Carlo and ultimately reached Egypt by boat from Marseilles over to Alexandra from where they joined their most adaptable friends.

Victor's impressively olive-skinned mother Bamba[143] (who was of German- Abyssinian descent) lived sometime on the banks of the Nile near Cairo. The area of the Delta was often visited by Victor and the Fifth Earl from 1887 onwards. During the Earl's coming of age year, Victor's mother died the same year in London. As playboys the two inseparable chums (who were together at Eton and Cambridge) were frequently at sea together, out of the Royal Yacht Club's moorings at Cowes, Isle of Wight and indulging in short sailing trips to the seafront gambling dens on the Belgian and French coasts.

Curiously, women were banned on board ship and wearing brown shoes was compulsory: that was Carnarvon's preference. The two pals sowed their proverbial oats in European and North African sin cities, frequenting notorious bath houses, gaming clubs and brothels in pursuit of excitement, vice and pleasure. The price paid by the Fifth Earl for the risks taken (negligent hygiene coupled with a sorrowful taste in lowlife 'ladies and gentlemen of the night') was that he contracted a permanent venereal disease which spread virulently to affect his face and lungs. This caused disfigurement, blighting his quality of life, putting a halt to normal sexual escapades and exposing him to the tender mercies of practically every quack doctor north of the equator. Their nefarious prescriptions included dangerous mercury compounds which left him debilitated and toothless; ultimately these poisons destroyed his entire digestive system.[144]

## Porchey's Birth and Christening

After a traumatic pregnancy during which Almina grew increasing large in body size, she became even more alarmed at the prospect that the forthcoming baby's looks and hue might resemble its real father. She was full of superstition, especially about having this child born at a house numbered 13. The Earl's physician Dr Marcus Johnson (a good friend to Almina too) calmed his patient down with sweet attentions and tender loving care and delivered a healthy child of Caucasian appearance who was known as Lord Porchester (Porchey) and later became the Sixth Earl of Carnarvon.

Porchey's birth was on 7 November, 1898 at 13 Berkeley Square, London. To great celebrations and family ritual at Highclere and on the Carnarvon estates he was later christened on 12 December 1898, as this extract from *The Times* describes:

"The baptism of Lord Porchester, infant son and heir of the Earl and Countess of Carnarvon, took place yesterday afternoon in the Chapel Royal, St James's Palace. The Rev Edgar Sheppard, Sub Dean of the Chapels Royal, performed the rite, and used water brought from the River Jordan. The child received the names of Henry George Alfred Marius Victor Francis, and the sponsors were Prince Victor Duleep Singh, Lord Ashburton, Mr. Alfred de Rothschild, Lady Burghclere, and Mrs. Wombwell." [145]

Lady Burghclere was previously Lady Winifred Herbert, the blue-stocking, straight-laced sister of the Fifth Earl. Mrs Wombwell was Marie Boyer, Almina's over-ambitious French mother, the merry widow of Frederick Wombwell of the Wombwells of Newburgh Priory, North Yorkshire. Ashburton was a rich shooting pal of Carnarvon. Alfred de Rothschild was the millionaire banker linked in social terms with Marie Boyer. Some said she was his mistress but this is a most unlikely posturing; Alfred was a predatory homosexual more likely to be caught up in a Cleveland Street or Cadogan Hotel type-trap which would end in his arrest and his place in Society. Alfred adored Almina to bits and called her affectionately 'Pussy Cat'. And Pussy Cat robbed her benefactor on all fronts to pay for her marriage and later foibles (including in war-time her nursing homes) and illicit black market dealings in pleasures. Alfred (bless him) also paid to keep Lord Carnarvon out of Almina's hair.

## Porchey appears on the Early Census Records 1901 and 1911

It is of note that the two-year-old Porchey is to be found under the roof of his mother's benefactor, Baron Alfred de Rothschild, at Alfred's country seat of Hatton House, Buckinghamshire on Census night of 1901, albeit in the safe watch of two nurses: forty-four-year-old Emma Rowe and twenty-four-year-old Margaret Russell. [146] Family visits to Halton were irregular. Alfred had a reputation for laying on some fine hospitality and the house boasted an impressive collection of art and antique furniture and exotic pets.

## Porchey's Childhood

In 1901, under the heading of *"Gentlewoman at Home"*, a long article appeared in the magazine *The Gentlewoman* describing the home life of Almina, Fifth Countess of Carnarvon, at Highclere. The article included a portrait of Almina and her infant son, Lord Porchester.[147] This marked Porchey's first public outing after his christening.

He was at times a sickly little boy and in 1903, on the eve of his parent's trip to the USA, he fell gravely ill. He rallied and was left to the tender mercies of his nanny, who had her work cut out as Porchey's sister Lady Evelyn [148] had been born the previous August and was now nanny's favourite. [149]

In 1904 Porchey made one of his early public appearances at a family wedding at Dulverton, Somerset, when the Fifth Earl's sister, Lady Margaret Herbert, married George Duckworth. Porchey supported his aunt (the bride) as a page boy, dressed in a Joshua Reynolds suit of pale blue velvet. He was tiny but was competent holding up her long Court train. [150]

Two years later, in 1906, Almina staged a large garden party in honour of her mother Marie, Mrs Frederick Wombwell. Almina's two children, "Lord Porchester, a tiny man of six and his still tinier sister Lady Evleyn Herbert",[151] were staying with their grandmother in Bruton Street, Mayfair. A conjurer and a slide show were hired to amuse the small guests. Porchey fell into the company of the American-born Duchess of Marlborough's "two big handsome boys, Lord Blandford and little Lord Ivor Spencer-Churchill."[152] The Duchess famously referred to her sons as "an heir and a spare".[153] The friendship between Porchey and 'Bert' Blandford (later Tenth Duke of Marlborough) lasted the remainder of their lives. They were like two peas from the same pod in their singleton or combined audacious conduct towards women. One ninety-one-year-old peeress who kindly supplied the author with a particular memory wrote of Porchey and Marlborough that "Porchey's great friend was Bert, Duke of Marlborough, they hunted in pairs!" [154]

In 1908 nine-year-old Porchey was among the young people who attended the Duchess of Leeds' children's party at 11, Grosvenor Crescent, London for her little son, Lord Carmarthen.[155] Porchey was in his element as an up-and-coming young beau; after all, the Duchess also had four playful little daughters.[156]

By 1911 Porchey, the twelve-year old reluctant schoolboy, was a boarder at Ludgrove School in New Barnet, Middlesex. Among his fellow pupils, others of noble birth born in 1898-9 were Peter Whitbread, Hon, Edward Keppel, Lord Romilly and Hugh Hebert Percy.[157] Porchey's school reports were nothing to write home about (but his housemaster did, all the same); when they inevitably reached his parents it appeared that he excelled only in bad behaviour and inattentiveness.

In his memoirs[158] Porchey recalled two bitter childhood memories that affected him mentally. The first was when he was thrashed with three twigs of birch wood on his bare backside by the Fifth Earl; the charge sheet included indolence and 'those school reports' (offences for which the Fifth Earl had often been chastised by his own father).

The second was when he was slapped on the head and kicked in the shins by his mother, Almina, all the way home from a children's Christmas party at Windsor in which he had disgraced her in the presence of Princess Mary (methinks it wouldn't take much to disgrace yourself in front of this formidable lady) and other Royals. Almina imposed additional sanctions to the physical punishment including solitary confinement, a diet of bread and milk and the seizure of all Porchey's Christmas presents.

Humiliated, (an emotion that Porchey could *not* deal with well), he plotted revenge (an activity he was to return to in later life when he was not someone to be crossed lightly) against these parental tormentors; in short he wanted both parents dead and even worked out exactly how he might achieve being left fatherless by stabbing the Earl to death "with ...a little dagger which seemed well fitted to the task in hand." [159]

Often during his lonely childhood Porchey's only regular companion was his younger sister Evelyn, born three years after him. Evelyn was an especially important presence when Almina and the Fifth Earl were in Egypt year on year for the winter seasons before the Great War. It was customary to despatch Porchey and Evelyn to Bretby Park, the Carnarvon's place in Derbyshire. Porchey found Bretby fascinating as it was a paradise for riding, hunting and shooting. The estate was eventually sold off by the Fifth Earl to balance the family's accounting books. As a result Porchey and his sister often stayed with Almina's mother, Marie Wombwell, in 20, Bruton Street, London, where they were thoroughly spoilt and fondly loved.

Both Porchey and Lady Evelyn retained much affection for their grandmother who spoke French to them, read stories in that same language, and adored them being under her roof. In turn, Almina's two children dearly loved Marie, but she died in 1913. Apart from the Fifth Earl's stepmother, Elsie[160] (who did not have much contact with Almina's children), Marie was the only regular grandparent they saw in the family. Marie was also a frequent visitor at Highclere and in the years before his death in 1912 Almina's beloved brother, Captain Frederick Adolphus Wombwell,[161] rode and shot with his brother-in-law, the Fifth Earl, on the Highclere estate. It is a cheerless reflection that Highclere *fail* to acknowledge Frederick's existence or acknowledge the fact that Almina (and her mother) raised a memorial stained glassed window to an adoring brother and son at St Michael's and All Angels, Highclere's Parish Church.

## Hero Worship

Porchey's heroes rode and shot, and he believed he could be as good as them. But at Eton one boy stood out as a friend (and is mentioned in both of Porchey's books of memoirs): that was Harry Kerr. Porchey was fond of Harry but his dear friend was killed in action in the Great War.[162] But Porchey did not grieve, he was taught to hide his emotions, and this blighted his development and attitudes.

## The Call of the Army

In October 1916, after attending a crammer for several months, Porchey was successfully admitted to Sandhurst Military College where he was gazetted a second-lieutenant in the 7th Queen's Own Hussars, the *only* lowly rank he ever held throughout the Great War. At the same time as he was commissioned his close Eton and Sandhurst friend, the Hon. John Alan Burns[163] (son of Lord Inverclyde) joined the Scots Guards. The two old pals continued to meet regularly in London at the all-gentlemen *White's* Club. As we shall see, in 1920, when Burns (who had by then succeeded to the Inverclyde title) was ADC to the Governor of Gibraltar, he suggested that Porchey might be suitable for the vacant (unpaid) post of additional ADC to the Gibraltar Governor. Whilst serving together on *The Rock*, (the term used for Gibraltar) Burns played cupid in bringing Porchey and Catherine together.

## Youth

Bert Blandford (heir to the Duke of Marlborough, later the Tenth Duke) made up another of Porchey's faithful Eton and Sandhurst generation. He was co-conspirator when the two seventeen-year-olds sought to lose their virginity and the two heirs in waiting didn't have to wait long. Their deliverers were co-operative actresses in the same touring company. Porchey's 'gal' was named Mosesta. The boys were clumsy and quick but the women were very understanding and each received the appropriate gentleman's rate. In fact, business picked up as word got around and the same actresses agreed to relieve several of their Sandhurst chums of their innocence. Such rites of passage all took place when the boys had a break away from their short period of army training (which was all that new officers received in the hard-pressed days of the Great War).

Mosesta was not alone: several other ladies are 'mentioned in despatches' in Porchey memoirs and interviews. [164] He recalls these early amorous adventures thus: "During our leave [from Sandhurst] it was not unnatural that we should look for love and laughter. After all, we were young and full of joie de vivre."[165]

The Hussars were on patrol until well after the Armistice but the War Diary of the regiment has no meritorious mention of Porchey apart from him going off on a training course.[166] Reduced to only twelve officers and ninety-six other ranks, the 7th Queen's Own Hussars was on duty until March 1919 when they left Baghdad to start the journey home to England via Basra and Suez.[167]

After the Great War ended Porchey came back home to England and to a potentially heavy schedule with a backlog of *12,000 debutantes* waiting to be presented at Court! The meat market of war was replaced by that of high society.

Porchey remained in the army for several more years and, in addition to re-entering the social scene, wasted no time getting back on to the saddle as an accomplished amateur rider. He clocked up dozens of mounts at English and Scottish racecourses[168] and his name appears in several reports covering the years from mid 1919-1920 onwards.

However, riding didn't come without a cost to Porchey. He sustained several falls in his early life and on one such occasion as a fifteen-year-old boy he had been badly shaken up, sustaining bruises and a broken shoulder bone after being thrown from a horse when riding to the Vine Hounds, near Highclere. [169]

For Porchey, taking a toss from his horse was an occupational hazard. The price he paid for this in later years was recurring bouts of sciatica.

When on furlough from their army labours Bert Blandford (who was in the Life Guards) was often in Porchey's company at London night spots and they were a part of a betting syndicate that placed bets at the big race meetings, including the Epsom Derby of 1920 which was won by J B Joel's colt *Humorist.* The syndicate won a substantial sum. The Joels were friends and neighbours of the Fifth Earl and Almina in Mayfair.

# Catherine's Broken Romance and Gibraltar Meeting

*Catherine and Porchey*

Being around horses and those who wager on them, Catherine's mother knew a good picking up point, especially for identifying eligible young men returned from the war. It was also a thriving place to pick up intelligence on the movement of the marriageable well-off.

Catherine liked horses and she had ridden ponies as a young girl in America and at Sandridge. Porchey didn't meet her at the races but by the early winter of 1920 the scene was set for Catherine to first meet Porchey in Gibraltar and later emerge as the budding Lady Porchester. According to the Sixth Earl's ghost-written memoirs *No Regrets* she first met Porchey formally when he was acting as an extra ADC to General Sir Horace Dorrien-Smith,[170] the Governor of Gibraltar.

Their encounter was not accidental. *The Rock* (as Gibraltar was termed) was an important British stronghold[171] and the social life on the island (including plenty of polo, horse racing and shooting) was outstandingly good; this had been a key reason for Porchey accepting the posting which Alan Burns orchestrated. The Gibraltar Governor was a social animal whose regular rather grand balls attracted many visitors from home as well as from the ships of the line.

The meeting of Porchey and Catherine therefore happened by a mix of stealth and importuning. It began with one of Marian Wendell's notions (a tip-off from Gertrude Griffiths) about going out to *The Rock* on the prowl to eye up prospective wealthy or colonial husbands for her two unmarried and very much less prosperous daughters. Marian's plan was to show Catherine off at the 1920 Ball.

The suggestion in a recent book from a Highclere ghost writer that Catherine and her mother were simply engaged on a tour of Europe is somewhat disingenuous as it could not be fitted in with their appearance back in England soon after being in Gibraltar.

The precise date of the Gibraltar encounter is discernible from the Ship's Passengers Lists in National Archives. Marian Wendell, a forty-nine-year old widow, and the nineteen-year-old Catherine Wendell left London on 5 November 1920 on board the *Kalyan*. They were travelling, for appearances sake, by First Class, but only to Gibraltar.[172] This was about as far as Marian's little money would stretch. Porchey Carnarvon's second wife Tilly (like Catherine's mother) was a believer in the policy of "Always have a good black dress, pearls, and stay in the best hotel, even if you can have only the worst room."[173]

*The Rock* had been chosen to distance Catherine from her broken engagement to Francis Collingwood Drake, something that could affect her 'pulling power' back home. Catherine was labelled as someone who did *not* keep her word and was talked about as a bit of a tease. It's clear that whilst engaged to Drake she was flirting non-stop with a variety of other men, several who had been misled into even proposing marriage. Highclere's testimony backfires on this point. They cite *fourteen proposals of marriage* before Porchey had his way. Catherine encouraged these other suitors and left them dangling; her apparent betrayal must have become known to Drake who must have rejoiced that he'd had a lucky escape.

To set her trap for the next new would-be husband the pushy Wendell mother plus daughter installed themselves at the *Reina Christina Hotel* in Algeciras, a location set closely between the borders of Spain and Gibraltar.

The usual thing was for any notable British visitors staying near *The Rock* to be invited to join the party. Alan Burns (Lord Inverclyde, like Porchey one of the Governor's ADCs) spotted Catherine on a reconnaissance trip to Algeciras and introduced himself. Later he mentioned to Porchey that "a lovely American girl was staying at the Reina Christina…….. [adding] actually she's lived in England for quite a long time but she is travelling with her mother to get over a broken love affair." [174]

Inverclyde sent Porchey over to collect Marian and Catherine on the official barge. Porchey was smitten at once by Catherine's good looks and as usual lust overcame his sense and rationality.

At the Governor's Ball Catherine appeared in a "becoming yellow dress and looked beautiful."[175] Marian's cunning plan was working with this appearance and display of her eldest daughter in such male company. Gibraltar was where soldiers and sailors *en route* from their long overseas postings spent a last night or last day before a bout of restorative home leave back with their families. Marian's thinking was inspired: act quickly to offer her daughter before any of these eligible young men actually returned home to England.

Porchey asked to see Catherine again and a romantic correspondence of sorts between them followed. This was also a part of Marian's cunning overall plan coming to fruition. Catherine was *told* to fall in love with Porchey. Porchey was now fully up for the thrill of the chase; he wanted to seduce her and peddled his usual string of platitudes, promises and tales, plummy chat-up lines he'd used to good effect on the many women he had already bedded and then discarded. On this occasion, however, Porchey chose the wrong quarry with Catherine and found himself well and truly captivated. He must have her at all costs! Marian Fendall Wendell's machinations were beginning to bear fruit. Catherine agreed to see Porchey again in London during one of his next periods of home leave. In fact, shortly afterwards Porchey's secondment to Gibraltar ended and he was back in London until a new army posting, and later he had a more settled return back again to England.

# Porchey's Circle: Porchey Romping and Lusting

As an officer in the 7th Queen's Own Hussars, wherever the regiment was stationed Porchey Carnarvon's choice of female attachments were chosen to satisfy his carnal desires and to hell with the consequences, especially if his activities caused affront to his parents or, indeed, to the regiment's stuffy commanding officer. Soldiers may march on their stomachs but he had other appetites to be assuaged. One informant describes him as a " polo-playing, pig-sticking snob, a bigot, a bully with a rough edge, a taste for giving subordinates the lash." [176] In the art of seduction he was sometimes disturbed by a father, a mother or a husband which necessitated him climbing and descending drainpipes, accessing rooftops and rushing down fire escapes in the company of his trousers after nights out. Indeed, if his war record had been as varied and busy as his sex life in local bars hotels and even the officer's mess, the man would have been more decorated than Oxford Street on Christmas Eve.

Among those army cronies who shared or shielded any fallout from Porchey's sorties on any given female population was Tommy Frost;[177] indeed they were a reprehensible influence on one another. Frost later acted as Porchey's best man at his wedding to Catherine in 1922. Of the many women Porchey lured bedwards, one tale is worth telling: his ensnarement of one Viscountess but everything didn't quite go to plan.

## Wife of the heir to the Earl of Craven and Porchey

Among Porchey's contemporaries at Eton, just a year his junior, was a badly-behaved peer named William Craven, Viscount Uffington,[178] the heir to the Earl of Craven. Uffington was expelled from Eton "for bad discipline, not vice"[179] and as a seventeen-year-old officer in the Hampshire Regiment he tried the patience of his commanding officer with wild histrionics and absence without leave.[180]

Uffington's mother (Cornelia,[181] daughter of the millionaire New Yorker, Bradley Martin) pulled strings to keep her son in the army and he was eventually packed off to a safe haven as a General's ADC. This was not before marrying a gorgeous redhead named Mary Wilhelmina George,[182] a town clerk's daughter from Invergordon, whilst training with the Hampshires at Strathpeffer in Scotland.

Uffington's attentions soon moved on to other women and Wilhelmina (who bore him a son and heir) looked elsewhere for love. Porchey knew the family (they were neighbours in Newbury) and he soon took a shine to Wilhelmina who he describes as "one of the loveliest girls I've ever met."[183] Foolishly, Porchey chose the Uffington's house to seize the opportunity to take full advantage. Porchey was happily locked in the redhead's arms when their passionate embrace was interrupted by the sudden appearance of the hopping mad Uffington (his reasons for hopping were in fact twofold as he had lost a leg in the Great War). However, what was concentrating Porchey's mind was the fact Uffington was brandishing a loaded revolver. Concerned for his life, Porchey hurriedly dressed and fled not a moment too soon as Uffington fired a shot through the door behind where Porchey had hitherto been standing.[184] There is anecdotal evidence that Porchey returned many times to woo and win favours from Wilhelmina. Divorce proceedings were taken later by Wilhelmina who cited Uffington's very public affair with the Countess of Cathcart which, in 1926, also swept in a member of a Wendell collateral, Cecelia, the wife of Philip Gordon Carr. [185]

Uffington's father died at Cowes in a drowning accident in 1921; he inherited the Earldom and died in 1932. Wilhelmina survived until 1974.

## Catherine Moves In Ever Increasing Royal Circles

Porchey and Catherine's relationship grew closer and with this Catherine ascended into ever more exalted circles. She had a certain cachet already from her earlier acting performances with racier members of the smart set such as Lois Sturt and things got even better when making enquiries about the Carnarvon heir (which included intelligence-gathering by Gertrude among other London Society Hostesses). Marian discovered to her sheer delight that her prospective son-in-law was a member of the Prince of Wales's choice inner-sanctum.

But there was a debit side too as a Royal rumour was recounted that Porchey had been considered (and then discounted as "quite unsuitable"[186]) for the hand in marriage of Princess Mary, the only daughter of King George V and Queen Mary. The reasons for the block were unclear to Gertrude's informant but the snub did not unduly bother Marian or Gertrude. Americans were not unduly concerned about Porchey's more bizarre origins.

As far as the Royals were concerned the truth about Porchey's paternity was an issue of race rather than class. There had been an extraordinary surrogacy arrangement between Prince Victor Duleep Singh (whose heritage was Sikh) and the Carnarvons. The paternity issue lay dormant in Almina's cabinet of secrets, and with it the cover-up of the identity of her only son's true father, until an American guide at Highclere was commissioned to write a biography of Almina which he did, to gasps at the outcome, as he discovered quite by chance that Prince Victor Duleep Singh was Porchey's father. [187]

The deal in 1898 when the Carnarvons spent time with Duleep Singh in Egypt was accepted, in fact, encouraged by Lord Carnarvon who was riddled with venereal disease and made a risky father.[188] Besides his exotic blood line Porchey had the personality of a bear with a thorn in its paw; he was often irritable and was a despicable, insatiable womaniser. He constantly flirted with the Prince of Wales's clutch of friends, especially his girlfriends.[189] Catherine realised after such displays as she witnessed at close range that there was deep trouble in store for the future, especially over the appalling way Porchey behaved at times, his dirty-minded innuendos passing for witty banter, his less than amorous talk, his wandering eyes and hands, including not shrinking about making a pass at another man's sweetheart or wife.

"An outsider summed [the Prince's group up] …. All the girls had slim, lovely legs. All the men were rich, and some were flashy." [190] Porchey was most definitely flashy.

Catherine had her own grave doubts about Porchey but Marian overruled this resistance and fooled her daughter into a safe belief that all would be well. Catherine was duped by both Porchey and her mother as one.

Catherine's eyes caught sight of her ideal man and it was not the lewd, short, dumpy-shaped Porchey. She first became a close friend of the pretty and lively banking heiress Poppy Baring[191] who, although christened Helen Azalea, "was always called 'Poppy', [an] exotic, velvet-eyed beauty..."[192]  Catherine and Poppy discovered they had a mutual friend in Lois Sturt.[193]

*Poppy Baring and Prince George*

They got on immediately and Catherine soon met her real Prince Charming.  Poppy, also dubbed "the Belle of Cowes"[194] (where her parents had a mansion house) was one of Prince Edward's coterie but Catherine was drawn more sensually to Poppy's occasional lover, Edward's younger brother, the dashing, tall, dark haired, blue-eyed Prince George. She simply adored George (who was known as 'PG'); it is said she "gasped for breath in his presence." [195]

*The Bright Young Things Enjoy 'A Baby Party'*

The Prince of Wales's group of 'Darlings' (simply everyone was called 'Darling') sometimes had PG in tow. They were all in the race for pleasure. They oozed wealth, glamour and chic and their time together was full of crazy pleasure-seeking and, as Noel Coward observed in song, "cocktails and laughter"[196]. They were part of the *Bright Young Things* brigade. They were mad about tennis and golf, fast cars, sailing, the latest high jinks, pranks including playing at chasing clues and also horse-racing, of which Porchey was the leading stud as well as everyone's betting tipster as he was an amateur jockey and horse owner, as was his father, the Fifth Earl. The madcap friends craved the latest jazz music, the 20s frivolous dancing fads, drinking champagne, smoking cheroots, cigarettes, some drug taking and always having a very good time, mostly travelling to and spending the evening at, parties (many of them themed parties) at secret places and in the era's nightclubs in London. But as the evenings passed some partygoers generally sneaked off in twos, not always a boy and girl, well off the beaten track, and let nature or whatever take it course.

For his part Porchey danced well, stayed up late and was often outrageous fun to be with but had a short temper and was not a sensitive or considerate lover. He talked of using the same technique in lovemaking as used when riding a horse over the sticks at Uttoxeter,[197] not perhaps then the happiest of prospects for Catherine.

# Chapter 4

## Moving in on the Carnarvons

Catherine was a bridesmaid at a large-scale Society wedding in London at St Margaret's Church, Westminster, on 25 April 1922[198] which, as timings go, was a good rehearsal for her own wedding a few months later in the same magnificent venue. A wedding at St Margaret's was an indication of rank and wealth and standing in London.

An announcement appeared in *The Times* which was a complete surprise to Almina and Lord Carnarvon, of the marriage of their only son and heir to, of all people, an American refugee. They had not met the girl but they had heard she was pretty and attractive and altogether much liked. However, by having at least one broken engagement (to Francis Drake) she was soiled goods and all of London knew about it; besides, there had been no proceedings taken on Catherine's part for breach of promise. This was an indication that *she* had been the party to reconsider and break her promise and accordingly was branded a risk for the next chump who took a shine to her beauty.

Paris was the agreed setting for Catherine's inspection by Porchey's closest family. According to Almina's godson, Tony Leadbetter, Almina told him that she was set against the marriage since all the signs were that the Wendell migrant from America was only gold digging.[199]

Although this charge was true, to Catherine's great credit she emerged as a likeable young woman, albeit she had no money and was an American. One factor above all others that influenced Almina's change of mind and ultimate acceptance of her would-be daughter-in-law was that Catherine showed respect and reverence towards her, pulling off a wonderfully appreciated gesture by presenting Almina with a spray of violets, a flower that represents one's humility in the presence of the party given the bouquet. This was an amazing coup on Catherine's part and the two women became lifelong friends and protectors.

As time was short before the date of the proposed wedding Almina was keen to show case her prospective daughter-in-law back in London.

Almina knew how to throw a party that dwarfed almost everyone except the Royal and State occasions. On 14 July 1922, to Vassie's band, she gave a dance for 500 guests at her London home of 1, Seamore Place, Mayfair to show off her prospective daughter-in-law Catherine at the same time as toasting her own daughter Evelyn in her follow-up year as a debutante.[200]  Guests came from far and wide; Catherine and Porchey's friend Prince George was the guest of honour and they mingled with Ambassadors, Dukes and Duchesses, Marquesses, Lords and Admirals as well as the Prime Minister's wife, Mrs Lloyd George and their daughter.

## American Wives

Catherine Wendell was not the first American citizen to join the Herbert clan. Lord Carnarvon's half-brother Mervyn Herbert[201] had an American wife, Mary Williard, who was the daughter of Joseph E Willard, a former American Ambassador to Spain and sister of Mrs Kermit Roosevelt.

Usually Almina had no time for Americans (after a decidedly unhappy trip from the East coast to West coast of the USA in 1903[202]); the Fifth Earl was equally against their extravagancies although he admired their horse racing stables, some American jockeys (who rode in the Carnarvon colours) and had respect for some of the men he had worked with from the Metropolitan Museum in New York in Egypt. But in any case, both Almina and her husband warmed to Catherine. Neither however was optimistic that Porchey could hold on successfully to the attraction he seemed to have for this beautiful woman he had won. He would botch it up with his ever wandering eye for the next pretty girl that came along. That, alas, proved to be true.

There was also an American connection with Porchey's sister as Lady Evelyn Herbert's proposed romance (leaning towards a future marriage) was to a Captain Brogrove Beauchamp of the First Life Guards.  Brogrove's mother was Betty Woods, an American, the daughter of Archibald Woods of Columbus, Ohio.

# The Porchester's Wedding

*Catherine and Porchey Wedding 1922*

It was the last day of the London season of 1922. Catherine felt serene and supported after a pleasant day spent lunching and last minute shopping with her girlie friends who had a variety of suggestions on how to tame Porchey's wicked ways, of which several of those present had (how shall we put it ?) 'first-hand' experience. Edwina Ashley was among the party. On the day following Catherine's wedding she was to marry her royal sailor boy, Lord Louis Mountbatten.

Catherine was looking forward to seeing another royal, the stunning Prince George in the line up of close friends. In the back of her mind she couldn't help imagining him and not Porchey standing beside her at the altar.

It was a stellar gathering. Prince George, the American Ambassador and his wife Mrs Harvey, Lord Louis Mountbatten and Edwina Ashley were all amongst the large congregation assembled to witness the wedding of Porchey and Catherine. St Margaret's Westminster, the scene of so many Society weddings, was a public spectacle, and one of the very few occasions when Almina walked arm in arm with her husband, Lord Carnarvon. A small snap shot bears this out. Prophetically it was to be one of their last ever public engagements together. Within twelve months Carnarvon would be dead, from cancer of the throat.[203]

The wedding was a showpiece event conducted by Canon Carnegie. The bride wore a classically cut gown of white satin caught at the side by a diamond clasp. The two trainbearers were Master Ronnie Maudsley and Miss Jean Crichton.

There were nine bridesmaids, notably Porchey's sister Lady Evelyn Herbert and Catherine's sister Philippa Wendell leading the rest of the line-up of girls of mixed ages.[204] The bridesmaids wore dresses of yellow chiffon with yellow and white crystal belts, yellow hats trimmed with pale yellow ostrich feathers and silver sandals.

As the bride alighted at the church a trumpeter of the 4th Dragoon Guards sounded the regimental call of the 7th Hussars, Porchey's regiment.

Marian Wendell held the post-wedding reception at her friend Lord Leigh's house at 31 Grosvenor Square, London.

Catherine's brother, twenty-five-year-old Jac Wendell (who gave Catherine away) was also considering his own marriage options. His name had been linked in the chit-chat of London parlours with several titled girls. One particular story was of his engagement to Lady Elizabeth Bowes-Lyon, who went on to marry the Duke of York.[205] The Bowes-Lyon family (of the ancient Glamis Castle, Forfarshire, Scotland) and in particular the Scottish peers, the two Lords Strathmore [206] (Elizabeth's grandfather and father) had been given to understand they would eventually be rewarded for their part in giving sanctuary to the notorious Prince Eddy (the Duke of Clarence[207]) who, it was rumoured, did *not* die of influenza in 1891 but ended his days on the Strathmore Estate, dying there under an assumed name in the 1930s. [208] What better reward than that a Bowes-Lyon became a Royal Duchess?

At the time of Catherine's engagement to Porchey, Jac announced shortly before his sister's wedding that he was to marry Eileen Carr (who was one of Catherine's bridesmaids), a girl from a rich stockbroker family whose father was also well known in horse racing circles. Jac and Eileen subsequently married on 17 April 1923 at a difficult time for the Carnarvons as it was in the immediate aftermath of the death of the Fifth Earl in Egypt on 5 April.

## The Porchesters Head for India

A few months after he was married Porchey was given a posting with his regiment to India. At Christmas 1922 (with Tutankhamun fever ringing in everyone's ears after the discovery of the Tomb of the boy King in November that year) he travelled with Catherine out to the East from Tilbury Docks. It was whilst in India in March 1923 that news came through of the Fifth Earl's closeness to death. Some details in Porchey's memoirs about this episode (written fifty years afterwards by the ghost writer, Barry Wynn) are totally unreliable and cannot be right, since several of the personalities mentioned were not in the posts attributed to them at this time, but such poppycock is still set in concrete by Highclere's history pirates and recycled.

There is truth in the fact that Porchey was whisked by train and by boat from India to where Carnarvon's death scene took place, in a hotel in Cairo. It was all played out like an episode from a character's demise in a modern-day soap opera full of drama and pathos.

# Lord Carnarvon's Death Scene in Cairo Revisted

Porchey arrived in Egypt in time to see Lord Carnarvon still alive but under deep sedation, moreover the future of the Earl's life was in Almina's personal control. The Countess did not accompany her husband when (after the Earl heard from Howard Carter of an actual tomb find), Carnarvon travelled out to Egypt in November 1922 and Lady Evelyn took Almina's place. The subsequent triumph of the natives and diggers finding the tomb justified Carter and Carnarvon's years of exploitation of the landscape.

*Lord Carnarvon and Howard Carter*

Almina and Carnarvon were strangers for most of their married life and only came together for travel, racing and some family events. In 1923 she was busy with the new male interest in her life, Lt Col Ian Onslow Dennistoun, and she was also involved in delicate negotiations with the art dealer Joseph Duveen over art sales from her Rothschild legacy.[209]

But subsequently the news of Carnarvon's illness reached Almina in London and it was grim. He lay as if poleaxed at the Continental Hotel in Cairo, the place where Evelyn and Carter had persuaded him, the man they both loved, to move to for the doctors to attend him. Almina knew that Carnarvon was in the last stages of what had been a daunting illness. The nature of it had been suppressed since there was a fear that sponsors of Tutankhamun like *The Times* would reduce their premium payments for rights, photographs, articles etc. The reality was that the Earl was in remission from cancer of the throat, and he had already several times escaped death by a whisker.[210]

Somehow Almina knew this was not another dress rehearsal; this was the real thing. The Countess made the maverick decision to hire a biplane and try to complete the journey out to Egypt in one fell swoop. Her motivation was first and foremost that of a nurse; the fact that she was also the Earl's wife seemed at that point somehow neither here nor there. However daunting her first experience in a plane and whatever else lay ahead it was a sense of duty to the suffering that called.

Despite the ubiquitous record in the public domain of Almina's heroic flight to Egypt and her plane being brought down prematurely over France after she took ill on board, the latest book from Highclere states incompetently that Almina's journey to the Earl's bedside only took her two days. Since the second leg of the journey actually had to be recommenced by train and a boat across the Mediterranean and a further train laid on in Egypt by the local railway company Almina did *not* reach Cairo until *five days* after leaving London. [211]

Notwithstanding Almina's ultimate game plan to bring an end to the Earl's misery, which she and Carnarvon had many times discussed together and with Dr Marcus Johnston ( who accompanied Almina ); now with the family all assembled Almina prepared herself to perform that last act of charity. In times past the Countess had done all in her power to restore the fragile frame of her husband; there are several letters making complimentary remarks to this effect from Almina's mother-in-law (Elsie) and her sister-in-law Lady Winifred Burghclere. Almina had done everything possible as the Earl's ministering angel[212] but one last act now remained and all would all be changed forever.

It was *not* a mosquito bite that caused or precipitated the Earl's death, nor was it pneumonia (which is the cause on the death certificate, which bears numerous errors of substance and fact). The co-discoverer of the Tomb of Tutankhamun finally died on 5 April 1923 in Egypt after (almost certainly) Almina arranged for morphine to be given to end all things painlessly; [213] it was an act of courage and mercy. "Carnarvon was riddled with cancer." [214] Almina had considerable inside knowledge of the use of toxic drugs and ready access to a supply of narcotics since she had run nursing homes for the war wounded and dying over many years.

### Tutankhamun Tales
### 1923- 1928
### The Treasure of Tutankhamun

The Fifth Earl's own recorded words are rare. Unlike his father, a Victorian politician, cabinet minister and Man of Letters, George was not a compulsive letter writer or diarist. [215] He did however pen an account of the discovery of Tutankhamun which contains this fragment about the initial discovery of one of the world's great treasures:

"By the uncertain light of a candle a wonderful sight was exposed to our eyes. Gilt couches, boxes of all sorts and other objects in the dim light were just visible…. We first thought that our find was a hiding place or 'cache' where we should probably find some royal and semi-royal mummies....but the more we examined the contents of the first chamber the more convinced we became that it was the tomb." [216]

But the two daring adventurers involved in the discovery were less than truthful men. The expose by Thomas Hoving[217] stands as a clear testimony of the unscrupulous (but perhaps in some ways understandable human action) taken by the Earl (and accepted by the otherwise meticulous, uncompromising man of integrity, Howard Carter) to protect their find; spending the night with the treasure and removing items altogether *before* the Egyptian Antiquities Department could get their act together; selling off some of the pieces and using the Metropolitan Museum of New York as dishonest brokers. The justification was that as far as the Earl was concerned (to hell with the contract he had with the Egyptians), it was *his* treasure. That was the thinking of a pure-born British aristocrat like George, as if the actual find had taken place on one of his own Estates. [218]

The Earl enjoyed getting his own way. Like many of his aristocratic fellows George Edward Stanhope Molyneux Herbert was feudal in his approach, despising the working classes and believing himself to be a superior being. But with this mould also came a quirky, unconventional streak. Probably damaged by his emotionally barren childhood, he rebelled against his father's rule and his stepmother Elsie's indifference because neither of them showed him much physical love. He went on to spend his inheritances rashly; he developed a love of racing, yachting, gambling, and motoring and in general preferred the company of men.

His years in Egypt were an escape from convention, too, and helped restore his damaged frame. The devoted Howard Carter was a subordinate but in the years of struggle of man against the sand dunes, with year on year of frustration and fruitless finds, he grew to be as close as anyone could be allowed to get to see into the psyche of what made the *real* George tick; in fact they became a couple, an item.[219] The Fifth Earl was a dysfunctional man, quick tempered and vain and Almina was always afraid of her husband who was ten years her senior.

## Death Shall Come on Swift Wings

## Death of the Fifth Earl

The Author is sorry to disappoint the reader as there's nothing like a good curse. [220]And that's the point - there was nothing like a Carnarvon curse, good or otherwise. There was no inscription anywhere on the tomb of Tutankhamun, outside of it or on any of the relics found there declaring "Death shall come on swift wings to him that touches the tomb of a Pharaoh." All fiction!

There was also no motor car accident in Germany in 1901 or 1902 or 1903 that sparked the Earl's first Egyptian adventure. That often-told tale of Lord Carnarvon going to Egypt after he nearly died, and for his fragile lungs, is culled from a perfectly true event but from 1909, long after he met Howard Carter in Egypt and by the time of this motor car skirmish in Germany he had been digging at Thebes for at least five years.

The Fifth Earl of Carnarvon was a very sick man all his life but his life was prolonged by the restorative dry climate of Egypt over several decades. It was Victor Duleep Singh who rushed to Lord Carnarvon's bedside time after time to help his beloved friend and hasten his return to life and well-being.

## Love Token

In 1918, Prince Victor Duleep Singh left his son Porchey " a sapphire ring presented to him by the Fifth Earl ... desiring [ Porchey] to treat it as an heirloom to go with the Carnarvon estates."[221] This was a love token from the first owner to the second and with the same sentiment it was passed to the third. [222]

## Carnarvon's Will[223]

All her married life Almina, the Fifth Countess of Carnarvon, knew her husband was dying. In 1918 he was three minutes away from the jaws of death and was just saved from the brink of extinction by Berkeley Moynihan, the Leeds surgeon. After he was given this period of further remission, and with Victor dead,[224] Almina encouraged her husband to make his Last Will and Testament, naturally leaving practically everything to her to rule over and control.

The Will remained perfected with only one codicil made a few hours before Lord Carnarvon finally shuffled off this mortal coil. He exclaimed " Give all my Bearer Bonds to my dear daughter. "[225]

The battles between Porchey and his mother almost always reverted back to the control that Almina exerted over the Fifth Earl's final estate.

*Almina, Fifth Countess of Carnarvon*

# LORD CARNARVON'S WILL.

## DISPOSAL OF EGYPTIAN COLLECTION.

The Right Hon. George Edward Stanhope Molyneux, fifth Earl of Carnarvon, of Highclere Castle, near Newbury, Hants, of Bretby Park, Burton-upon-Trent, and of 1, Seamore-place, W., who died at Cairo on April 5, aged 56, left property in his own disposition of the gross value of £398,925, with net personalty £274,376.

Probate of his will, dated October 29, 1919, with two codicils, has been granted to General the Right Hon. Sir John Grenfell Maxwell, G.C.B., K.C.M.G., of 103, Lancaster-gate, W., and Major-General Sir Robert Hutchison, K.C.M.G., of 57, Catherine-street, Buckingham-gate, S.W., and Mr. Arthur Fitzhardinge Berkeley Portman, of 29, Montagu-square, W.

His Egyptian collection is dealt with in the first codicil, made on the same day as his will, but written in his own hand. He leaves this collection to his wife, adding:—

I would like her to give one object to the British Museum, one object to the Ashmolean, and a fragment cup of blue glass (Thothmes III.) to the Metropolitan Museum, New York. The first two bequests need not be capital objects. Should she find it necessary to sell the collection, I suggest that the nation—i.e., the British Museum—be given the first refusal at £20,000, if below its value, such sum, however, to be absolutely hers, free of all duties. Otherwise, I would suggest that the collection be offered to the Metropolitan, New York, Mr. Carter to have charge of the negotiations and to fix the price.

Should my wife decide to keep the collection, I leave it absolutely to her whether she leaves it to my son or to the nation or to Evelyn Herbert. I suggest, however, that she consult Dr. Gardiner and Mr. Carter on the subject.

The second codicil was made a few days before his death, and was written out by Dr. Alan H. Gardiner at his request on a cable form of the Eastern Telegraph Company. It is dated April 3, and reads: "Give all my Bearer Bonds to my dear daughter." Affidavits were required as to the circumstances of the execution of this codicil, but it was admitted to probate as a valid document.

As directions as to his funeral and mourning, the testator stated that he wished to be buried, if possible, on Beacon Hill, and he directed his executors to erect on Beacon Hill a mound of earth with trees or a stone, which is not to cost more than £50. If this burial were not possible he desired to be buried in Highclere Churchyard, next to his mother. He expressly desired that there should be no black horses or any sort of mourning used at his funeral, or any mourning afterwards; that the funeral should be exceedingly simple, and that two doctors should view his body before burial to make sure that life was extinct. He left

£500 to Mr. Howard Carter (described as of Luxor, Egypt): £100 to Dr. Budge, of the British Museum: £100 to the Inspectors at Paddington Station, to be divided between them; to eight old men and eight old women on the Highclere estate to be selected by his executors "a good thick blue coat with a red collar each"; £500 and one of his cigarette cases to his agent, James Augustine Rutherford, expressing the hope that he will continue to act as agent to his wife and his son; £400 and his personal apparel not retained by his wife to his valet, George W. Fearnside, if still in his service and not under notice; £200 similarly to his butler, Alfred Streatfield; £150 similarly to his head keeper, Henry Maber; £50 similarly to his under keeper, J. Rutherford; £25 similarly to his woodman, David Garrick; one year's wages to each other indoor servant at any of his residences who shall have been in his service for the two years preceding his death and shall not be under notice; £100 each to Dr. Alan Gardiner and Dr. T. S. Bruce.

To his wife the emerald ring he always wore, hoping that she will always wear it after his death, and the pearl pin which was her gift, and which he hopes she will have mounted and wear herself. Also all his racehorses and any of his jewelry and furniture, pictures, statuary, plate, articles of vertu, &c., that she may select.

To his daughter Evelyn his pearl stud with £200 to have it mounted, his gold cigarette case and £1,000, as well as all his Bearer Bonds mentioned above.

Among other bequests the testator left:—

£2,000 each to his sister Lady Burghclere and Richard C. Dawson, of Whatcombe; £1,000 to each of his sisters Lady Margaret Duckworth and Lady Victoria Herbert and George Herbert Duckworth; £500 and his 20-bore Purdey guns to his brother-in-law, Lord Burghclere; £500 to each executor and to Marcus Johnson, of Henrietta-street; £200 to each of his half-brothers, Aubrey and Mervyn Molyneux Herbert; and all his real estate (except the Highclere and other settled estates) to his wife for life, with remainder to his son and his heirs in tail male.

He appointed the Highclere estate to his wife for life with remainder to his half-brother Aubrey Molyneux Herbert and his heirs in tail male, whom failing to his half-brother Mervyn Molyneux Herbert and his heirs in tail similarly; but in each case charged with the payment of £25,000 each to Henry and Auberon, sons of his sister Lady Margaret Duckworth. Subject to the right of selection of his wife mentioned above, he left his jewelry, pictures, statuary, articles of vertu, furniture, &c., to devolve as heirlooms with his property.

All other his personal estate he left to his wife.

---

*Lord Carnarvon's Will*

## Funeral of the Fifth Earl on Beacon Hill

Before and after Lord Carnarvon's burial on Beacon Hill overlooking Highclere Estate, Almina played out her best and most compelling acting role, observing all kinds of rituals to fulfil the Earl's last wishes. Attentive in his death in a way she was not always so during Carnarvon's life, she had already moved her own quarters to London several years earlier and occupied Alfred de Rothschild's beautiful house at 1, Seamore Place, Mayfair, overlooking Hyde Park.

## Hospitality at Highclere

*Highclere Castle*

Despite moving into her London home at 1, Seamore Place in the heart of Mayfair from 1918, Almina had kept the social side of Highclere going throughout the years following the Great War with many weekend parties and seasonal events so the house was always full of guests, with hospitality to match any Royal Palace or civic reception. But there was virtually no time for Catherine to actually learn the ropes from Almina about the running schedules of any large house because as an army wife Catherine was abroad in barracks with Porchey from the end of 1922 until the events in Egypt of March/ April 1923 which resulted in the death of the Fifth Earl.

Now, as the new Countess and chatelaine of Highclere, the twenty-two-year-old Catherine faced formidable challenges, about which Almina is said to have remarked that her successor would be as sound as a bell in performing but would need to issue clear instructions that would both command and charm the staff and to rely on the senior members of the household of butler, housekeeper and cook to show her the way. Almina had a word with those in the domestic hierarchy who in some cases had served her and the Fifth Earl for many years, to all rally round Catherine. There was to be no talk of her youthfulness or inexperience being a measure of anything. Almina herself had been only nineteen when she had faced the same task in 1895 and the Fourth Countess, Elsie Howard, had been almost the same age as Catherine when she arrived at Highclere in 1878. A new Countess of Carnarvon would (as her predecessors had all done) rise to the duty of being the mistress of Highclere.

It was Porchey's plan to open the house to guests for the racing at Newbury, a first test that Catherine passed successfully. Meanwhile Catherine heard that her sister-in-law, Lady Evelyn, was soon to be married; Porchey would give his sister away and Catherine would attend to some of the intended celebrations. This would add to her experience.

# Lady Evelyn Herbert, the real victim of Tutankhamun and Her Marriage in 1923

*Lady Evelyn in 1972 at the Tutankhamum Exhibition British Museum*

Whilst the Fifth Earl was alive, Almina stopped going to Egypt in the 1921 season. Her daughter Lady Evelyn, Porchey's sister, became the Fifth Earl's companion thereafter and accompanied him on the last two history-making trips. Evelyn adored the time she spent in Egypt and over several digs she was loyal, protective and loving towards the Fifth Earl; Carnarvon doted on her, whether she was his daughter or not.

Encouraged by Almina, Evelyn assisted Carnarvon and Carter in their work and shared their highs and lows with all the excitement of the search (and certainly frustrations) looking for the Tomb of Tutankhamun.

Evelyn's brief was also to keep a watchful eye (carefully instructed by Almina) on the Earl's health and to report any changes to her mother by telegram. It is unlikely Evelyn knew he was dying but Carter probably did, from the meeting between Carnarvon and Carter at Highclere in the autumn of 1922 when his Lordship could only promise to fund one more season of digs. The truth was that his health had collapsed and it likely (but not completely clear[226]) that he knew he might die and he revealed this (or Almina confided this) to Carter. History records that it was one last season in Egypt because Carnarvon had run out of money but there is no doubt that Almina would have funded further seasons as she had the funds, so that reason is discredited.

Evelyn was fond of Howard Carter and respected his expertise. She was more than likely unaware of the intimate side to the relationship between her father, the rich patron of the year-on-year excavations, and the shy archeologist. [227] She would however have known that both men had short fuses and were by nature impatient. There were to be several moments of heightened tension between the two men as the money supply drained away into the sands of The Valley of the Kings.

Evelyn became a knowledgeable bystander; she witnessed the moment when the great tomb was finally breached for the first time on 26 November 1922 and of the wonders exposed. In later years she was the last survivor of that small group consisting of herself, Lord Carnarvon, Howard Carter and Mr. Callender and in 1972 she was given a place of honour when the priceless treasures of Tutankhamun were exhibited at the British Museum to commemorate the 50th anniversary of the discovery.[228] These exhibits of course no longer travel the world: they are held in their native Egypt at the Cairo Museum.

It was Lady Evelyn who was *the* real victim following the fatal illness of Lord Carnarvon in Egypt. For it was Evelyn who had to give up much more than anyone else, especially her love of archeology and the chance to carry on her father's work alongside Carter. Almina would not hear of such a plan; Evelyn must consider her future in England and so she had to switch her life back into being another twenty-two-year-old searching for a suitable husband. There was someone who had met Evelyn in London and kept in touch after visiting her at the tombs in the Valley of the Kings in Egypt, and he wanted to make Evelyn his bride. The suitor, Captain Brogrove Campbell Beauchamp, was three years older than Evelyn; he was a soldier in the Life Guards and a would-be politician who had once stood for Parliament and he was also the heir to a baronetcy. He proposed, Evelyn accepted and an engagement was announced on 16 July 1923. The marriage subsequently took place at St Margaret's, Westminster on 8 October 1923. Almina (assisted by Catherine) gave a reception afterwards to several hundred guests at 1, Seamore Place, Park Lane, Mayfair.

*Lady Evelyn Herbert marries Brogrove Beauchamp in 1923*

# Chapter 5

## Porchey Returns to the Saddle and Catherine is Pregnant

*Porchey and Catherine at the Races*

In August 1923 Porchey made his first appearance in the saddle after becoming Lord Carnarvon.[229] He told Catherine he intended to ride frequently and expected her to accompany him to race meetings up and down the country. On one level this wasn't a chore; Catherine enjoyed horse racing and, like her mother-in-law Almina before her, set new highs of fashion and style in her choices of dress, make-up and hair designs that drew praise and which other women copied. However, Porchey's habit of non-stop flirting and incessant following around of several lady race-goers and then sneaking away, tempered considerably Catherine's pleasure when attending these meetings.

At this time, too, Catherine had news of her own for Porchey; she announced that she was pregnant with her first child. There is some somewhat tenuous hearsay from two informants (who knew Catherine) that suggests quite startlingly that PG (Prince George) may have been the father of the Carnarvon baby, Catherine's adoration of Prince George having taken its inevitable course over several years in an equally sought and loving relationship.[230] George had encouraged Catherine to marry Porchey but made a promise that he would always be in the background if and when she ever needed attention, love and, especially, his protection. Between the lines of a recent book[231] (based on the Castle's Visitors Book) PG was at Highclere amongst the Carnarvons as regularly as the Herbert's earlier progenitor, Prince Victor Duleep Singh, in the generation before. Was history repeating itself with a new progenitor?

## The Birth of Catherine's Son, Henry, Lord Porchester

On 19 January 1924 Catherine gave birth to a son, Henry, who immediately ousted his Herbert cousin, Auberon Mark Henry Yvo Molyneux Herbert, as the next heir to the Carnarvon Earldom. Auberon had been heir presumptive following the death of his father Aubrey (half-brother of the Fifth Earl) in 1923 after a botched operation leading to blood poisoning.

Naturally, with Henry's emergence there was much rejoicing by the tenants on the Highclere Estate and throughout the wider family at the birth of a male heir to the Carnarvons.

Catherine appeared in the fashionable *Bystander* magazine showing off her child to the world at large.

Meanwhile, during the period of waiting for a Carnarvon heir, the limelight had switched to Catherine's younger unmarried sister Philippa and her quest, (superintended, of course, by her mother Marian and Aunt Gertrude).

# Sister Act

## Catherine's Sister Philippa Fendall Wendell

Catherine's sister Philippa Fendall Wendell completed a round of being a bridesmaid (a precursor for all young ladies of the era before their coming-out) and was finally presented at the May Court of 1923.[232] Marian (supported by Gertrude Griffiths and Catherine's brothers Jac and Reggie) turned up at numerous dances and receptions thereafter with a single cunning plan to marry off Philippa. The climax to this matchmaking was a grand dinner and dance given by Marian and Gertrude at Claridges Hotel, with a colossal guest list of the nobility and with music provided for the occasion by the Clifford Essex Band. Heading the guest list was Philippa's husband-to-be, Randolph Stewart, the 12th Earl of Galloway, who was known as Ronald. [233]

But Ronald did not bite quickly. He was older than Philippa, he was seeing other women and for a time in his youth (and even later, in marriage) ran Porchey close in the philandering stakes. The Earl had not made up his mind on anyone to marry and so Philippa's exhausting round of dinners, receptions and dances continued unabated with her returning each night, unclaimed, to the Griffiths home at 34, Bryanston Square,

The 1924 season saw Philippa still doing the rounds with her mother although her brother Jac had now found himself a wife with a stockbroker father of note, Philip W. Carr. He was also a racehorse owner and was well acquainted on and off the turf with Porchey (now Lord) Carnarvon, and Jac's younger brother, Reggie Wendell.

On 6 February 1924, Gertrude (who was as keen as Marian to see Philippa married to a title, of the same rank as Catherine) agreed to give an afternoon "At Home" at the Griffiths residence at 34 Bryanston Square. It would be a musical extravaganza, with "Mme Tatiana Makashina, a Russian *prima donna*, and the Westminster Singers." [234] Guest of honour (among throngs of diplomats, European Royals and a cluster of London hostesses and Dowagers) was Amy, Countess of Galloway.

Porchey joined the gathering to put a word in for Philippa's cause. Catherine was recovering from giving birth to her son Henry, the new Lord Porchester, a few days before, and describing the progress of the baby to the widowed Countess Amy was a means of concentrating Amy's mind on the fact that her only surviving son Randolph, Earl of Galloway, (her other son had been killed in action in the Great War) had better get cracking in finding a wife and putting her in the family way pronto.

Philippa was a very popular debutante and, like her sister Catherine, could act, turning in an impressive performance at the Royal Opera House, Covent Garden in Wilfred Byre's 'Chiquita'.[235] With a large following of male suitors it seemed surprising to many bystanders that Philippa had set her cap at Randolph Stewart, 12th Earl of Galloway, an odd-ball. An informed onlooker however would be aware that Randolph had been best man at the wedding of Lord Charles Carnegie to Princess Maud Duff, a granddaughter of King Edward VII and Queen Alexandra (in other words the boy had form). Certainly Gertrude Griffiths and Marian Wendell were delighted that they had pulled off a match of their very own girl marrying into such proximity to the Royal Family.

Andrew Bruce, the present Eleventh Earl of Elgin, now almost ninety (but still as bright as a button) remembers both Charles (his cousin) and kinsman Randolph as fellow freemasons, serving together in the great lodges of Scotland.[236]

## Griffiths Divorce Threatens Marian's Plans for Philippa's future

Marian and Gertrude were clever marriage fixers. All the would-be husbands knew that the Wendells in England had no money or property and were dependent on hand-outs from Percy and Gertrude Griffiths who were quite comfortably off. References to Marian Wendell having her own wealth are highlighted and repeated in a recent book from Highclere on Catherine. This seems more exaggerated than true. Ronan Donohoe (of the Portsmouth Athenaeum, the repository of the Wendell family papers[237]) comments on this point: "I really can't see that there could have been that much spread around. Her [Marian's] southern family may have died at convenient intervals." [238]

In light of the fact there is no audit trail or footnotes to Highclere's texts and of their record in misrepresenting key facts, the source for saying Marian had money in her own right is challengeable, however there is evidence that in 1921 both Marian and Gertrude Griffiths received a small share ( but no more than $1500) from  the estate of a family friend. [239]

Wendell or Fendall coffers aside, all was not well in the twenty-five-year marriage between Percy and Gertrude Griffiths. One event in the background hanging over Marian's situation kept her up at night: Gertrude was suing Percy for divorce. Percy was a member of the Excelsior Club which often held luncheons at the *Ritz* hotel. At one of these a 'friendly' peeress kindly informed Gertrude that her husband was keeping a woman named Dorothy Robertson.  This didn't go down well with Gertrude.

Meanwhile, whilst Gertrude considered how (or whether) she would proceed with the divorce action Marian turned to her son Jac's relations, the Carrs. One of the Carr collaterals was about to launch her three daughters onto the London scene.

Any further ructions between Gertrude and Percy Griffiths to end his support of the kept woman Dorothy Robertson remained in limbo, especially as at the summer of 1924 Philippa Wendell was still unclaimed in the matrimonial stakes. A public spectacle in the divorce court and in the press involving the Griffiths' was bound to have an affect on Philippa reaching the altar since she lived with them at Sandridge so Gertrude withdrew her divorce petition.  Percy continued to see Dorothy, revealing that Gertrude like Marian gave up her own happiness for the sake of pushing the Wendell daughters into the British aristocracy.

On 24 August 1924 to huge sighs of relief the announcement finally came of Philippa's marriage to Lord Galloway[240]:

"The marriage between the Earl of Galloway and Miss Philippa Wendell will take place on Tuesday, October 14...at St Margaret's Westminster." [241]

*Wedding of the Earl of Galloway to Philippa Wendell*

Lord Charles Carnegie returned Randolph's favour by being best man at the wedding. The two men had served side by side in the Scots Guards during the Great War and the Houses of Carnegie and Stewart also had family overlaps and strong personal beliefs. Both men acquired a reputation in the years that followed as extreme right-wing conservatives and high ranking freemasons.

The wedding brought together the various portions of the Carnarvon and Wendell families in Britain and USA. Although held in London it was a very Scottish wedding, all the bridesmaids wearing tartan ribbons and all the pages kilts in the colours of the Clan Stewart. The two kilted trainbearers were Lord Bute's youngest son Lord Rhidian Crichton-Stuart[242] and the bridegroom's small kinsman Master Michael Stewart.

Marian Wendell occupied the role of queen bee at the reception at Claridges with a full turn out of the Carnarvons and collaterals and with the Dowagers Almina and Amy, Lady Galloway, playing up to their roles at the centre of it all.

*How the Press Put it!*

Despite the headlines ( as above ) sadly, on a human level all Marian's efforts to elevate her girls' social standing meant that both Catherine and Philippa ended up with husbands who did little to bring them happiness; one an inveterate womaniser, the other a recluse in later life with extreme right wing political views that would have made Genghis Khan blush. [243]

# Chapter 6

## 1924
## Porchey and Catherine resume their roles

*Catherine and the new Lord Porchester*

Porchey rewarded Catherine's successful production of an heir with a trip to Paris where the top priority was a new wardrobe for the Countess. The Earl was in a good mood, since the birth of a son and heir brought with it a cheque for £10,000 from an old friend, a wealthy Frenchman named the Vicomte de Fontarce (who knew the Fifth Earl in Egypt) who had promised such a sum if a boy was born.

However, during the spending spree in Paris, Catherine was not at all well, nor physically strong enough to enjoy herself. Her post-natal recovery was slow and there were concerns over her condition, necessitating an early return to Britain.

Overcoming further various health scares back home at Highclere at the end of March, and with one postponement of the new Lord

Porchester's christening already necessary, the new Carnarvon heir was finally christened on 6 April 1924 at Highclere. Lord and Lady Carnarvon's friend the glamorous dark haired Prince George (later Duke of Kent) was one of the godfathers, albeit by proxy for the ceremony but he later joined the festivities and appears in the photographs taken on the day. Another proxy was the child's paternal grandmother, Almina, who was holidaying in South Africa with her second husband, Lt Colonel Ian Onslow Dennistoun. [244] Those sponsors who were present to see the tiny boy christened Henry George Reginald Molyneux Herbert were Princess de Faucigny-Lucinge (one of the girl friends of Catherine and her sister[245]), Vicomte de Fontam and Reginald Wendell, Catherine's older brother. The child was wrapped in an heirloom robe of embroidered ivory satin and a lavish party was held after the ceremony.

To Catherine's greater joy, Prince George stayed on at Highclere for a few days. During the time there he also accompanied Catherine and Porchey to the cinema at nearby Newbury, which improved Catherine's state of mind and health.

## A State Ball and Wendell Wealth

The new Earl and Countess of Carnarvon attended the State Ball at Buckingham Palace on Wednesday 28 May 1924.[246] There was still some uncertainty about Catherine's background and in an effort to glamorise and partially reinvent the status of Jacob Wendell Jnr (Catherine's father) at least one commentator (at the time of Philippa's engagement to Lord Galloway) described Jacob flatteringly but inaccurately as "an American financial magnate". [247]

Charles W Wendell, a present-day member of the family, clears up the misrepresentation in these remarks which began with a report by the American Ambassador in London, in the *New York Times*:

"[The] information which appeared in the New York Times in 1922, at the time of Catherine's wedding, concerning her family's wealth arising from New York City money is completely incorrect. Given the fact that little was known about Catherine (something to note in itself), the [American] Embassy was contacted for background. The result was a profile proving that Catherine had her own wealthy family connections, namely in John Wendell of New York whose grandfather was an assistant in the fur business of John Jacob Astor (ca-ching-ca-ching) before breaking out on his own and investing in real estate. All this got the headlines when in 1931 John's last of six sisters, Ella Wendell, died in the family house, the last private home on Fifth Avenue, next to the current Lord & Taylor's Department Store at the corner of West 39th Street. Ella left millions of dollars worth of real estate, partially because her brother John believed in never selling (nor maintaining) and not allowing any of his sisters but one (Rebecca) to marry. It's quite a story. The bottom line is that the first Wendell [later with Astor links] came to New York in the mid-nineteenth century. I doubt if Catherine's family in New York had anything more than general public awareness of John Wendell, his father John Daniel Wendell and family. The Embassy's assumption was messy, but it probably didn't hurt Catherine's image." [248]

However, to be fair, another more accurate description focused on the lineal descent of the Wendells and Fendalls "from two of the oldest American families – the Washingtons and Lees of Virginia." [249] These were impressive antecedents as they were surnames that every schoolboy would recognise as heroes from the American War of Independence and the American Civil War.

## Almina Livid over Porchey's Snub

Meanwhile, back from South Africa, Almina was mortified that she missed her first grandchild's christening. Despite a request from Almina to await her return to Britain, Porchey had pressed ahead with the event at Highclere. This was deliberate to avoid the presence of Almina with her new husband, Colonel Ian Onslow Dennistoun. Porchey was far from happy over his mother's disclosures about his Sikh paternity, her lavish spending, and her madness in proceeding to a second marriage with someone he considered a bounder and a cad. [250]

In particular Almina was *persona non grata at* Highclere since the revelations triggered by Reggie Herbert, 15th Earl of Pembroke and Montgomery, and the machinations of the Pembroke lawyers following the death of the Fifth Earl. In short, the Pembrokes (who are the main progenitive line on the Herbert family tree) expressed grave doubts about Porchey being the rightful Herbert heir. A request for clarification had been sent with an affidavit for Almina to swear but the Dowager Countess scorned at swearing anything other than in the face of the Pembrokes. Almina held up her stonewalling position and Porchey's position was secured, thanks to his mother's action and determination to ignore the Pembroke challenge, whether true or not.

## Catherine Suffers a Health Scare

Catherine had been suffering from the after affects of the birth of her son and rushing too quickly back into a normal pace of running Highclere. Her condition was described in the official bulletins as "influenza" but she was quite ill and exhausted. However she was sufficiently recovered at the end of July of 1924 to attend (with Porchey) the christening of her brother's first child at Sandridge Church, St Albans, and the celebrations for the infant son of Mr and Mrs Jac Wendell.[251] The child was called Jac, after his father, and Catherine and Porchey were among the god parents. [252]

## Porchey and Catherine Go North to Visit Almina and the Colonel at Alvie

Porchey had to face his mother's wrath for being snubbed over his son's christening. At the tail end of August 1924 he and Catherine spent a short time with Almina and her new husband, Lt Colonel Ian Onslow Dennistoun, at Alvie Lodge, the Dowager Countess's newly acquired Scottish Highland Estate at Lower Badenoch in Invernesshire.[253] Porchey had to swallow his pride and aim to make a good peace with his mother, not least on financial terms.

Almina had been languishing in Scotland for several weeks bored rigid; she missed her life in London. Alvie Lodge was a mansion house set in a beautiful landscape, and it was Almina's hope that the Colonel could find peace and rest there in the centre of a pine forest, midway between Kincraig and Aviemore. Here he could ride and shoot and play golf to his heart's content. It was an area that he knew well; there were Dennistoun relations at nearby Ballindalloch Castle[254] and in his youth the Colonel had stayed there regularly with a beloved aunt. On one occasion he had been in a shooting party with Prince Victor Duleep

Singh, a close 'collaborator' of Almina and her first husband, the Fifth Earl.

Almina wanted to know everything from Catherine about how her new grandson, Lord Porchester was faring, since he was now seven months old.

The boy's progress was truly remarkable and his granny's interest in him was to be one of the constant joys of the rest of her life. Her affection was reciprocated by the young Lord Porchester; they understood each other perfectly.

Catherine's arrival from down south was a glorious opportunity for Almina (desperate for any hot news) to catch up with her daughter-in-law on all the Society gossip and chit-chat from Highclere and London. Against the odds, especially given their fragile early relationship, the two Countesses had become friends and allies and confidantes.

Catherine stood in for Almina during this holiday break for the opening ceremony of a bazaar organised by the Aviemore Tennis Club in aid of the club's funds.[255]

Relations between Almina and Porchey were still delicate especially since the Lord Porchester christening snub earlier in the year. The Pembroke affidavit was not mentioned and that bitter secret document gathered dust for several decades until it was unearthed in the mid-1990s by the Seventh Earl's choice of biographer of his beloved granny, Almina; the biographer's proposed book was suppressed by Highclere as he had discovered quite by chance that Prince Victor Duleep Singh was Porchey's real father.

During the visit to Alvie two more pressing subjects dominated the discussions between Porchey and his mother. First and foremost was the thorny issue of the family finances and how these were allocated. Porchey was greatly pained by his father's Last Will which in effect had left him only the Earl's title and a few trinkets but no money; however, with succession to the title came the burden of managing and maintaining the Highclere Estate. Another absurdity (as Porchey saw it) was that whilst he had ownership of the Highclere Stud (inaugurated by the Fifth Earl in 1898), Almina had been left the bloodstock.

Porchey was not a wealthy man in his own right in terms of hard or loose cash. He had been a soldier for most of his adult life. Although he had received legacies from his late grandmother Marie Boyer and Alfred de Rothschild, these had been spent or, in the case of Marie's Boyer's estate, in 1913 Almina had looted that which was due to Porchey and his sister Evelyn. Catherine was not well off and she had no dowry or marriage settlement for Porchey to plunder.

Porchey, now the Sixth Earl, was in dire financial straits as he faced payment of the death duties of the Fifth Earl of close on half a million pounds. Despite Highclere being Porchey's safe haven, and he really did love the estate, he threatened to sell. Some money was raised by selling off family assets. [256] Almina was not amused. She said she would help her son from out of the proceeds of the proposed sale of some of the art treasures of 1, Seamore Place, London that her guardian Alfred de Rothschild had bequeathed. Three pictures by Thomas Gainsborough had already been disposed of by the art dealer Joseph Duveen, to aid Almina's cash flow. [257]

Another tricky issue on the agenda for discussion was the simmering dispute between Colonel Dennistoun and Dorothy, his first wife – the main reason for Almina and the Colonel exiling themselves to their Scottish hideaway. This was a row over Dorothy's pay-off (labelled alimony) to keep her mouth shut and not to reveal Ian's chequered past to the world's press by suing him in open court. Dorothy was out to cause trouble by revealing the plain fact that, in order to gain promotions, Ian had sold her to Sir John Cowans, Quarter-Master General of the British Army during the Great War. Such revelations coming out in court were bound to reflect on Almina's judgement in her choice of second husband.

Almina conceded several blackmail payments to Dorothy and then stopped paying. She dismissed Dorothy as no more than "a teasing and conniving bitch", [258] she would not dare go to the law or the press and "disgrace herself as a whore".[259] Almina would not listen to any argument over making a full and final financial settlement with Dorothy but her lawyers were working behind the scenes to try to fix things. The Colonel did not show himself much; when he did so he remained silent, exactly what he had been told to do by Almina. He wandered the grounds with his man until meal times. He was fit at this time and still riding horses, although years later he became very much an invalid. It is simply not accurate (as stated by Highclere's ghost writer in a recent book about Catherine) that the Colonel had broken his back and was in a wheel chair. The press photographs of the Colonel at his wedding to Almina in December 1923, and two years later of him coming from the High Court day in and day out in March 1925, show that he was walking about normally. Almina bought him a motorised chair when his mobility decreased, but this was not until the mid 1930s.

At Alvie Almina dug in and would not budge off her high horse with regard to Dorothy. Having reached no tangible agreement with his mother on either of the issues that were set to dog the family with lurid and embarrassing headlines for years to come, Porchey and Catherine returned by train to London in utter dismay.

## The Carnarvons Clubbing in London

In London Porchey and Catherine  installed themselves for a few days at the *Ritz* hotel and their spirits were lifted with a trip to *Ciro's* in Mayfair,  just about the most successful club in London and full of well-known people. They enjoyed dinner and supper and danced together under the watchful eye of the Club's proprietor, Rizzi.  This was an exclusive club for members only and their friends. However, as it closed about the time the Capital's night clubs opened, it was only a stepping stone from there to a night on the town before turning in back at the Ritz.

## Poppy Baring & Catherine Meet again

Confidante and friend Poppy Baring met Catherine on the latter's return from Scotland to tell her about meeting her fellow American, Grace Vanderbilt, who had been a rival for PG's attentions during the past summer. Grace had only just missed out marrying Louis Mountbatten and had switched her attention to PG. Poppy revealed her secret sorrow over PG being sent virtually into exile (as a naval sub-lieutenant he was sent to join the British fleet in China); this was in order to stop the pair continuing their liaison which Royal watchers felt was becoming too serious. In an effort to clear the field of unwanted runners and riders Queen Mary vetoed Poppy as a wife for George. (Poppy had committed the ultimate sin of saying she didn't like the King and Queen .....and in any case 'Princess Poppy?' I ask you!) . The Queen also halted Lady Alexandra Curzon's notion of winning Prince George by sending her off abroad. Poppy complained that she was sick and tired of all the gossip about her love for PG and anyway she was going to give them really something to talk about because she was going into trade: she had plans afoot to open up a dress shop in Down Street, to be called 'Poppy'. But before this Poppy's close friend, an Australian named Sheila Chisholm (Lady Loughborough, a former lover of the Duke of York[260]) invited Poppy to accompany her on a tour of America.

## Christmas at Highclere

In December 1924 the Carnarvons spent their first family Christmas at Highclere Castle since the time of the Fifth Earl's death.

Earlier in the summer at Alvie Lodge in Scotland Catherine had asked Almina if she objected to an overhaul of the interior decorations of the Castle. It was no secret that Catherine did not share the passion of her mother-in-law for the relics of Marie Antoinette. When Almina became the chatelaine of Highclere in 1895 there was no outgoing Countess to snub since the Fifth Earl had evicted his stepmother Elsie not long after the Fourth Earl breathed his last in 1890.

Almina had been a tour-de-force for great change inside Highclere, squeezing money from her benefactor Baron Alfred de Rothschild to install electricity soon after her marriage, (sadly there wasn't much electricity in the marriage itself). The house had telephones and the kitchens had been redesigned to suit the ever more refined palates above stairs. Almina was proud of what she had achieved, there was hot and cold running water and several bathroom suites had been added. The house under her stewardship became a beacon of modern convenience, not to say luxury. Despite these achievements, or perhaps in part because of them, Almina wished only to co-operate with the new Countess, saying:

"My darling Catherine, you must do whatever you wish, for I am the past; you are the new modern age for living." [261]

Catherine's own rooms were renovated first. It was decided that the Great Hall would be used as a living room and here would be served the Christmas dinner.

## Catherine and Highclere Stud

Catherine enjoyed visiting the Highclere Stud, especially when Porchey and the trainers were breaking in new horses and she was fascinated seeing them through and sold off as yearlings. Later she adored seeing these same horses running at the racecourses. She also made sure she was pre-eminent in the winner's enclosure in terms of setting the standard in fashion, every detail of what she was wearing being recorded by the London newspapers.

## Married Life with the Galloways

The new Earl and Countess of Galloway were considerably inconvenienced by Randolph's stubborn Irish mother, Amy,[262] who refused to make way for Philippa to become the resident chatelaine of Cumloden. Instead the newlyweds were forced to begin their married life in London which, in point of fact, Philippa quite enjoyed but this did not suit Randolph who preferred his Scottish Borders home.

By Christmas of 1924 Randolph was in despair but a solution was found when a gaggle of formidable females including Marian Wendell and Gertrude Griffiths descended upon Cumloden to spend the holidays with Philippa and her husband, with the shared purpose of easing Amy from the family pile.

Eventually Amy took the hint; alternative accommodation arrangements were made for the formidable Dowager Countess of Galloway and a short time afterwards Philippa became the incumbent Countess of Galloway at Cumloden. She was presented at Court as the Countess of Galloway but the Galloways gave up their town house in London. Randolph's anxious years of confinement as a prisoner of war in Germany during 1914-18 had taken a toll on his handling of people skills and had knocked his confidence.[263] His younger brother, the Hon Keith Stewart,[264] had been killed in action and the family's grief was great; this was one reason the Eleventh Earl had gone to his grave a broken man.

The head of the historic Stewart Clan, Earl Randolph (and as a result the family as a whole) paid the price of war. The Earl cut something of a lonely figure at times, roaming the open countryside around Cumloden, his high acre family estate in the borders of Scotland.

In effect the Galloways subsequently dropped out of any elaborate level of London socialising. They were also at times reluctant to head for the Highlands which were cluttered up by the gentry decimating birdlife and stalking deer by day and night. There was enough such sport to be had on their own lands or on adjoining estates where grouse, partridge and pheasants roamed, although few birds were actually reared at Cumloden.[265]

Many had hoped that Philippa would become one of London's leading hostesses but as her husband wanted peace and local pursuits she had to be content with a quieter existence; however she continued to see and visit Gertrude Griffiths at *Sandridgebury*, sometimes with Randolph when he could be dragged off the moors. Randolph (always called Roland, which was one of his Christian names) escaped his wife's relations and headed to his London club or the bed of a mistress.

## News of another baby for Catherine and one for Lady Evelyn Beauchamp, overshadowed by Dorothy Dennistoun

As 1924 closed, both Catherine and Almina's daughter, Lady Evelyn Beauchamp, were pregnant. Overshadowing this welcome news was much more unwelcome news as it became apparent to all that Almina's nemesis, Dorothy Dennistoun, was determined to take Colonel Ian Dennistoun to court for alimony. The case of *Dennistoun v Dennistoun* was to be the *cause celebre* of the decade.

# Chapter 7

## The Dustbin Case : 1925
## Mother Courage

The Dennistoun case, which lasted seventeen days, was costly and time-consuming for Almina and her family. Prior to the Court case, with the inevitable media spotlight and prurient delight of many, Porchey and Catherine considered escaping to Egypt where the Fifth Earl's surviving partner Howard Carter had reached an accommodation with the Egyptian authorities over access to the Tomb of Tutankhamun. Almina was granted a new concession, albeit the contents of the tomb were to be wholly owned by the Egyptian government with an arrangement for offering duplicates to interested parties. Carter was calm and determined to proceed with his work; with this truce came his solemn commitment to complete a catalogue of the contents of the great treasure, discovered in 1922.

Because Catherine's health remained poor the Carnarvons' plans to go abroad were cancelled, whilst in court it became clear that Dorothy Dennistoun was going ahead to seek punitive damages against Almina's second husband. Porchey had to bite his lip and close family ranks supporting Almina in the current litigation. This was not entirely a case of 'noblesse oblige,' more one of following the money as Almina had repeated her offer to him to help resolve the family's financial problems over death duties and keeping Highclere.

There were several large sums to come into Almina's hands that Porchey was keen to see something of, including the proceeds of the sale of the Fifth Earl's own personal Egyptian Collection (which was bequeathed to Almina in 1923 although the document stemmed from 1918) and the compensation claim before the Egyptian government by the trustees of the Fifth Earl for the reimbursement of all the costs incurred by Carnarvon in digging in the Valley of the Kings.

The Dennistoun case was finally listed to begin in March 1925. The first week of the case coincided with the birth of Catherine's second child, this time a girl.

## Birth of a daughter

After the birth of Lord Porchester in January 1924 Catherine had wasted no time in getting pregnant again. Enduring a second difficult labour in just over twelve months, an exhausted Catherine gave birth to a daughter, Lady Anne Penelope Marian Herbert, on 3 March 1925.

Catherine was too ill to attend the opening days of the Dennistoun case but Porchey appeared in Court alongside his mother from the outset. Of course, he despised Dorothy and the Colonel (and, not least, his mother!).

*Catherine with her two young children*

*Left to Right, Reggie Wendell, Catherine, Lady Penelope and Porchey*

# Dennistoun v Dennistoun Revisted [266]

*Colonel Ian Onslow Dennistoun and Almina Leave Court in 1925*

Described by the satirical magazine Punch as *The Dustbin Case* and *The Sale Wife* case, *Dennistoun verses Dennistoun* was heard before *"the bachelor judge"*[267] Mr. Justice Henry McCardie and a Special Jury on 3 March 1925. The proceedings in the Kings Bench Division of the High Court in London took almost a month to reach a conclusion.

According to *Time* magazine it was *"one of those periodic scandals that causes the various strata of British society to experience the gamut of emotions."* [268] Judge McCardie called it *"the most bitterly conducted litigation he had ever known."*

The case comprised a number of monetary claims by Dorothy Dennistoun against her divorced husband, Lieutenant-Colonel Ian Onslow Dennistoun, for the return of certain small sums of money which she said she had lent him and/or paid for on his behalf.

However, scratch the surface of this 'open and shut' exterior and you find a scabrous mixture of love, malice and hatred, in particular the fallout from the couple's past exploits, and these dark deeds were reflected in Dorothy's charges and in the Colonel's defence. Ian Dennistoun's legal team refuted *all* of Dorothy's claims and raised a number of allegations against Dorothy, citing her being involved in immorality and blackmail. Naturally, Dorothy denied these assaults on her character. In exchange, and to a sharp intake of breath from observers, she asserted that Ian had forced her to live as the mistress of a notable army General of the Great War, Sir John Cowans and, as Dorothy's lawyer put it, this "enabled her husband to live on her immoral earnings."

The atmosphere was electric. Added to this was the assertion that when the Dennistouns were divorced, in Paris in 1921, an arrangement was agreed whereby Ian Dennistoun went along with the divorce and Dorothy did not press her husband for an order for alimony. It was claimed that Ian promised to support her if and/or when he was in a financial position to do so. As far as Dorothy was concerned that cash point was reached when Ian married the extremely wealthy Almina in December 1923.

From the start the case turned out to be part matrimonial slanging match and part not so genteel cat fight between Almina and Dorothy, having all the ingredients to make it the *cause celebre* of its day.

The evidence occupied seventeen days at London's High Court. Neither party cited was well-known although they were *"well to do"* but as the case unfolded and the grim details were revealed, the Dennistouns became the most talked about couple in the English speaking world. This bad press reflected heavily upon Almina, the Colonel's second wife, who was very well known in Society.

Dorothy, who had been brought up in Yorkshire, had married Ian Dennistoun in 1910. Ian's origins were from a long-standing Scottish-Colonial business family with Highland estate connections.

The case was only topped for *"disgust"*, so wrote the King's Private Secretary, Lord Stamfordham,[269] by *Russell v Russell,* another Society divorce case, from 1922.[270]  A file at National Archives, Kew confirms George V's despair in his Private Secretary's letter to the Lord Chancellor about the Dennistoun mud-slinging.

Stamfordham wrote:

The King feels that you will share his feelings of disgust and shame at the daily published discreditable and nauseating evidence in the Dennistoun case.... The King [also] deplores the disastrous and far reaching effects throughout all classes and on all ranks of the Army of the wholesale Press advertisement of this disgraceful story" [271]

This Royal disquiet proved a persuasive lever in efforts to reduce salacious  reporting of seedy divorce cases by Parliament passing the *Judicial Proceedings (Regulation of Reports) Act 1926.*

Dorothy's barrister, Sir Ellis Hume-Williams, deemed the *"most important"* aspect of the case to be the 'General Cowans factor' and the letters written by Ian to Dorothy relating to a conspiracy. The key element centered on Ian Dennistoun making a *"gift "*of his wife Dorothy to this British army officer, General Sir John Cowans, in exchange for *"preferment"* in his own appointments in the Army.

*General Sir John Cowans*

The military files for both Lieutenant Colonel Ian Dennistoun and General Sir John Cowans are held for viewing at National Archives, Kew.[272]    Dennistoun struggled as a Lieutenant to be made up to Captain and all his appointments and promotions up to the rank of Lieutenant Colonel were entirely due to Cowans' recommendations. The General was a well-known womaniser and Dorothy was attractive; for her part Dorothy seemed to have been much taken by the legendry Cowans charms and impressed by his war record[273] as a talented soldier and strategist.

It is clear from Cowans' personal file that the War Office knew all about his close liaison with Dorothy. This is reflected in a letter sent to them by Dorothy after Cowans' death, returning a large collection of the General's papers during a period when they were living together. The same administrator who dealt with this matter, Lt Colonel Creedy,[274] had also reviewed Ian's position at the end of the Dennistoun case.  On that count Ian himself capitulated.  His letter resigning his Commission and waiving his pension crossed with a curt letter from the War Office saying they were about to do just that, anyway.

It was a battle of wills and wits between the Dennistouns during their married life and in the years following their alleged collusive divorce in France in 1921. They refused to compromise with each other and lived in their own seedy, fantasy world, assuming the roles (in letters) of *"Brown Mouse"* (Dorothy) and *"Tiger"* (Ian) in and out of the bedroom. Several letters produced in evidence show the squalid nature of this bizarre relationship.

They really were as bad as each other. Claim and counter claim flew across the court with no hint of remorse for their own poor behaviour; the modern phrase in divorce cases of *"irretrievable breakdown"* cannot be better represented than in this duo. It is not beyond the bounds of possibility that the Dennistouns were initially involved in a joint enterprise to fleece Almina but when Ian found himself the subject of Almina's favours and she offered marriage he decided to fly solo and ditch Dorothy. After all, who needs half a fortune when you can snaffle the lot?[275]

Dorothy was the woman scorned, as she saw it. Detectives followed her everywhere she went; enquiries were paid for by Almina who was besotted with Ian but she also used him for her own purpose for laundering huge sums of money, exceeding £100,000, from the sale of the proceeds of Alfred de Rothschild's legacies.

By Ian taking up so publicly with her rich mutual friend Almina, Dorothy wanted restitution and revenge. Dorothy's world had collapsed when her Spanish lover, Senor Chico Bolin, snubbed her. Almina had persuaded her one-time friend Dorothy to finally reject Bolin and had also helped abort the baby Dorothy was carrying. During the overlapping time the two woman also shared a lover besides the Colonel: he was Tommy Frost, Almina's son's best man at his wedding, the "Mr. F" who features in the court proceedings and was someone still willing to offer Dorothy marriage.

Dorothy was jealous of Ian's happiness; he was sitting pretty with Almina's clout and money. Dorothy wanted at a certain sentimental level to carry on playing their previous cat and mouse games, except she had now reversed her role as the cat and Ian was her prey. Dorothy also wanted to tarnish Almina's standing; in other words, to 'get her own back'. It was Almina's decision alone to refuse to settle with

Dorothy out of Court.[276] In evidence Dorothy's French maid said "I was told that Mrs. Dennistoun was trying to hurt Lady Carnarvon through her husband...."

Ian in turn was a serial gigolo who did not mind being a kept man or breaking women's' hearts. He had several lovers and tainted affairs. In the days after the jury's finding for Dorothy (later reversed by the Judge in respect of a payment recommended by them of £5,000) an American actress, Lois Meredith, came forward to say she was about to sue Ian for breach of promise. An out-of-court settlement (funded by Almina) stopped this being splashed all over the British press. The fate of 100 love letters written by Ian to Lois is a curiosity; these were burned by the lawyers after Almina settled with Lois for damages of £30,000.

In the aftermath of the Dennistoun jury partly finding for Dorothy (albeit the £5,000 they suggested was withheld by the Judge as not supported in law), it was said that Ian's defence team had even more former lovers of Dorothy lined-up, besides a dozen hotel reception clerks and chambermaids, to give evidence of what a busy girl she'd been between the bedsheets. Her success with men was highlighted by attacks on her in court from Ian's barrister Sir Edward Marshall Hall.

In court it was a gladiatorial contest between two leading King's Counsels; the case features in their biographies and memoirs.

But for the Colonel's defence it was not Sir Edward Marshall Hall's finest hour. The mistakes made by the flamboyant lawyer were revealed by the social and legal commentators. Even the jury was taken aback by some of his elementary courtroom gaffes. His cross-examination of Dorothy was harsh, of course; for the sake of his client (and friends) the Colonel and Lady Carnarvon it had to be like a rapier, and it was. But Marshall Hall was very ill, suffering from phlebitis of the leg, and during the case the pain showed in his short temper. Moreover, not just content to repeatedly refer to and taunt Dorothy with many references to her as "brownie" or " little brown mouse", he committed the exceptional blunder of asking her about a conversation she had had with him over some other legal proceedings brought four years previously.

The case, however, established the name of a new up-and-coming young King's Counsel named Norman Birkett who supported Marshall Hall and it was Birkett's skills that turned things around. It is said that Birkett sat up all night working on his performance to master his closing speech, keeping awake by drinking gallons of coffee. [277]

Dennis Bardens, in his biography of Birkett, says that Marshall Hall only acted for Ian as he was a close friend, as was Almina.[278] The Court was told that Marshall Hall's health had relapsed. But the truth was that Ian's defence felt it would lose if Marshall Hall was allowed to continue. Behind the scenes it was Edgar Bowker,[279] Marshall Hall's astute clerk, who pushed for Birkett (who in later life was a distinguished High Court Judge) to take over. Birkett made an epic closing speech and saved the defence from any further criticism.

Sir Ellis Hume-Williams, Dorothy's barrister and a veteran of many contentious divorce cases, describes the Dennistoun case as a "painful and dramatic story". He also remarks in his book *The World, the House and the Bar* that Sir Edward Marshall Hall was "handicapped by his friendship with his client which warped his independence and judgment".

The Judge in the case, McCardie, was a leading rebel on the High Court bench. A file at National Archives on Mr. Justice Henry McCardie reveals that he was often at loggerheads with a succession of Lord Chancellors.[280] Crippled with ill-health and gambling debts, he later committed suicide. [281]

For the man and the woman in the street the frenetic bed-hopping lifestyles of the Dennistouns added a bit of welcome colour during the grey wintery days of the Great Depression. When Dorothy went into the witness box and admitted that her lover was a General 'X' and that he was the man who had promoted Ian from Captain to Lieutenant Colonel and then revealed the man's name as Sir John Cowans, a Great War general dubbed "the greatest Quartermaster since Moses", the case unearthed an undercurrent of hypocrisy, conspiracy and corruption in British Society and in the ranks of the army.

Many people knew all about the General and his inherent weaknesses for woman and gambling. Many also knew that Dorothy Dennistoun was his mistress of several years but he was also linked to several other women. One contemporary quipped of a stream of females ringing up The War Office and constantly inviting the handsome General out to lunch and dinner parties, asking warmly for "Dear Jack".

Cowans was a maverick operator as the Army's Quartermaster General and someone who, in peace time, the army found they were able to do without. He became very ill and it was around his nursing home bedside (whilst he was recovering from an operation for the cancer that would eventually kill him) that Dorothy Dennistoun first met Lady Almina Carnarvon. Almina had always been friendly with John Cowans, not least turning to him (as did Alfred de Rothschild) to facilitate the requisition of hard-to-get supplies for her wartime nursing homes. Almina was on constant watch when old friends of hers were in poor health. She had heard of Dorothy (and of Ian Dennistoun) but their paths had not crossed up to this point.

The two women became friends and in the next few years were inseparable and loving. That was a rare state of being for Almina, in showing an attachment to another woman. Almina was smart and there may well have been an element of keeping Dorothy as a hanger-on to quell any quick disclosures about her life as Cowans' mistress for four years. When John Cowans eventually died in 1921 in France, the War Office (not least also seeing a need to paper over any cracks left by Cowans) granted him a State funeral which was co-ordinated with style.

The Dennistoun scandal cost Almina the good reputation she had built up during the Great War, opening up and running hospitals to treat wounded officers. It shocked many that she was willing to take the caddish Colonel as her second husband and lover, and not necessarily in that order. She went into the witness box and, before the whole world, swore her love for a complete cad and bounder: in her own words "a wash-out" and admitted she fell in love with him the moment they met in 1921 (when Lord Carnarvon was still alive). She also confessed to money laundering on a gigantic scale and making a series of payments to the Colonel and a few to Dorothy.

Every household followed the Dennistoun soap opera and as more sensational evidence was revealed day-after-day the line-up of people who wanted to gain entry into the courtroom grew. The Judge was inundated with requests from peers and peeresses for a seat in the gallery, provoking McCardie to insinuate that he felt more like a Mayfair hostess than a High Court Judge. One of McCardie's attempts to restore a semblance of dignity to proceedings was to order the banning of opera glasses being used by members of the public. The popular press produced photographs of the arrivals and departures from Court. The titillating aspects of the story were relayed all around the world.[282] People always wanted to read about other folks' dirty deeds. Sex, lies and broken promises were the irresistible features.

Newspaper coverage of the trial was ubiquitous for many weeks. It is clear from an examination of coverage that Editors imposed their own censorship. One example of this is the substitution in reports of "misconduct" for the less acceptable word "adultery". Names are frequently omitted in the reports of personalities. [283]

In reality there was no outright winner. Some small claims by Dorothy were proved. Much of her central testimony and claim was rejected.

There was money from the spin-offs. All participants in the case were paid large sums of money to tell their side of the story in the American newspapers and the large audience there lapped up the continuation of the saga, compiled specially for them. These cleverly manufactured articles were the revelations of Dorothy, Ian and Almina largely cobbled from the Court reports. Banner headlines – such as the one below-whetted the reader's taste buds:

"Lady Carnarvon tells her own thrilling story of her love for her second husband, Lt Colonel Ian Onslow Dennistoun, recently sued by his first wife with the allegation that he connived at her relations with General Sir John Cowans for the purpose of securing military advancement. Colonel Dennistoun, during the trial in London, admitted that Lady Carnarvon, while the Earl of Carnarvon was alive, had provided him with $100,000 and a luxurious flat. "

Even Lady Cowans, Sir John's widow, despite claims of being in abject poverty and having to sell her husband's medals, stood proudly behind her late husband memory and sold her story. This pandering to the prurient was curtailed by a change in the law in 1926, restricting the way divorce cases were reported on.

The Dennistoun case was quickly forgotten. Dorothy married a Russian army officer who had sworn to look after her. He did just that. Almina restored her reputation but it took time. The Colonel continued to cost Almina thousands of pounds providing a home for him as his health failed.

## After the Dennistoun Case

It was to her remote Highland retreat of Alvie Lodge that Almina fled with the Colonel after the hellish seventeen days of the Dennistoun court case in London.

Almina regretted nothing, although the pantomime had cost her over £40,000 in legal costs and another large sum exceeding £30,000 in payment of a breach of promise case involving the Colonel and the American actress Lois Meredith.

The escape to Scotland meant that Almina was not present when her granddaughter Penelope was christened in Highclere Parish Church with a smattering of sponsors, mostly of family members.[284]

Catherine gave a tea party in Highclere after the ceremony.

## The Beauchamps Have a Daughter

On 11 July 1925, Almina's daughter Lady Evelyn Beauchamp also produced a daughter, Patricia. There had been strains on Evelyn's health arising from the worry over the Dennistoun case and Brogrove Beauchamp (who had succeeded his father as a baronet in February 1925) refused to have anything more to do with Almina thereafter. He blamed his mother-in-law for causing his wife unnecessary agony as she almost miscarried her child. After the birth of Patricia, Evelyn was told she should not try for any further children as it would jeopardise her life.

116

Almina and her daughter got round the life-long ban imposed by Brogrove. They constantly chatted by telephone and kept in touch by postcard and telegram. They met up occasionally in London (usually at the *Ritz*) when Brogrove was out for the afternoon and also during Almina's four week trips to the South of France in later years. However Almina was never invited to the Beauchamp house in the country and Evelyn only visited her mother once in Bristol in the 1960s, after a brief crisis arose over Almina's health.

Almina's granddaughter Patricia (Mrs Leatham) records fond memories of her granny (and others) in a short book of memoirs.[285] There are also references to Patricia, (who aged exactly with Catherine's daughter Penelope) in the Wrens during the Second World War, in *The Carnarvon Letters*.

## Almina Restores Herself

Almina took delight in being the first person to use a new telephone exchange that was opened at Kincraig, in Lower Badenoch.[286] Lying low at Alvie was now perfect for Almina, who adored the telephone as a way of keeping in touch with news and gossip and family members.

Porchey was not happy with his mother, and refused to talk to her. The tens of thousands forked out on the Dennistoun case included sums initially earmarked by Almina to relieve her son's burden (and fast growing debts) in running the Highclere Estate. It was left to Catherine to bring the two conflicting egos together, brokering a meeting to discuss how money could be raised to save the family pile.

Almina was forced to admit she was stretched financially but, undaunted, she planned to restore her reputation (after the Court case) by opening up a nursing home that would specialise in providing services to wealthy patients.

A gigantic sale was the solution. Porchey and Almina would stage an unforgettable joint auction over three days in May 1925 at Christie's salerooms in London.

# Chapter 8

## The Sale of the Century

**The catalogues were breathtaking. No other sale before it came close.**

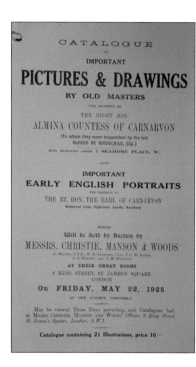

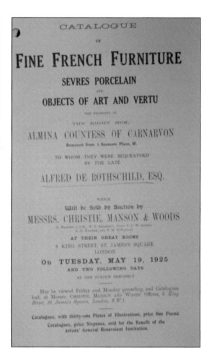

There was a sensational amount achieved on the bidding for Porchey's Chesterfield pictures by Gainsborough. The portrait of Anne, Countess of Chesterfield, made £17,850 and that of Philip made £6,825. But the big winner was Almina who raised a small fortune in disposing of the contents of 1, Seamore Place. She also made several sales through the art dealer Joseph Duveen.

## Porchey is Best Man

In June, 1925, Porchey acted as best man for Major Gabriel Charles (Alan) Breitmeyer, a fellow soldier in the 7th Queen's Own Hussars. Catherine was poorly but made an effort to attend the ceremony at St Margaret's Westminster.[287]   Alan Breitmeyer (as a Lt Colonel) later commanded the 7th Hussars and was a leading polo player.  It was largely through Breitmeyer that Porchey gained rapid promotions in the Hussars, eventually ranking as a Lt. Colonel.

## Cowes Week 1925

Cowes week in August each year saw an exodus from London for the sailing and yacht races.  The events often saw members of the Royal family taking part; in 1925 the King's cutter with His Majesty on board was a favoured craft in the big handicap race.

Catherine's close friend Poppy Baring asked her mother to invite the Carnarvons to the Baring residence at Nubia House. They accepted and Catherine (who was recovering only slowly from the birth of her second child, Penelope) benefited from the change of scene, although she was not able to take part in all the dances at the ball given by Lady Baring at Trinity Hall for local charities.

Lord Montagu of Beaulieu advises that the Carnarvons were present at a lunch party (recorded in Lady Montagu's diary).[288]

## 1926

One of Catherine's many official roles was being patron of the Craven Hunt. She graced the annual ball at the Corn Exchange, Newbury, on 12 January 1926, to great success before a company of at least six hundred people.[289]

Later in January Porchey was keen to go to St Moritz where, somewhat incongruously, horseracing continued despite the ice and snow on a track beside a frozen lake. Other sports attracted thousands of visitors in the winter season.  Porchey joined forces with strays from *Whites*

*Club* including Lord Inverclyde to watch the curling whilst Catherine enjoyed watching the ski jumpers and the tobogganing.

Catherine's reported illness at the beginning of December of 1926 was managed by Almina at close quarters. She immediately passed her distressed daughter-in-law into the tender mercies of Sir Berkeley Moynihan who had private consulting rooms in London and performed surgery at Leeds Infirmary and in a private clinic. Almina's relationship with Moynihan spanned several decades from the Great War onwards. They were lovers and good friends as well as professional colleagues.

Moynihan deemed that urgent surgery was necessary and Catherine was moved to a private nursing home near Leeds. There she underwent a successful procedure for a condition first described as "a slight complaint". [290] Later another source reports this as Almina's universal euphemism of "appendicitis",[291] the apt description she frequently applied to mask the horrors of sexually transmitted diseases like gonorrhoea, a miscarriage or an abortion. However Catherine had been unwell, suffering with seriously infected scar tissue arising from the birth of her daughter, Lady Penelope, in the previous year.

It was a much more serious situation than whipping out her appendix. Catherine was advised not to have any more children; it was suggested this could otherwise be a life-threatening issue. This traumatic event was a confidence that reinforced the relationship between Almina and Catherine; on other occasions Almina successfully managed several miscarriages and abortions for Catherine.[292] In between the highs and low of Catherine's miserable marriage to Porchey, Almina rose to her aid with the problem of bringing Catherine out of bouts of heavy drinking sprees and an attempted suicide.[293]

Moynihan carried out a sterilisation, warning Catherine she must rest for six months and abstain from intimacy. Porchey was livid. During the next few months Catherine did as she was told by Moynihan and as a result her health improved.

In February of 1927 the Carnarvons were invited to spend time in Cairo as guests at the Residency of the High Commissioner and Lady Lloyd.

One newspaper snippet from March 1927 captures the gradual return of Catherine fulfilling her role as Countess of Carnarvon and Porchey's wife:

"Back from Cannes: Lord and Lady Carnarvon were at Hurst Park races the other day. Lady Carnarvon has just returned from Cannes, where she spent the winter recuperating from a serious illness." [294]

Poppy Baring, on a trip with her new best friend Shelia Loughborough (now Lady Milbanke), persuaded Catherine to escape to the sun beds of Cannes; this proved a real tonic and Catherine returned to London as brown as a berry.

## 1927-8
## Porchey's Turn to Fall Ill

Porchey was now a prominent figure on the turf as a horse owner and amateur rider and Catherine was a popular appendage to her husband in racing circles. She delighted fashion commentators and despite feeling low, she was always looked radiant in smart, colourful outfits topped off by the latest in chic millinery. Almina often chatted to her daughter-in-law about what should be worn, and where, as the season played out.

Almina sought to spend the proceeds of the sale of her Highland estate at Alvie[295] to install the Colonel into some new rural refuge while also diverting money for the expensive conversion of 7-9 Portland Place, London, for use as her planned new nursing home. The Colonel had been affected by serious back pain and had for that reason once missed an appearance in Court in the course of giving vital evidence in the Dennistoun case.

In the summer of 1927 it was Porchey's turn to seek medical help for a back disorder; his relentless years spent in the saddle were taking their toll. A Harley Street physician was proposed by Almina who suggested he go abroad to a sanatorium. He left England, with Catherine, for Czechoslovakia "to undergo a cure for sciatica." [296]

Porchey moaned and groaned but found solace and pleasure in taking a series of mud-baths in order to ease his excruciating pain.

## Another glimpse at the married life of the Carnarvons

Balls in that stateliest of stately homes, Blenheim Palace, gave Porchey (who often stayed over alone) license with others of the Bert Marlborough set to indulge in country pastimes during the day and other equally strenuous pursuits by cover of night.

*The Ritz Hotel, London*

London meant one thing: booking rooms to stay at the *Ritz* hotel, which suited both Porchey and Catherine's often separate interests. Porchey became a legendary figure there, decades after his married life with Catherine was over.

As with Almina and the Fifth Earl, racing was an interest (in Porchey's case a passion) shared between Catherine and Porchey. Excursions to race meeting at home and abroad brought them highs and lows.

Deauville in France was a particular favourite of Catherine's, where there were many well-heeled émigrés from London seeking the same enjoyment of the racing and the social scene.

# Chapter 9

## 1928

On 7 January 1928 Catherine and Porchey left Britain on board the suitably named Union-Castle Line Steamship *Carnarvon Castle* for a trip to the Cape of South Africa.

In the spring there was further travel to Paris but finally some breathing space back in London at the end of April, for a few weeks at the *Ritz*.

The close of the 1928 Season in London saw many strangely themed Balls; while not quite 'Tarts and Vicars' an evening staged by Lady Hillingdon and Mrs Gerald Leigh involved guests donning "masks and dominoes or fancy dress".[297] Those who were present did not reveal their identity until midnight. Porchey and Catherine fell in with Bert Blandford's wife's party, which included Poppy Baring, and one presumes a merry evening was had by one and all.

## A Sad Death at Highclere
## Reggie Wendell, Catherine's Brother

### His Last Hours

In mid-1928 a family death occurred which would send ripples through the Wendell and Carnarvon families for generations.

The tragedy struck at Highclere Castle on 16 July 1928 when Catherine and Philippa's brother Reginald died suddenly from a meningeal haemorrhage. He was just twenty-nine.

Mary Van der Woude (Catherine's Wendell cousin) records the sad details of Reggie's last hours in a letter to her mother in the USA:[298]

"I will try and tell you all I can:

Saturday - Gertrude went to Germany, Aunt Marian, to stay with Philippa – Jac and Eileen to Frinton with no telephone. Percy to Cornwall – Reggie to Catherine's. They had a houseparty of all his best friends. He had just come back from a walking tour with Tim Boden[299] and Gerard Lymington. They were both here.

Sunday – He played golf all the a.m., tennis in the p.m. Bridge with Porchey before dinner.

At dinner complained to Poppy Baring ......the heat was terrific …

After dinner he felt better – they all danced and sang. He danced with Catherine and then said he thought he'd go out and get a little air – and stepped outside. Catherine walked out later with Margaret Coats and Poppy and found him lying unconscious.

11.30 Tim rushed out and he and Porchey carried him upstairs. There was a trained nurse in the house and they had a doctor in 15 minutes. Porchey then sent to London for a specialist and two other nurses who arrived at 3 ( o'clock).

We didn't know where Jac was or Gertrude or Percy. We wired Aunt M to come at once….I finally found Jac by wire – wired Gertrude and agreed to meet Aunt M. …..

At 4 ( o'clock) Jac telephoned me that he had arrived at 3 (o'clock) and Reggie died at 3.15.

He never regained consciousness. Tim Boden sat from 11.30 till 3.30 pm till he died – holding his hand. He told Jac he kept him till he got there.

Catherine was in a trance and unable to move – could not be with him.

Aunt M arrived at 9.15pm. I went to the station and there was Jac standing absolutely dazed. He did not know me till I shook him. Aunt M got out and just said "Is he alive?" I said "No". I had *sal volatile* [smelling salts] in a glass which Curtis was holding – I thought she was going mad – her eyes were glassy and I had to shake her and call her….

At 12.15 she was better when she saw Reggie. "[300]

## Reggie's Life and Funeral

During his adult years Reginald Lee Wendell appeared on the social scene in London and New York. He had no occupation but was a regular racegoer and a party animal with a passion for fast cars, playing golf and bridge. He mixed with a particular group of close male friends including Tim Boden (who touchingly held his hand as he slipped away into oblivion). Porchey's Wallop cousin Viscount Lymington[301]was another compatriot and another special friendship was with Hon. Maurice Lubbock.[302]

*Back Row Maurice Lubbock ( groom) and Reggie Wendell ( best man )*

Reggie was best man to Maurice at his wedding in 1926 to Hon. Adelaide Stanley[303] and from her early memoirs[304]Reggie pokes out as a chum of her husband-to-be as a fellow member of the Bachelor's Club based in Piccadilly, as well as the same club-fellows dining extensively together at the Savoy Grill. Girls mattered too but so did the bonds between these young men forged at Eton and Oxford and on the sports field together.

Reggie's funeral took place at St Michael and All Angels, Highclere and he was buried in the churchyard.[305] A cross marks the spot with his names as an inscription.

*Resting Place of Reginald Lee Wendell, Catherine's Brother*

The turnout that summer's day in July was a small but dignified display of respect and sympathy. Old enmities were laid aside, because there was no love lost between Almina and several of those attending the funeral including two of the pall bearers[306] The Dowager Countess of Carnarvon stood gallantly beside the deceased's mother, brother and sister in an imposing state of genuine empathy for their sad, irreversible loss.

Mary Van der Woude records in her letter to her mother, "I sent a beautiful white wreath from you. Aunty Marian wanted it near Reggie. ..Eileen and I arranged everything. He was buried at 2. Jac and Porchey – Percy - then Tim and Gerard – Maurice Lubbock – Bro - - then Aunt Marian, Catherine, Gertrude  and Eileen, Nana and I, Almina and Evelyn. There were very, very few people in a tiny Church. They had a memorial service in Grosvenor Chapel [London] at the same time. Reggie had told Catherine he would love to be buried at Highclere – so that settled it. Percy, Gertrude and Jac wanted him at Sandridge – but could say nothing. Aunty Marian has been wonderful ….she send you all kinds of love …and said she knew how you loved Reggie.

Catherine had fainted three times after the funeral and I feel worried about her. I talked to Ronald [Randolph Stewart] and he says Philippa [who was expecting her second child] is marvellous and only thinks of the others. [Mary's husband was not present as he was in Holland]. Reggie told Beryl Anson that he wanted 'Londonderry Air' played at his funeral; that is why that was in. Aunty Marian was so grateful for all your wires. I feel so terribly for all of them. Reggie had been so sweet this year more so than ever – I can't think what Porchey and Catherine will do without him….." [307]


## The Galloways Again

In October 1928 Philippa Galloway gave birth to a son and heir, to much rejoicing at Newton Stewart as well as on the Cumloden estate. Bonfires and fireworks were lit and the family celebrated. The boy, who assumed the courtesy title of Lord Garlies, was later to be a great worry to his parents, with a string of behavioural problems. Out of respect for Philippa's late brother, Reggie, Garlies was named Randolph Keith Reginald Stewart.

Whatever opportunities Philippa got to appear back in the swim of the London society scene, especially during the Season, she took. Always the epitome of style, at times she outshone her more high-profile sister Catherine in the 'It Girl' stakes. One hack commented "Philippa [Galloway] ....is as pretty and vivacious as American girls can be; is in complete contrast to her fair-haired sister, the Countess of Carnarvon, for she is a brunette." [308]

In the spirit of a modern titled lady of glamour, Philippa had no hesitation in putting her face and her name in the early 1930s to promoting Pond's Two Cream, a makeup product.

"A PERFECT brunette with enchanting brown eyes, soft dark hair and a flawless olive skin, this is the lovely Countess of Galloway. Through wind, rain and hot summer this slim young Countess protects the Smoothness of her flawless complexion with Pond's Two Creams". [309]

Among Philippa's fellow peeresses who apparently were bowled over by the efficacy of Pond's were Thelma, Viscountess Furness and the Marchioness of Cambridge. One promotion carried the name of over thirty titled ladies who endorsed the product. [310]

Such exposure led to Philippa's two young children being in demand at Society weddings as presentable pageboy and bridesmaid material. One such outing saw Philippa's son, the three-year-old Lord Garlies and his six- year- old sister Lady Antonia Stewart, dressed up in pure white at one Society bash in London in 1931.[311]

Garlies was not by any means an easy child, being prone to uncontrollable tantrums, and for several of his nannies his behaviour was a resigning matter (they flew the coop) leaving Philippa feeling at her wits end. There was some support from the relatives in the south and Catherine phoned them often. Almina for her part was a constant source of strength and advice when approached over the subject of Catherine's nephew's instability.

Philippa received some respite from the challenges presented by her son being passed around private schools. The Countess adored taking trips away visiting Edinburgh, a three hour drive from Cumloden. She found the Court at Holyrood in the summer months a lure where she would bump into several of her fellow Scottish titled wives and mothers and enjoy some shopping and fine dining in the Scottish capital.

But getting away completely was not easy as Lord Galloway expected her to give him and NOT Garlies her attention. While Catherine and Porchey enjoyed the French seaside resorts to indulge themselves among the revellers at Deauville, Dieppe and La Touquet and on the Riviera coast, Philippa and her husband only managed a trip across the Tweed to stay with local landed families.

## Almina Restores Her Reputation with the Royals

Also in 1928 Almina opened a nursing home called Alfred House. Her timing was superb as it facilitated a way of getting back into the Royal Family's good books. The cloud overhead that had something of a silver lining was the King's sudden illness.

In fact George V almost died in the winter of 1928. The court and country held their breath as his life lay in the balance. Almina rallied to the plight of her beloved monarch and Queen Mary and offered love, sympathy and the private use of her plush new nursing services at Alfred House, a facility already dubbed 'The National Wealth Service'.[312] The King was tended in his palaces and eventually recovered but Queen Mary was touched by Almina's generous offer.

Indeed, by way of acknowledging the Royal forgiveness in the aftermath of the Dennistoun Court case and throughout the 1930s, Queen Mary asked Almina to treat several members of the Royal Household for a variety of ailments. [313]

The Duke of Gloucester and his wife Alice received a full, free service from Almina in Alfred House and at The Glebe, Barnet, where Almina ran a hospital specialising in maternity cases. The ill-fated Prince William of Gloucester was born at the Glebe, under Almina's charge, in 1941. Wallis Simpson was another patient at Alfred House for some grim procedures.

*Alfred House Nursing Home, Portland Place, London*

During the King's illness London Society had tiptoed along in rather a subdued fashion. The one notable exception to this moratorium on gaiety was Lady Mary Ashley Cooper's marriage at St Margaret's, Westminster to Lord (Naps) Alington; it proved to be the wedding of the season. Lady Mary was tagged the "Jewel Bride" on account of the fact that she had been the recipient of more pieces of jewellery than any bride of that period. There were throngs of sightseers outside the church and a full turnout of the aristocracy at the reception for over two thousand guests at Londonderry House.

Porchey, true to form, cast his eye over the bridesmaids and one in particular caught his eye, the twenty-year-old Tanis Guinness.[314] She was to be a future 'conquest' some years' later and escaped marriage to Porchey by the skin of her teeth.

In the week preceding the Alingtons' wedding, the christening of Philippa Galloway's son Lord Garlies, also at St Margaret's, Westminster brought some joy after the weeks of torment that Catherine suffered after the death of her adored brother, Reggie. And

Reggie was fondly remembered among the names given to the heir to the Earldom of Galloway, to Catherine's (and Marian's) huge delight. The reception afterwards was given by Gertrude Griffiths.

## Catherine's closest friend, Poppy Baring, Marries

In December 1928, possibly in order to reduce the gossip that was threatening to re-surface over Prince George and Poppy Baring, she married William Piers (Peter) Thursby,[315] the son of a vicar from Berkshire, who was otherwise described as an Eton cricketer who played for Berkshire in the Minor Counties Championships.[316] Catherine rallied round to help her friend with all the arrangements for the service performed at St Margaret's, Westminster. The four-year-old Lord Porchester was a page. The tempestuous Poppy was married in white satin on 17 December 1928, her aunt Lady Helen Cassel[317] lent her a beautiful old Brussels lace bridal veil for the ceremony.

*Catherine ( right ) and  Poppy Baring at a Wedding Together*

Almina, building on her rehabilitation into very polite society, brought a measure of good tidings and Christmas cheer by hosting a dinner (with Ian Dennistoun as co-host) for King George and Queen Elizabeth of the Hellenes at 1, Seamore Place on 19 December 1928. Among the four hundred guests were the Carnarvons, the Beauchamps and Catherine's dear friend Lady Helen Cunliffe-Owen. The newly married Margaret Coats, Viscountess Knollys, (who had shared the terrible ordeal of Reggie Wendell's death with Catherine and Porchey) was also present, as was Catherine's girlhood chum Lois Sturt, now the Hon. Mrs Evan Morgan.[318]

## 1929

At Epsom 1929 the Carnarvons were among those who welcomed the Prince of Wales (accompanied by Princess Mary and her husband) to the season's meeting. The Princess was also entertained by the Carnarvons and others at Epsom that year.

## Porchey Loses His Rag and Almost His Scalp

Porchey lost his rag with Catherine at a party hosted by Prince Aly Khan, in London in March 1929. The Carnarvons arrived at what was billed as a ' Wild West' party. It was the height of the era of the *Bright Young Things* crazily themed parties.

Gaily ornamented tickets had been issued to guests ( to prevent gate crashing ), but Catherine had left the tickets at home. Dressed as a fearsome looking cowboy, festooned with guns and knives about his person, Porchey was in no mood to be turned away. But the Carnarvons were left standing at the door as abandoned outcasts whilst the Prince was located to vouch for their invitation. Catherine ( dressed as a cowgirl ) could not reason with Porchey as he was trod on by the ticketed arrivals including a unruly mob of red Indians who wanted to take Porchey's scalp.

# Chapter 10

## Gertrude and Marian Co-host in Mayfair and enjoy jaunts away

Gertrude Griffiths continued her role as an enthusiastic Mayfair hostess holding receptions and soirees for London's social elite. She was never in the same league as the legendry aristocratic Ladies Cunard, Colefax or Desborough, who were unrivalled in their gracious hospitality; here the latest and juiciest of scandals could be dissected at length, making their privileged lives a little less tedious particularly if it was a love match they had engineered or an infidelity one or other of them had got wind of.

With Gertrude came the moneyed whiff of the Eastern seaboard of the USA with its plush New York parlours groaning at the seams with Old World antiques. Marian Wendell commonly co-hosted the receptions etc. with her cousin, Gertrude; they made a very good double-act because between them they had entree into so many different networks of the great and the good, hence their guest lists were not to be sniffed at. Moreover, the depth of Percy's bank balance meant that the assembled company at Gertrude's events were more than well catered for.

Countesses Catherine and Philippa often attended these soirees and for appearances sake initially arrived alongside their husbands. The Earls however would often find themselves called away on urgent business or a vote in the House of Lords; in truth they were on other missions where 'cherchez la femme' (and, oh my, did they cherchez!) was the order of the day. As for their wives, they mostly had to just grin and bear it. Percy himself made but fleeting appearances at Gertrude's bashes before cunningly slipping away to spend time in the arms of his mistress, Dorothy Robertson.

In 1930 Gertrude gave a lavish cocktail party and dinner to reintroduce Eleanor Wendell, daughter of her cousin Arthur Wendell,[319] who was visiting London from the USA[320] but the Carnarvons were not present as they were entertaining at Highclere. The party for Eleanor was to mark her third season since being presented as a debutante in 1927[321] at Buckingham Palace (and earlier being show-cased in Washington).

Sponsored by her wealthy father, Eleanor's genteel and somewhat lengthy (by society's standards) search for Mr Right (or shall we call him The Earl of Rightfordshire?) was no doubt influenced by the lack of matrimonial bliss encountered by her two cousins Catherine and Philippa.

Catherine adored one-to-one sessions with her sister and on one occasion, whilst Philippa was on a brief trip to London from Cumloden (shopping for Christmas gifts), Gertrude gave a further cocktail party which Catherine attended alone and could catch up with family news with her sister, especially about their respective young children.[322] Undoubtedly there were lessons learned on the sidelines by the two sisters, especially Philippa as a regular visitor to *Sandridgebury*: she saw the effects of the breakdown of the Griffiths marriage from 1923 onwards. Gertrude had given up on her divorce action; she made that sacrifice in order for Philippa's marriage to proceed and she accepted (indeed, she may have suggested) the quaint arrangement for co-existence with Percy. In effect, the deal struck at the time of Philippa's engagement meant turning a blind eye on Percy's continuing adultery; their marriage was a sham.

When Reggie Wendell died in 1928, Mary Van der Woude (a Wendell family member, her father was Barrett Wendell) wrote that she had hopes that the tragedy might bring the Griffiths back together again. It didn't. [323] Throughout the 1930s Dorothy was Percy's constant companion, accompanying him on overseas jaunts[324] and pleasure cruises and the Griffiths money paying for the woman's upkeep until unexpectedly Dorothy married. Her husband was the journalist Dominic Bevan Wyndham Lewis, [325] famous for his *Beachcomber* column in *The Daily Express*.

Yet, in reality Gertrude enjoyed her life without Percy's amorous demands. She coaxed Marian into accompanying her on a holiday to Italy, in part to ease their joint grief after losing Reggie. Meanwhile, during the years that followed, the two women were often to be seen together during the season at Court functions in London. They also enjoyed going to the theatre and opera and relished entertaining the

Carrs, Carnarvons and, more often, the Galloways at *Sandridgebury*. Undoubtedly Gertrude's greatest coup was in 1931 when Queen Mary paid a private visit to *Sandridgebury*.[326]

Occasionally showing a united front with Percy (in public) the Griffiths couple (with Marian) installed themselves at 34 Bryanston Square for the key events of the 1930s season and declared their status in the *Court Circulars*.

When Percy craved the attentions of Dorothy, Gertrude and Marian went off to enjoy themselves on the Continent, spending several months there each year Italy was a favourite place for both ladies, who enjoyed its history, heritage and culture. Several close friendships were cemented on these carefree trips. Gertrude announced her pleasure trips each year in the *Court Circular*. Percy's stock response when asked about his wife's absence from appearances at Deloittes dinners and the hunting field was that she was in Italy for the sake of her health. He turned Gertrude into "an invalid".[327]

Gertrude showed herself to be quite the reverse; she was an active, thriving hostess, especially caring for her own family members. She also extended her generosity by giving receptions for the Italian Ambassador and was often invited to the *Ritz* hotel for luncheon with Signor Grandi and his wife Antonietta, with Marian joining them.[328] The two cousins Gertrude and Marian also splashed out on the latest fashions to attend the Royal Garden Parties at Buckingham Palace. Gertrude also hosted several large supper parties and balls.[329] Charity events were a favourite indulgence, all paid for of course by the adulterous but wealthy Percy.

# 1930

By 1930 Catherine Carnarvon was something of a solitary figure at Highclere but still to be seen attending local functions in and around Newbury. In London, however, Eve Beauchamp or Almina provided diverting companions.

Meanwhile Porchey maintained an unrelenting pace that kept him away from Highclere for weeks at a time, during the daytime at any number of race meetings around the country and abroad and at night checking out the local nightlife, often with Bert Blandford or a racing chum or two in tow.

## Porchey's Stable Lads

At this time the other buddies in Porchey's life besides Blandford were Eddy, Lord Stanley and David Beatty, the latter two were in line to inherit family titles, both Earldoms. On the death of Porchey's great ally Eddy, Lord Stanley[330], his son, Edward Derby[331] ( grandson of the Seventeenth Earl of Derby, and later the Eighteenth Earl) was a favourite racing chum of Porchey's , David Beatty [332]was the son of the famous Admiral of naval victories in the Great War. As a pack they were inseparable on race courses, their London Clubs and in fierce competition as to how many times they could get in and out of 'my lady's bedchamber' .

They were all of a certain type, high born and at times high tempered with a penchant for putting all those they considered socially beneath them firmly in their place.

## Bert Blandford ( Late Tenth Duke of Marlborough)

For a Duke in waiting it was all about breeding, beauty being a bonus. Bert ( as the Marquess of Blandford ) married Mary Cadogan, in 1920. She apparently had a voice that could call many a herd of cows home at the double. When Tony Leadbetter ( Almina's godson) was a footman at Cornbury Park ( the seat of the Watneys ) he once mistook her ( on the telephone ) for a man.

Bert and Porchey were both at times uncivil and unfaithful to their wives, civility returning only when they wanted something. The wives carried on regardless and despite often being hurt by their husbands' errant behaviour turned their attentions to maintaining a comfortable home at Highclere and Blenheim.

## Poppy, Catherine and Prince George

While Porchey stayed often away with his racing chums, Catherine and Poppy Baring remained great pals and both were somewhat enamoured of Prince George and did not mind sharing him with each other.

Poppy was a great patron of the London ballet and theatre; she was very much 'in the know' and was thus able to ensure that where the Royal Prince went she and Catherine were sure to follow. However, the deep love of *both* woman for George became a sport in which several other wives became their accomplices.

In July 1930 Poppy and Catherine were guests of Lady Astor at Cliveden. During their stay she whisked them off to a small dance where PG had the fairest of several of his old flames around him including Catherine, Poppy, Mrs Dudley Coats and Tanis Guinness.[333] At this stage the latter was not the grave danger to Catherine's position that she ultimately became a few years later when Porchey was smitten by Tanis's feminine allure.

Another place for good living, relaxation and safety was at Eaton Hall where Loelia Lindsay, Duchess of Westminster, was a valued friend of Catherine and Poppy, albeit Porchey received invites here too and did appear with Catherine once or twice. Photographs survive, with all three enjoying playing endless games of croquet on the lawn at Eaton Hall.[334]

This sanctuary became a favourite place also for Tilly Losch to escape from the pressures of appearing on the London stage. She mixed in the company here of her sometime lover Tom Mitford (only brother of the famous Mitford girls), a promising young man who was to die of wounds in Burma during the Second World War.[335]

## 1931

## Melton Mowbray Hunts

Each January a large contingent, usually numbering three to four hundred members of the aristocracy, met together at the Corn

Exchange at Melton Mowbray for the Melton Ball. This was where the 'huntin' shootin' and fishin'' brigade got together to plan their year's sport. Porchey and Catherine feature prominently in the 1931 line-up.[336] The social side of the event proved to be a time when other planning and assignations took place, it often being a case of "Tally Ho! and stand by your beds", or preferably someone else's bed.

*Mollie Dalkeith and Porchey ( looking every bit the Indian Prince )*
*at Melton Hunt*

## Catherine organises a hunting party

To the surprise of many Catherine demonstrated she could organise and entertain outside of Highclere or London when she acted as hostess for a house party at Lowesby Hall, Leicestershire, for the hunting. [337] She also encouraged her daughter, six-year-old Lady Penelope, to take part in the Children's meet of the Quorn Hunt. [338]

## Embassy Club

One of Porchey's favourite London refuges for rascality was the exclusive *Embassy Club* in Bond Street, (frequently visited by the Royal Princes, visiting Americans and stage stars). Porchey often entertained here or was entertained by the Hon. Lionel Montagu.[339] They were truly close chums, especially on the racing circuit. Lionel worked for SOE in the Second World War;[340] he was a wise mentor to Porchey's son, the young Lord Porchester, and there are several references to him in the *Carnarvon Letters*. Montagu had a soft spot for Catherine too.

The *Embassy Club,* which comprised a large dining area and a spacious dance floor, was an ideal place for friendly rendezvous and for meeting, wining, dining and dancing with available women. The ultimate aim, of course, was to woo the lady back to your apartment or hotel room; in Porchey's case 'cut to the quick' foreplay was not the Earl's strong suit and he was definitely a first date man.

In fact Porchey sometimes couldn't even wait to find a bed in which to romp; any vacant corner of the Club would do to achieve his one perpetual end, the girl's capitulation to his seduction. The Carnarvon Rolls Royce was Porchey ace card in terms of pulling a girl, his chauffeur being instructed 'Eyes Front and Centre' while he set about pressing his ardour. One member of the peerage who was molested by Porchey mentions that the *Embassy Club* is where he first tried it on; she threw up over his dinner jacket and thankfully even Porchey lost interest at that point.

The diplomat Duff Cooper (who had a reputation as a heavy drinker, womaniser and gambler[341]) had a fling with Catherine's friend Poppy Baring. Cooper, like Porchey, was an *Embassy Club* regular and it was here that he finally made his move on her. In his diaries he records details of his fatal attraction for Poppy: in the entry for 12 January 1924 he records, "I dined at the Embassy and brought Poppy home with the inevitable result". [342] Duff Cooper was also an occasional visitor to Highclere with his wife Lady Diana whose only child, the present-day travel writer Lord John Julius Norwich, was born under Almina's watchful eye at Alfred House in 1929.

Apart from the amorous goings-on at *The Embassy*, most found the food and wines and dancing a draw too. A lover of fine dining, Porchey endeared himself to the *Embassy's* owner, Luigi Nainte. He was also a friend of the epicure Harcourt Johnstone who occasionally entertained Porchey, sometimes with Catherine, at the *Embassy* and the *Ritz* hotel. Johnstone, who died of a stroke aged 49, was a lover of the good life; it was said that he "dug his own grave with his teeth".[343]

## Ciros Club

Opened in 1915, *Ciros* was another favourite place for the Bright Young People. A members club it was based in London's Orange Street.

## Porchey at the Ritz

Porchey's main other London lair was the *Ritz hotel* Piccadilly where, in the years before the death of the establishment's chairman Lord Lurgan,[344] Porchey (with or without Catherine's presence or residence) was allotted a suite of rooms (gratis); this was in exchange for his personal recommendation of the magnificence of the hotel to all in sundry in the racing world and especially among his and Catherine's wide American connections in New York and contacts in the capitals of Europe.

Porchey was a legendary figure-cum-resident at the *Ritz* for over fifty years. His coterie would gather round to be told to 'put their chemise on Windbrake in the two thirty at Haydock', only to find the horse had lived up to its name and been withdrawn from the race with colic. Many similar escapades of Porchey and his like are to be found in a history of the *Ritz* hotel published in 1980. [345]

In reality Porchey loved to talk about horses and, of course, himself. He was vain, arrogant and loud. He was also a famous raconteur, as was demonstrated in later life with his appearances when he invited himself onto TV shows. Many stories were embellished and further distorted. Tales of the Fifth Earl's Egyptian years were fabricated but continue to be offered wholesale in books and to visitors at Highclere. His two ghost-written volumes of memoirs reveal dashing tales of Porchey's part in the affairs of state with Royalty and Prime Ministers, including a role in the Abdication crisis of 1936. A recent book revives this popcorn, which has no supporting evidence in the Royal Archives. It only happened in Porchey's often disturbed but whimsical imagination.

Of Porchey's contacts with Prime Ministers, he did have conversations with Winston Churchill when they met at Blenheim and enjoyed shooting parties with Harold MacMillan and drinks with Anthony Eden and his wife, Clarissa, who was on Porchey's hit list to bed. Clarissa was a friend of Tilly Losch.

For those who wished to listen (and buy him a bottle of best champagne and dinner) Porchey entertained his fellow guests at the *Ritz* by re-running furlong by furlong many of his past racing triumphs, citing and re-conquering as many fillies at the *Ritz* as he tamed on the horse race tracks of Britain and France. He held court here as a horseman and breeder, and if the chance arose he worked out the best route to seduce any pretty girl who passed by, waitresses included. When he was flush with cash he became a gambling man, suggesting bets to others in his company; when he was light in pocket he raised the stakes even still higher. The Aga Khan was another *Ritz* dweller, famously remarking that he "could always be contacted"[346] at the establishment. The same was true of Porchey Carnarvon.

Porchey's style with *Ritz* staff was often brusque and arrogant; he relished acting out the feudal lord. A record of this display of the nightmare guest who is hard to satisfy (worthy of Fawlty Towers) survives in a film documentary about the hotel. The scenes include Porchey taking breakfast. The foreign waiter is seen struggling to keep his guest happy as he picks faults in the table laying and the failure in standards whilst serving him coffee, with Porchey pulling the man up on his pouring method from the pot and putting the milk in the cup first.

## Eleanor Wendell's further appearances

In 1931 pressure was re-applied by the collateral branch of the surviving cousins of the Wendell family from America for Eleanor

Wendell to find (if possible) an ermined husband, especially from those eligible men made accessible through their Earl and Countess's relations. The net was cast wider on the distaff side of the family, enlisting the help of not only the Countesses of Carnarvon and Galloway but also bringing up those big guns of matchmaking, Marian Wendell and Gertrude Griffiths.

Still confident that her daughter would be picked for marriage to at least an earl, Mrs Arthur Wendell gave a dance at the *Ritz* on 28 May 1931. The ballroom was decorated with pink rambler roses and pink hydrangeas and music was provided by the *Embassy* band.[347] Tables were headed by Gertrude, Catherine, Mary van der Wode (daughter of Catherine's uncle, Barrett Wendell) and Jac Wendell's wife, Eileen Carr. There were several hundred attendees including the Galloways and the Dowager, Amy, as well as Lady Evelyn Beauchamp and her husband, Brogrove.

It all proved too much for Catherine, who had over-indulged herself and was consequently in the middle of having a nervous breakdown, lying sedated in Almina's care at Alfred House. [348] This process of heavily sedating Catherine (having been recommended by Almina after discussions with several of her doctor friends in Harley Street) seemed to be beginning to work. Almina also arranged for one of her trained nurses at Alfred House to be in attendance on Catherine at Highclere, day and night.

In Catherine's absence Porchey took on the task of the official Carnarvon welcoming committee for Cousin Arthur and family, along with his Wallop cousin Viscount Lymington (the heir to the Earldom of Portsmouth), directing Arthur's wife to the appropriate London hostesses, including Almina, for help and advice on all the expensive things. At this further dance, also given by Mrs Arthur Wendell, Porchey and Lymington accompanied Misses Priscilla and Helena Perrott.[349] The Perrott girls had attended Gertrude's 1930 parties with their chaperone, Lady Amherst. In the following year, another wave of dances was given for Eleanor. At one of these she met Thomas Sharon Fermor-Hesketh, the son of a baronet. Eleanor and Thomas became an item; they appeared everywhere together and naturally rumours followed that this dashing young soldier in the Scots Guards (with an American mother) was going to pop the question but the grim reaper took a hand, as Thomas was killed in a plane crash in France in 1937. Eleanor was left to mourn for her lost soldier lover. [350]

## 1932

## Some Personal Horrors Hit Catherine
## Inseparable Foursome

The Carnarvons and the Beauchamps frequently entertained four long-standing friends from among the era's set of fervent racing couples, Sir Hugo and Helen Cunliffe-Owen and Sir Jock Delves and Vera Broughton. The links between them over the previous ten years started at the wedding of the Porchesters in 1922. Catherine and Lady Helen were confidantes and close friends.

The Cunliffe-Owen's home at Sunningdale Park was often the venue for house parties at the time of Ascot, Newmarket or Newbury race meetings. Horse owner Sidney Beer[351] was another friend usually in the company; he was in a business partnership with Lady Helen Cunliffe-Owen which owned a horse called *Venturer*. The common denominator of the coterie was a passion for gambling, with a king's ransom in debts owed by several of them to shady betting syndicates. Bad debts, a divorce and an insurance fraud later forced Jock Delves Broughton to flee abroad to Happy Valley in Kenya.

A few years later, in 1941, Sir Jock and new wife Diana Caldwell were implicated in a murder case with Jock as the main suspect  when the body of their friend Josslyn Hay, 22nd Earl of Erroll, an insolently glamorous seducer was discovered with a bullet through his head just outside Nairobi. Porchey later declared to one investigator working on a retrospect of the killing that Diana was having an affair with Hay, the inference being that Jock had acted out of jealousy.[352]  Arrested and charged but acquitted of murder, Jock Broughton was banished from the Happy Valley colony, Diana deserted him; he returned to Britain and committed suicide in a Liverpool hotel. Two later books,[353] a newspaper enquiry and a series of commentators conclude that the murderer of Hay was almost certainly NOT Jock. But was he innocent? If so, was he meant to be the fall guy for the real murderer or murderess? In any event Happy Valley proved for him to be something of a misnomer.

Almina knew the various members of the wider Delves Broughton family as Lady Evelyn, one of her bridesmaids in 1925, was a member of the clan. Almina fell in with inviting the various couples from her son and daughter-in-law's orbit, along with Sidney Beer, and they had a table together when she requisitioned the whole of the *Ritz* Restaurant for a dinner and dance in honour of the Duchess of Aosta and the Duke of Spoleto. Colonel Ian Dennistoun even came out of his country retreat to attend the party.

## Sidney Beer's help to Catherine

Sidney Beer could see that Catherine was often depressed, and he was aware at close quarters of Porchey's bad behaviour towards Catherine and his pursuits with women. Beer became a key figure who helped Catherine with support, offering her a listening ear. He eased her crisis through Porchey's constant adultery during their marriage. Born in Liverpool of wealthy parents (his father was an American-born cotton merchant), he was a well-known and enthusiastic race horse owner and a gambler "who came near to breaking the bank, not at Monte Carlo but at Cannes";[354] and was also a leading figure (particularly during the Second World War, when he founded the National Symphony Orchestra) as a conductor. Sidney Beer also knew Tilly Losch from his association with the State Academy of Music in Vienna and the Mozarteum in Salzburg. Heidi Beer (Sidney's wife, who was an artist) corresponded with Tilly when she fled from Porchey's clutches to America, in 1939.

Trained under the musical legend Sir Malcolm Sargent, Beer introduced Catherine to Sir Malcolm which led to a stable period during which Catherine was regularly invited to dine out with Sargent, receiving a steady flow of tickets to his concerts, and they later became lovers. During the 1930s Sargent was a patient at Alfred House when he was convalescing after a bout of serious illness. Almina (a life long friend) knew about Sargent's reputation for his long line of love affairs with aristocratic women before abandoning them and warned Catherine not to get too attached to him. She didn't fall in love with Sargent, nor did he fall in love with her, but their short fling filled a gap in Catherine's engagement diary and, more importantly, helped her to regain an inner confidence in her capacity to be a woman again.

## The Carnarvons Regret

The Carnarvons were forced to send their regrets (and declare the same in the Court Circular of Saturday 23 July, 1932) as they "were 'unavoidably prevented from obeying their Majesties' Command to attend the Garden Party at Buckingham Palace." [355]

They were going through a rocky patch in the marriage and Catherine was under sedation again. A harsh indictment on Catherine at about this time was that "plainly and simply, Catherine was a drunk; she was never sober and was messing about with Malcolm Sargent and Prince George who was later Duke of Kent."[356]

## Porchey's Affair with Tanis Guinness begins

Porchey strayed once more, and in the process bit off more than he could chew. His attention was on Tanis Guinness who had been out in Society since the age of eighteen in 1926. Porchey had first clapped eyes on her at a dance at Warwick House, St James's, and cast a further a wandering eye on this always lovely and extremely rich Guinness heiress (the clue's in the surname) at the Lord Alington-Mary Ashley Cooper wedding in 1928 where he made furtive advances towards her seduction. He began a conquest of a more exacting nature after she had just married the Hon. William Drogo Sturges Montagu who, with his roving eye, was as much a womaniser as Porchey.

The setting for Porchey's first conquest of Tanis was at a large-scale function at Stornoway House, St James's, given by the newspaper magnate Lord Beaverbrook, which Catherine could not attend owing to one of the children being taken ill.[357] Beaverbrook's hostess was his daughter Janet Campbell whose five year marriage to the incurable gambler Ian Douglas Campbell, the heir presumptive to the Dukedom of Argyll (later the 11th Duke), was floundering. They ultimately divorced in 1934.[358]

Tanis's first husband Drogo was also playing away with others, including 'The Beaverbrook Girl', Janet Campbell, and all this mutual adultery fuelled Tanis also taking divorce proceedings in 1934.[359] In 1935, without any dust having settled, Drogo married Janet Campbell.[360] This was the cue for Porchey to move in and pursue Tanis to the altar. He had been chasing her cunningly around Europe and now showered her with compliments and expensive trinkets; in fact the cash registers of Tesler's of Bond Street were never busier ringing merrily as Porchey bought up more diamonds for his new prospective Countess. However, he had over looked the small matter of the fact that he was still married to Catherine. This very public violation (one among many) of his marriage vows caused much distress to Catherine. She was consoled by Almina and Marian Wendell, but she started to drink heavily again.

## A Wonderful Escape at Christmas Time

Catherine was a dedicated and loving parent and this was her single best achievement: her son Henry and daughter Penelope. Whilst not exactly hands-on (few of her class were) she tried to ensure that she at least saw them regularly and accompanied them for treats and hosted parties for them and their friends.

On one excursion by Catherine to collect the eight-year-old Lord Porchester from school at the end of term and deliver him to a pre-Christmas treat, mother and son experienced a scare when their chauffeur-driven Rolls was involved in a motor car accident on the Bath road near Newbury. A tyre burst violently and caused the vehicle to swerve, skidding twice, striking a kerb and completely overturning. Catherine was flung on top of her son and the chauffeur was hurled against them both. Fortunately Catherine, Porchester and the driver all managed to open the doors and crawl out exhausted, shaken, but not injured.[361] They were safely conveyed to Highclere in another car.

Later, Porchey quizzed the chauffeur whose explanation was simple: "My Lord, the car shot across the road as if it had been hit by a cannon ball."[362]

146

Lord Porchester's two grandmothers, Almina and Marian Wendell (who Porchester and his sister always called 'Gar') were among the first to enquire about his welfare (and that of Catherine). They had had a very narrow escape.

## 1933

In 1933 Porchey went to Egypt on 4 February without Catherine during the Cairo season, where there was racing, duck shooting and golf during the day. He was kept amused in the evenings by being included on the guest list of Sir Percy and Lady Loraine at the Residency, Cairo, with others for dinners and dancing including the Duke and Duchess of Alba, the Earl and Countess of Wharncliffe and Mrs James Horlick and her daughter Miss Katherine Horlick. It was pure pleasure and self-indulgence. Porchey returned to England on 12 March 1933 with Lady Jane Egerton and Lord and Lady Greenwood. [363]

Almina and Colonel Dennistoun appeared in London at the end of May of 1933 for the last two pre-Ascot Courts. Evelyn saw her mother at this event and brought news of Catherine's fragile state of health which prompted Catherine's further admission into Alfred House.

## A Horse Racing Cycle Begins

In the early spring of 1933, much to Porchey's annoyance, a cold weather snap and frost cancelled several horse race meetings. He had other problems in racing: a French-bred horse *Tibere* which had first shown promise had floundered so it was resold. To escape boredom and frustration, Porchey offered patronage (along with Lords Lonsdale, Rosebery and Tweedmouth, the Duke of Westminster and Lord Beatty) to a boxing tournament at London's Albert Hall.[364]

This was in good time to be around the Royals because the King and Queen with the Duke of Gloucester (almost fully recovered from being a patient in Almina's nursing home) all attended Newbury Races. Among other racegoers Lady Evelyn Beauchamp was also present and the King's horse won the Spring Cup.[365] Almina warned Evelyn (by telephone) to keep a watchful eye on Catherine's behaviour to ensure she was removed from the temptation of drinking too much. The secret to success in this lay in keeping Porchey and Catherine apart as much as possible to stop Porchey sniping at his wife and Catherine finding further solace from the nearest bottle. The two sisters-in-law were often to be seen together at racecourses, weddings and London functions, Evelyn keeping an ever-watchful eye. Their respective husbands had also joined forces into a business partnership which made both of them considerable sums of money.

Attending at race meetings, running his horses and frequently riding his horses was the central part of Porchey's life with this thrill only matched by his lust for the ladies.

The two things he paid less attention to were maintaining his marriage and the Highclere estate. There were expensive family and estate tax avoidance schemes in place but Porchey relied on his agents and solicitors to operate these on his behalf. He was bored with Catherine, as her constant state of depression was unchangeable despite his behaviour being the root cause. He deemed her out of his control and unable to improve.[366] There was talk of having Catherine placed under specialised care at an establishment like the *Priory*[367] or the *Holloway Sanatorium*,[368] for her own good. Such a move was abandoned in favour of Catherine going into a retreat, which brought some good results. But day to day Porchey never knew how his wife would be; on the other hand with race horses Porchey knew exactly where he was with them at all times.

Porchey had a reputation for being a good judge of a horse; he was still riding in amateur races and was on the lookout for a suitable new beast for to ride in the summer races. At Lincoln he made several bids for horses in selling races, with one purchase. As the good weather returned Porchey's horses ran at Liverpool in the Grand National meeting.

Out of the blue Catherine turned up at Aintree, where the keen wind demanded smart tweeds and fur coats. However she slipped off, unaccompanied, to accept an invitation from Almina to a luncheon at the *Ritz* which was also attended by Brogrove and Lady Evelyn (who, as it happens, were in residence at the hotel). After the first course

Brogrove made a hasty exit; Evelyn claimed he had a business appointment but the truth was he couldn't stand the sight of Almina. The two Countesses of Carnarvon and Evelyn enjoyed a good gossip[369] and the chatter also turned on the forthcoming Newbury race meeting over several days. Catherine was hosting a small house party at Highclere and Porchey had several of his horses running in the races.

As April continued, Porchey had a win at Lingfield. However bad weather again forced the Royal party to drive from Windsor Castle to the Epsom Spring meeting in a snowstorm. Since Catharine was unwell, Lady Evelyn Beauchamp accompanied Porchey. Sandown Park and Ripon brought mixed results, despite the efforts of Carnarvon's favourite jockey Gordon Richards and trainer Dick Dawson.

Newspaper pundits praised the antics of Lord Carnarvon, the owner-rider at the Salisbury meeting, recording that few were as keen as him or as successful on a horse of their own. At the previous year's gathering Porchey had won on a horse called *Kiang* and now he went on to win the Lingfield Club Welter Stakes on his mount *Knight of Lorn*.

The 1933 Derby was looming, always a high point in the racing calendar, with the all-male Derby Club luncheon at the Savoy Hotel. Whilst Porchey would have preferred a room full of ladies to flirt with, he had been asked to make a speech at the lunch.

The lunch was presided over by Lord Riddell. To accolades galore, and alongside other speakers Lord Derby, Lord Lonsdale, Lord Zetland, Sir Alfred Butt, Gordon Richards, Steve Donoghue and others, Porchey, to great cheers and chuckling, remarked that he didn't fancy his own horse *Madagascar* to win but did rate one of his former horses that now belonged to someone else, namely Sir Hugo Cunliffe-Owen's horse *King Salmon*.[370]

But in the end it was Lord Derby's horse *Hyperion* that actually went on to win the race, 153 years after his forefather who founded the race

Catherine suffered another breakdown in May. Almina and Colonel Dennistoun appeared in London at the end of the month for the last two pre- Ascot events at Court, where Evelyn saw her mother and brought news of Catherine's fragile state of health. This news prompted Catherine's admission to Alfred House to dry out.

On Thursday 1 June, with Catherine discharged, the Carnarvons appeared in public together at a dinner party at the *Ritz* given by Sir Delves and Lady Broughton, which was by way of a small family reunion with Almina and the Beauchamps also attending. Catherine was anxious to see Sunny Marlborough (who was not in good health) with his son (Porchey's fellow-womaniser) Bert, Marquess of Blandford. Moreover, Blandford was not harnessed to his wife, which meant one thing: that he and Porchey would want to slip off after dinner. The talk was of horses; Porchey was due to ride at Newmarket and Hurst Park the following week: he was full of vim and ready for his night out with Bert and his forthcoming riding commitments.

## Howard Carter

The newly published third volume of Howard Carter's epic book on The Tomb of Tutankhamun[371] reminded everyone of the glorious discovery of 1922. To Almina and Porchey the whole matter was a closed book. Almina had sold off the Fifth Earl's personal Egyptian collection (to the Metropolitan Museum, New York) and the Egyptian government had settled with the trustees of the Fifth Earl's Estate a figure for compensation and reimbursement for all the expenses incurred by Lord Carnarvon during the years before the discovery.[372]

Porchey and Catherine spent much of their time on the racecourses of Britain and France. Both of them had a betting and gambling fetish which often got the better of them. Everything was hunky-dory if they were winning but losses meant misery.

## Ascot and Newbury Races
## A £400 Bet That Backfired

A dazed Catherine went to Ascot with Porchey and smiled painfully at everyone. Porchey was glum because both his horses *Kyles of Bute* and *Madagascar* had failed to show in the winning three. At Newbury, Porchey was back in the saddle himself for a bit of fun, although a serious bet involving £400 was attached to it. After taking a ragging at a Derby dinner over his horse *Patmos* losing a race at Salisbury, where another horse *Brother–in–Law* (owned by Mr J A Dewer) won by a length and half, Porchey proposed racing *Patmos* against *Brother–in–Law* at Newbury over a mile. The race was duly organised with Porchey's old pal Alec Cottrill, a successful amateur rider, as the opposition. In the two-horse sideshow that ensued Porchey was solidly beaten.[373]

Some said that the old King Tut curse caused the death of Alec Cottrill. Son of a horse trainer (H L Cottrill), Alec died after a race at Lewes a few weeks later. In fact Alex's saddle slipped whilst he was riding in the Hamsey Welter Handicap on 4 August 1933 and he died six days later from his injuries. He was just twenty three.

The £400 bet is a good example of Porchey's pig-headedness in trying to make a point; a jocular wager often masked a dark determination not to be bested by another human being.

Cottrill's death did not discourage Porchey from riding. This was no time for marks of respect, there was a race to be run and so it was at Lewes on 25 August 1933 that he won the Southdown Welter Handicap on *Claudine,* which he described as "an enjoyable ride."

Catherine joined Porchey for the 1933 St Leger at Doncaster which was won by *Hyperion,* the same horse that had won the Derby. Much of the rest of the year for Catherine was spent waiting at Highclere for Porchey to come back home. She enjoyed several weddings in the year, and her dazzling eye for fashion led to many favourable comments in the society pages of the London press.

In the summer of 1933 virtually the whole of London Society moved to Taplow Parish Church to see the Hon. Phyllis 'Wissie' Astor marry Lord Willoughby d'Eresby[374] with Almina and Catherine amongst the congregation of celebrities of the time.[375] Almina (who had the lives of Lords Lansdowne and Dudley in her hands at Alfred House during the course of the year) saw much less of her daughter Evelyn for some months as she was busy helping Sir Brogrove in his constituency labours in Walthamstow. Catherine was also a patient at Alfred House in December, 1933, with a mystery injury to her spine.[376]

Throughout the 1930s Catherine's cousin Arthur R Wendell's horses appeared at British racecourses, with mixed results. The Wendell horses were trained by Dick Dawson, a friend of Porchey as well as one of the Highclere stud regulars.

## 1934

At Highclere there was a mass outpouring of grief and sympathy after the death of Lady Helen Cunliffe-Owen on 14 January 1934. Catherine was devastated and had once again to be medicated. Lady Helen was a fellow-American from New York, a mother-of-four, a neighbour at Sunningdale Park, Berkshire and a horse racing enthusiast (her husband, Sir Hugo Cunliffe-Owen, was chairman of the British-American Tobacco Company). Helen and Catherine had been particularly close confidantes. Almina phoned Catherine immediately as she feared the news would lead to Catherine taking to the gin bottle but heavy sedation had helped her get over the initial shock. Helen had been a patient of Almina's nursing home at Alfred House until 3 January so Almina knew all the details of Helen's frail condition and had warned her beforehand that Helen was seriously ill. Almina was often good in a crisis and her support was a great comfort to Catherine after losing such an important friend and ally.

When Catherine's health problems persisted into 1934 Porchey went off alone again to Egypt [377] and Catherine was eventually fit enough to try to convalesce back at Highclere. In May 1934 they arrived together in London.

Neither Catherine nor Porchey were great fans of socialising in Scotland; they tended to bypass invitations from the Holyrood and Highland set and those peers and peeresses with Scottish shooting estates. Catherine usually went on solitary pilgrimages to visit Philippa at Cumloden. On the other hand Philippa did keep in with some of her fellow Scottish including the Dalkeiths at Eildon Hall, the Roxburghs at Floors Castle and the Beatties at Grantully Castle where an occasional Royal visitor came during the traditional autumn shoots and dinners in Scotland.

One of Porchey's targets for seduction was Mollie Dalkeith [378] who, minus her somewhat diffident husband Walter, the Earl of Dalkeith (a dedicated Member of Parliament from 1923 until he inherited a Dukedom in 1935 and his seat in the Lords), frequently attended functions of the important social events in the horse racing calendar such as Ascot, the Derby and Goodwood to mark the end of the London Season. It was at Goodwood 1931 that Catherine went home alone, leaving Porchey to have his wicked way with Mollie.

More fun and games ensued during Melton hunting weekends, with Mollie and Porchey outfoxing the cuckolded Earl as he galloped through the Leicestershire countryside.

In London, under the cover of supporting music and the arts, ballet and opera, or a charity ball helped with a candlelit supper at the Savoy (since Catherine was at the *Ritz*, Porchey was at least thoughtful enough not to rub Catherine's face in his serial adultery), the affair continued. Almina, however, often witnessed her errant son with Mollie dining together at the Savoy Grill. [379]

## A Royal Visit to Highclere by Prince George

As previously recorded, Prince George (PG) was a regular guest at Highclere. Several visits were not announced in public: he simply flew into the grounds which had been made famous as a home for early flying by the Fifth Earl who was friendly with a number of the flying pioneers.

PG adored the drama of disappearing off the scene for a few days from Court and naval duties. There was no mention of his true whereabouts in the Court Circular. The same secrecy surrounded visits by the present Queen when she visited the Seventh Earl and Countess in the 1960s-1990s by helicopter (not her favourite mode of travelling).

On Saturday 16 June 1934, after witnessing an air display by the RAF Club at Hatfield aerodrome, Prince George flew to Highclere to spend the weekend with Porchey and Catherine. The Carnarvon's miserable marriage had reached a nadir for both parties.

Officially the Prince had been invited to open a garden fete in aid of the Blagrave branch of the Royal Berks Hospital. He even won a shilling raffle for a live fat lamb but he graciously put it up for auction to help the local hospital's funds and after some spirited bidding it was knocked down for four guineas.[380]

Prince George's mother, Queen Mary, also sent a collection of gifts to Catherine for her stall. These were sold by auction, realising fifteen guineas.[381]

The Prince tried everything to induce the Carnarvons to engage with each other over their matrimonial difficulties. It was all to no avail, the relationship was doomed. Both wanted their freedom. Catherine was drinking heavily; Porchey was in hot pursuit of several new lust interests, including Tanis Montagu. There only appeared to be one outcome and, even among the aristocracy, divorce would cause a certain amount of disapprobation.

For the sake of not drawing attention to their unhappy state, the Earl and Countess of Carnarvon continued to accept invitations to social events in London but did not turn up together or at all. They both attended the second day Ascot Race meeting on Wednesday 20 June but did not stand together for long. Catherine joined the Beauchamp party. To some surprise from onlookers Prince George accompanied Catherine for the third day's racing (which was Gold Cup day). This display of moral support boosted her well, in appearing in public with the man she really loved and adored and in front of the whole of rest of his Royal Family.[382]

## Almina Supports Catherine to Boost Her Morale

Despite Catherine being asked by her mother in law, Almina, to help to co- host her extravagant dinner–dances at the *Ritz*, Porchey was always on hand to indulge in an opportunistic fling with a female guest. This was sometimes unwisely done in front of the poor girl's gallery of predecessors who had, from time to time, no doubt exchanged notes on his technique (or lack of it). They were all, one suspects, relieved to talk of their time with Porchey in the past tense. Meanwhile Porchey's cheesy chat-up routines involved rides in his Rolls Royce and lines like "What's a pretty little filly doing in a place like this? Let's make ourselves scarce". There was little danger to all but the most naive of the season's crop of debutantes but Porchey still occasionally had his way when the less watchful mothers were not paying enough attention. Catherine turned a blind eye to the spectacle. At one of Almina's gatherings at the Ritz in 1934[383] her own Prince Charming, PG, attended and Catherine was as usual spellbound by his presence. They danced several times together to Ambrose's band and this helped blur whatever particular mischief Porchey was involved in at the time.

At first Catherine tried to control her drinking sprees but she regularly fell off the wagon. A particularly embarrassing event occurred at Moulescombe, Sussex, at a house party she organised for Goodwood races. The guests included regular racegoers Sir Delves and Lady Broughton and Sir John and Lady Buchanan-Jardine but sadly Catherine herself was unable make an appearance owing to being in a state of near exhaustion brought on by excessive drinking.

Porchey was far less interested in Catherine as a wife, although with his abuse and regular philandering with other women he had been the chief architect of her falling into a chronic state of alcohol dependency. The death of her brother Reggie and the passing of Lady Helen Cunliffe-Owen also took a place in affecting Catherine's troubled heart and mind. Some days she could not get out of bed, on other days she cried for hours at a time.

Porchey saw Lord Porchester off to Eton in September 1934[384] and returned to taunt Catherine, sounding off once in Almina's company who stopped him dead. When he had Catherine on her own his fury was hysterical; his put-downs centred on her humble origins as an American refugee. He said that he alone had rescued her from a fate worse than anything when he made her his Lady Porchester and then, later, his Countess. She had her looks for the moment but never any money. She owed him: all the money was *his* money. She was dependent on him for life itself. Yes, he'd felt sorry for her once but now he detested her. He wanted a divorce. Catherine was defenceless under this ex-cavalry officer's spiteful tirade. There was an undeniable truth: she was entirely dependent on Porchey for financial support and a roof over her head. It was this fact that terrified Catherine about the future.

Besides this crisis in their marriage, she had a terrible secret too that was about to explode and bring the relationship finally to its knees. It was to lead to Porchey physically assaulting Catherine a second time in their married life. The first time was with his fist, this time it was to be with a riding whip.

*Wedding of Prince George and Princess Marina*

In November 1934 at the time of the marriage of Prince George to Princess Marina of Greece and Denmark,[385] and with it a week-long spate of celebrations, gala dinners and grand receptions in London and by civic authorities up and down the land, an incident occurred at Highclere that hammered the final nail in the coffin of the Carnarvon's marriage.

Upon hearing from Catherine that a missing family tiara (given to her by the Fifth Earl) had in fact been sold to pay off her gambling debts Porchey (who had been out riding in the grounds) lost his temper completely and lashed out at Catherine. He struck one blow upon his wife and recoiled in shame and disgust but that blow symbolised a

Rubicon of abuse crossed and Catherine had had enough, whatever the consequences for her held.

A recent account by the Carnarvons' ghost writer[386] of the events surrounding the attendance by the Carnarvons at the Buckingham Palace reception for PG (the newly created Duke of Kent) and his bride-to-be, showing Porchey refusing to dance with Catherine at the reception, takes on a clearer meaning after the news broke about the tiara and his vile assault on his wife.

As 1934 ended Catherine and Porchey led separate lives. Appearances together were strained. At a reception given by the Egyptian Charge d'Affaires on 15 December 1934 the Carnarvons were far from easy being in each other's company,    Rumours followed that they were planning to have the marriage dissolved.  Porchey continued to be seen on the London scene, alone and predatory, and took parties of guests to various balls and functions.

## Porchey and  Maureen Dufferin

*Maureen Dufferin nee Guinness*

Having renewed their acquaintance at a house party at Bowden House, near Newbury, and being reunited again  at Christmas of 1934, Porchey took a particular  shine to Maureen, Marchioness of  Dufferin,[387] she was his guest at a film premiere. Sheila Milbanke reported their togetherness to Poppy Thursby who promptly told Catherine.    In between turning up at race meetings  Maureen Dufferin travelled back to her husband's estate at *Clandeboye,* County Down, Ireland or  stayed over in London at their town house in Hans Crescent. [388]

The attraction was obvious to those who saw through Porchey. Maureen was an enormously rich woman.  Soon afterwards  the Earl became a regular feature  at  the annual garden parties she gave  at her home in Lamberhurst, Kent.

## Almina's National Wealth Service

As the year 1934 ended Almina was still clocking up a record number of surgical services to the gentry and the wealthy, with several actresses of stage and film happily leaving their  "appendix safely in [Almina's] motherly hands"[389] – and sometimes more than once!

## Cecil Beaton : A patient at Alfred House

Cecil Beaton[390] (the society photographer, artist and stage designer, whose photographs of Tilly Losch were Porchey's particular favourite) underwent an operation for appendicitis at Alfred House on 19 November 1934.   Almina recalled this patient with relish as this admission brought in so many sprays of flowers, plants and decorated fruit bowls from well-wishers that Beaton's bedroom resembled "one of the exhibition stalls at the Chelsea Flower Show."

Years later Beaton curiously acknowledged Almina's first husband's status as a pioneering photographer[391] :

"Lord Carnarvon was a man of many interests, a famous Egyptologist, and a picture-restorer.   When he was taught photography by his friends, Bertram Park and Lewis J Steele, he built himself a large studio where he developed and enlarged his picturesque studies of nude female models posing among the water-lilies of the lake at Highclere Castle, his country estate." [392]

# Beaton on Tilly Losch

*Cecil Beaton : Society clicker*

Cecil Beaton photographed Tilly Losch over many years describing her "blunt features [ that]  evince certain delicacies  [ adding ] she looks like a lot of other people would like to look".[393]

In November 1927, Beaton held his first exhibition at the Cooling Galleries in London's  Bond Street, Among the many glamorous sitters[394] was Tilly Losch in a tree-trunk.  Beaton's great rival was Emile Hoppe [395] and he produced one of the most stunning of all close up images of Tilly that this time, one that has been described as a "mesmeric stare" . [396]

As we shall see,  Beaton became an intimate friend of Tilly Losch.

# Chapter 11

# 1935

## Catherine's Dry Run

Whilst Porchey increased his sun tan wintering in Egypt, Catherine took refuge in the *Ritz* hotel on 2 February, 1935. She saw Gertrude Griffiths at a reception for the White Rose ball at Grosvenor House, London, on the 7 March in aid of a local hospital.[397] This was a dry run, she was was now preparing to leave Porchey!

## Catherine and Flash Harry

In March 1935 Catherine went to see her friend and lover, the musician Sir Malcolm Sargent. 'Flash Harry' (as Sargent was nicknamed) was conducting a concert at Claridges Hotel of a programme of Gluck, Handel and Debussy, specially put together as a dinner and dance to raise money for the Greater London Fund for the Blind. Evelyn Beauchamp attended with her sister in law.[398] The other Sargent event attended by Catherine that same year (when all the fuss about the divorce was settled) was a "Fashion Plate Ball" at Grosvenor House on 2 December 1935.

Catherine's absence from Porchey's side at the 1935 Derby House Ball and Newmarket race meeting (which she had *never* previously missed) signalled their final public separation. The Earl was not short of old flames to soothe his unofficial bachelor status again, with Mollie Dalkeith in attendance as well as the new Duke and Duchess of Marlborough. 'Bert' had succeeded his father, 'Sunny', in the previous summer.

Porchey, at forty and ever the optimist, was getting ready expectantly for Queen Charlottes' Ball which was due a few days later, and with no fewer than 178 debutantes (as maids of honour) hauling the traditional birthday cake.[399] He would be on the lookout for a few 'presents' to unwrap himself.

# The Divorce

Catherine had broken her marriage vows and she felt ashamed, despite the fact that in the infidelity stakes Porchey was streets ahead. Little by little, and despite Porchey's undermining of her confidence, she began to make plans for her own independence although she had little idea of how she would survive financially. Anything was better than the hellish marriage she found herself in. She no longer wished to be the Countess of Carnarvon.

Thus she eventually she made a decision and, acting on guidance from her brother Jac (who had never been that keen on Porchey), in May 1935 Catherine left her husband, albeit still putting the outcome in a muddle. The Highclere butler was instructed to tell his Lordship .... "Her Ladyship, Sir, has left you". Porchey's reply (probably thankfully for those of a delicate constitution) is not recorded.

The Carnarvon children were away at school. Catherine was feeling faint at heart and not confident but she safely installed herself at the *Ritz* hotel in London and rang Almina. The divorce was to be a long-distance haul of almost a year with the first proceedings being halted as Catherine suffered another mental relapse, with immediate seclusion to a Surrey retreat followed by Almina admitting her into Alfred House. The delays and second thoughts over naming a woman, Lucy Nugent, in a contrived affair with Porchey as co-respondent, which backfired (albeit this was left on file), requiring a second writ to be issued and, (on Almina and Jac's insistence), the hire of a private detective to get concrete evidence against Porchey which Catherine might use to her advantage in the financial settlement.

By 21 June, 1935, Catherine was still a patient at Alfred House "although her health was reported 'greatly improved' after [her] recent nervous breakdown." [400]

Catherine's mother Marian was approached by the curious press. She told a reporter that she could "neither confirm nor deny reports that [Catherine] had instituted divorce proceedings against Lord Carnarvon." [401]

Whilst Catherine was ill, Porchey made no effort to visit her at Alfred House; in any case Almina would not have allowed his presence. As Catherine lay sedated, Porchey continued to set standards he seldom failed to live down to in terms of gambling and womanizing.

Catherine eventually recovered her wits. Even facing the prospect of financial loss, she finally decided to turn her back on continuing the sham of being the Countess of Carnarvon, married to a wicked man. Staring at the private detective's report was sickening. There was the evidence that Porchey had been almost certainly paying for the accommodation occupied by several of his lady friends. One insider of the gentry remarked "Porchey's dalliances were in his bloodstream; he was a serial offender, a modern-day Lothario," [402]

Beyond this evidence Catherine was not short of reasons for ending her marriage to him on cruelty grounds; the episode with the tiara remained a painful, humiliating memory.

The arguments between them over money, the gambling and the upbringing of the children often exposed Porchey's aggressive side, his quick temper and irritability and his fits of brutal, terrifying barrack room language. These fault lines were enough grounds to sustain a divorce for serial adultery or cruelty.

But to save Porchey some public humiliation (perhaps for the sake of the children, and in return for which Catherine was given custody of them) her case before Mr Justice Langton in the London Divorce Court on Wednesday 22 April 1936 was solely made on the grounds of Porchey's catalogue of misconduct with one other woman.

Catherine had her demons as well; she was plagued by bouts of incurable depression, a ferocious gambling addiction and a heavy dependency on drink. She too had committed adultery, albeit in a minor key compared to Porchey's debauchery.

The Sixth Earl entered no defence or protest. He was not bothered. He was prepared to discard his marriage to Catherine as though it was a cheap betting slip on a race horse where the filly had fallen before finishing the course. He wrote to her saying that there was no hope of their living together again and admitted that he had been unfaithful to her. A token, professional co-respondent was named called Jean Cooper.

## Gertrude Raises Catherine's Morale

After the sleepless nights caused by Catherine's divorce proceedings against Porchey, Gertrude restored the morale of both Marian and Catherine by staging an extravagant entertainment and dinner at 34 Bryanston Square on 6 July 1936. In the same week Almina whisked Catherine off to a reception being given by Mme Edwards, wife of the Chilean Ambassador in London. The Chilean community long appreciated Almina's provision at Alfred House for several of their people when illness struck.[403] Almina was also on hand to invite Catherine out to the many functions that she put on after a day's labours in her Alfred House Nursing Home.

## Catherine under Almina's care at Home and Abroad

Catherine was treated all her adult life for a nervous condition. In part this illness was congenital; several members of the Wendell family suffered a generic condition that caused them to have bouts of depression and anxiety. Catherine's father Jacob Jnr. and two of her uncles, Barrett and Gordon, suffered nervous breakdowns. In the case of Jacob and Gordon, the effects could be said to have been fatal.

In the 1950s Tony Leadbetter well remembers Almina receiving letters from Catherine when (as Mrs Don Momand) she was hiding out or drying out in a Swiss sanatorium alongside several European Royals and celebrities, all inmates being linked by a dependency or regal insanity.[404] "The letters looked like they had just come from one of the grand hotels on Lake Constance." [405]

What now would be recognised as Catherine's bipolarism was at its height in the years of the late 1920s early – mid 1930s before her divorce from Porchey was finalised. There was no way out of her mental misery at times and only a long stay in Almina's nursing home at Alfred House in Portland Place (or later, going off to a Catholic retreat) or regular sedation helped to conceal and protect Catherine from the world at large and offer her a place of safety.

Catherine's sister Philippa, Countess of Galloway, was favoured more by her relatives Percy and Gertrude Griffiths; this is clear from the terms of the couple's last Wills.

*Sandridgebury, Sandridge, Near St Albans  2013*

As children the Wendell sisters (with their two brothers) had grown up at the Griffiths' fine mansion of *Sandridgebury* near St Albans, a house of treasures which included a clock once owned by William Hogarth[406] and a portrait of a lady by Sir Peter Lely.[407]  The children were terrified of touching anything until they were of an age to appreciate the history of one or other of their uncle's collection.

Philippa was regularly invited by Gertrude (whom she always referred to as "her aunt", out of respect for the age gap between them) to tea, cocktail parties and dinner at the Griffiths' London home at Bryanston Square, with its fine drawing room where a magnificent picture by Rubens decorated one of the walls and there were priceless artefacts from Percy's addiction for endless collecting, he having the wealth to indulge himself.[408] A Charles II silver mounted brass trumpet was one oddity whilst a fine assortment of mirrors, of which a pair of George I giltwood and gilt gesso pier mirrors, was another particular showpiece.[409] Collecting mirrors was a passion of the unapologetically vain Percy, with his greatest pride being a pair of eighteenth century Chinese mirror pictures of the Ch'ien Lung period, in mahogany frames.[410] One of the ladies depicted in one of the pictures was Hsiang Fei whose husband, a Mohamedan Prince, was killed fighting against the Emperor. Struck by her beauty, the Emperor fell in love with her but she refused all his advances and was finally poisoned, either by her own hand or by the Emperor's mother. It was a story Percy loved to tell over and over again.

Here in the heart of London's Mayfair was to be found gathered together all the gossipy women of the era engineering the latest scandal, including Ladies Cassel, Paget, Max-Muller, Jessel and Baring. The inevitable subject of Catherine's health was carefully broached. It was always reported with a much more positive reflection on her psychological state than was borne out by the truth. Almina told her godson that Catherine had at times to be sedated when she nurtured thoughts of self-harm, including when suicide entered her head. There were several suicide threats by Catherine in the 1940s, managed by Almina and her staff.

After the divorce from Porchey was over, it was Philippa who often accompanied Catherine out once again in London Society for her to find inner confidence.

In 1936 the *Merry Wives of Westminster's party* (then in its third year) was a big fixture on the social calendar for November, where several royal guests were a colourful feature and virtually all the premier league Duchesses including Westminster, Sutherland and Buccleuch held court.

Choosing precisely the most suitable costume to wear proved just the right tonic that Catherine needed to kick-start her life again. Almina had a word with her daughter Lady Evelyn Beauchamp (who attended with her husband Brograve who was fast becoming one of the political personalities of the moment) to keep a vigilant eye on her ex-sister in law.

Catherine was relieved to see old and close friends and was immediately summoned to take part in a fund-raising event for the Anglo-Jugoslav Hospital for crippled children in Belgrade, at which she renewed her tender friendship with Prince George, now Duke of Kent. The ancient hostesses of Cunard and Fairfax glanced over and tut-tutted at the two old lovers flirting once again.

## 1936
## Famous Beauties Ball

Porchey was treasurer of the *Famous Beauties Ball* held at the Dorchester Hotel each year. The event had flourish since the opening of the Hotel in 1931. Naturally Porchey was in his element. Catherine avoided the event. Those taking part dressed up in the costume and head dress as a famous lady from the past. Actress, Gladys Cooper opened the 1931 pageant as Helen of Troy. She exclaimed humorously " Don't bother to announce me, for whatever I'm supposed to be in these shows, I always look like Britannia."[411]

## Porchey is jilted by Tanis Guinness

Porchey finally got his come-uppance when, after a lengthy chase across the Atlantic to secure a new bride, the red-haired Tanis Guinness failed to turn up for their wedding scheduled for 4 November 1936 at the British consulate in Baltimore. Some reports have it that she called things off a few hours before the ceremony. Either way, 'he'd been done up like a kipper'.

Porchey, however, would not let the matter rest. Back in New York he pleaded with Tanis to reconsider things (she was holding out at the

Hotel St Regis) and Porchey, pursued by the press pack, reported somewhat lamely "My wedding is not called off. It is merely postponed." [412]

## Who Jilted Who?

**Mrs. Montagu and the Earl of Carnarvon**

Scheduled marriage in Baltimore of Mrs. Tanis Guinness Montagu, English society beauty, and the Earl of Carnarvon didn't take place and eastern social circles wonder why. The question seems to be one of who jilted who or why? Both secluded themselves in New York and refused to talk.

Porchey returned to his suite at the *Ritz-Carlton*, only a few blocks away from Tanis's hotel. But Tanis's door was firmly closed shut.

The usually jovial Porchey "looked glum as he sailed alone for England without a bride." [413] Tanis was still in the mood to marry someone and within a short time she rushed to the altar with the songster Howard Dietz, but they later divorced in 1951.

Tanis was defiant: "I don't care what people think – here or in England – but we both know it is for the best. We certainly intended to be married, but we changed our minds."

Placing the responsibility on Tanis, Porchey attributed the collapse directly on her shoulders:

"Yes, my good fellow, she did it" declared Porchey. "It was her choice."
[414]

Dismissing that the curse of Tutankhamun was to blame Porchey sneered "King Tut had nothing to do with it. It's strictly between us two".[415]

On 11 November, saying that "the wedding was definitely off", Tanis left New York to sail to France to see her father, the wealthy Benjamin Guinness.

## Catherine Celebrates in London

Whilst Porchey headed home across the stormy seas of the north Atlantic in winter, Catherine was stepping out in style with her closest relatives[416] in London to receive dinner guests at 41 Upper Grosvenor Street at a concert (attended by Prince George, Duke of Kent, as well as a variety of European Royals) in aid of the English Hospital for Crippled Children, near Belgrade, Yugoslavia.

Standing steadfastly by the side of Catherine in her first major outside event since the divorce from Porchey were Prince Ataulfo of Spain and the Marquess and Marchioness of Carisbrooke, but her staunchest support came from her sister Philippa with the Earl of Galloway, her brother Jac Wendell and wife Eileen and Gertrude Griffiths as well as old friend Margaret Coates (Viscountess Knollys). Illness prevented Almina from attending.[417]

## 1937

## Death of Percival D Griffiths

In February 1937 Gertrude Griffiths went abroad as usual, to Italy, but everything was about to change for her in the blink of an eye when Percy was killed in a hunting accident the following December. He met with his fate at Stony Stratford while riding with the Whadden Chase

Hunt.[418] Percy must have died instantly; he was approaching "a flooded brook [where] a horse fell into the water ....his mount jumped sideways and slipped on landing ....[Percy] was thrown on his head and broke his neck."[419]

*Percy D Griffiths grave at Sandridge[420] and the local Hunt*

In September Gertrude had left England for America and remained there until November. She had no way of knowing that she would return to widowhood. Each year the Griffiths' lived at *Sandridgebury* until November, then went to their home at Bryanston Square for the winter but always returned to Sandridge for Christmas. Percy died on 11 December and is buried in Sandridge Churchyard, in a modest grave which also bears the name of Gertrude's mother, Sarah Bailey Tredick.[421]

But Gertrude was not going to falsely play the grieving widow and didn't. She hosted receptions, entertained foreign visitors and eventually she remarried.

Percy's Will (valued at £105,337 gross but with a net personality of just over half of this amount, at £59,754) made adequate provision for

Gertrude after bequests (which included the sum of £15,000 to his mistress, Dorothy). The residue of the estate was earmarked for Gertrude for life, thereafter two thirds were allocated upon trust for Philippa, Countess of Galloway, and one third to Jac Wendell.

*Sandridgebury* and Percy's extensive collection of antiques,[422] furniture and silver were subsequently put up for sale. A local history of Sandridge records "The house was cleared in 1938...the contents were sold in 1939, an important part being purchased by the Herbert Court Gallery in Coventry." [423] There are also items of Percy's in the Metropolitan Museum of New York City. [424]

## Porchey Sighs

Back in Britain and with no regular girlfriend, Porchey was down in the dumps. He was a marked man after the Tanis Guinness affair. The whole of womankind, it seemed, had hearts of stone where Porchey's needs were concerned; all the pretty girls (and even the less pretty ones) seemed set to avoid his approaches, and dim his excesses. But Porchey never ceased to appear jovial, once remarking with no hint of self-doubt, "I love giving pleasure". [425]

At the *Ritz* the talk was dominated by dreams and schemes for exotic travel abroad. The gay Viscount Tredegar was planning to take a party of his friends for a four month tour of Java and Bali and South Sea Islands, going as far as Honolulu. Porchey always gave Tredegar a wide berth; he couldn't stand homosexuals and turned red with anger and embarrassment when Noel Coward naughtily addressed him (in his exaggerated accent) as 'Porchey Dolling' He declined invitations from Somerset Maugham to visit Villa Mauresque near Cannes, the writer's 'boys only' paradise on the Saint Jean-Cap Ferrat. Porchey did however admire Maugham's wife, Syrie, who was often on the London scene.

Porchey's cousins, the Pembrokes, were also going overseas, taking their son, the Hon. David Herbert, to the Dutch East Indies. A land once deemed ideal for shooting big game, it was a place explored by the Fifth Earl of Carnarvon, Almina and Prince Victor Duleep in the years before the Great War.

Porchey also craved some big game shooting; his plan was first to go to Egypt and then off on a safari to Kenya. The trip to East Africa brought the chance to see old friends out in the British Colony in 'Happy Valley', where a good number of the gentry has moved after the financial collapse of the world stock markets in the Great Crash of 1929.

## Affairs at home and Abroad

On the rebound from Tanis Guinness, Porchey had a brief but torrid affair with an American girl named Patty Hoyt, and spent time with her ( a friend of Myrtle and 'Flash' Kellett[426]) in Kenya. Porchey knew the Kelletts as regular guests of Loelia, Duchess of Westminster at Eaton Hall and in other country retreats. 'Flash' ( a name applied as he was a man always immaculately dressed ) was a top foxhunting and horse racing man!

Porchey was always on hand when a lonely, unappreciated or estranged wife needed comfort and equally ready to perform his to the manor born duty where he might offer sympathy and support to a newly rendered widow of any old pal.

When Myrtle Kellett's husband 'Flash' was killed in action in 1943, Porchey was one of her first visiting mourners.

In earlier years Porchey too had charmed, dined and bedded several ' dear ladies' spouting declarations of eternal admiration and odes to their beauty. Among those comforted was Phyllis Filmer, a "petite and large breasted [ gal with] short blonde [ page boy like] hair" [427] unhappily married to a Shell Oil Executive and resident at the English colony in Kenya, where adultery and even murder broke the boundaries. Phyllis, like Porchey was staying at the *Ritz* in London for the Coronation of King George VI when they enjoyed each other's company and caresses. [428] In the same year Porchey fell on his ceremonial sword when his " very old friend" [429]Margot Mills, Lady Chesham eventually divorced her ever- cheating husband, John. [430] In the following year, 1938, Porchey was at the tender call of Eddy Stanley's widow Portia, when she was widowed at the age of forty-five.[431] Porchey refers to her in his memoirs as " a most entertaining lady and she and I were great friends. I well understood her foibles."[432]

171

On his trips to the USA, Porchey relished his stays in Florida with entrepreneur Charlie Munn,  dubbed, ' Mr Palm Beach', the owner of *Amado,* a luxurious mansion where  the area's most select social groups met  to relax,  around Charlie and his second wife Dorothy  Spreckles, ( affectionately known as 'Sugar', the source of her family wealth ), one of the most glamorous couples of their time, who ran greyhounds.[433] Here    the English Lord Porchey  indulged  himself  in  perfect surroundings  at  the  glorious  unceasing  hospitality  of  the *House of Munn*!

## Fire at Highclere

A shock hit Porchey on his previous return home from Africa; he was due back from Nairobi in late March 1937.  A fire at Highclere had engulfed three rooms, two bedrooms and a bathroom at his family home in Hampshire.[434]

On his travels Porchey had missed England, but the company in East Africa had been varied and he enjoyed the sport and the heat and the charms of easy women, unavailable it seemed for him now at home. Everyone was talking about his cousin Laura Herbert marrying the satirist and member of the Bright Young Things brigade, Evelyn Waugh, who had been married previously to another of Porchey's cousins, Evelyn Gardner. [435]

Almina, having personally examined the fire damage at Highclere, set about persuading Porchey to get himself back into the swing of being seen in London Society circles again.  A series of Coronation Balls had already begun at the Dorchester and plans were afoot by a number of Duchesses and Lady Peers on an array of committees to raise sums for good causes, in order to welcome in the new King George VI and Queen Elizabeth. Porchey and Almina each separately took parties to a variety of these dazzling events.

Porchey also busied himself on the horseracing circuit again. He had purchased several new horses from abroad and was keen to see them pushed through their training and have them tried out on racecourses.

Almina was finding it difficult to balance her nursing work in London at Alfred House and travelling periodically to her home of Eastmore on the Isle of Wight to ensure that her husband, Colonel Dennistoun, was in good spirits. He was well looked after by Alice Butler, the housekeeper, but Almina liked to keep a sharp eye on things.

There was a long-standing invitation from Almina to Princess Beatrice to visit her at Eastmore. Beatrice maintained her own summer home on the Island, at Carisbrooke Castle. In August 1937 the Princess did Almina the honour of attending a party held by her and the Colonel at Eastmore; other guests included Lord and Lady Mottistone and Lady Seely, as well as many of the people from London staying on the Island for the yachting.[436]    The late 4th Lord Mottistone, half-brother of Almina's aforementioned Mottistone guests, well remembered that there was good rapport between Almina and the Islanders[437] and many tradespeople were sad to see her sell up after the death of the Colonel in 1938. Several neighbours (including her friend, Princess Beatrice) tried to persuade her (at aged sixty- two in 1938) to retire permanently to Eastmore, near Yarmouth, where she had a spacious house, extensive gardens,  peace and quiet and a lovely backdrop of the edge of the Solent.

## A-Hunting We Will Go

Porchey was among the shooting party arranged by the Earl of Derby in Cheshire, staying with Lady Stanley at Craig Hall. Duff Cooper, the Duke of Rutland and the Hon Fred Cripps (one man who was eternally grateful for his life being saved in Almina's nursing care[438]) were among those who enjoyed excellent shot bags. Porchey accepted an invitation to meet with some of the party again at Deauville.

## Deauville Offers Female Company, Racing and Polo

Despite all this bravado on the outside, there was something missing in Porchey's life; in short, he craved a regular lady friend. A trip to Deauville in September 1937 proved the perfect pick-me- up, (he seemed to have been forgiven for being jilted, one of the lesser crimes on his crime sheet, one has to say). There was a bevy of Porchey's old-gal crowd at hand to brighten up the post-Tanis dreariness, amongst whom Lady Stanley and the Hon. Mrs Frederick Cripps were adept at playing cards and both were good company, with or preferably without their husbands.

*Mrs Frederick Cripps* [439]    *Lady Milbanke (nee Chisholm)*

Porchey flew over to France with ace flying brothers Sir John and Toby Milbanke who were both to die young; John, aged just 45, in 1947 from wounds sustained whilst flying with the RAF in the Second World War and Toby, aged 42, in 1949 by his own hand.[440] John, who was known as "The Boxing Baronet", boxed in the ring with Porchey, beating him once on points and once after a disqualification. On his marriage to the Australian-born Margaret Chisholm (formerly Lady Loughborough[441] and a great friend of Poppy Baring[442]) John and his bride-to-be famously sent out wedding invitation cards from "Shelia and Buffles." John's brother Toby held on to his blissful state of bachelorhood; always living in the fast lane, he occasionally strayed into smuggling booze (especially champagne), cigars and cigarettes across the English Channel.

While the horseracing was its usual pull for Porchey he also played polo with Lord Louis Mountbatten's team and caught up with Lady Edwina, who was another of Porchey's old flames from the halcyon days with the then Prince of Wales in the 1920s at London's Embassy Club. More good news on the equine front arrived when Porchey received an invitation from that doyen of the turf, the Aga Khan, to visit him at his villa facing the sea, called *Les Abeilles* (The Bees).[443]

Meanwhile in late November Almina decided to have an evening out with Evelyn and Catherine; they attended the first night of *The Silent Knight* at St James Theatre.

Catherine was romantically involved with stockbroker Geoffrey Seymour Grenfell[444] who was well connected. Geoffrey's first wife, Sybil, divorced him after eleven years of marriage and the birth of a daughter Elizabeth in 1931, citing that on "17th 18th 26th and 27th September 1935 he committed adultery with some unknown woman at the Rembrandt Hotel, Thurloe Place, South Kensington".[445]

As 1937 came to an end Porchey was short of cash. Having set Catherine up in her own accommodation (largely for the sake of providing a comfortable home for the two children) a series of further bills were cutting deep into his pocket. Porchey viewed the likelihood of Catherine's forthcoming marriage to Geoffrey Grenfell as providing some relief from these continuing costs but meanwhile, to raise funds, he was forced to sell a number of drawings, paintings and engravings at Sotheby & Co on 3rd, 22nd and 23rd November 1937.

# 1938
## The Gathering Storms

Almina was among those who claimed a place at Court in 1937 and 1938; with a new king on the throne (George VI) it seemed the only current Countess of Carnarvon should be close by the king, particularly as world events were beginning to look decidedly tricky.

# Porchey Sulks Through 1938

Still sulking over the Tanis Guinness affair, Porchey spent the next couple of years living it up on the Riviera. He saw Sir Brogrove and Lady Evelyn Beauchamp regularly at Monte Carlo[446] along with many other old male cronies, and spent his time picking up loose woman and entertaining a few Society women passing through the South of France's playgrounds. He still had a voracious sexual appetite.

Despite his gallivanting, the Tanis affair had left its mark. He recalled wistfully the occasions he had been a guest of Tanis's father Benjamin Guinness whose villa, *Notre Dame de Vie*, was at Mougins, near Cannes. Even after being so publicly knocked back by Tanis he still had the brass neck to seek an invitation there despite all that happened with Benjamin's daughter.

Porchey became listless and depressed on the continent, with other appetites sated for the moment. He longed to be back in England standing on the gallops watching his fillies run; he trooped back to Highclere for the flat season and to catch up on family matters. He rarely missed a classic horse race in Britain or France and accepted invitations to house parties, especially at the season's end at Goodwood where he spurned the Duke of Richmond in favour of a request for his company at Lavington Park by Captain Euan Wallace, MP, along with old friend Lionel Montagu.[447]

Porchey's sister Evelyn was as much of a racegoer and gambler as he was; they both lost large sums (although won some, too) on horses and in the casinos in Monte Carlo and in Le Touquet.

Almina also took her own trips to France (accompanied by her maid, later housekeeper, Alice Butler), especially to Paris and onto the Riviera where one essential holiday was snatched after Colonel Dennistoun died in August 1938. In late 1938 Almina began to realise that her nursing home commitments were becoming burdensome and a huge drain on her finances, although selling her property on the Isle of Wight (at Eastmore, Yarmouth, where the Colonel had lived with Alice Butler looking after him from 1936 until a few weeks before his death) would help; however, she was still determined to carry on, despite the pressure on her funds. She, like many others, was very aware that the threat of another war with Germany was very much on the horizon.

## Horse Sales and Romance at Saratoga Springs

During the autumn of 1938 Porchey made a trip to America to the horse sales at Saratoga Springs (somewhere he had previously visited in the early 1930s) and here he purchased five yearlings. This decision was highlighted by the racing world in Britain as being a smart move, especially when the horses began to win races.[448] Porchey became a well-known figure at Saratoga Autumn Sales, bidding alongside representatives of notable American horse-owning stables, including Marshall Field and Louis Mayer of motion picture fame. His presence at Saratoga brought in flurries of invitations from American hostesses.

In later years a would-be romance blossomed at Saratoga between Porchey and Georgiana de Ropp Meyer,[449] a long-time resident, horse fancier and garden designer who, for a time, truly doted on Porchey. One informant writes that they "were an excellent couple, but the [Carnarvon] family regarded [Georgiana] as an American gold digger, which she was not … and ….aborted the relationship." [450]

## Catherine Remarries and Porchey is smitten by Tilly Losch

Catherine was making plans for her wedding and looking forward to being settled into married life with the stockbroker, Geoffrey Grenfell. The engagement was announced in September and they married quietly on the 21st of that month with only a few family members in attendance. After the wedding the new Mr and Mrs Geoffrey Grenfell set up home at 9 Upper Grosvenor Street, Mayfair. Geoffrey's first wife was living with Geoffrey's daughter Elizabeth in a flat at 34 Ovington Square, Kensington. When financial matters were sorted and the first Mrs Grenfell gone, Catherine and Geoffrey moved into this flat.

Porchey was feeling frisky again. There was this woman, you see: no ordinary woman, a goddess (well, according to Porchey). Tilly Losch, the dancer and film star he had first met in America in 1931. Ever since he had again seen the Austrian nymph in Monte Carlo (newly released from a Swiss Sanatorium where she had been taking a cure for fatigue but it was really a serious attack of tuberculosis), he was besotted by her image. There was after all a vacant position as Countess of Carnarvon and Porchey had a shortlist of one for the post.

# 1939

## Porchey and Almina Charm Each Other

In 1939, with war looming again, Almina offered to sell her remaining stake in the half -million pound fund set up in 1895 by Baron Alfred de Rothschild. This was offered to her son Porchey and daughter Evelyn, who agreed to cough up the asking price of £62,000.

On the strength of her funds from selling off Eastmore, Isle of Wight, Almina acquired a leasehold interest in a large house and garden at Avenue Road, Regents Park.

She also had to relocate Alice Butler, the housekeeper on the Isle of Wight who had faithfully served the Colonel in his last years at Eastmore. Accordingly, Alice moved into Avenue Road.

True to Almina's style a large house-warming party was held at Avenue Road in July, where the guest of honour was Queen Victoria Eugenie of Spain and her daughter, the Infanta Maria Cristina.

Porchey hosted the event on behalf of his mother. This reconciliation between them was as sincere as could be achieved and since returning from America in 1936 (after the Tanis farce) they found themselves rubbing along quite nicely.

The Avenue Road event caught the attention of the press who commented "Debutante parties so often capture all the limelight that it is pleasant to be able to write about entertaining planned for the benefit of your married and older people." [451]

There was a dinner party, with dancing in a marquee on the lawn. Halfway through the evening there was a cabaret performance and the best item on the programme was that of a youthful conjuror and thought-reader whose performances were so convincing that the audience felt almost reluctant to risk their "minds" being read.

Meanwhile Porchey, whose mind was often an open book (think *Lady Chatterley's Lover* crossed with *The Racing Post),* informed Almina of his intention to marry Tilly Losch.

## Porchey learns of Tilly Losch's availability as a Wife

Tilly's availabity was news first heard when Porchey was in the USA during the early weeks of 1939, on a visit to Saratoga in search of yearlings to add to the Highclere stud. In New York he was the target for the news gatherers, whose memory of the Tanis Guinness affair had still not been totally erased. The truth was that Porchey was on the prowl for a new Countess, with plans ahead, come what may, for leisurely and carnal pursuits. At a house party in Florida he found comfort in the company of old girlfriend, Maureen, Marchioness of Dufferin and Ava a London socialite ( whose husband Basil, inherited the family titles after his father was killed in a notorious plane crash in 1930[452] ). Maureen was also a member of the Guinness Brewery family, a man eater, dubbed by Cecil Beaton "the biggest bitch in London". It was after moving to Nassau, to soak up the sun, that Porchey got wind that Tilly Losch ( whom Porchey had met in America a few years before ) was almost certainly looking to remarry, despite the humiliation over the divorce fiasco with Edward James. It was all a question of offering the right inducements, the hard bitten Tilly was still quite a catch, and could name her price.

# Chapter 12

## Tilly, the Dancing Countess of Carnarvon

*Tilly Losch*

Porchey Carnarvon's second wife, the Austrian starlet Tilly Losch, danced her way right to the very top of the world of show business and glamour. In the mid 1930s she was a woman of means, earning tens-of-thousands of pounds a year. As a young girl she held the high position of *prima ballerina* in prestigious Viennese opera and ballet companies. Later she was thought (equally in British and American culture) the apotheosis of all that was stylish and *a la mode* in the late 1920s and early 1930s.

Yet, Tilly was always escaping from the shadows of her past, one way or another.

In 1939, when the dark-haired dancer was first mooted as a lady friend for Porchey, there were those with very long memories who recalled her as one of the *'Cochran Girls'*. This set of actresses and dancers who worked for the legendary theatre producer and impresario C B

Cochran (Charles (Cockie) Blake Cochran[453]) were sometimes more primly referred to as the '*Cochran Young Ladies*'.

*Cochran and his Young Ladies*

Establishing her place at the pinnacle of Cochran's rankings, Tilly was painted by the Society portraiture Ambrose McEvoy[454] as the artist lay dying: a portrait which demands attention, full of nostalgic overtones for those who saw her incomparable Gothic numbers in the C B Cochran revues. She was also photographed by the celebrated Cecil Beaton, who became a close friend and was once a co-conspirator over a bogus book of autobiography[455] entitled *My Royal Past*. [456]

Tilly was literally the 'talk of the town' and as a result was invited to the swellest of cocktail parties mixing, with Royalty and the nobility both real time and private places off-stage.

Tilly's rise to prominence (first encouraged by the great German composer Richard Strauss[457]) came at the tail-end of the glamorous

**1920s, when London was dominated by the *Bright Young People* and the talking movies had just arrived.**

*Tilly's mentors  Richard Strauss ( Left ) and Max Reinhardt*

**Although Cochran made the Austrian dancer a star on the London stage she was first seen dancing in Europe by the influential director Max Reinhardt. [458] In 1928 Tilly returned to please Reinhardt by dancing at the Salzburg Festival, of which he was the godfather.  She often repeated this selfless act of devotion; after all, it was Reinhardt, a fellow Austrian, who had acted as her Svengali, transforming her from the national scene onto the international arena.**

## Tilly Shines for the Austrian Minister in London

**Tilly became a full-blown Austrian export of the era. Almost as soon as she arrived  back in London she was approached by the Austrian Legation  where from 1920 to 1938  Baron Georg von und zu Franckenstein[459]  was the Austrian Minister. The Minister was an influential snob, renowned for his sumptuous hospitality, hosting musical concerts and masked balls, with many of Britain's Royals,**

Ambassadors, aristocrats and leading politicians in attendance. In his memoirs[460] the Baron acknowledged Tilly's part in the success of these gatherings. [461] The Legation had magnificent rooms in London and arranged a temporary stage for Tilly and special lighting effects for her numbers.

One attendee records " Sir George Franckenstein gave an evening's exquisite music for Schuschnigg [ the Austrian Chancellor, later put under house arrest by the Nazis ] and Tilly Losch did her dance of the hands." [462]

## Tilly's Dance of the Hands[463]

At the height of her career Tilly was filmed in ' Her Dance of the Hands'. A remarkable seven minute piece, recorded for posterity. One commentator remarks:

" Theatrical set designer Norman Bels Geddes and dancer Tilly Losch created a kinetically intimate camera study of repetitive body movements."[464]

In the years from 1928 until 1935 Tilly shone (under the auspices of being a one-time member of the Vienna State Opera) faithfully and patriotically (and sometimes carnally) serving her country's Minister in London for his grand, all-embracing receptions and private functions including events with the English ballet star Anton Dolin.[465] As well as appearances dancing with Tilly at the Austrian Legation  Dolin records an appearance together at  one Foyles Literary Luncheon,  in London. [466] He also arranged a very fine gala All Star Dance Gala at the Winter Garden Theatre  in New York, in 1940, in which Tilly appeared and performed her 'Dance of the Hands' "[467]

But it was  Max  Reinhardt  who  recognised  the  instinctive understanding that Tilly possessed  for  movement and  dance. Complaining to  Anton Dolin (born the less exotic sounding  Patrick Healey-Kay),  that it was " beyond his comprehension why the ballet [ Dolin was working on for Reinhardt] was not ready to  perform] Max exclaimed 'Why can't you improvise?....Tilly Losch used to be able to do it!' "  [468] Dolin's response from was a long plea about the need to practice and time everything.

Among the other great English ballet legends, Tilly danced also once at a gala with Frederick Ashton.[469]

## Charles Cochran and his Starlet

*'Cockie' Cochran*

Tilly owed a particular debt to Cockie Cochran who saw her whilst talent-spotting on the Continent. *Punch Magazine* described Tilly as "one of Mr Cochran's most intelligent discoveries." [470] Cockie was always prepared to go far afield in search of fresh talent and spotted Tilly dancing at Salzburg. He records in his memoirs:

"One comes across art in many unexpected places. You might expect to hear a new actor or singer in Salzburg, but you would certainly not go there to look for a dancer. Yet when I was on a visit there with my wife I found Tilly Losch. One of my most successful foreign importations. She is an incomparable artist with great creative instinct." [471]

But whilst Cochran made Tilly a star, he looked for reward ( as he did from several other of his 'Ladies') by them accepting dinner and pawing and sometimes sexual favours. Tilly was different from most of the others, for he thought he was in love with her. They were close and secret but Cockie's wife, Eveyn, missed nothing in her husband's stream of sleeping partners. At parties Cockie and Tilly convinced everyone it was only a business arrangement. Their party piece of dancing a polka[472] together left bystanders in no doubt he was enchanted by her form.

## A Brief Note on Tilly and Cockie Cochran

Tilly's champion, Charles Blake Cochran, (Cockie) married Evelyn Alice Dade in 1903. Before this Cockie knocked about America for several years ( he was once reduced to selling fountain pens at the Chicago World Fair, of 1893 ) and began his career as an impresario ( staging musical hall, boxing an circus shows) thanks to a £50 loan from his sister. For Cochran the spectre of bankruptcy (an occupational hazard for showmen of his ilk) duly arrived however help was at hand when legendary strongman Georg Hackenschmidt [473] ( a friend and one of Cochran's earliest big stars in Britain and USA ) helped return him to solvency by making a deal with creditors.[474] The Cochrans lived in Park Lane with a house in Aldford Street, and entertained in style. [475]

Over the course of his next fifty odd years as an impressario, with its crowded first nights in London and openings in New York Cochran made and lost fortunes and was knighted by George VI for his services to the theatre.

*Charles and Evelyn Cochran with Richard Tauber*

Cochran's wife Evelyn Dade was ten years younger than Cockie. She was a watchful wife, but soon adjusted to Cockie's inability to resist flirting ( and at times canoddling) with his latest female discovery. Evelyn carried on regardless.

One biographer of Cochran neatly sums it up :

" There were dinner parties for theatre folk...Evelyn was a perfect hostess... the early sexual excitement [ in the marriage] had faded...Cochran's appetite for pursuing women increased rather than diminished with the passage of time...with all the pretty girls around

Evelyn.... [she] knew very well that he was consistently unfaithful to her..."[476]

Evelyn looked after the new members of the company; she successfully nurtured, new talent as the harmonica virtuoso Larry Adler[477] testifies.[478] He was among Cochran's successful male stars beginning with Alder's teenage years, in New York and London. In 1930, sixteen- year- old Adler played in the 'novelty spot' for *Smile*, with Fred and Adele Astaire, he also turned up in the same cast as Tilly in several Broadway shows and charity functions.

But beyond the male stars made by Cochran or not there were scores of others who ( whilst earning the title of being one of the 'Cochran Young Ladies') never made it into a headline spot. Cochran almost certainly slept with those who did succeed and probably with many who didn't. Some even made it without taking a detour to his boudoire.[479] In such cases Evelyn certainly new about it as Cockie would sulk for days afterwards.

When a girl had been willing to be seduced Evelyn also knew it! Besides the familiarity of calling her husband 'Cockie', as opposed to Mr Cochran, the girl usually moved from third from the left in the chorus line to a more prominent position in the line-up. When no further promotion was seen, Cockie's attentions had diverted to another girl.

In Tilly's case there is no doubt she had an affair with Cochran, and Evelyn was well aware of its flight path from exhilirating lift off to inevitable touch down.

The morning after one such dalliance Cockie's shrewd, and witty wife ( to paraphrase Dorothy Parker ) simply brushed her teeth and sharpened her tongue. It was during the Manchester opening of one of the early shows Evelyn launched a spirited attack on Tilly at the breakfast table with the remark : " And how is *our* husband this morning, my dear?"

Cochran enjoyed playing roulette with dinner guests, he was a man who reveled in gambling and taking risks at work and at home. But Evelyn had a retort for every occasion. At the height of Cockie's affair with Tilly at a dinner party one evening in the Aldford Street flat "the green

baize cloth was brought out [ for to play roulette] and he remarked " It's awfully dirty." "Yes, Cockie darling" replied Evelyn " just like your little Austrian's friend's knickers". [480] The conversation stopped dead but then moved on quickly.
[481]

After Tilly Cochran moved on to a new girl, dubbed by Evelyn his " mistress of the month. " [482]

In 1948, Cockie was honoured with a knighthood from the King. Ironically it was by literally getting into hot water that Cochran met his grim and untimely end. He was badly scalded in his bath. He suffered from severe arthritis and was unable to reach the hot water tap to turn it off – so he died from the burns. At the inquest Cockie's doctor explained that this account was given to him by the dying man, who lingered "almost unrecognisable" [483] for some several days in Westminster hospital. He was seventy-eight. [484]

On his death the newspapers published tributes to Cockie's half century in the theatre.[485] Seven months later, on 14 September 1951 over fifty of the former ' Cochran's Young Ladies' stood in the foyer of the Adelphi Theatre, in London's Strand, where the actress Anna Neagle [ previous she was understudy to Jessie Matthews and knew Tilly from *Wake Up and Dream!* ) unveiled a bust of Cockie by Peter Lambda.[486] Cochran's long suffering wife, Evelyn died in 1960.[487]

# This Year of Grace! 1928

In 1928 Cockie Cochran made Tilly the star in his revue *This Year of Grace,*[488] authored by the already well-established playwright–songster-performer, Noel Coward.  Amongst the cast was also Leslie Hutchinson 'Hutch' the jazz pianist,  drug supplier and male lover of Cole Porter.[489]

This show was lift-off for Tilly. Moreover, Cochran and Coward realised their acquisition was full of interesting ideas and a chorographer of high merit.  They allowed her to supervise the ballet sequences in *This Year of Grace,* firstly during the production's pre-runthrough at Manchester and then at the premiere in London where Tilly shared a dressing room at the  London Pavilion with the English evergreen actress, dancer and singer, Jessie Matthews. The two girls did not get on well.  Jessie writes in her memoirs, "Tilly was exotic, extremely feminine and rather touchy."[490]

*Tilly Working Her Magic*

Despite Jessie's sensitivities, all of London fell for the ravishing Losch. Well, the men did, certainly. Tilly's salary from Cochran of a thousand pounds a week brought in that sum at the box office many times over. The chorus girls on contract in the same troupe were on a mere twelve-pounds a week.[491]

After her London sell-out performances a tour of America was obligatory, allowing Tilly to recall the memories of her first dance recitals there (with the Reinhardt Company) in 1927 (and in her original ballet dancing shoes) partnering the German interpretative dancer Harold Kreutzberg[492]. Tilly also appeared in the smoky Berlin salons later made famous by Christopher Isherwood in the film *Cabaret,* mixing in with the bohemian, drug-fuelled, café life in pre- Hitler Germany.

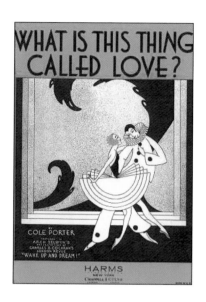

In 1929, under the guise of a new Cochran review, Tilly played at the *London Palladium* and subsequently at New York's Selwyn Theatre in Cole Porter's *Wake Up and Dream*.[493] The show-stoppers were the songs Let's *Do It, Let's Fall In love*   and   *What Is This Thing Called Love* (these titles both epitomise Tilly's life story).   Despite the New York stock market crash of 1929 and the underlying gloom, Manhattan brightened up by falling under Tilly's magic spell.

Her next musical glory was The *Bandwagon*, from Arthur Schwartz and Howard Diezt (who later married Porchey's old flame, Tanis Guinness).

*Fred Astaire and Tilly in The BandWagon*

Tilly appeared on Broadway for more than six months with siblings Fred and Adele Astaire[494] and the show was a smash hit. It was the last time the Astaires danced together in public as Adele then went off to marry the alcoholic Lord Charles Cavendish.[495] The big dramatic number in *The Bandwagon* was *Dancing in the Dark* [496] in which John Barker ( dressed in evening clothes ) sang whilst huge mirrors were placed all around the stage so that Tilly could dance with her own reflection. She knew with almost certainty who was 'the fairest of them all.' And with this show came the perfect duet for Tilly and the energetic Fred in *The Beggar's Waltz*.[497]

# Tilly and The Astaires

*Fred and Adele Astaire*

The Astaires and Tilly hit it off immediately. The perfectionist Fred was taken by the choreographic skills of the ballet dancer from Vienna . When Tilly and Fred danced together in *The Beggar's Waltz*, in *The Bandwagon*, they made a statement about modern dance which brought the comment that the show was " a new era in the artistry of the American revue" [498]. This set in motion the spark for many of Astaire's later definitive dances on film with over thirty musicals and dance partners including Cyd Charisse, Jane Powell, Leslie Caron , and of course the many celebrated films he made with Ginger Rogers. [499]

Tilly became a close Astaire family friend where the mutual affection never dipped. Fred's sister , Adele ( 'Delly') Astaire, became Tilly's best friend, ( and as we shall see ) she was ready to tell lies in court to save Tilly's case against the cunning tactics of Tilly's first husband, Edward James. [500] The jury remains out on whether Adele and Tilly were ever lovers. At least three titles cite Adele's affair with Mercedes de Acosta  an American playwright   " famous for her lesbian trysts with Greta  Garbo,  Marlene Dietrich and Isadora Duncan."[501]

*Adele and Tilly*

Tilly often saw Adele in company with Cecil Beaton.     Whilst Tilly preferred to be just friends with  Beaton,  Adele enjoyed  at least one night of  passion with the great Society clicker, who at times played the straight man.[502]

## Tilly in 1930s Manhattan

In 1930, the twenty-six-year-old Tilly describes herself as an *Artiste*. She appears to be living the quiet life in Manhattan, New York, with her forty-three-year-old maid, Anna Haase, with whom she could continue to converse in their first language of German. [503]

Tilly gave an early interview about dance in Paris in 1933 based on what she had seen in Europe  and America. " American girls are beautifully built and seem to be born supple, but they are outclassed by European girls when it comes to solo dancing." [504] However she praised American girls for their choral and ballet work adding " their system of rhythm and movement is perfect."

Tilly's professionalism came first and last when dance was involved. Dancing always seduced her more than any lover. Many of the surprising choreographic partnerships she forged ( including co-working with the debonair playboy Jack Buchanan ( in the New York version of the eighteen-week run of *Wake Up the Dream*!) and the risky Canadian dancer Maud Allen ( whose provocative version of *Salome* was an abiding influence on Tilly's own interpretation of the role[505] and arguably her entire stage craft. ) Tilly saw Allen at close quarters during the runs of *The Miracle* when the Canadian played the Abbess.

Tilly's work as a choreographer dwarfed her work as a performer but between appearing in the Cochran revues she also choreographed *This Year of Grace* (1928) for New York audiences as well as the London production of Coward's Bitter *Sweet* ( 1929) and *The Gang's All Here*, back in New York ( 1931).

Tilly had a good ear for the music too. She once challenged the conductor Pierre Monteux when she danced at a recital ( conducted by Monteux). During the rehearsals Tilly pointed out that a Ravel piece should be played faster. To convince the eminent conductor of the San Francisco Symphony Orchestra Tilly commented " Ravel played it for me himself and he approved". Monteux bowed to Tilly's request. [506]

# Chapter 13

## Tilly's Fragmented Background

Tilly Losch's background and early years are fragmented. Her year of birth is variously recorded as 1904 or 1907. On a sea voyage, going into the port of Southampton on 18 May 1930 (when she about to star in a Cochran revue), she gave her age as twenty-six, which is consistent with a 1904 birth. As she got older it was her prerogative to understate her age; for instance on 13 June 1950 on a trip from New York to Southampton she says she was only forty-two but this might just confirm the 1907 birth!

*Tilly in Vienna c1909-1915*

There is also some doubt as to *where* she was born despite Vienna, Austria, being the most likely place although her two husbands are at variance with this statement.

Porchey declares that Tilly's father "was a Polish Jew from Lodz and upon arrival in Vienna had taken the name of Losch."[507] Her first husband, Edward James, records that she was born in a place called Chemsall in Romania[508] and attributes her "very Slavic high cheek-bones, wonderful green eyes wide apart and a nose like a little cat's"[509] to the indigenous peoples of this region of Eastern Europe. Porchey adored Tilly's green eyes with yellow, amber pupils; these were one reason he was smitten.[510]

*The Losch Family*
*Tilly is the little girl in the back row beside her father*

Tilly's precise family origins are the subject of speculation encompassing the best and worst of the fact and fiction of a Hollywood or Fleet Street scribe. She was born Ottilie Ethel Leopoldine Losch, the daughter of Otto Emil[511] Losch and Eugenie (or Eugena) Dreucker (this name is sometimes recorded as Druker). Tilly had at least two brothers, one named Fritz, who was still alive in 1935 since there is a letter from him in Binghamton University Libraries, the home of Tilly's large personal archive.[512] Another brother, named Otto, is recalled by a surviving distant maternal cousin.[513] Porchey states in his memoirs, "Her mother was a Catholic and her brother a cavalry officer who had been killed in the First World War." [514] A stunning photograph of the

197

Losch family appears in one biography of Edward James, showing Tilly's parents and *six* children. [515]

Tilly's father is sometimes described as a banker.[516]This is probably a version of the truth; he was more likely a bank clerk or cashier. Some articles on Tilly suggest her father died when she was aged ten. A more flippant reference to Tilly's father is that "he happened to be a small banker with just enough money to give his pretty and vigorous daughter a fair education of the mind and a magnificent education of the legs..."[517]

Another sure thing is that Tilly's widowed mother Eugenie later went to America from Austria where she eventually became an American citizen. There may have been a religious conflict between Tilly's parents fuelled by their Jewish– Catholic upbringing.[518]

## Dance and Dazzle Them

Tilly was born to dance and dazzle and shock her generation, yet she could be enigmatically shy. New York was in thrall. She adored performing and was not short of male attention. As in London's theatre world every red blooded man on Broadway wanted to seek out Tilly and dreamed of gazing into her extraordinary cat-like eyes, unwrapping the enigma and making her theirs and theirs alone. She was captured and gave in to many powerful men. Such vipers were the bane of Tilly's life. One of the early ones was Sonny Whitney [519] who took what he wanted from Tilly, on false pretences, between the first and second of his four wives.

Yet from an early age Tilly learned to appeal to and please and tantalise men. Some narratives say she became the plaything of an Austrian Count before she was rescued by Strauss and Max Reinhart.[520] She was the prototype *femme fatale* for later sex goddesses (not unlike Greta Garbo and Marilyn Monroe) and among her stalkers were several of the most prominent movers and shakers in Hollywood and on Capitol Hill. [521]

Tilly leched too; seduction came to her as second nature. According to one of the biographers of Randolph Churchill[522] (son of Winston) whom Tilly took to bed (his first sexual experience with a woman), Randolph adored the ground Tilly walked on. Using what he learnt in bed from her during his two marriages and the affair he had with Tilly's first husband, Edward James[523]), sharing it around seems to have been quite the thing in those days in some circles. [524]

For Porchey (who had known of Tilly's accomplishments as a lusty lady) the attraction was Tilly's hands and a reputation for having a boundless sexual capacity which Randolph (well known for his lifelong indiscretions, especially when drunk) had boasted about to his fellow Clubmen.

*Tilly taught Randolph Churchill and Tom Mitford a thing or two!*

Randolph had also shared Tilly's passionate embraces with his friend and intimate cousin, Tom Mitford[525] who was nicknamed 'Tud' or 'Tuddemy' (to rhyme with 'adultery') because of [his] success with married women.[526] In her affair with the handsome, fair-haired, fluent German-speaking bisexual,[527] Tom's hot and cold flings with Tilly took place both when she was a spinster and during her first marriage to Edward James.[528] Randolph records that the Mitford family were relieved that James married Tilly as they "were so afraid that Tom would!" [529]

Whilst appearing in London stage shows Tilly's photographs appeared constantly in the press, along with several in-depth interviews. The best of crop were with photographer Dorothy Wilding[530] (a perfectionist) and the maverick journalist James Wedgwood Drawbell; [531] together they created a loving portrait of Tilly, with words to match, in one of Drawbell's many readable and surprisingly forgotten books, *A Gallery of Women*. [532]

*Tilly Losch*

From Drawbell's interview we glean from Tilly own words that she first appeared on stage at the Stadt Operhaus (the State Opera House), in her home town of Vienna in 1912. She was ten when she appeared as a child dancer in Louis Frappart's *Wiener Waltzer,* and her follow-up to this was as *Princess Teablossom* in a ballet. Some dance records mark these as Tilly's output in 1913. [533]

Drawbell swoons around his subject just like a wonderfully gracious, romantic Austrian waltz:

"She danced because she *had* to dance – to please herself, to delight her mother, to entertain her mother's visitors in their Viennese home. It was one of these visitors... [who] watched the child and recognised her talents." [534]

After her training and with the success of *Wiener Waltzer*, Tilly appeared in Korngold's ballet *Das Schneemann* and subsequently became *premiere danseuse* of the Vienna Opera House. She danced divinely for Reinhardt in Vienna and Berlin and ultimately she went with his company to tour America in 1927. Her first role in New York was as a fairy in *A Midsummer Night's Dream* and later she was the principal dancer in *Everyman*.

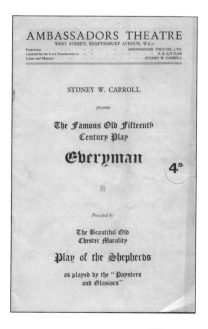

*Tilly, a fairy in 1923 and Programme for Everyman*[535]

There was ever a melancholy side to Tilly, identified by the perceptive Drawbell: "Success has not taken away from her that haunting pessimism that has always been hers. Her face is pensive, almost sad."[536]

In the 1930s Tilly's dancing career was enhanced by her curious marriage to Edward James (who was only besotted by her image and waxed lyrically about this in his poetic verse). James was a strange character: "he owned an immense Rolls-Royce car for instance, inside which – at the pressing of a button – a completely equipped bed appears." [537] The idea of a car with a bed inside was the spark of Lord Louis Mountbatten who was well known to Edward, as were the Windsor-Mountbatten coterie of many and varied sexual persuasions.

## Edward James's Descent

In his subconscious mind Edward James fell madly in love with Tilly the dancer. Some say he was her only true love. He records this state of affairs came about "while watching her and Laurie Devine dancing in a number called *'Gothic: A study in Arabesques'*. [538] But James wanted her less as woman and wife in flesh and blood than as an ideal, a concept, a possession. With the life choices open to him through his great wealth he was someone who collected things. It was a fetish. One tale told was that he "bought four houses in Rome, one to live in, one to visit in the afternoons, one for his friends to stay in, and one in which to play the piano". [539]

James was the son of an Anglo-American[540] marriage between Evelyn (Evie) Forbes,[541] daughter of a Scottish baronet and William (Willie) Dodge James[542], an American copper mining and railway magnate. Evie was one of the best known of the Edwardian society hostesses. The vast James home at West Dean Park near Chichester, Sussex), set in 8000 acres of lush gardens, was described by one social historian as a house that "eclipsed Goodwood [home of the Dukes of Richmond] as the resting-place of royalty at the close of the season.....a place socially so characteristic of the Edwardian age." [543]

Edward's mother - who was always tagged as "Mrs Willie James" - was a renowned figure in High Society.[544] Evie was one of King Edward

VII's closest companions and she may sometime have been his mistress. However a book written in 1978 contends that Edward may have been Evie's father, the Royal seduction of Evie's mother having been accomplished when Edward was Prince of Wales. The claim is that she was in reality conceived during a Royal visit to Balmoral.[545]  Other writers who claim Evie was the King's mistress also suggest Edward may have been the King's own son. On paper, after birth he was the King's godson. In any event the family walked in Royal circles.

*Mrs Willie James and her children*

Notwithstanding Edward's pedigree, he had four older teasing sisters. They teased him as he was the only boy and would inherit all the James family money.  The eldest sibling Helen married Henry Mowbray Howard, a great nephew of Elizabeth Howard, the Fourth Countess of Carnarvon, who was the Fifth Earl of Carnarvon's stepmother. Edward's high powered   Royal loving sister Audrey (formerly Mrs Dudley Coats "the brilliant daughter of a brilliant mother"[546] ) was married to the multi-millionaire Chicago banker, Marshall Field III. [547] Audrey always despised Tilly and tried all sorts of tricks to prevent her brother falling for her wiles.

A further link with the Carnarvons is poignant because Evie James died in Almina's nursing care at Alfred House in 1929; she was aged just sixty-one. [548] Evie James and Almina Carnarvon both had complicated and at times strained relationships with their sons which persisted for many years. Porchey and Edward's prep-school days were spent in similarly hellish conditions at Eton defending their virtue;[549] Edward at least gave into his instincts but Porchey fought back.

*West Dean, Near Goodwood*

Edward James was rich, his spending power limitless. At the age of five he inherited the West Dean estate and his father's many millions. At the age of twenty one, in 1928, he inherited more money from his uncle. Throughout his life he used part of this inheritance to provide patronage for the arts. His own passions were poetry and painting, writing and collecting (especially the artist Salvador Dali, with whom he had an affair[550]). James is credited (as a publisher) in producing the first collection of John Betjeman's verse. When he discovered surrealism he found his forte but somehow he lost his way. In Magritte's *Not to be Reproduced* he is depicted in a double portrait showing the back of James' head as he stands beside a mirror with "Lautreamont's Song of Maldoror, the black bible of surrealism." [551]

# The James Home In London

To please Tilly  Edward James embarked on a spirited modernist renovation of  his 19th-century town house in London, in collaboration with the artist and designer Paul Nash.

For Tilly's private suite, he and Nash came up with a scheme that resulted in one of the most spectacular bathrooms of the era, and not just because it included a nickel-plated exercise ladder that stretched from floor to ceiling. Airy, spacious and well lit, the high-ceilinged space was lined with a patchwork of glass in a shade of purple chosen to complement the new Mrs. James's dark hair and ice-blue eyes. (The bidet, sink and tub were deep purple too.)

Some of the squares and rectangles were standard mirror, but most of the larger sections were made of cathedral glass. This single-color, machine-made glass is often used in church windows, and its dimpled texture makes it look as if rain is falling against it.

# The Edward James Foundation

The Edward James Foundation at West Dean remains a lasting tribute to James,  the man who (as an inverted compliment) was once described as "one of the most tiresome people imaginable [but] no one else so deserved to sit beside Alice and the March Hare [in Wonderland]." [552] He later made his home on a Mexican hillside, a sort of Xanadu amongst the snakes and parrots of the jungle. It was full of beautiful boys.[553]

# Tilly the Nun and the prankster

Tilly is best remembered as a very fine dancer and for impressive stage performances in revue and for her extraordinary role as *'The Nun'* in the revival of Reinhardt's play *The Miracle* in London and America. At the Lyceum Theatre Tilly playing this role caused some critics to shake their heads but Charles Cochran knew what he was about when he chose her.

"I felt that here was the one woman whose power of acting and expression in dance and mime would make her an ideal Nun." [554]

One of Cochran's biographers says, "Some critics claimed that Tilly Losch as the Nun seemed far too light-hearted in the first scene, but Cockie could not agree with this." [555]

*Tilly Losch ( the Nun ) in*
*The Miracle*

The mix of Max Reinhardt and the elegant Lady Diana Cooper (who recreated her role as the statue of the Madonna and was required to remain absolutely still for half an hour), with brilliant sets and costumes by the flamboyant Oliver Messel (another of Edward's coterie), transformed the theatre into a cathedral that made Walpole's *Castle at Otranto* look like a third world airport lounge.

Tilly could be a prankster, as is evidenced from the trick she played ( on stage) against Diana Cooper during *The Miracle* when she switched Diana's habit round back to front leaving her co star " thrashing around ingloriously looking for the exit."[556] This was followed next night with Tilly inserting two large hatpins into Diana's veil. It is remarked by one of Diana's biographer's that they was no point complaining to Cochran as " he was besotted by Tilly Losch."[557]

The fussy critic James Agate wrote "Miss Tilly Losch stands out pre-eminently, her performance of 'The Nun' being one of the most delicately perceptive and brilliantly executed things ever seen in London." [558]

The King and Queen attended a performance of *The Miracle*. Cochran escorted their Majesties to a specially designed Royal box. Queen Mary called for Tilly to meet her and they conversed together in German. [559]

## Tilly marries Edward James

*Edward and Tilly and Tilly's Footprints on the stairs at West Dean*

In the early 1930s and full of desire, the orphaned Edward James pursued Tilly across America, and despite Tilly saying 'No!' more than once, on 2nd February 1931 she was finally lured into a sort of marital state. It has to be said that this was more of a fogbound than a whirlwind romance. The wedding ceremony was held in Manhattan, New York.

Tilly didn't love him. She saw a loophole or two: an unmatchable opportunity and a means of topping up her bank balance. She wrote to a friend that "she had only married the 'little Englishman' as a joke."[560] This was part of Tilly's style with both her husbands: to go on and rob them and then run away. She judged it would be only be a brief affair with James, followed by an annulment and a settlement to suit. Besides, she suspected that Edward (like his chums Noel Coward and 'Chips' Channon[561]) preferred male company underneath the eiderdown. James was rich, an artist and bohemian and always photographing beautiful boys, but she was surprised when he asked to make love. Apparently Tilly laughed out uncontrollably on board a train whilst they were travelling across the USA on the first night of their honeymoon, when he tried to enter her cabin. Tilly put it to him thus: "But Edward, my darling, you're a fucking pansy!"[562]

Although Tilly could run circles round the fresh-faced, eternally boyish Edward, she soon discovered that whilst Edward *was* able to consummate the marriage (and he goes on endlessly about his love-making prowess in an early autobiography[563]), this was a strain. He was fascinated more by beautiful men and boys. 'Beautiful' was his favourite word. Tilly observed this awkward, irritating infatuation evolved with several beautiful males on the beaches during their honeymoon to Honolulu. She later raised this (depicting it somewhat disingenuously as being a personal snub), which James denied but it found its place on the charge sheet as an act of cruelty during the subsequent divorce action of 1934.

Tilly's worst fear was of getting pregnant; that dread was her everlasting nightmare. She went through several abortions for men who were vipers, others who were lovers and once for James, as though these were merely minor operations as inconvenient as a scratch, graze or a scald. Of course she got rid of these babies *before* any mention was made of their brief existence, swallowing (or being given) quinine to effect the removal of the embryonic encumbrance of the James baby. There is some suggestion that she actually told James she was pregnant without adding that the baby was his; she told him in Court that he was the father at the height of their divorce in 1934 but the Judge struck out the testimony.

About babies Tilly was openly hostile, dismissive and unsentimental; that is, until later life. In her dancing years she displayed no maternal instincts: she blatantly refused to carry James's (or anybody else's) children. This dismayed James and made Tilly vulnerable to condemnation, especially in the later court action.

## A Cheque Book Marriage

James' heart was an open cheque book for Tilly as he attempted to revive their ill conceived union.

*George Balanchine*

Through James's patronage Tilly worked with the choreographic genius George Balanchine (returning to ballet work again after the death of his friend Diaghilev) and Boris Kochno. Despite Balanchine and Tilly not getting on there were some magical sequences in their collaborations *Anna-Anna*[564] and *Errante.* [565]

*Kurt Weil and Lotte Lenya*

These productions in Paris and London are long remembered in dance history.[566] Tilly starred in, and helped choreograph the shows under the guidance of the German composer Kurt Weill and the writer Bertolt Brecht. James had brought the latter to London to save him from being arrested by the Nazis and to devise a *ballet chante*, the *Seven Deadly Sins of the Petit Bourgeoisie*. The theme, conceived by James himself, was sung by Weill's wife Lotte Lenya (as the singing Anna) and Tilly was the dancer (as the dancing Anna).[567] "The two Annas, representing two sides of one self-journey through seven American cities.; in each they commit one of the seven deadly sins in order to earn enough money so that their family can build a house." [568]

## Tilly's affairs with women

In Paris, in private, Tilly and Lotte Lenya enjoyed some sinning time together. In a biography of Kurt Weill and Lotte, Tilly is outed as a lesbian. [569] Later we learn from the author that the bisexual Lotte " Of course ...had an affair with Tilly Losch, but she [Lotte] was still with Otto Pasetti (a singer in *The Seven Deadly Sins* male quartet) and this was when Lenya divorced Weill." [570] Curiously the Weills remarried each other again in 1937 after Lotte's affair with Pasetti ended. Later, in the USA, Lotte "went on a binge of mostly superficial affairs." [571]

*Losch and Lenya as the two Annas*

The same author of the Weill biography describes Tilly as the "strange artistic lesbian ballerina."[572] Tilly is quoted in a book about Marlene Dietrich (whom she knew and worked with in Berlin, New York and Hollywood), reflecting on the time there when Dietrich was type-cast as the Blue Angel; Tilly herself is described as "a leading doyenne of the Berlin lesbian bar scene." [573]

"It was chic for girls not to be feminine. I knew Dietrich in those days and she was a tough little nut." [574]

Several texts make reference to Tilly and Dietrich being involved in an affair when the twilight world of Berlin's bisexuality was at its zenith in pre-Nazi days. One history records a description of her as the "Austrian starlet Tilly Losch, rumoured to be among Dietrich's lovers ...." [575]

## Les Ballets transfers to London

This artistic and human circus of dance and sexual experimentation was at its peak during 1933 when Tilly's multi-millionaire husband James put up the tens of thousands of pounds (some writers say £100,000) to stage an epic production of Tilly's own company, *Les Ballets,* at the Savoy Theatre, the Palace and the Ambassadors, repeating the work done previously in Paris.

James's purpose was to present an adoration of his wife, a framework in which to show off his gorgeous but naughty, mischievous spouse. He was a generous man; the whole of the 1933 *Les Ballets* Company was put up at West Dean and treated to lavish Country House living in style with everything laid on without charge. Tilly did not appear, despite her showing up at the theatre; she was living elsewhere at James's expense.

For the 1933 ensemble Roman Jasinsky[576] was the principal male dancer, with Tamara Toumanova[577] and Pearl Argyle. The shows had breathtaking sets with reconstructions of actual rooms that showed off Tilly in all her primeval power and glory. The costumes were so thin, the dancers appeared to be in the nude. Edward had satisfied another fetish and these architectural extravaganzas were later reflected in his palace in the central Mexican jungle."[578]

1933 also saw Tilly shine when she danced in de Basil's ballet at the Alhambra, of which Arnold Haskell[579] wrote: "Tilly Losch ...is an artist of taste, talent, beauty, and positive personality whom I have always greatly admired in her own sphere. I was perhaps the first in our little world to acclaim her, and have always had a strong belief in her future." [580]

But Tilly's best dancing years were virtually over, besides which her domestic life was a mess. The James' marriage was full of mistrust and littered with dramatic rows and showdowns.

# One Row Revealed

On 21 October 1932 Tilly was recovering at the matrimonial home of 35 Wimpole Street, London, after her physician, a Dr Richardson, had carried out an abortion. An ugly incident followed. Edward appeared and discovered the full extent of the Tilly's deception, as she had just aborted *his* baby. Tilly describes this as "a violent scene in the room in which she was, saying he would kill her, abusing her and cursing her." [581] In the documents submitted as a part of the divorce Tilly alleged that Edward had called her "a dirty bitch, a Viennese bitch, a louse, vermin."[582] Similar taunts were made later that night by Edward, allegedly calling his wife "a lousy bitch, a dirty swine, a dirty gold digger, filthy vermin."[583]

There was only one outcome but neither Tilly nor, as it turned out, Edward was prepared to let things go quietly. One biographer of Edward James reflects, "Another couple, if unable to avoid it altogether, would at least have arranged for a discreet parting of the ways,"[584] adding, "With Tilly and Edward it was a case of irresistible bloody-mindedness against immovable obstinacy."[585]

## Tilly Worries Over The James Divorce

Kurt Weill reported to Lotte Lenya that as Tilly's alimony hearing drew nearer ( which Edward James had now turned into a full blown divorce action) she was devastated " she doesn't look well and is nervous because of the lawsuit." [586]

## The James Divorce

London loved sex scandals. Almina, Dorothy and Colonel Ian Dennistoun had given the gossipmongers a feast in 1925 and now Tilly and Edward were poised to rip the lid off their hopelessly ill-matched marriage of barely three years duration. It was a comedy and a tragedy at the same time. Tilly had separated from Edward and was living (at his expense) in an apartment in London's Culross Street. When Edward wanted a piano returned that was stored there, Tilly exploded. She began an action for a separation allowance of £1000 a year (this is sometimes referred to as £4000) on the grounds of his cruelty and homosexuality. Edward replied by taking divorce proceedings on the grounds of Tilly's infidelities.

Tilly grabbed the first headline as she was recovering from the shock of a minor car accident. It was a lucky escape in a taxi cab smash in London's Grosvenor Square. She was taken to her home in Culross Street, Mayfair and confined to bed for over a week; five doctors attended her.

The ensuing ugly divorce proceedings occupied several days in the London divorce court and the reporting led to dozens of lurid headlines and testimony and a clutch of witnesses offering opposing evidence. Edward named the twice-married Prince Serge Obolensky, "a man of great charm and dash who had fought in the Czarist Russian army in the First World War,"[587] as Tilly's lover.

James alleged that Tilly had committed adultery with the Russian aristocrat Obolensky in New York during their first year of marriage, sometime between August and October 1931.

In the evidence heard in Court it was further alleged that after the honeymoon in Hawaii he returned to England from time to time leaving Tilly in New York as she had theatre commitments with *The Bandwagon*. While away he employed detectives to watch her every move. The evidence from Edward's agents and hotel attendants was read at length, with addresses (where Tilly met the Prince) quoted as Park Avenue and East 57th Street, New York, both places rented by James. The evidence of the night watchman was damning against Tilly in listing Obolensky's frequent visits, and one of Edward's secretaries claimed he had seen the Prince naked in Tilly's bedroom.

Serge Obolensky was a 'café socialite' who could charm the birds off the trees. Two failed marriages behind him (the second to Alice,[588] daughter of Titanic victim John Jacob Astor) made him a ruthless, ambitious predator. Tilly's case was that she was on nothing but the most casually friendly terms with the Prince and his wife, the latter whom she described as an intimate friend. The Prince's wife divorced the Prince at Reno in 1932, co-incidentally on grounds of cruelty, and a month later married Raimund von Hofmannstahl[589] who later became a close friend of Tilly's.

## No winner

In reality (as with *Dennistoun v Dennistoun*) there was no winner in *James v James v Obolensky*. It was a disgraceful affair, beginning with the fact that Edward James was the plaintiff and *he sued Tilly for divorce*. A husband (and in Edward's case a gentleman, the godson of a King) suing his wife in England was unthinkable. A long exile abroad would be the price he paid for such behaviour.

The whole unpleasant business was viewed from different standpoints; those collaterally damaged would have it either that Tilly took advantage of James to feather her own nest or that James was an ineffectual faithless gadfly with a nasty streak.

The cruelty charge comprised physical harm by James upon his wife, alleging that "James slapped his wife's face, twisted her arm, abused and cursed her, and terrified her during her pregnancy by saying that he would give her poison." [590]

One precedent was cited against James, since it was well known that when Serge Lifar refused to dance with Alicia Markova, referring to her as 'cette bourgeoise anglaise,' Edward James slapped his face in the hall of the Savoy Hotel.[591]

Another of the charges involving Edward's assault on his wife was in connection with a dinner party in America which Tilly refused to attend. Tilly alleged that Edward was "so angry when she finally would not go that he slapped her, whereupon she tried to bite his hand and he caught her wrists to stop her."[592]

Edward's dalliances with men, including a young Italian bus driver named Fernando for whom Edward offered to pay singing lessons, was cited as one lewd interest as well as the beach boys Edward importuned during the honeymoon.

## Beautiful Boys

The detail in the documents from Tilly's side was specific. She "alleged generally that Edward "persistently neglected [her] in favour of men for whom he to Tilly professed 'love.'" [593] That during the honeymoon in February 1931 the newly-weds were staying at the Royal Hawaiian Hotel, Honolulu and Tilly claimed that Edward neglected her and spent most of the time with Hawaiian native bathing boys.

That Edward took a liking to one of the natives, in particular one named Harry who "sang so beautifully and looked so lovely." [594] Later Tilly claims that Edward "locked himself in one of the rooms of the hotel suite with the native boy and would remain with him for a considerable time, refusing to open the door."[595]

Tilly also alleged that in October 1931 Edward had befriended an American boy who was a friend of a Count Ledebur. This boy was "supposed to have Indian blood and was referred to as 'the Mexican'." [596] Edward later told Tilly that "he was very much in love with 'the Mexican' but that he was too dirty." [597] The boy later accompanied Edward on a trip to Mexico.

Of the man named Count Ledebur [598] Tilly additionally alleged that in November 1931 at 444, 57th Street, New York at one o'clock in the morning  Edward had brought Count Ledebur back home from a party; they then spent several hours together in a locked room and later (in tears) Edward told Tilly that he was in love with the Count.

Another incident was raised by Tilly from time spent in Venice at the Excelsior Palace Hotel, Lido, involving Serge Lifar with whom Edward had fallen in love. It was in Venice that Edward also befriended an Italian singer, Fernando Gusso, who worked as a bus driver and Edward later brought him to England.

So far as these allegations from Tilly were concerned of James' undue friendship with such beautiful men and boys the court found no substance in Tilly's charges.

## The Outcome and Aftermath of the Court Case

What went against Tilly was that she wasn't seen as 'one of us' by the powers that be. On stage she was untouchable, being every man and some women's fantasy, but in court she was seen as a foreign little vixen and, as they always do, the upper classes closed ranks around this godson of a King of England.

Tilly gave it her best shot, trying to evidence James' abuse of her. She called several doctors as witnesses to give evidence on her behalf of the forced abortions and was supported by friends including Randolph Churchill, Henry 'Chips' Channon ( who was accommodating  Prince Serge Obolensky during the hearing)  and Tilly's co-star in *The Band Wagon*, Lady Charles Cavendish (who was formerly the dancer and actress Adele Astaire, sister of Fred). Others who spoke on behalf of Tilly were Dr Alec Landell Clarke of Brook Street and Nurse Lilian Smith who attended Tilly in October 1932 at West Dean Park.

Adele Astaire did her friend no favours with her evidence and by demonstrating a rude gesture in Court about an incident on 4 December 1931 in a taxi cab travelling between the Empire State Buildings, 34th Street, 5th Avenue and 444 East 57th Street, where Tilly and  Prince Obolensky were seen kissing and hugging each other.

## Lady Cavendish Thumbs Nose in British Court

(By United Press)

LONDON, June 22.—A select audience in divorce court was convulsed with laughter today when Lady Cavendish, the former popular American dancer, Adele Astaire, thumbed her nose while testifying in the divorce suit of Edward F. W. James against Tilly Losch, dancer.

Lady Cavendish was not making the gesture of derision at anyone in court. She was testifying in support of Miss Losch's denial of her husband's charge that she misconducted herself with Prince Serge Obolensky. The gesture demonstrated how she and Miss Losch "made faces" at one another from two taxicabs traveling side by side on Fifth avenue in New York.

Lady Cavendish—then Adele Astaire—was in one cab with a companion and Miss Losch and Obolen-sky in another. It was on that historic ride that James alleged the prince and his wife were observed in a kissing clinch. Lady Cavendish testified that she had a clear view of the other cab and that no kissing occurred.

Lady Cavendish repeatedly amused the audience. When she was asked on cross-examination why she remembered a certain visit to the Empire State building in New York, she replied:

"Because I paid a fee of one dollar," adding that she thought it was too expensive to go up in a building.

She told the court she was a member of a party of four, including Obolensky and Miss Losch, which visited the James apartment on Park avenue late at night after the theater. She supported Miss Losch's denial of misconduct at the apartment.

*Adele Cavendish ( nee Astaire ) and the  gesture that shocked the Court*

Adele said she had been in another taxi cab with 'Chips' Channon following Tilly and the Prince but Edward's barrister suggested that Tilly and Serge had been making love on the top of the Empire State Building. It was said that Adele and Channon were also there but they rejected the charge and afterwards followed Tilly and the Prince in the taxi cab; on passing, as the couple were allegedly kissing and hugging,[599] Adele "cocked a snook at them"[600]. This reference upset the Judge who asked Adele to demonstrate the motion, and despite the Judge's abhorrence (which was met with huge laughter otherwise by the Court) Adele repeated it to the journalists and photographers outside the Court.[601]

After eight days Tilly failed in her risky strategy against James. She dared to allege that James had a certain proclivity towards young men, which indeed he did, but as we know sex wasn't invented until 1963 and man on man action presumably some time later. Britain in 1934 was not ready for such things!

The bizarre spectacle in court was played out in all the newspapers of the day.  The dead babies on Tilly's part were dismissed as so much flim-flam, the hits and slaps from Edward seemed to suggest a control freak. The centrepiece of the couple's showdown were their gaggle of witnesses.

Like Tilly, James called several witnesses to defend his camp and portray him as the innocent party. Some surprising people spoke out against Tilly including her New York maid Anna Haase. Others who offered evidence in rebuttal of Tilly's cross-petition were Maria Boshere of Berners Street, London; Ada Cabner of South Croydon (another of Tilly's maids until 1932); Sir Thomas Beecham, the conductor; Dr Alexander Low of Gloucester Place and Portman Square, London; Dr Beckett Overy, a gynaecologist of Lowndes Street, London and Dr Francis Leslie of West Street, Chichester.

Tilly always needed a real man and James always fell short. Although Edward James was undoubtedly in love with Tilly (and this can be seen from the various poetic gems he penned to her, even long years after they had finally parted) he was an eccentric aesthetic and just not good at being anybody's husband. But he found it hard to exorcise the ghost of his past through his epic time with Tilly. In a touching tribute at West Dean there is a stair carpet into which were stitched her footprint, a sort of very British equivalent to the Chinese theatre in Hollywood.

The almost certain Society backfire at these same lurid allegations that were being cited in 1933 in the divorce case of Catherine's friend, the Hon. Lois Sturt (later Viscountess Tredegar), made Lois think twice about proceeding with her own open warfare against her husband, the Hon. Evan Morgan, who was also homosexual. The legal papers make it crystal clear that Evan's trivial pursuits were having young men in his bed and Lois' lawyers dared suggest that 'buggery' had taken place. Tilly stopped short of this kind of accusation of Edward.

The jury of ten men and two women took about three quarters of an hour to side with Edward, They found that Tilly and Obolensky had committed adultery together and Edward had not been guilty of *any* of the charges of cruelty.

Neither Sir Boyd Merriman, the President of the Divorce Division of the High Court and acting Judge, nor the jury of 1934 had any stomach for tackling James's homosexual leanings. Beyond the Courts Tilly's invites to the stately homes of England suddenly dried up.

Edward also was shunned. Former friends refused to speak to him and although the outcome was in his favour he was never comfortable or happy living in England (or America) again.

In concluding the case the Judge was scathing in his personal attack against Tilly and the Prince:

"The Losch charges of cruelty against James were without foundation. They have been pressed ruthlessly and abandoned when they were seen to be hopeless in a way that was not calculated to remove their sting. If I said all I thought about the matter he added I would have difficulty in restraining my language..." [602]

The barristers were Norman Birkett KC for Edward and Sir Patrick Hastings for Tilly. Prince Obolensky was represented by Roland Oliver, KC.

Despite compelling legal arguments by Hastings and Oliver costs were awarded against Tilly and Prince Obolensky.

The Judge ordered Tilly (who it was said earned £10,000 a year as a dancer) to pay the costs of the cruelty issue while Prince Obolensky would be required to pay the general costs. [603] More importantly, Edward was granted a decree nisi and Tilly's petition dismissed.

After hearing the verdict Tilly started to faint and had to be carried out of the stuffy courtroom. When she had recovered she said she would never marry again as long as she lived.

The James divorce had been a bitterly contested public spectacle that attracted more attention in 1934 than all of Tilly's performances on stage put together.

Unity Mitford (writing to her sister Diana) remarked "I'm so glad Edward won....I do think she [Tilly] was a little brute to say such horrid things about him." [604]

Tilly was defiant to the end, but she was in tears. "It is terrible for me". She told reporters that she was penniless but was planning to resume her dancing career to restore her finances. She added "Dancing – that is my whole life."[605]

Adele Cavendish took Tilly home in her motor car, refusing to comment on whether her friend would seek an appeal.

## Prince Serge Obolensky

*The Prince*

After the James divorce Serge Obolensky recovered his reputation in the USA and Britain during the Second World War. One of his war missions in the Office of Strategic Services was to parachute into Sardinia amid tens of thousands of German and Italian troops with instructions from General Eisenhower to contact the commanding officer of the Italians and persuade them to side with the Allies.

Obolensky had worked for Vincent Astor's St Regis Hotel for 11 years (apart from when he was married to Vincent's sister Alice Astor) and his breeding and wit fitted him for the job.

He volunteered to go to Sardinia. He was then aged fifty three. First he reported to Major General William J Donovan's HQ in Algiers where an interpreter and two radio officers went with him on the next part of the mission. They were dropped into a valley and successfully carried out the task.

The Prince also trained paratroopers in England for work in France and then jumped into Eguzon himself as part of a mission to save the power station there, which was the largest one in all France. He left the American army as a Lieutenant Colonel and took a job with the Hilton hotels group as publicity and promotion director, his old specialty.[606]

The Prince, who died in 1978, wrote a memoir[607] in which Tilly is mentioned as a dear friend but there is no admission of any impropriety.

## Recovery and Tilly's Last Show for Cochran

Later in 1934 Tilly returned to Vienna to visit her mother. Her career subsequently took a bit of a nosedive in England but in March of the following year she appeared in a word and movement show, *Everyman*, at London's Ambassadors Theatre. With an all-star cast, the "oldest of all the morality plays explored how mankind is invariably doomed to death in spite of such good friends as Good Deeds and Knowledge." [608]

It was not the best direction to cheer Tilly but she impressed as an Angel, the image of which appeared in the press to promote the show.

Reports suggest that Tilly had a good enough income in the period that followed the divorce to settle her legal debts. In any case the costs were tax deductible in the USA so the loser at the end of the day was Uncle Sam.

Cochran also came up trumps. She went into rehearsal for another show, this time from the lyrics of A P Herbert and Ronald Jeans and music by Vivian Ellis. It was entitled *Streamline* and was scheduled to open at the Opera House, Manchester on 1st September and premiere in London at the Palace on 28 September. Cecil Beaton and his great rival Oliver Messel designed the sets.

The show gave Tilly a successful comeback and the James debacle could be almost forgotten.

*Streamline* was Cochran's twenty-first revue and also starred the brilliant female impressionist Florence Desmond and artists Jack Hart and June Holland. Comedy was supplied by Naunton Wayne. Nijinsky's daughter Kyra was also in the cast.

SCULPTURESQUE "STREAMLINE":
TILLY LOSCH IN "HARMONIA MOBILIS."

Streamline : Cochran's Twenty First Revue

It was described by *Country Life* as the "most dazzling show in London ....with brilliantly clever dancing throughout ..." *Vogue* said it was "a crashing success."

"*Streamline* owed its success to the dancers, headed by the delightful Tilly Losch. The dancers including Young Ladies of Mr Cochran's chorus, alive and kicking" ..."[609]

*The Talented Tilly*

Others said Tilly was exquisite but with the merit of others in the cast being equally praised. Tilly was a star but she was also a very good team player.

It was the last time Tilly danced for Charles Cochran. He reflected on this by summing up Tilly's talent: "Tilly has a rare beauty which does not conform to conventional standards..."[610]

## Tilly slips into a depression

Tilly reached rock bottom in January, 1935. Kurt Weill wrote to Lotte Lenya " I visited Tilly ..in the theatre. She complains bitterly because she has no prospects in sight." [611] Two days later Lenya is more waspish in her reply " And Tilly? That one will be only too glad just to find something for herself. Her influence can't be all that great, or she wouldn't be wailing like that….. But she probably knows a lot of people." [612] A few weeks later Weill is caustic in his comments over Tilly's latest show in London " In the afternoon I went to see that revue with Tilly. God-awful. Tilly is too fat ( like a dumpling), and her dancing is terrible. She's desperately looking for a rich husband but goes about it the wrong way and entirely without charm." [613]

Work seems to be hard to find for Weill and Lenya too. However in August 1935 Weill was offered a job in Paris by Max Reinhardt. The contract didn't include Lenya, and Weill complains to her in a letter suggesting that Renhardt's accomplice [ Rudolph] Kommer was working behind the scenes for Tilly's advancement at Lenya's expense. [614]

*Rudolph Kommer and Lotte Lenya*

The exact nature of the personal relationship between Tilly and Kommer is complex. Gottfried Reinhardt[615] ( son of Max) describes that he[ Kommer] first took Tilly under his "lethal wing [( for Max) with a] concentrated, faithful, theoretical passion." [616]

On 17 July 1935, Tilly is reported as having lunch as Lady Colefax's ( they met through Cecil Beaton) where Tilly talked ( in German) about the latest London Russian ballet offerings at Covent Garden to journalist and diplomat and Great War super spy, Robert Bruce Lockhart.[617]

But there was light to come for Tilly from a movie mogul in Hollywood.

## Relief as Tilly is signed up by David Selznick

In December 1935 the infamous movie writer Louella Parsons broke the news that Tilly had been signed up by Hollywood producer David O Selznick.[618]

Everyone wondered if Selznick was going to make a film about ballet!

The writer Louis Golding [619] was asked to write a story for Tilly:

"Tilly Losch shall be the star of the great Russian ballet film. We shall make a world star of her overnight. All we need is a story. I had a few friends in New York who knew of my devotion to the ballet. Would I write a story for Tilly Losch? I would be proud to." [620]

Alas, the story was never made into a movie!

## Tilly's Interlude in Hollywood

Taking up Selznick's offer, and still bruised by the bitter split with Edward James and seemingly shunned by most in society, Tilly went to Hollywood and made several bizarre movies, notwithstanding an impressive performance alongside Paul Muni and Luise Rainer in an adaptation of Pearl S Buck's epic saga of the soil, *The Good Earth*. The film was still playing in Britain to record audiences many years later and remains one of Tilly's enduring roles. In 1937 Tilly appeared with her sometime friend Marlene Dietrich and with Charles Boyer and Basil Rathbone in David O Selznick's *The Garden of Allah*, a torrid love story that Gertrude Griffiths could easily have penned, set in the Algerian desert.

One review of Tilly's dancing career remarks, "Probably Mata Hari, executed by the French as a German spy during the [Great] War, was the only other oriental dancer ever to achieve such tremendous acclaim on the Continent." [621]

*From The Good Earth*

## Hollywood Name Change

When Tilly first went to Hollywood, one film producer wanted her to change her name. Appalled by the suggestion, she asked why. He said her tag was not romantic enough and he associated the name with a newspaper comic strip character *Tillie the Toiler*.[622] She argued him out of it. But clearly her unusual name did conjure up an image in itself. When Tilly first met the composer George Gershwin, he said " Gee, you're so much younger an prettier than I imagined." Tillie replied " What made you think I was older and uglier?" Gershwin admitted " Oh your name – Tilly Losch, it sounds so short and fierce." [623]

# 1938

In March 1938, before leaving for England ( where she thought she could find a rich husband ), Tilly went to San Francisco and performed a few dances backed by the City's Symphony Orchestra. Reviews were mixed, but the board of the governors of the Musical Association gave a large reception in her honour. [624]

## Christmas 1938

*Lady Juliet and her son, Sir Michael Duff*

Back in Britain, Tilly was in a safe haven in Wales, with bright new flame, Sir Michael Duff [625], staying at his mother's home at Vaynol ( Faenol)[626]. Michael's mother Lady Juliet Duff [627] ( who had been one of the first women to cause uproar smoking in the lounges of cross Atlantic liners during the Edwardian era ) could not have been more hospitable. Tilly also discovered that Lady Juliet was a considerable follower of the ballet, she was a personal friend of the great dancer Serge Diaghilev[628], with a collection of programmes and photographs and dance memorabilia ( that years later sold for large sums). Despite Tilly finding Michael a generous and romantic lover and enjoying the host comforts and the good food and wine of a Christmas in Wales, Tilly caught a cold which turned nasty, forcing her on return to London to seek urgent medical advice. Her lungs were congested, the diagnosis was critical, and a period in a sanatorium was advised. Tilly ( who was also deeply depressed ) booked herself into a quiet retreat in Switzerland. Only her closest friends ( like Cecil Beaton, Duff's some time lover[629]) were told where she was in hiding for six months.

*Tilly ( far right, in sun- glasses ) with Cecil Beaton and his guests at Ashcombe*

# Chapter 14

## Porchey Marries Tilly

*Tilly With Old Lover, Randolph Churchill and New Lover Porchey*

There were those who remembered Tilly the dancer, those who squirmed at Tilly the tramp (since she had countless affairs throughout the late 1930s) and those who remembered Tilly the slayer in the Divorce Court in 1934. Most people mused at how Porchey could ever think to take such a shop-soiled and frankly dangerous woman for his next Countess.

Whilst Porchey was still wounded from the Tanis Guinness affair three years earlier he was always under starter's orders at the turn of a pretty ankle and there was no question in his mind that Tilly fitted the bill. Equally Tilly was still, deep down, bruised by the memories of matrimony with Edward James that had ended with great expense and humiliation.

It looked at first that there was going to be a repeat of that same Tanis farce, in a game of "Will She? – Won't She? Marry Him?"

Ilka Chase, an American actress who knew Tilly, records: "We lunched ....at the Ivy with the enchanting Viennese dancer [Tilly Losch]. Tilly is as pretty as a kitten, with a shrewd eye for this world's goods." [630]

In effect Tilly was prepared to do *anything* again for money!

Another actress friend of Tilly's (who herself had been mauled by Porchey) cautioned her: "It would be a pity, darling, if you were making a mistake...Dukes and Earls and things like that are his only friends, and they get very dull."[631]

Tilly's answer was curt and feline: "Perhaps you are right, my darling....but they are surely no duller than the top executives of Hollywood studios." [632]

Another adviser reminded Tilly that Porchey had probably slept with all their girlfriends. It is said she even threw this charge at Porchey but excluded the fact that she'd slept with some of them too.

However, to ensure she did not jump too quickly into Porchey's bed and to maximise her demands, Tilly laboured longer. By early August 1939 the wheels on the proposed marriage between Tilly and Porchey stopped turning. Reporters sniffing around Tilly ran around asking about the wedding but Tilly was full of frowns and snapped that there was no date fixed because she did not know whether there would be any wedding.

Another reason was the Carnarvon family's concerns over Tilly; they wanted no dancing Countess. Of course it was *not* her dancing they objected to but her scandalous past!! The Carnarvons saw Tilly's move on Porchey as a means of getting a British passport for a Jewess.[633]

Surprisingly, whilst she was mulling over Porchey's marriage proposal, Tilly was persuaded by a group of friends, centred around Randolph Churchill and Tom Mitford to go on 16 July, 1939, to hear a speech from the British fascist leader, Sir Oswald Mosley. The meeting was hailed later as Mosley's " last and greatest meeting in London." After sitting in terror for nearly two hours, Tilly coaxed Randolph to leave.[634] It was a horrific experience that caused Tilly to rethink her position regarding her own safety in London, with or without marrying an English Lord.

However, a marriage was finally announced and on 1 September 1939 Porchey Carnarvon and Tilly Losch got hitched at the Registry Office at Caxton Hall, London. The omens were not good; war was looming and the irregularity of such a match was enhanced when, for reasons which remain unclear, Porchey telephoned the Superintendent Registrar at midnight, asking him as a favour to marry them before the Registry Office opened. This was agreed and the official was brought to the office by car by a colleague who assisted at the ceremony.

Almina and Eve Beauchamp were the only family members present as witnesses and for the first time ever they sang Porchey's praises. However, this was not a match made in heaven but one governed by expediency for both parties.

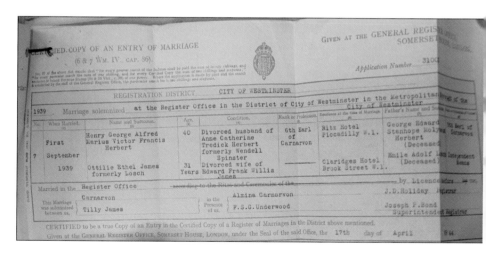

*The Marriage Certificate*

# Tilly Meets The Highclere Evacuees

International

Hostess to 27 evacuated city moppets and their mothers is Dancer Tilly Losch, on the estate of her husband, the Earl of Carnarvon. Evacuated slum people shocked a few aristocratic butlers.

Among the first to greet the new Countess of Carnarvon at Highclere was a large number of children evacuated from London.[635] Part of Highclere was turned into a nursery school.[636]

Tilly's health was fragile and she was not well disposed to be in close proximity to these undernourished children who brought with them, in her mind, the possibility of diseases like ringworm, scabies or head lice. She was obsessively fearful of such exposure, to some degree understandably as at the time she was in remission from tuberculosis which had required complete rest for six months in a Swiss sanatorium.[637] At one point Tilly had been so seriously ill in Switzerland that she almost died.

However, Tilly was first and foremost a performer. On several occasions she overcame these health fears for the sake of a good photo opportunity, being 'snapped' for several magazines in Britain and America playing games with the displaced children from London and telling the reporters that she was dashing up to buy pyjamas for the poor children inhabiting her husband's castle.

To give Tilly her due, she took briefly to the role of benefactor to these homeless children. According to letters in Binghamton University Library Tilly worked with Highclere staff and "agreed on details of the children's [1939] Christmas gifts and meals. The 'tiny tots' received stockings that contained a ball, a toy, some sweets, an orange and a penny." [638]

To the untutored eye Tilly may have appeared to be caught in Porchey's gilded cage but she revelled for a while in the status of a Countess, playing it for all it was worth on both sides of the Atlantic. The payoff was putting up with Porchey demanding his conjugal rights but with a headache here and a convenient period there these were severely rationed as she chalked off the days.

Seeing friends in London helped. But still not entirely recovered from illness, Tilly found the strain of blackouts and the crash of bombs and shells more than her nerves could stand. She became sombre and subdued, worrying over the Earl's lack of funds because he had told her his (financial ) assets were frozen by the British government at the outbreak of the war. (This turned out to be another of Porchey's 'porkies').

## Boredom!

Tilly was at her wits end with boredom and craved better company than Porchey could offer. However her spirits were raised by attending the wedding of an old flame, Randolph Churchill, on 4 October. [639] It was one of the first occasions that saw Porchey and Tilly on parade together amongst London's gentry. Tilly, the dancing Countess of Carnarvon had deliberately dressed down, even so the men drooled, whilst under their regal breaths the women ( who remembered too well the Edward James fiasco) muttered 'gold-digger' and 'scarlet woman' and 'Jezabel'.

# Austria's Fate

Tilly used her past services for Baron Georg von und zu Franckenstein at the Austrian Legation to call in favours and establish news of loved ones in Vienna. There was much concern by Tilly and her fellow Austrians, including her friend Raimund von Hofmannsthal [640] over the safety and welfare of contacts and family under Nazi rule, in Europe. Tilly took tea with the von Hofmannsthals at their home in Regent's Park, ( which was later bombed ). To catch up on the news both good and bad.

Elizabeth ( Liz) Hofmannsthals was a member of the Paget family and a niece of Lady Diana Cooper ( wife of the influential, well -placed diplomat Duff Cooper ) thus in daily contact with those in government circles who knew how Austrians were coping and who was dead. The Hofmannsthals had just pipped the Churchills in getting married, in June, 1939. They had also just come back from a motoring holiday in Europe. The news was grim enough to increase Tilly's determination to book a passage back to America.

## Tilly's Interview at the Ritz [641]

Installed at the *Ritz* hotel in London Tilly agreed to an interview with a reporter:

Had she given up the stage? " Yes, she said she had to bow to Porchey's request that she abandon her stage career and take up her place in Society."

What of her new love, the Earl of Carnarvon? " I have always been in love all my life. And most of my loves have been unhappy ones. I seem to attract unhappiness in emotional affairs. Perhaps, without realizing it, I enjoy not being happy."

She was coy about mentioning her Germanic roots:

" For years I gloried in saying Vienna  whenever anyone asked me was my birthplace. It always seemed to bring a special smile to people. Now it is different. I dread saying that I am Vienna born, and  in England trying to do what I can to help,  I know my accent stands in my way."

The dancing Countess of Carnarvon had nothing but praise for the "magnificent spirit of the British.  They fully realized their danger,  I appreciate  all that is being done to spare us  the horrors of Nazi attack."

Referring to her fellow guests at the Ritz  as *The Indomitables*,  by all accounts  the place  became  something of a beacon of  a very british kind of  bravado (however oxymoronic that might seem). Tilly told of the frequent night air raid alarms, at the conclusion of which the guests- still in their night clothing and with robes thrown about their shoulders, stampede into the famous cafe for a toast to their own salvation and a prayer for King and Country."

On one of these occasions, the hotel manager and staff, under strict instructions from Porchey,  did everything in their  power for the safety and comfort of the Countess, by  arranging for  a bed to be  moved into the bar for her use. There she slept soundly  while the air-raid sirens wailed outside.

## Freedom

Tilly's marriage was built on a bed of straw.  She  had fears for the future and felt insecure:  even within days of  tying the knot  she wanted to call time on things.   Porchey was just another man who was misusing her body, she had  seen off dozens of  that kind, each of them no better and sometimes worse than the previous.  As with the Edward James ' kid- on' marriage  she was doing it for money, she had  had similar relationships before out of the bonds of wedlock. However  she learned to control all these situations, especially now older and wiser. She set about  diverting  Porchey's attentions and carved out her way to freedom.  Almina had seen  nothing in her new daughter- in- law to give any praises, her advice to Porchey  was to  " Let the whore, go". [642]

*Tilly Leaves Britain for USA*

On 27 November, 1939 Tilly got her freedom. She sailed from Southampton on the *Statendam*, bound for New York and travelling as Ottilie Carnarvon of Highclere Castle, Berks, Peeress. She gave her age as thirty two (in fact she was at least thirty six). [643] First thing she did on arriving in the USA was to see John Wharton,[644] a notable Corporate Lawyer and friend of Cole Porter.

# 1940
## Tilly makes excuses

Tilly was so desperate to get away from Porchey's clutches that reports suggested "that she arrived in America with only the British wartime travel allowance of a few pounds sterling." [645]

Porchey agreed to wire Tilly some money and did at first maintain her as his wife. But in the mid-1940s he withheld any new funding in an attempt to have her return to Britain and resume fulfilling her marital role in Porchey's castle and bed. Porchey was not happy when he received a snub. Tilly was not willing to return, of course, and she fobbed Porchey off by saying she was unable to return. She excused herself by saying she'd been signed by the New York American Ballet Theatre as a guest artist. This was a group founded in 1937 that offered classical ballet. The pre-publicity was clear; Tilly was due to appear with the New York Company at the Lewisohn Stadium at the beginning of August 1940, for Antony Tudor[646] in a new Spanish ballet to the music of Granados. [647]

This was the sort of manoeuvring that Tilly accomplished successfully for several years to avoid being back in England. As previously recorded, she did return for a few weeks in March-June 1940 and she and Porchey had something of a reconciliation, helped no doubt by the sumptuous surroundings of Genoa, Monte Carlo and Paris before she left Porchey for the last time in June 1940. But even during that brief period she needed time off, disappearing to Ireland (without Porchey) to see Adele Cavendish for three weeks.

## Tilly's War

Tilly's name was rarely out of the American press gossip columns, with reports of her highs and lows and associations with male and female friends, some of whom no doubt became lovers. She was sought after to appear in charity events in Hollywood and New York. During the war years and afterwards she supported good causes, reprising some of her best performances from her Cochran days in London a decade and more previously. One series of appearances was for the British War Relief at the Rainbow Room on Broadway. [648]

As a display of her intention to return to Highclere in April 1941, Tilly gave a farewell dinner at New York's Waldorf-Astoria prior to returning to Britain to see Porchey, but as she prepared to pack she changed her mind.[649] This was the pattern over the next few years, because Tilly was genuinely afraid of being killed on board ship since the U-boat activity in the Atlantic was always at the back of her mind.

On this occasion in 1941 she was "Flying to England"[650] but it all fell through.

The next few years were another constant farce, played out between Porchey and Tilly by letter through their lawyers. One reason that Tilly cited for not coming back to Britain was the precarious health of her mother Eugenie. At the time of the premiere of *The Good Earth* in 1937 Tilly had learned that her mother was lying critically ill in her native Austria; she had her bags packed and a chartered plane standing by to fly her from Hollywood to New York, from where she would travel to Europe by sea. This journey was only cancelled after she received a long distance call telling her of her mother's improvement. Later, Eugenie went to live in the USA.

## Love Letters

The exchanges between Porchey and Tilly (by letter and cable) straddled the war's highs and lows.

They had sweet nicknames for each other – Tilly is described as 'my adored wifie' or 'pink pearl' and sometimes (even after they were divorced) as 'My beloved Tillykins.'

Porchey is often addressed as 'Porchey Poo'.[651]

A telegram sent to Tilly in New York demonstrates Porchey's urgent desire to see her:

"POSITIVELY PINING FOR PINK PEARL YOUR RETURN TICKET POSTED BY CUNARD HOPE MY LETTER RECEIVED MILLION KISSES. POO." [652]

Porchey persuaded family and even staff at Highclere to add their appeals to Tilly to return:

Crystal Stubbings,[653] Highclere's Land Agent, wrote to Tilly, "It will be no news to tell you how much his Lordship is longing for your return... He misses you terribly, and seems more lonely every day. ... I don't know what will happen to him if you do not come soon! Please forgive me if this seems presumptuous, but I thought you should know how he is feeling." [654]

# 1942

By day as war raged through Europe and in the Far East ( America entered the war the previous year after Pearl Harbour ). Many of Tilly's girlfriends had enlisted for useful war work. Tilly told Cecil Beaton in a letter that she " had been working for the Red Cross and [ hoped] someday to train as a nurse". [655] Meanwhile she was doing a lot of painting and had sold a few of her pictures to make ends meet.

At night  Tilly went to the opening of Fefe's *Monte Carlo Beach*, off Broadway,  with a cross section of the celebrity set, including Moss Hart and Sylvia Fairbanks.    A visit to the *Stork Club* and *El Morocco* followed where the company was more illustrious and full of starry Manhattan dwellers and incomers from  Hollywood . Among Tilly's oldest and closest chums ( with whom a spot of gin rummy was often played ) were the one time  "leading figures of Continental society"  [656] Sir Charles and Elsie Mendl,[657] who had fled their luxury home at Versailles when the Germans occupied Paris and bought  themselves a sizable property in Beverly Hills. Sir Charles was a diplomat,   Elsie [ De Wolfe ] oozed  chic, class and glamour, she had also been an actress and dyed her hair pale green.

## The Lawyer's Tongue

Also during  1942 Porchey made another impassioned plea (through his lawyers) to entice Tilly back to Britain. The text formed a part of the evidence in the subsequent proceedings taken by Porchey (in 1945) against Tilly for desertion.

"My Dear Lady Carnarvon

I am writing you this letter not only as Porchey's legal adviser; he has consulted me at some length recently and given me full access to all your letters and cables. As a result of this I find myself forced, for the sake of convenience, to enumerate.

(1) In June 1940 you persuaded P. much against his will to let you go to USA. You alleged that you desire to go and work there. You also said you would be bored living at Highclere whilst P. was serving with his Regiment and you left for U.S.A. the third week in June.

(2) You offered by cable to return in November of that year, and when P. joyfully accepted this offer you then pleaded ill health and it was agreed to defer your return until the spring of 1941.

(3) In April 1941 you intended to return but through a variety of muddles on your part you failed to do so. You again pleaded ill health and deferred the matter till the Summer. All this time repeated applications were made by P. for you to return and all without avail.

(4) In the late Autumn of last year you cabled categorically stating you would return in April and P. urged you to do so by air or sea. Up to date you have continued to make various excuses, namely, that you refused sea transport for fear of the risks involved; you state you hope to get a Clipper passage in due course.

So much for a brief resume of past events.

Now, as to the future,

P. has been extremely loyal to you during the very long time you have been away, and has put up with more than most husbands would tolerate. You must remember that you, his bride, left him after only ten weeks of married life, that you did not return till the middle of March 1940 and that even then you were away in Ireland for three weeks during the battle of France. You should remember, too, that his love for you is very real, so much so that he has resisted the efforts of many friends and relations to sever your marriage, efforts that have been far stronger and more persistent that you have any idea of.

I must impress upon you that P's strength and steadfastness has amazed me and that in my opinion it speaks volumes for the depth of his affection for you.

The time has come, though when P. can accept no more excuses for your absence. There is no difficulty in your returning from America, nor much delay if you use the normal means of travel, and still less risk.

P. is adamant and I think he is justified in being adamant that you return to him by September 1$^{st}$ at the latest. Now I want you to realise that and to understand what it means. It means that if you bestir yourself to come to him at once he will receive you with all the love and affection that he has always displayed towards you – and only you know the full and generous measure of that. It means that even if you delay your departure until the last possible moment that will get you home within the period I have mentioned, he will still accept without question the additional delay and welcome you back with open arms.

But it also means that if you do not accept this chance, if you do not at this late hour recognise your responsibilities and your obligations towards him - the door to Porchey's heart kept open for so long and in the face of so much discouragement will be closed and sealed against you for ever. And in Porchey's heart, in place of your own image which he has cherished so dearly all these years will be writ in unfading letters the word DESERTION.

I do hope, Lady Carnarvon that you will weigh carefully these words which I have written, that you will realise before it is to late not only that extent of your failure towards P. but the legal consequences which will inevitably follow if you disregard this last final and conclusive offer on his part.   It will be the end of everything between you. Surely it would be the acme of tragedy for you to allow a marriage so blessed as yours with every prospect of happiness and comfort to come to such a melancholy and bitter and conclusion?

I beg you not to make such a course necessary but instead, to pluck up your courage and return by sea so that you may enjoy many happy years together and I rely on your cabling me that you are heeding my advice."

# 1943

*Lord Porchester : Catherine's Son*

The Carnarvon Letters,[658] reproducing many dozens of the young Lord Porchester's correspondence (mostly exchanges with his parents and sister when he was serving in the army with the Royal Horse Guards in Egypt and Italy during the Second World War), contain a frantic flow of references to Tilly's litany of reasons to justify her continuing absence from Porchey's castle and his bed. The cable campaign was increased: Tilly received a number of telegrams from the Carnarvon brood, Herbert and Beauchamp alike and their followers, who pointed out (sometimes with added bile) that her rightful place was with her husband, in England.

Smartly, Tilly sometimes offered credible hope of her making a re-appearance. She claimed she was attempting to get clearance to come to Britain for an engagement with ENSA, to which organisation (involved in entertaining the troops) Jeanne Stuart was attached.

Although Porchey became agitated about Tilly, substitute hostess Jeanne Stuart was installed in a discreet fashion at Highclere, especially at weekends. Whilst the Earl's day job was variously spent in army training and administration, during which he rose from Captain to Lt. Colonel, Highclere was maintained as a centre for house parties (mainly shooting parties) made up of Porchey's inner circle of old Etonian chums and racing friends. Bert Marlborough, Lionel Montagu and Fred Darling, were regulars. Various family members stayed, to recuperate from the real or imagined privations of war.

Catherine never set foot in Highclere. Penelope had returned from the USA; she was working in the Foreign Office and lived with her mother (who did a bit of charity work during the war) and rented flats in Windsor and in London.

At Christmas Almina and her old sparring partner Dr Marcus Johnston[659] (Dr Johnnie) were at Highclere for family celebrations. Almina had given up nursing and had moved to a thatched cottage called Orchard Grove (with six acres of apple orchard) in the village of Bicknoller, North Somerset, with her new love interest, James Timothy Stocking.[660]

## Death of Rudolf K Kommer

1943 was a sad year for Tilly. On 28 March she was one of the first on the scene at the *Hotel Ambassadors*, New York when her great protector Rudolf K Kommer died in his sleep. She called Gottfried Reinhardt ( Max's son ) who joined her, and Tilly, Gottfried and the hotel manager entered Kommer's room to inspect the body and make arrangements for its collection. Exhausted after the loss of her mentor and guardian

Tilly told Cecil Beaton she was going to retreat to California,[661] to see her mother.

## 1944
## Tilly the Painter

*Tilly: The Artist*

As Europe braced itself for the D-Day landings in the spring of 1944, Tilly opened her first one-woman exhibition as a painter and artist. The show was held at New York's Bignou Gallery.

She told her followers: "I am very serious about my pictures...and I don't want people to think this is just a whim." [662]

One critic said "...her pictures are of slender figures, dreamy, airy, poetical in color and movement." The titles were emotive and personal, including "The Road Taken", "Evocation", "Anguish", "The Lady of the Sea" and "Two Angels". [663]

Tilly told her friends, "I never feel a painting is finished, and now that they are hung I am exhausted. Four straight ballets wouldn't do this to me. Pictures have a will of their own, but now that they are hung I feel exposed – as if I were dancing before people naked." [664]

Tilly attributed her artistic inspiration to the English artist (and her close friend) John Churchill, (nephew of Winston), who painted her portrait.

Another influence was in 1934 when Tilly met the artist and designer, Cathleen Mann [665]( Marchioness of Queenberry ) when Cathleen designed the costumes and backcloths for Cochran's musical revue *Streamline* at the Palace Theatre. They became friends, In 1936 Tilly's portrait by Cathleen Mann was exhibited at the Royal Society of Portrait painters, to acclaim from the critics. Mann was an influence on Tilly's own portraitures.

# 1945
## Desertion or Not?

After the war was over in 1945 Porchey sought a divorce from Tilly for desertion. The petition was heard in the High Court in London on 22 November 1945.

Porchey admitted misconduct with other women but his barrister said that Tilly had never been committed to the marriage, claiming that "in the motor car to the Register Office she said she wished she was not going to be married and she was not in love."[666]

Putting Porchey's case it was further argued that Tilly "preferred the luxury and friendship of Hollywood to the harsh and dangerous conditions in England, moreover that in the ." [667]

The Judge examined whether Tilly had left for America against Porchey's express will or whether he said she could go if she wished. The view was that Porchey had agreed to Tilly's request to leave, as she was to star in a play in New York. Quoting later correspondence between Tilly and Porchey the Judge commented, "So far as I am able to read her [Tilly's] mind from her letters and cables, she was in a confused and frightened state about her journey back."[668]

In discussing the petition Mr. Justice Bucknill said of Tilly, "I am not satisfied that she deserted her husband."[669]

The Judge read the lengthy correspondence between the Carnarvons, including a letter in which Tilly said, "I am terribly unhappy to be such a nuisance of a wife. I want to be in your arms, darling. I miss you, and love you so much." [670]

Mr. Justice Bucknill added: "I see no sufficient reason for thinking that her letters were insincere. Indeed, she wrote to her husband urging him to go to America. [671]

The Judge was critical of Porchey, with a snipe about the Earl's misconduct with Jeanne Stuart and lashing out a direct assault: "If he [Porchey] had not started to commit adultery in 1941 his wife might have returned to him."[672]

Porchey was devastated, the desertion action failed, and despite the costs incurred he was still married to Tilly.

## After the War but before the final Divorce
## 1946 : Porchey Sees Tilly in USA

When Porchey saw Tilly briefly on a trip to the USA in 1946, he appealed again to her to come back to England : promising her whatever it needed to make her happy: she declined. Dejected, but determined to make the most of his stay, Porchey embarked on a fishing holiday ( to reel in horses and women ). Always looking for publicity, and " beating his walking stick upon a concrete floor [ the] nattily dressed...forty-eight- year- old is          [ described as] stocky and tweedish….. in a Panama hat bashed back from his forehead, a tan grey suit, gold and green striped tie and brown and white sports oxfords…. He talked of both horses and people and went off to lunch with [ the publisher ] Frank Gannett . " [673] Later Porchey spent time with Gannett on Lake Ontario on board the Gannet yacht. The fishing trip was followed by a week at Saratoga Springs for the racing and horse sales. [674]

## Tilly snoops around Hollywood

*Tilly's erotic dance in The Garden of Allah*

In Hollywood Tilly became a regular partygoer, movie moguls, producers and directors inviting her to their social gatherings where she shone as brightly as ever, looking for a part in the next post-war epic.

One lighthearted report was that when she was seen with the film director Sir Alexander Korda (a native of Budapest, Hungary) at a party given by David Selznick, the host remarked that, "Ah, this must be a reunion of the Austrian-Hungarian Empire." "What do you mean, Australian-Hungarian Empire?" said Korda haughtily, taking the arm of Tilly, Countess of Carnarvon. This is a meeting of the British aristocracy."[675]

There can be little doubt that in earlier years Tilly had to fend off the amorous attentions of  Korda in London and in New York hotels. Dubbed     " a legendary womanizer in London ...as well as the city's foremost movie mogul" [676] his second wife ( from 1939-45)  was Merle Oberon ( who should have played alongside Tilly in 1936 movie *The Garden of Allah*, but was replaced by Deitrich).   Cecil Beaton adored photographing Tilly and Merle, they regularly travelled across the Atlantic together in the mid 1930s and later, but as the  girls suffered easily from sea sickness, they hid themselves away in their cabins.[677] But in 1946, Tilly,  Merle Oberon and Hedy Lamarr were considered " the most beautiful women in the world"    [678] by one motion picture magazine.

## Tilly Divorces Porchey

The Countess of Carnarvon (Tilly Losch, the dancer), now in New York, was granted a decree nisi against the Earl of Carnarvon yesterday, alleging his adultery with a woman named Jeanne Docker. The suit was undefended.

In 1945 Lord Carnarvon unsuccessfully petitioned for a divorce, alleging desertion. They were married in 1939.

*Daily Mirror, 23 July 1947*

Tilly eventually consented to a divorce Porchey in 1947. Jeanne Stuart, the actress, ( who spent more time at Highclere in Porchey's reach than on ENSA tours ),  was named in the later proceedings under the guise of Jeanne Docker. When the decree nisi was issued on 22 July, 1947, Tilly was back in New York.

*Jeanne Stuart, Lady Docker,*
*Porchey's bed warmer at Highclere during the War*

Porchey agreed to make a generous allowance which she appreciated. She continued to travel backwards and forwards between Britain and the USA for many years where, in the fullness of time, she was quite well thought of as a former stage and film actress.

She had one last request for Porchey. She sent him a four-page list of her wardrobe items remaining at Highclere, hoping that "it won't be too much trouble to sort them out and pack into my best white suitcases and either bring yourself or send by boat." [679]

## Tilly and Film

Charles Cochran thought that Tilly only toyed with the idea of film work. Her voice was considered too 'foreign' to turn her into a full-blown actress in speaking parts.

But the American playwright Joyce Sachs is kinder:

"Have you ever heard her [Tilly's] voice? I have. It was the most cultivated one I have ever heard – a slight Viennese accent and an overlay of a British one. A clear, modulated voice and highly intelligent." [680]

Cochran reflects on Tilly the film actress: "She got so far as to receive an offer from Hollywood, and appeared in a couple of 'pictures' there. But, despite the enthusiasm of powerful men in the film industry, this delightful artist did not have another chance in Hollywood. It was the old cry that a suitable story could not be found." [681]

Tilly's last major film role was in 1946 when her movie career was reinvigorated temporarily with an appearance with Jennifer Jones, Gregory Peck, Herbert Marshall and Joseph Cotton in King Vidor's torrid Western *Duel in the Sun*. Tilly was cast as Mrs Chavez, the Native American mother of the fiery half-breed Pearl Chavez, played by Jennifer Jones. At one point in the film Tilly dances on the top of a 102 foot rectangular bar. She was in Britain for its wider screenings of the picture in Europe.

In 1948 Tilly left Britain for New York, on the Queen Elizabeth liner on 7 July. Giving her London address as 60 Ebery Street, London SW7, she travelled with her maid Dorothy Dyer. Tilly gave her age as forty and her occupation as "Countess". [682] It may be said that she had been somewhat selective in fulfilling her job description.

Tilly's final years will be covered in a later Chapter.

# Chapter 15

## The Rest of the Carnarvons at War

*Porchey in the Uniform of the 7ᵗʰ Queens Own Hussars*

Some quarters of the British and American press defended both Porchey and Tilly's chequered pasts, saying they had been unlucky in love in their previous marriages. Whatever the truth these two larger than life characters with a taste for danger in the bedroom were soon to be tested by the very real dangers posed by the Luftwaffe.

Porchey received orders from the army which took him away from Highclere but only to the Kent coast. Meanwhile the Carnarvon's castle had become the home to several dozen children evacuated from London. One commentator cynically remarked that "the government had effectively taken over the marriage."[683] Porchey suggested that they take rooms in a London hotel; Tilly eventually conceded reluctantly. The earth only moved for her (and not in a good way) when the bombs started to fall around the *Ritz* hotel.

## Porchey gets a safe Desk Job

At the outbreak of the Second World War Porchey had returned to uniform, assuring Tilly (much to her dismay) that he would *not* be going off abroad to fight with the British Army against the Nazis.

True to his promise he was appointed Adjutant of the 6th Cavalry Training Regiment at Shorncliffe, Kent, albeit this Unit was closed down in 1940.

By 1940, the uneasiest year of the year by far, the country was in peril with the Battle of Britain to be won or lost. The previous year Porchey's original regiment, the 7th Queen Own Hussars, was in effect a Tank Regiment, having been transferred to the Royal Armoured Corps. The Regiment's War Diaries show that they took part in many great battles and campaigns in Europe and North Africa. [684]

Porchey was too old to be of use in the theatres of war. At the age of forty-two he was saved combat duties and given an ultra-safe desk job: it was a posting almost certainly fixed from on high. He began the war with the rank of Captain but was well enough placed to eventually become the Colonel commanding the Southern Region Claims Commission of the War Office, becoming Assistant Director in 1944.[685]

After Tilly left for America Porchey spent his weekends back at Highclere with a smattering of racing chums, often playing bridge, shooting and entertaining. He still had a resident French chef at Highclere who produced excellent cuisine so from Friday night to Sunday evening the pursuit of life, love and happiness carried on much as it had before. War? What war?

There were, however, sacrifices to be made for Porchey. Several members of the Highclere staff were caught up in the conflict and went overseas, including Porchey's valet (later butler) Robert Taylor who "later [commanded] a troop of tanks in Normandy." [686]

However, outside the house on the Highclere Estate matters were in good hands as Porchey had hired a remarkable woman, Christabel (Crystal) Ivy Stubbings as the Estate Agent. Her tenure at Highclere was a long one, and Porchey was blessed in having a successor to the members of the Rutherford family (whose links with the Estate went back to the time of the Fifth Earl), and with whom Porchey dealings were at times strained. In 1976 Porchey's dedication in his memoirs *No Regrets* was 'To My Dear Friend Crystal'. For many years she was a go-between for Almina and Porchey, especially when mother and son were are at odds with each other over money or family affairs. Almina remarked to her godson Tony Leadbetter that Stubbings made well-intended attempts at reconciliation between them. To Porchey's horror his managing agent often took Almina's side or was at the very least sympathetic to the Countess.

## A Telegram about Geoffrey Grenfell

War took its heavy toll of worry and grief on everyone. Catherine's husband, Lt Commander Geoffrey Grenfell, was transferred to the trawler HMS Juniper on 14 February 1940. These small craft were in service on the seas protecting other vessels, merchant ships and oil supply boats that were much less able to defend themselves, especially against submarines.

For all wives, mothers and their families the thing most dreaded in wartime was a telegram from the War Office or the Admiralty about their loved one. It usually was a harbinger of bad news.

On 16 August 1940 Catherine received a telegram at 34, Ovington Square, London which was devastating:

"FROM THE ADMIRALTY DEEPLY REGRET TO INFORM YOU THAT YOUR HUSBAND LIEUTENANT G S GRENFELL RN IS REPORTED MISSING ON ACTIVE SERVICE THOUGH POSSIBLY A PRISONER OF WAR".

This news was quickly followed by two stark letters repeating the information and explaining the arrangements to continue to pay a missing officer's allowances for a short time ( up to thirteen weeks), after which any payment was "suspended until a definite decision as to his fate can be made." [687]

## Gertrude Griffiths Remarries in Scotland

*Marian and Gertrude*

As August of 1940 continued, although Catherine was concerned about the fate of her husband Geoffrey she had to get on with other things regardless of the lost sleep and distress.

Though grappling in her mind with the possibility of her husband's death, Catherine's spirits were raised by getting away from the bombs and blackouts of London and going north of the border to Scotland to attend the wedding of Gertrude Griffiths to Lt-Colonel Francis Jolliffe Raitt of St James' Court, Buckingham Gate, London and the Yorkshire Club, York. Gertrude's pain over the years because of Percy's deceit and adultery had subsided; she felt herself blessed, more than forty years after her first marriage in the USA, in now finding a man who loved her dearly and with whom she could enjoy her remaining years.

Percy had been dead almost three years and the troubles over tying up his estate had also almost finally been resolved.

All that Gertrude wished for was to have those she especially loved to be at the wedding. The quiet, family only ceremony was held at All Saints' Episcopal Church, Challoch, Newton Stewart, in the Scottish Borders and in the very heart of the Stewartry. Apart from Catherine (listed as Mrs Geoffrey Grenfell), the other witness was Catherine's mother, Marian Wendell, with the main arrangements being made by the Earl and Countess of Galloway. The Countess, of course, was once Philippa Fendall Wendell, Catherine's younger sister, Marian's daughter. The two children of the Galloways, twelve-year-old Lord Garlies and fifteen year old Lady Antonia Stewart, were also present. The Galloways laid on a glorious wedding breakfast afterwards at their nearby residence of Cumloden, Newton Stewart. [688]

Thinking always about Geoffrey, Catherine was in a solemn mood and at her most vulnerable. She spoke to Almina by telephone every day and was in touch with her housekeeper at Ovington Square, in case of any news.

With the backdrop of this remote Scottish border landscape Catherine stayed away from the temptations of the bottle by accompanying her nephew Randolph, Lord Garlies (who was her godson), on rambles through the heather with his dogs and attending to the whims of her blossoming niece, Lady Antonia, as she approached her debutante years. Catherine greatly missed her own daughter, Penelope, being nearby but it was a godsend that she had been able to see through her education under the care of cousin Arthur Wendell and his wife, in America.

However, safe as Penelope was, the same was not true of Geoffrey. Catherine's private grief had created a deep inner darkness but seeing her closest family again had given her a sense of worth; moreover she had to stay strong for her son Henry, Lord Porchester, whose army call-up was bound to come if the war continued.

# Mary Wendell Van der Woude

Barrett Wendell's daughter Mary was a regular family contact at Highclere and London. Whilst Almina couldn't stand her she was a reliable ally and confidante to Catherine at times of great pain and adversity.

Mary was the chief chronicler on the death of her cousin Reggie (Catherine's brother) in 1928. Mary's letters to her mother whom she calls 'Pearl' (the family thrived on its nicknames for each other) comprise a substantial legacy in the Wendell Family Archives in the Portsmouth Athenaeum, New Hampshire, USA.

Ronan Donohoe of the Athenaeum advises:

"Re: Mary van der Woude. She is a big favorite of mine for several reasons but mainly because the Athenaeum has boxes and boxes of her correspondence and much of it is highly entertaining as well as informative. She wrote to her mother (Mrs. Barrett Wendell - nee Edith Greenough) and to her sister (Mrs. Charles Osburne - nee Edith Wendell) several times each week from the time she went to Shanghai with her first husband (Tom Wheelock) in the early years of the last century to her death as Mrs. Reinier van der Woude at Heronden in Kent a half-century later. There's a great letter describing her capture of a German pilot who dropped out of the sky onto her tennis court in the war years: that is right out of Mrs. Miniver. She was very aware of Catherine's difficulties and applauded her conversion to the Roman Church (Farm Street) as possibly providing the stability she needed. She refers to her own marriage as 'another casualty of the war.' Prince Bernhardt was often a house guest at Heronden while Reiner van der Woude was with Royal Dutch Shell....... She frequently speaks of Porchey as depraved and disgusting." [689]

The reference to her marriage being affected by war is of note. Her second husband was President of Shell Petrol Corporation, New York. Mary preferred life in England.

She was not without her own blemishes. "Mary took stationery from every hotel, ship and boozing shed she ever visited." [690]

In the dark days of December 1940 she made a seemingly major error of judgement after being involved with Squadron Leader Murray Armstrong Payn who was convalescing (from a strained heart) with Mary in her spacious Georgian house, Heronden, in the village of Eastry, Kent. She had driven Armstrong Payn to a harbour area between Margate and Hythe where he proceeded to sketch the scene. A corporal was watching and he thought that Armstrong Payn (who was not in uniform) was writing things down. Overhead there were German planes droning.

Both Mary and Armstrong Payn were prosecuted under the Defence of the Realm Act. They appeared before Magistrates at Wingham (near Canterbury) to answer the charges.

Mary was summoned for allowing her car to be driven without a permit in a defence area. She bears comparison with Joan of Arc in the commanding way she conducted her own defence:

"I am the only alien [American] allowed to live in the defence area. I have lived here for years. All this could have been avoided if I had got a car permit..."[691]

In defending her RAF friend she was indefatigable:

"I can't possibly let Murray (acting Squadron Leader Murray Armstrong Payn) get into this trouble. He is an RAF flying instructor. Eleven of his pupils have won the DFC". [692]

Payn was charged on two counts of driving a car within a five mile coastal belt without a permit and of attempting to make a sketch of a harbour and other defence works. Both culprits eventually pleaded guilty and were fined.

Mary Van der Woude survived until 1975. Her death intimation in *The Times* summed up a one-off character:

"DEATHS: Van der Woude: On Dec 17 1975 peacefully, Mary (nee Wendell) aged 92, after a full and rewarding life." [693]

# 1941

## Lt Commander Geoffrey Seymour Grenfell's Death Confirmed

Catherine's anxiety over Geoffrey was greater than ever. After nine months of waiting for news that he might be a prisoner of war there was finally word. It was the worst of news. On 8 February 1941 Catherine learned officially that her loving husband Lt Commander Geoffrey Seymour Grenfell had been killed in action commanding HM Trawler Juniper [694] on 8 June 1940, in an incident off Norway. The Juniper had been escorting an oil tanker, Oil Pioneer.

The official SECRET record of 15 June 1940 indicates that: "Juniper left Malangen Fiord at 13.45/5 in company with Oil Pioneer. She is now long overdue and must be presumed lost; it appears possible she was the "Modern U-Boar Chaser" claimed by the Germans to have been sunk with OIL PIONEER". [695]

There was no doubt, even though he was "presumed dead" following the events more than six months before. The formal presumption of Geoffrey's death was given as 18 June 1940.

There were small crumbs of comfort; Catherine knew that Geoffrey lived to be at sea and fight for his country. As a youth he had been a Dartmouth sea cadet and a brave midshipman during the Battle of Jutland at the time of the Great War. Later, in business, he was never at home in the Stock Exchange but although he was a successful stockbroker with Grenfell & Co he always looked to sail and cast his eye away from the land out to some point on the ocean.

The Admiralty papers on the loss of the Juniper indicate that the authorities were in possession of the facts on 7 September 1940. This information was contained in a letter intercepted by Naval Section (Censorship) from a son (Steward H D Curtis, one of the few survivors among Geoffrey's crew) to his mother in Great Yarmouth:

Son writes to his mother:

"Out of the crew of 27, only 3 were saved – my chum Stoker Turrell of Yarmouth and one wireless operator of London.

On June 7 [1940] at 5.30am we sighted 2 Destroyers and 2 Cruisers and as we were only 28 hours away from Scapa, we thought they were the British Navy, then we saw they weren't flying the White Ensign, we fired once on one side, the engines were still going full speed, the Chief Engineer rushed away from the engine-room and died in my arms. Every man stood to his post until last.....the ship sank in 5 minutes. The Tanker we escorted was torpedoed, out of the crew of 45 only 16 were saved." [696]

Catherine was seeing out the war (with other family members) at the Imperial Hotel, Torquay. On 13 February 1941 she wrote to the Admiralty for the names of the survivors from Geoffrey's ship, with a view to contacting them (for any further details about Geoffrey and the Juniper's ill-fated voyage) and to offer her best wishes for their recovery. [697]

*The Times* of 6 March 1941 carried an obituary of the man whom Catherine had first known though the social contacts of her late (much missed) brother Reggie, but with whom she had only enjoyed a very brief but contented married life; one that, with the outbreak of war, had always been spent on the edge, waiting. Catherine told Almina that she "never regretted marrying Geoffrey". [698]

Whilst Catherine was further comforted by hearing that Geoffrey and his crew "had courageously engaged a German armoured cruiser", it was harder to take in that the Juniper had been "inevitably overwhelmed, but [the guns of the ship] went on firing until the end came and after all her officers had been killed." Her grief was total, but through support from her mother, Marian and Almina, she came through the tragedy better than expected. Her Catholic faith also became more important and she initially turned more to this for refuge than to alcohol.

Geoffrey's Last Will and Testament was a tribute to the man's inner conflict with himself. He abandoned his first marriage but felt a conscience over the future of his divorced wife and small daughter. He also felt an equal commitment to Catherine. Accordingly his estate was (with some long legal paragraphs) divided up amongst the three women who most mourned his loss: a wife, Catherine, an ex-wife, Sybil, and an only child, his daughter Elizabeth Mary. [699]

The RNPS Memorial at Lowestoft contains Geoffrey's name as well as the rest of the crew of H M Trawler Juniper who died with him.

In 1946 Geoffrey's stockbroking firm Grenfell and Co (of 62 London Wall, EC2) wrote to the Admiralty to say that they proposed hanging his photograph in the Board Room with an inscription about his death during war service.

## Lady Penelope Herbert in the USA

*Happy Family Outing, Porchey, Penelope and Catherine*

Catherine received news from her daughter Lady Penelope who was continuing her schooling at Foxcroft School, Virginia, USA during the early years of the Second World War; this was a precaution taken by several of the gentry with American families. Edwina Mountbatten was another such mother; she sent her daughter Pamela Mountbatten to stay with Mrs Cornelius Vanderbilt. [700]

The adjustment for Catherine of not having Penelope nearby was a more difficult one. As for Penelope, she was least affected as several of her best friends were with her in America.

Acknowledging Porchey's paternal rights Catherine had sought permission from the High Court to effect the overseas journey for Penelope to stay with 'Cousin' Arthur Wendell. Penelope was close to both her parents and during her time in USA she was also entertained by her Wendell-Van der Woude cousins. Reiner Gerrit van der Woude lived at The Old Mackie House, Southampton, and Long Island, New York.[701]

On her return from America in 1943 Penelope lived with her mother again at Windsor and later in London, although she was often at Highclere too. She worked in the Foreign Office along with her close friend Elizabeth Winn,[702] whilst a number of her other contemporaries including Elizabeth's sister Anne (who had been with Penelope in America) worked with the code breakers at Bletchley Park.

Catherine found solace during Penelope's time in the USA in that her daughter was being cared for by an old family retainer; the same woman, Mlle Huc (known as Doll) who had first been a maid and later was Lord Porchester's adored French governess.[703]

## Lord Porchester at Eton and Army Service in WW2

Catherine's son, Lord Porchester, was one of fifty boys who left Eton in December 1941.[704] He was at Eton at the same time as his Wendell cousin Gerrit Van der Woude who was later to marry Porchester's sister, Penelope.

Among Porchester's great school friends who left Eton at the same time at him was Patrick, Lord Plunket,[705] whose parents were killed in a plane crash in California in 1938. Both Plunket and Porchester had known each other from childhood[706] and became further involved with each other (after the war) as members of the Royal Household; and both were known for being in the inner circle of Princesses Elizabeth and Margaret. .

Lord Porchester served in the Second World War as a Lieutenant in the Royal Horse Guards, 1st Household Cavalry Regiment, in Egypt and Italy. Porchester's wartime letters to and from his father (Darling Pups) and Catherine and others from 1943-44 were published in 1994.[707] The outpourings of affection and love in the inter-relationships is impressive and moving. Only Tilly Losch was slated by everyone. Catherine remarks of Tilly in one letter to Porchester saying "She really is rotten".
[708]

## Porchey, a Godfather

It may be pushing it a bit to say there was a spiritual as well as a temporal side to Porchey but during the war he became godfather to the daughter of his racing pal Sidney Beer, who also looked out for Catherine's welfare. Beer made a heroic contribution to national morale in the Second World War by organising concerts and musical events. He was also linked with the Salzburg Festival where he knew Tilly Losch very well.

References to Sidney Beer feature from time to time in *"The Carnarvon Letters"*.[709]

*The Carnarvon Letters* are full of domestic tittle-tattle from Porchey, lording it (in all senses of the word) at Highclere over the comings and goings over two years. Interestingly they list many of the personalities, especially in the racing world and Porchey's fellow Clubmen. It is also a source to glean the ups and downs of the health and wellbeing of family members.

Lord Porchester, away fighting for King and Country and with advice from his father to keep his head down and resist being a dead hero, was already a name in the racing world with his own horses and ambitions to own more. He was also a good racing tipster. Catherine's letters to her son and the few from Lady Penelope (Pen), Marian (Gar), Gertrude (Aunty Bunny) and one from Almina (Granny) are full of hope that their soldier boy will survive the conflict and come safely back home again.

## Porchey's Royal Butler Sent to Prison

In 1942 one of Porchey's staff who was acting as a stand-in butler was arrested by the police. The man had been lying low since 1940 when he was employed as butler at Windsor Castle. He had disappeared from there after stealing a gold cigarette case, a diamond and turquoise tiepin and diamond cuff links valued at £100 from Sir John Hanbury-Williams, Extra-Equerry to the King. The butler was also accused of drinking the King's whisky and replacing it with coloured water. At the trial at Windsor the man was sentenced to three months imprisonment.[710]

Porchey loved retelling the story at his London Clubs of the King drinking watered down whisky and of apparently not detecting any dilution.

## Mysterious Death of Prince George, Duke of Kent

Catherine was pole-axed by the death of her one-time lover, a gentle man who was always her friend and helper, the dashing PG, Duke of Kent. The Prince was killed (in circumstances that remain mysterious even today over seventy years later) when the plane (flight W4026) he was travelling in crashed in Scotland.

One summary is that the Prince's "flying boat left Invergordon carrying the Duke of Kent and three members of his staff. After about 60 miles after taking off the plane ploughed into a hill called Eagle's Rock in the Caithness area in low cloud. All but one of those on board was killed."[711]

Porchey's cousin Sidney Herbert (heir to the Earldom of Pembroke and Montgomery and one of PG's equerries) was supposed to have been on board but he took ill before the flight and had a lucky escape.

On top of the distress brought on by Geoffrey's loss, coupled with the loss of friends, Catherine was inconsolable. So many deaths came back to remind her of those she had regarded as a guiding light: Reggie, Helen Cunliffe-Owen, Geoffrey and now PG. However, there was still support she could rely on: her mother, Marian, who was also upset by the toll the grim reaper was taking. Almina saw Catherine at once, too, and suggested a short spell in her nursing home at Barnet, which Catherine appreciated; she preferred a complete withdrawal into a retreat. Philippa also offered refuge at Cumloden.

## Carnarvon Women: War Services

All the Carnarvon, Carr and Wendell women made their own individual contribution to war work, raising funds and working in canteens and hospitals.

In Somerset Almina was a regular visitor to the American Military Hospital at Musgrove Park, Minehead (known as the 67th General Hospital), and was especially active in the days after the D-Day landings with morale-boosting visits to the wounded GIs. She made friends among several American doctors including Gordon Johnston[712] of Maine whose daughter Jane has fine memories of her father renewing his acquaintance with Almina in the 1960s.

## Visit to Almina by Porchey

*Orchard Grove*

266

Porchey visited his mother at Orchard Grove, Bicknoller, only once during the war years. This meant a major operation on Almina's part to remove every trace from the cottage that there was a man living with her, namely James Timothy Stocking (whom Almina forced to change his surname to Stocks but he was always known as 'JTS' or sometimes 'Tim'). The cover-up was successful. Porchey was convinced Almina was living quietly on her own with her housekeeper Alice Butler, although the truth was that JTS (a man twenty years younger than Almina) was a fixture in her life and remained so for the next twenty years, quite unknown to Highclere.

*Almina Ruling the Roost at Orchard Grove, with JTS,*
*and Tony and Anne Leadbetter*

Porchey refers to the visit in a letter to Lord Porchester dated 20 March, 1944

"I completed a successful tour of the West Country last week, which I rather enjoyed.....I lunched with Granny [Almina] and I must say she gave me an excellent meal, including Dover Soles, which I have not seen for many a long day." [713]

## Marian Wendell Safe at Hemingford Park

After Gertrude Griffiths moved to Scotland, Marian Wendell spent more time with Catherine in London and at the Imperial Hotel in Torquay but the disruption caused by the war forced her to seek out a new sanctuary with her Carr in-laws at Hemingford Park, St Ives, Huntingdonshire, in a Georgian Mansion sitting within several hundred acres. She was on good terms with her son Jac's mother-in-law Louis[714] and spent some time there in safety whilst London was bombed to smithereens. The Carrs lived well and Louis, a widow since 1931, was comfortably off. Wartime restrictions on the use of petrol (something that Almina was most indignant about complying with) led to both Louis Carr and her daughter Eileen Wendell (Jac's wife) being prosecuted for breaching the rules and on summons they appeared at Cambridge Assizes, to be fined the princely sums of £250 and £100 each.[715]

## 1944

Catherine was feeling very unwell and she consulted Almina, who recommended an operation. This was subsequently performed by a surgeon, Eric Gordon Steeler of 5, Devonshire Place, London; he specialised in ENT surgery. [716]

Illness put an end to Catherine being socially and even romantically linked with Sir Gifford Fox,[717] of whom Porchester was concerned enough to enquire of his father on his credentials. The gentleman in question was in any case still married and Catherine resisted his charms.

In September 1944 Alice Butler welcomed her sister Anne Leadbetter to Almina's home at Orchard Grove, Bicknoller, along with Anne's six-year- old son Tony, who survives and who advises:

"The domestic scene at Orchard Grove was that my Aunt Alice was the cook and housekeeper. My mother arrived there in 1944 (for a holiday) and offered to do some general mending and Almina soon discovered her talents for making clothes. We stayed on, my father was left behind in London (and when he once appeared, was banished by Almina). My mother was with Almina until she died only a few weeks before Almina, in 1969."

Gertrude (Griffiths) Raitt was widowed on 29 September 1944.[718] After the war she later moved back to London.

## Catherine's Religious Conversion

With the return of Lady Penelope from America,  coupled with the comfort gleaned from receiving regular news in  Porchester's letters from overseas - which  eased her mind- there was a lull in Catherine's heavy drinking. Porchey comments  were that " she is now off the drink for ever!" [719]

The cure ( which it was by no means ) was more of a steady remission but it  had been achieved in part by Catherine's conversion to the Roman Catholic faith and the ministering of  her friend Doll who stood as her sponsor – her   " godmother at  Westminster Cathedral"[720]  when she took the baptismal name of ' Mary Herbert' .  Catherine's retreat was at the Augustinian Sisters of Meaux,  [721]'Bethanie' Convent, in North London at Highgate.

# 1945

## Fixing Porchester's Safety

On Lord Porchester's return to Britain from Italy ( before his Regiment had been excused further service in the theatres of War[722] ) it was fixed from on high for him to continue as a soldier in the Mounted Squadron in London. He was not invalided out of the Royal Horse Guards until 1947, but was assigned from at least the summer of 1946 onwards to the Royal Household at Windsor Castle. Before this he carried out various ceremonial duties, including being part of the Sovereign's Escort in the procession to St Paul Cathedral for the Thanksgiving Service on VE Day on 8 May, 1945.

## Lord Porchester Celebrates his 21st Birthday
## Almina and Catherine Conspire on a Cake

*At Highclere for Porchester's 21st Birthday*

Lord Porchester's coming-of-age was celebrated in January 1945.

Tony Leadbetter has good reason to remember these celebrations for Lord Porchester's twenty-first birthday. For several weeks, as a seven-year-old he had been in on the big surprise between Almina, Catherine, Almina's housekeeper (Tony's aunt Alice Butler) and Alice's sister Anne (Tony's mother).

As far as Almina was concerned the event of her grandson's legal coming-of-age must be given a very special memory. It was the climax of a great conspiracy between her and Catherine to mark Porchester's glorious moment with a huge celebratory cake made by Alice.

With rationing the ingredients for the cake had been obtained over many months of hard struggle. The cake was to be iced in the colours of Eton College, to remind Porchester of happier days than his time spent in war-torn Europe.

Tony recalls the journey of the cake, ultimately to Highclere from Bicknoller and through London's Paddington Railway Station:

"I didn't see the baking of the cake; that had all been organised by Almina and Alice.

Alice made the cake especially for Lord Porchester in the Eton College colours of blue and black. There was a limousine at Paddington Station waiting for us to alight from the first class carriage of the train from Taunton. We went straight into the back of the limousine, where Catherine (who was then Mrs Geoffrey Grenfell) was sitting in a fur coat. Almina was in her furs too, it was January and very cold. The cake was carefully put in the boot of the car. We all went off to the Cumberland Hotel for lunch.

That evening in London Lord Porchester saw Almina (and later sent a message of thanks to Alice); he was going out night clubbing and invited his granny to go along. I don't know whether she did, but she was invited.

Later there was a big gathering a Highclere and great celebrations. Almina was very fond of the photograph taken of the whole family at the time. It was one of the few times everybody was happy."

## Lady Penelope Herbert marries Gerrit van der Woude

*Catherine, Porchey, Lord Porchester and Almina*

Catherine and Porchey's daughter Penelope married her cousin Gerrit van der Woude of the Grenadier Guards and whose paternal family was of Dutch origin. The wedding took place quietly at Highclere on 21 April 1945. On 10 May 1945 Catherine and Porchey held a reception at the Dorchester to celebrate their daughter's marriage and a large number of the friends of the couple were present.

During the war Catherine was living sometime at 5, Berkeley House, Hay Hill, London W1. The war caused her to move away from time to time.

## Almina's Opposition Ignored

*Almina, Countess of Carnarvon , who ran a series of nursing homes from 1914 until 1943*

Almina was against Penelope's wedding on the grounds that the parties were Wendell cousins. She had seen the devastating effects of such close marital unions, not least with the dire health problems and early deaths that beset the Fifth Earl's two half-brothers, Aubrey and Mervyn, who were born after the Fourth Earl married his cousin Elsie Howard. Almina's instincts were right; Penelope and Gerrit's daughter Catherine was born severely disabled and only lived until she was twenty-five but they also had two sons who survived without problems.[723]

# Chapter 16

## Brave New Worlds

## Princess Elizabeth Expects

By 1945, Catherine's son, Henry, Lord Porchester was already on close personal terms with Princess Elizabeth.[724] He had been her watchman when the two young Princesses ( dressed incognito) had brushed shoulders with the massive crowd cheering in the Mall on VE Day.

One of the next sightings of the two friends was in the enclosure at the running of the St Leger race meeting, at York, in September 1945. Thereafter it was expected that Porchester would ensure the heir to the throne was minded. It was *never* a burden to Porchester.

*Princess Elizabeth with Lord Porchester, September 1945*

Porchester resumed horseback on 12 May, 1947 when he formed part of the Sovereign's escort when the Royal Family ( in open landaus) returned to London ( to roaring crowds) after a tour of South Africa, which took the King, Queen and the two Princesses away from Britain for over three months. Soon after this Princess Elizabeth's announced her engagement to Prince Philip.

*Lord Porchester ( extreme left, on horseback ) as part of the Sovereign's Escort, 1947*

The King and Queen were both very fond of Porchester, he was knowledgeable of horse racing and a good shot ( two things King George VI particularly enjoyed as man sports and as conversation). Besides, cajoling his monarch being dubbed " the son the King never had" [725], Henry proved an amusing companion, confidante and guide for the two Princesses when the girls needed to be made aware ( from someone of about their own age ) of how best to cope with the Society pressures but also have some fun with an escort for balls and parties who was safe company. Princesses Elizabeth and Margaret liked Porchester, so it was no chore to have him around. Charming, rich and fanciable, Porchester was a popular member of the Royal Household, as an unofficial ADC with the welfare, amusement and happiness of the two Princesses as his principal portfolio. [726]

Almina was thrilled at Porchester's meteoric rise and Henry wrote short notes to his granny of the Royal shooting bags and social goings-on with the two Princesses and courtiers. [727] Catherine was told frankly to be more cautious about her drinking habits, appearances in public and gambling sprees and avoid acquiring any involvement with new men friends that might attract the attentions of an inquisitivey hack looking for a story ( which might embarrass).

There was to be no sharing of the limelight for the doting Catherine in Henry's exalted social statusion : she could only watch Henry' glory days fulfilling his Royal duties from the sidelines and behave with exemplary tact and self control. This period of denial was one of Catherine's darkest hours, she felt humiliated and wounded by Porchester's snub.[728] It was Almina who helped Catherine to come to terms with such ostracism and avoid further thoughts of suicide.

For Princess Elizabeth the shared passion with Henry ( that fired their mutual worship ) was for horses ( riding and breeding). She clicked with Porchester – ensuring an umbilical relationship that lasted until his death, in 2001.

In a pathetically touching scene when Porchester suffered a massive fatal heart attack ( whilst changing channels on his TV remote control, at Highclere, whilst watching the Twin Towers crash down on 9/11[729]) his last conscious thought on earth was to ensure his family passed vital information to the Queen about one of her horses. An informant ( amongst the Queen Mother's friends and private household) advises that " the Queen was devastated " [730]at Porchester's sudden loss, weeping visibly in public when she later broke with court custom and *personally* attended the Earl's funeral.

The blissful memory of working with Porchester must forever be in Her Majesty's thoughts, she was frequently at Highclere during her free weekends, sharing the family's usual, no frills Sunday lunch at Milford House, something that continued after the Earl's death, her present racing manager – now ranked as racing adviser and bloodstock manager is Porchester's son-in-law, John Warren. Jeannie, the Dowager, Countess ( Porchester's widow ) has occasionally stood in as an extra Lady in Waiting as the queen and her party parade in horse drawn landaus down the course at Royal Ascot.

Much had been written about whether the Queen's son, Andrew, Duke of York who appeared unexpectedly ( in 1960) was Porchester's son, especially after Prince Philip's long drawn out marital exclusion by the Queen over his nocturnal escapades [731] including associations with the notorious Society painter, medic (cum-playboy- pimp), Stephen Ward, remembered for his suicide at the time of the Profumo scandal of 1963. In the late 1950s Prince Philip's presence at Highclere for charity matches of polo and cricket indicates his acceptance of Porchester's position. In the late 1940s the Duke and Duchess of Edinburgh began a long drawn custom of making private visits to Highclere. [732] More often this was to Milford House, which although beautiful, was limited by space ( owing to its single storey architecture ) leading to special security apartments being built to ensure the Queen's greater comfort, wellbeing and maximum safety. [733]

Whilst the evidence of paternity of Andrew is conflicting : nonetheless the two old friends monarch and Highclere squire cherished their undisclosed time together and personal correspondence.[734] In their early days the adjoining houses and landscapes of Sandringham and especially Birkhall ( on the Balmoral Estate, a great favourite of Queen Elizabeth, later the Queen Mother [735]) were secret hideaways where *only* the closest of their privileged class could meet, relax, shoot grouse and be sure of privacy. The role of racing manager ( from 1969) gave the the Queen and Porchester continuous pleasure, there was however one dark blemish in 1988 concerning the sacking ( under the guise of the termination of a lease) of the Queen's champion trainer Dick Hearn ( who had been badly injured in an accident ). Described as "the saddest, nastiest, episode in racing history"[736] neither Porchester nor the monarch came out of it smelling of roses. [737]

*Princess Margaret Rose and her escort, Lord Porchester*

Back in the 1940s, given Porchester's profile it was inevitable that the heir to the Carnarvon Earldom would a trusted member of Princess Margaret's inner circle. Porchester was often on board the plane of the King's flight ( which daily took despatches to the monarch around HM's Royal Palaces or wherever the King was residing out of London). The King expected Princess Elizabeth's ever-faithful beau to see that Margaret ( always less obedient than her sister ) was kept contented but if necessary restrained. Porchester learned that the secret was to have several people around the Princess with whom she could flirt. [738] Other young aristocrats were brought on board to provide Margaret with a coterie of coronets. It was a case of history repeating itself a generation later, as one of these pro- Margaret men was Sunny Blandford, ( son of old Porchey's partner in crime, Bert Marlborough) the Blenheim heir, today the Eleventh Duke.[739] Whilst Princess Elizabeth retreated quietly into the background ( for Prince Charles to be born ) the headlines in the popular press of August 1948 were full of reports of sightings of Blandford and the eighteen-year-old Princess enjoying late nights out together dancing at night spots including *Club 400.*[740] Margaret also accepted an invitation from Porchester's father's old sweetheart Maureen, Marchioness of Dufferin and Ava, to 'a bit of a do' at the exclusive *Hurlingham Club* where she danced the night away in a whirl of organdie and diamonds.

Others in the early rounds on Margaret watch were Michael Tree, son of the wealthy, bisexual Ronald Tree, who provided his stately home at *Ditchley*, Oxfordshire as a refuge for Churchill, " when the moon was high"[741] during the Second World War. Ditchley also provided a bolt hole Alice Butler Almina's housekeeper was discovered *in flagrante* with JTS, (Almina's paramour ) Alice was summarily banished ending up in *Ditchley* where she fell on her feet, becoming a close companion and nursemaid to Marietta[742], Ronald's second wife and their children, She stayed with the Trees for decades sharing their luxurious way of live in New York and the sunshine of Barbados,( the Trees having left Britain in the late 1940s).

Princess Margaret's would-be suitors came and went. Michael Tree ( who served in the Royal Horse Guards with Porchester ) married Anne Cavendish in 1949, Blandford married Susan Hornby in 1951, with the Princess peering at them nervously as they walked down the aisle. The later crisis around Margaret's one true love, Peter Townsend brought only anguish and eventually Margaret was beaten into submission. [743]

Porchester took a back seat but never ceased to be on call for either Princess. For a time it appeared wedding bells might be on the horizon for Margaret and Porchester, Tilly was asked her view. She said she was excited " at the news that Princess Margaret Rose's new beau [ was] Lord Porchester….If they get married, ( she calculated ) it would make me the ex-stepmother-in-law of a Royal Princess…" [744].

# 1947

## Jeanne Stuart
## Announces She Will Marry Porchey

*Jeanne Stuart*

It seems that the actress Jeanne Stuart (who had kept Porchey's spirits up at Highclere during the War and later, despite being missing for some of the time on an ENSA tour in 1944 ) was proud that her name was cited by Tilly in the divorce proceedings. After the case was heard in Court, Jeanne was approached. She was in Hollywood working on a movie.

She left no doubt about her six years relationship with Porchey and she told reporters she was going to marry Porchey:

"I expect to be married to Lord Carnarvon when the decree is made absolute"[745] [a process that takes six weeks].

She added "I've been in love with [Porchey] for six years. I'd like the wedding to take place in England, but I can't say when or where exactly until I see the Earl."

Meanwhile Porchey had arrived in New York two days before Jeanne's declaration of love. He was already *en route* to Hollywood to be reunited with his Countess in waiting.

There was no wedding. Jeanne and Porchey parted friends, she later married Baron Eugene de Rothschild and lived out her life in America and the South of France.

## Tilly in London and New York

Meanwhile Tilly was often spotted dining out in the best restaurants and clubs in London and New York with Hollywood royalty and hacks reported her presence. The records from diary and memoir writers at the times were plenty, for example:

"Dined at 'La Maze', where among other people were Greer Garson and Tilly Losch." [746]

## 1948

## Catherine is feeling the pinch

In 1948 Catherine was up against it financially and Christie's sold various objects that she had inherited from Geoffrey's estate.[747] In the following year Catherine was greatly saddened at the death of Eric Allden[748] who had been one of her mentors and spiritual advisers when she converted to the Roman Catholic faith during the war.

# 1949

In Hollywood, Tilly Losch had a new romantic interest and her new man was a prominent psychiatrist, Dr Frederick Hacker.[749] Dance guru George Jackson succinctly puts his finger on things in his reflection: "Romance and having suitable admirers was, I believe, very important for Tilly even towards the end of her life." [750]

Back in London, Catherine headed the mourners at a memorial service for Gertrude Raitt (formerly Mrs Percy Griffiths) held at St Mark's North Audley Street, on 27 July 1949.[751] Lord Porchester attended, along with Eileen Wendell, Eileen's daughter June and Mary van der Woude.[752] Lady Evelyn Beauchamp represented Almina who was still in Somerset, tied up with selling off Orchard Grove, her thatched cottage home at Bicknoller with six acres of apple orchard, and moving to a property at nearby Higher Hopcott and then to a rented cottage at Cleeve.

Catherine mentioned Almina's changing circumstances to Porchester as she was concerned about her ex-mother-in-law's income tax situation. Porchester was not able to act quickly and consulted his father, who had the means to pay off Almina's debts. Ironically the situation was akin to the one in 1923-5 when Porchey faced paying off the Fifth Earl's death duties (which Almina had the funds to settle, but didn't).

This tax issue snowballed. Almina received £9,000 from the proceeds of selling Orchard Grove, Bicknoller and from this she ought to have repaid Porchey a loan of £5,000 he had given her in 1943 to buy the property. Almina was in no mood to pass on anything to Porchey who, as far as she was concerned, didn't need the money as he was at doing pretty nicely, thank you, after several good horse sales.

Almina underestimated her son's demand for the money, especially since she had not even told him she had sold the house. Porchey was in no mood to be denied his outstanding loan of £5,000. The exchanges between them were vile; he wrote several times calling his mother "a scheming swindler". Almina would not retreat; Porchey was equally uncompromising and decided to report his mother to the income tax authorities who very quickly discovered that Almina's affairs had been badly neglected, with outstanding sums of surtax owing. It did not help that Almina's accountant had withheld (and spent) sums she had set aside for tax. In 1951 Almina was eventually made bankrupt and she declared defiantly, "My family wanted me bankrupt, they got what they deserve".[753]

## Death of Catherine's Mother, Marian Wendell

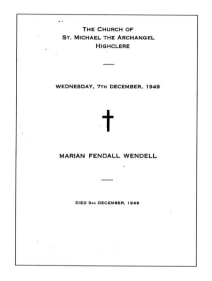

THE CHURCH OF
ST. MICHAEL THE ARCHANGEL
HIGHCLERE

—

WEDNESDAY, 7TH DECEMBER, 1949

✝

MARIAN FENDALL WENDELL

—

DIED 3RD DECEMBER, 1949

*Marian Fendall Wendall ( 1870-1949)*

Marian Wendell, whose courage on becoming a widow in 1911 caused her to bring her family to Britain to settle, died on 3 December 1949 at Catherine's London home, 11 Wilton Crescent. Although described as being of a quiet nature, "a reserved and unostentatious woman", Marian was the unreserved driving force (along with Gertrude Griffiths) in having her children married off in style into wealthy or titled British families  So much so that one commentator said she merited comparison with Queen Marie of Romania (a friend of Almina, well known in the Balkans for staging royal alliances) after three such highly successful matches, moreover with no great wealth behind her to pull it off. [754]

The funeral for Marian was at St Michael's and All Angels Church, Highclere on 7 December; she was interred alongside her beloved son Reggie at the little cemetery on the Highclere Estate. Her grave is sadly neglected, along with others containing member of the Carnarvon-Wendell family.

As 1949 ended, Catherine must have reflected on the deaths of her beloved 'Auntie Gertrude' (Aunty Bunny) and her cherished mother Marian (always called Gar in the family) as representing a final chapter in her past life over the previous four decades.

New heartbreak problems lay ahead in the years to come. Catherine's sister Philippa was to be mercilessly split with her husband, the Earl of Galloway, over managing the deteriorating mental health of their son, Lord Garlies.

In a recent book from Highclere Randolph (still surviving today as the present Earl of Galloway) is described as suffering from epilepsy. The diagnosis was in fact one of schizophrenia.

Randolph had a complicated upbringing. When a teenager he was lobotomized but the operation was bungled and changed his mind forever; it did not improve his appeal to his parents or calm his behaviour. After a time in a mental hospital and a monastery Randolph was reduced to an introverted, unbalanced, tramp-like figure with no social skills. He upset his father further by marrying a servant girl, Lily Budge, which resulted in his father cutting him out of his Will, to cries of fury and crippling legal proceedings.

Although Randolph became the Thirteenth Earl of Galloway in 1978 (on the death of his father) and his wife Lily became the Countess they were a sad and controversial couple, almost pantomime figures in a sea of snobs. Cumloden was passed on to another branch of the Stewart family. The full tragic story of Randolph and Lily is told in a book entitled *An Unlikely Countess*.[755] Lily died but Randolph lives quietly in a nursing home near the old family homestead. His sister married (and is now widowed) but had no children.[756]

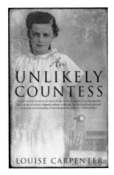

Whilst Philippa (who died in 1974) struggled to survive the horrors of seeing her only son Randolph destroyed by her husband's obduracy and denial over the boy's illnesses, Catherine was also burdened with her own children's demands and attention. Catherine's grandchildren came to know her only slightly in the early days and they were protected from the distress of her unsettled state caused by drink. In Philippa's case she was never blessed with any grandchildren.

Sadly Catherine found that her faith could not overcome her overriding addiction to alcohol and her health was also erratic at times. Lord Porchester expressed concerns to Almina (in early 1950) about his mother in a letter (written during his hops around the Royal Palaces with various courtiers and "P. Elizabeth"[757]):

"Sandringham Palace… 7 January 1950. Am rather worried and upset about Mother and as I am catching the 9.00 o'clock train I will attempt to see her on my way through [to Highclere]. She does not seem to have her usual determination to get well – however I now hear it is a disc which is the trouble."[758]

# Almina on Suicide Watch with Catherine

*Catherine and Almina: Confidantes for Life*

The truth was even more concerning: Almina was on suicide watch with Catherine. The deaths of Gertrude and Marian and other accumulated tragedies had brought Catherine down on her knees. She was staying on her own at the *Ritz* hotel in London and when everything became very dark, she felt very frightened and alone. With her mother and beloved cousin dead there was only Almina left for real comfort within Catherine's inner circle.

Fortunately Almina had seen Catherine in London the night before when the former was staying at her regular haunt of the *Cumberland* hotel in Marble Arch with Anne Leadbetter (who had long-since succeeded her sister Alice Butler as Almina's housekeeper/maid[759]). Her stays at the *Cumberland* hotel were routine. Almina spent Tuesday to Thursday in London all year round and she did her tour (in JTS's car or in a taxi, with an ever-loyal driver named Nosey) of visiting her hairdresser, dentist, optician, Tesiers (the Bond Street jewelry firm) and the Savoy Grill, as well as attending any Society weddings or funerals.

Catherine phoned Almina from the *Ritz* but Almina was already out on her travels. Anne Leadbetter realised Catherine meant what she said: she was going to throw herself from out of her bedroom window at the *Ritz*. Anne rushed in a taxi to the *Ritz* (only a short distance away) and persuaded Catherine to see sense. The incident shocked Almina to the core.

After her suicide attempt Catherine spent time in retreat. She came through that crisis well; in fact not everything was now gloom. As her fiftieth birthday loomed there was a glimmer of real hope. A new man was in her life, a man who offered her security and love and had asked her to marry him.

## 1950

## Catherine Marries Don Momand
## The Gathering Begins

Don Stuart Momand[760] was a successful businessman on both sides of the Atlantic. He was almost ten years older than Catherine, a divorcee with a daughter, Virginia. His name was known to Almina since Don was involved the medical and pharmaceutical world. He had also done sterling work for the Red Cross during the Second World War.

At the age of fifty Catherine was given a chance to spend the next twenty-seven years of her life with Don, "someone who loved her, without condition". [761]

Don was a stable presence in Catherine late life and Almina, for her part, liked him and approved of the match. Such was the affection that existed between the two women; Almina was among the first to know that Catherine intended to remarry.

Excited, and on a short driving tour of the West Country (with an obligatory stay at the Imperial Hotel, Torquay), she called in on Almina who was now living at a rented property at Park Cottage, Cleeve, near Minehead. It was a time of some anxiety for Almina, since the Income Tax authorities were threatening her with bankruptcy. Catherine was alarmed at the prospect of this happening but could do nothing to prevent the inevitable fall of Almina's name into the black book of bankruptcy. Relations between Almina and Porchey had never been worse. Porchey wanted to teach his mother a lesson once and for all.

## Catherine:
## The Only Family Member Who Knew About Almina Living with JTS

*JTS : Almina's secret partner for 20 years*

Tony Leadbetter first knew Catherine as Mrs Grenfell, and understood she was Lord Porchester's mother. He always admired her and she always had time for him with a pleasant word or a gift (often of pocket money) on her visits to see Almina. He remembers her coming to Park Cottage with Don Momand because in part this resulted in an incident that was serious at the time but is now recollected with much affection

288

and warmth for the indelible memory it left with him of those whom Tony much loved all those decades ago.

The incident was over Tony's pet Labrador named Tiger, a dog trained as a gun dog at Highclere. Almina gave the dog its name after her second husband, the caddish Colonel Dennistoun, who was known as 'Tiger'. It was assumed that the twelve-year-old Tony would keep Tiger under control whilst there were guests in the house. Catherine had been wearing some expensive flat shoes, made of crocodile leather, which she had left in the hallway of the cottage. Meanwhile, as everyone stepped outside into the adjoining garden area, Tiger had chewed off the heel of one of Catherine's shoes. Tiger didn't burn so bright that night and joined Tony in the doghouse, if only temporarily.

The visit to Park Cottage, Cleeve, and later visits by Catherine and Don Momand to see Almina at 19 Hampton Road, Bristol, to where Almina moved in 1951 (this was a house bought for his granny by Lord Porchester) also stands out in Tony's memory as Don Momand always drove an American-style Cadillac. This caused quite a stir wherever it was parked in the drab streets of Bristol in the 1950s. The Momands drove across Europe in this car; it was rumoured that Don had arranged with General Motors (at some significant expense) to have the front windscreen made of special glass developed specifically to his optician's specifications.

Tony has many memories of meeting Catherine and Don Momand in France, at Monte Carlo and Cannes where Almina always had a villa for a month each year. This was even after her bankruptcy, since she was adept at syphoning money out of both Porchey and Lady Evelyn Beauchamp, in part to facilitate Almina's acquiescence in signing as required paperwork concerning the Carnarvon Settled Lands.

These meetings on the Riviera provided an opportunity for Almina and Lady Evelyn (never Sir Brogrove, he avoided Almina like the plague) to meet and catch up. Tony usually received a few francs for himself from Almina's daughter. JTS kept well out of sight in the background.

Tony highlights that Catherine was the *only* member of the Highclere family who knew about Almina's secret love nest with JTS, an affair that began in 1942 (when he moved in with Almina and Alice Butler at

Avenue Road, Regent's Park) and ended with JTS's sudden death in 1963. This was a measure of the close bond of trust between the two women who had both been the Countess of Carnarvon, the successive chatelaines at Highclere from 1895 until 1936; a genuine love-based friendship that in all spanned over fifty years.

Almina usually saw Porchey in Paris, *en route* or returning on the Blue Train. It sticks in Tony Leadbetter's memory that this mother and son *never* embraced each other at this point in their lives. There had been just too much enmity passing between them through the years.

## 1951
## Tilly and her Painting

*Leonard C Hanna*

In the USA, as Tilly was seen less and less in the early 1950s, her name was nevertheless linked to Leonard Hanna[762] to the extent that the affair was the main talking point at the New York Colony.[763] Tilly was playing it all down and still working in the theatre from time to time, but most of her time was now taken up painting. In 1951 she staged an exhibition in New York, the first public expose of her work in three years.[764]

She had not deserted the stage and screen entirely, however, and could be relied on at opening nights to make an appearance. One writer records her showing as "[the] danseuse Tilly Losch with a long lynx coat and white gown…"[765]

## Syrie Maugham

Tilly met Syrie Maugham ( estranged wife of the writer, Somerset ) in the 1930s during the time that Edward James had commissioned the interior designer Paul Nash to create Tilly's ideal bathroom of stippled and plain mirrors and reeded and floated pillars at the James matrimonial home in London. Like Nash, Syrie was a leading Mayfair and New York interior designer. In the early 1950s ( only a short time before she died ) Syrie advised Tilly on the interiors for her New York and London homes. At the time Tilly was contemplating marriage again and the rumours were flying around that the man was a British or European Marquis. [766]

## 1952

*Dancing in El Morocco*

Tilly also walked with the Royals. Among a large company of old friends and lovers at *El Morocco* ( a Manhattan nightclub ) for a farewell dinner for the Duke and Duchess of Windsor, before they returned to England. Among those saying their goodbyes were Porchey, the Duchess of Westminster and the Marquis of Blandford as well as a clutch of American and European dignitaries and various other members of the nobility.[767]

# Chapter 17

## The Art of Seduction

Tilly seduced ( or was seduced by ) some of the richest and most powerful men in the Western world. She loved and was loved by scores of men She is amongst the best and worst in the amatory roll call of history, with Princes and moguls ( from the movies and business ), ambassadors, and sometimes their wives. None of her lovers except her first husband minded her sleeping with others.

## Tilly's Hold on Men
## The Serpent of the Old Danube

In the context of Cecil Beaton once lusting after Tilly, *The Spectator* magazine described her, albeit posthumously as " that serpent of the Old Danube." [768]

Serpentine she certainly was her lithe contortions turned men's heads and snaked into their hearts, at times her hold over them verged on the mystical. The brevity of her costumes on stage, created by the very best and presumably thrifty designers of the era gave her a goddess like quality, She was to be worshipped but approach at your peril. Off stage and in rehearsals she could be audacious and arrogant and bitchy. Some of the others girls in the show tried to bring her down a peg or two. "The chorus girls in *Errante* deliberately spiked the long, glittering green silk train on [ Tilly's] costume, producing a large tear. [ afterwards ] Tilly...screamed at them in German.." [769]

Away from the set Tilly went out to attract men. A story is told by the actress Merle Oberon after she went with Tilly to a birthday party for newspaper magnate William Randolph Hearst. The location for the gathering was a beach house owned by Hearst's lady friend Marion Davies, ( whom Tilly kept in touch with socially and in correspondence over several years ). The theme was a Spanish fiesta party. Oberon's biographers records in a memoir " Tilly Losch created a sensation when she came dressed as Goya's naked Duchess of Alba in a skin-coloured, skin-tight costume that left nothing to the imagination. " [770]

She had all the men at her feet and her female competitors throwing in the towel.

Being a practiced Narcissist, Tilly knew *exactly* how to attract men for gain. Such manipulation was her strength , yet it was a gigantic flaw too, she could see her own reflection in the mirror still as she was as a girl, and viewed her own perfection and beauty still as the child she once was, she found less likeable the reality of the older adult mask. Cecil Beaton once said of Garbo she " has the tragic quality of a child".[771] That comment might equally apply to Tilly.

Tilly was ravished by men in power. The trouble ( as Tilly saw it ) was that those who wanted her for sex were unattractive and imperfect but they were rich and powerful and well connected. She made sacrifices to please these men, just as a child would do. She was a trophy and was passed around. She slept with no one for love's sake, she was incapable of love, but those she had to sleep with she controlled and called time. She knew what she was doing. It was a transaction, an end justifying the means. Deeper down she might have wished romance, but she could not think of anyone she actually wanted to sweep her off her feet. The men got what they wanted but then so did Tilly and it was *she* who moved on. Like others of the same psyche, actresses like Monroe and Garland and Princesses like Marina ( Duchess of Kent ) and Lady Diana it was a simple act and then 'love them and leave them'. The deed done it worked best to move on as they could not handle true love. The women put up with the charade to satisfy witless men, but it was an act, a falsehood. For diversion and fun and out of personal choice Tilly became a 'fag hag' enjoying the sanctuary that came out of friendships with Beaton's coterie, among the era's grandest homosexuals including the eccentric composer ( Lord) Gerald Berners, and the fussy journalist Beverley Nichols ( whom Tilly had known for several years as one of the writers of stage shows for Cochran ). These gay men ( as we would term them today ) still adored her even after the careless talk about their kind during her divorce to Edward James.

# Some of Tilly's Men Friends :   In and Out of the Ballet World

*George Antheil*

In the 1930s Tilly met the composer George Antheil[772] through choreographer   George Balanchine. Antheil, whose music was once called   " so radical it is incoherent"[773]   worked in Hollywood on original scores for pictures by Cecil B DeMille. He liked Tilly and they became close friends. Antheil's side line was an expertise in   " glands and human behavior,"[774]

Tilly was enchanted that Antheil was  a follower   ( as she was ) of the writer Gertrude Stein. [775]

While Anthril tolerated Tilly, the ballet master  Balanchine's personal feelings for Tilly ran both cold and hot, despite her unquestionable allure  he had seen how vindictive she  could be  and how she struck out against Edward James. Describing her once  as " hysterical and useless" [776] Balanchine avoided inviting her out.[777]   Before Edward James commissioned him to work on *Les Ballets 1933* Balanchine had choreographed *'What Is this Thing Called Love'* for the Cochran  revue. Tilly   was widely acclaimed for her dancing to this well liked  piece but professionally  Balanchine saw Tilly more  as a music hall performer than a ballet or mime artist, once describing her as a contortionist.[778] Tilly was not best pleased at this down-grading of her art.

# Tilly a disciple of Gerald Heard

*Gerald Heard*

Tilly was a follower In England of the guru Gerald Heard,[779] "a slim red-bearded man resembling D H Lawrence. "[780] He taught at Oxford mixed with Edward James, Evelyn Waugh and John Betjeman. Heard later emigrated to the USA, his counsels helped Tilly over many years to deal with pain, stress and thoughts of self injury. Tilly also fell back on her strong beliefs as a Christian Scientist. [781]

# Winston Churchill

As Tilly rose to stardom the invitations came in from all comers, among them from Winston Churchill to visit his beloved Chartwell. Here Tilly found equal status with other shooting stars of the era including Charlie Chaplin and Ethel Barrymore. [782] Tilly, always accommodating in such circumstances, ended the dilemma for two young men demented about losing their virginity by helping out Winston's son Randolph and nephew John ( Johnnie) Spencer Churchill[783], a notable artist who years later painted Tilly's portrait and gave her advice about painting styles and " urged her to go ahead and paint fearlessly". [784] Johnnie's sister Clarissa[785] was an acquaintance of Tilly's, but she was more a friend of Edward James.

# John Sutro

Tilly was judged and eyed up for her talents as a dancer and a woman. One admirer in the 1930s was a promising young British film producer John Sutro, [786] a contemporary of Evelyn Waugh and other *Bright Young People* at Oxford. [787] Sutro, a Jew, described as " brainy, opinionated, mildly anti-establishment " [788] wined and dined Tilly in style at swanky London restaurants and their affair continued at *Ashcombe* as mutual friends turned guests of Cecil Beaton. [789] Tilly was amused by Sutro ( who was an accomplished mimic[790] and practical joker) and unlike other Tilly chasers, he was endearing and loveable. Professionally the lovers planned to make a film of Oscar Wilde's *Salome*, with Tilly in the title role as the temptress and eccentric aesthetic Harold Acton[791] as King Herod. The project was later abandoned.[792] Patrick Kinross, [793] a regular correspondent of Tilly's over forty years was another player from the same clutch of guests who first participated in the antics of Acton and Sutro at Beaton's retreat at *Ashcombe*.

# Rouben Mamoulian

*Ruben Mamoulian and David O Selznick*

Also from the 1930s Tilly stepped out to celebrate the success of her brief, but memorable role as the fiery Irena in *The Garden of Allah*, it was public knowledge that she was seeing the unmarried film director Ruben Mamoulian.[794] The Hollywood gossip columns reported the hatching and matching. [795] After the success of Tilly's film flick, she was reported as being lined up for a movie of the play *Idiot's Delight* playing the character Lynn Fontanne, against Clark Gable. [796] In any case Tilly secured a new screen contract as everyone ( including David O Selznick, who had given her first big chance to shine ) liked her performance in *The Garden of Allah*.

On a more intimate and personal note, with Tilly winning a new contract with MGM she sent for her Mama to come from Vienna and join her permanently in America.

## Howard Dietz

Whatever romance there was with Mamoulian was short-lived, reports in the same week of November, 1936, [797] linked Tilly with a new love-interest, the song writer, Howard Dietz, who was on the point of divorcing his first wife. Tilly and Dietz were not first time dating, he chased her during the run of *The Bandwagon* four years before. By January 1937, Dietz had moved on and married Tanis Guinness on the rebound from Porchey.

## Joesph Schenck

A romantic link between Tilly and movie maker Joesph Schenck was hot news in 1937. [798] This was heralded by observers as "a new combination." [799] After a spell in prison for tax fraud, Schenck transferred his infatuations to Marilyn Monroe.

## Ernst Lubitsch

The movie director Ernst Lubitsch[800] took Tilly out to parties in between wives and afterwards they ran into each other on the film and theatre scene in New York. He is described as " sweet" [801]when the furtive pair ran into Tilly's old estranged girlfriend, Lotte Lenya in New York, in 1938. However when he became Paramount's production manager he favoured Marlene Dietrich over Tilly for several film productions in Britain in America.

# Orson Welles

In the 1930s in New York  Tilly saw Orson Wells perform on stage in several plays. This coincided with Lotte  Lenya's excursions  there and being reunited with Tilly whilst Kurt Weill was in Hollywood looking for work contracts.

During 1945-7,   Tilly  met  up  again  with  Orson  Welles  when  he powerfully narrated the King Vidor/ David O Seiznick epic western *Dual In the Sun.* Tilly is credited as ' Solo Dance Creator ' with Lloyd Shaw.      Her  heavy  brown  make  up  was  mesmerising.  One  critic comments    " Losch's full- blooded, unbridled, savage performance goads the hundreds of leering cowboys and card players into a very Freudian, pistol- shooting frenzy." [802] Welles fell madly in love with Tilly, who was fourteen years his senior. The evidence suggests he was not " able to advance [ the relationship ] beyond the platonic stage". [803]

# John Gunther and William L Shirer

*John Gunther and William L Shirer*

In the 1940s Tilly was going out with the journalist John Gunther[804] described  by  one  contemporary  as  "  a  charmer".   [805]      Through Gunther  Tilly  met another American journalist and historian, William L Shirer[806], a notable chronicler of the rise of the Third Reich, who argued that if Hitler's ideas had been more widely disseminated and understood outside of Germany in the 1930s, then the world might have taken action in time to stop him. Gunther knew Shirer as a newspaper colleague in Vienna, where Shirer had married a Viennese girl. Still married, Shirer describes in one of his books of memoir [807] his first and later meeting with Tilly "So the two of us began to meet, and rather quickly Tilly Losch and I became close to one another." [808] Thereafter he frankly describes ( in fond and loving terms ) what the relationship meant to him concluding at the end on parting " I still loved her, but it had become obvious to us both that we would never make it together. She was tired of waiting for me. " [809]

The affair with Tilly fizzled out, she was far from willing to be associated with a communist sympathiser ( as Shirer was listed ) during the MacCarthy years in USA. Just before Tilly died she renewed a last contact with this old friend to say hello again. They met again briefly in New York. Shirer made arrangements for Tilly to see a specialist, but he had failed to realise that Tilly's life was almost over. Tilly's death was a shock to Shirer, he almost certainly still loved her.[810]

## John Brahn ( Hans)

The German born John ( Hans ) Brahn [811] was another movie maker who knew Tilly in her early days at Salzburg and in Berlin. They were on good terms in years following her divorce from Porchey and until the end of Tilly's life they still exchanged greetings.

## Tilly and the Prince Aly Khan

Playboy Prince Aly Khan ( whose life ended at the wheel of a sports car, in a head on collision, in 1960 ) was a lover of many of the world's most beautiful women, including Tilly. Among others who were besotted by the dark skinned Aly was Tilly's friend Merle Oberon. In his memoirs it is Porchey of all people ( a horse racing pal of Aly's father ) who takes the credit for helping Merle, " my favourite ' *muy simpatia*' companion ... with many dinners and luncheons together" [812] when the Prince moved out of her bed and onto his next prey.[813]

# Chapter 18

## Later Years

## Porchey and the Duchess

*Margaret Whigham Later Duchess of Argyll*

Margaret, Duchess of Argyll, [814]was known to be somewhat generous with her sexual favours among her own set while apparently (and perhaps on account of the Scottish climate) insisting on keeping her clothes on amidst the hurly-burly of the chaise longue. It was as Miss Margaret Whigham, at her coming-out dance at Queen's Hill Ascot in 1931, that Porchey first showed an interest.[815] Catherine sighed, as she knew Porchey was on heat again. It was in 1932 at a reception at Stornoway House that, like two rutting stags, Porchey and Ian Campbell (the Duke of Argyll, later Margaret's husband) came to blows. Margaret loved dining at the *Ritz* alongside the European diplomats who had also to live there as war loomed. Porchey literally lived at the *Ritz* hotel for several months each year and bedded dozens of woman under its roof.

Margaret chased her men and notched up a rough night with Porchey several times. She was famously divorced after proceedings were brought against her, with famous actors, politicians and Royal Princes being cited as among those whom Margaret culled. It was mouthed by those in the know that her particular skill lay in the art of fellatio.

Porchey was almost certainly on the "list of as many as eighty-eight men ... [John, 11th Duke of Argyll] believed had enjoyed his wife's favours". It was a fact that Porchey had made love to two of the Duke's wives, the first being Janet Beaverbrook in the 1930s.

## Lord Porchester, later Seventh Earl of Carnarvon

Of Lord Porchester there is some much-guarded secrecy behind just how much of a lady's man and charmer he was before he settled down in marriage to his cousin Jeannie Wallop. Almost by Royal command, ex- girlfriends are not willing to tell much. Two of them approached by the author were certainly less than forthcoming, remaining coy but suggesting by way of a tiny suggestive wink that there might be something to tell. But he was not in the same league as old Porchey. The girls had very happy memories of Porchester who was invited to shooting parties on many of the large estates where his womanising father was excluded.

But Porchester could be as rude and threatening as his father. The late Ross Benson[816] of *The Daily Express* had regular run-ins with Porchester (as can be seen in the gossip columns over many years) which brought the very worst out in them, both peer and journalist. [817]

The hangers on at Highclere included the Rupert Nevils. It was inevitable that Camilla Nevil ( a Wallop cousin of Porchey ) should have her nice unmarried cousin from Wyoming on holiday in Britain and meet with her nice unmarried Herbert cousin.

The tentacles of these people reached further than inside Highclere, to find a place of purpose in Royal circles, all the way up to monarchy.

# 1954

## Porchey's New Lust Interests

Old Porchey continued to look out for his next Countess. In America he was linked romantically for several months of 1954 with Mrs Edgar Leonard, a local socialite in Chomming.[818]

He had also lined up Countess Daria Mercati - one of his old flames - who hung out among a throng of rich, unattached maybe-willing-to-weds at New York's Colony.[819]

## Porchey's Tricks to Lure a Victim

Now well into his fifth decade, Porchey remained rampant and unbowed. He still thought he was as attractive to women as in his younger days. With his dark hair and the features (from his complicated gene pool) of a European- Indian mix he had a modicum of pulling power but as he grew older his stocky build and balding dome meant he had to work that bit harder.

He was not a dandy dresser. Vanity ruled here. Porchey could reel off the opposition in the Don Juan stakes including his friend Bert Marlborough and the equally ageing peers Lords Londesborough and Westmoreland.

In the 1950s Porchey had a marvellous time gadding about the hot spots of America where his suave English charm and the availability of a Countess's coronet made him much sought after. His Lordship did not shrink from the challenge "to bed and barrel". In his own words: "I have in my time known perfectly beautiful women, not a brain in their head, dumb as anything, and I've said, " I'm going to give you a barrelling and I'm going to enjoy it".[820]

Whoever was foolish enough to accept a chance to sit on Porchey's knee was doomed: a particular flirty invitation from Porchey's cabinet of infallible tricks for enticing a female waif, irrespective of her being a daughter, a wife, or a mother.

Another trick involved making a reference to "the little mouse in his pocket", with a bizarre invitation to the unsuspecting female to "stroke his little mouse". This was a favourite trick played in the back of his Rolls Royce when taking a lady out for a chauffeured drive. The poor woman was trapped and terrified; to even more disgust she was also often one of Porchey's son's newest girlfriends.

Despite the relationship between Porchey and Porchester being close and loving, the old man was increasingly embarrassing to his son. The hope that he might grow old gracefully was a vain one. It is even alleged in one story that Porchey exercised the feudal right to deflower his pick of the Highclere Estate's maidens - working for the Carnarvon family. [821]

## Highclere's Secret Passageways

Porchey smacked his lips and drooled over every pretty girl who crossed his pathway. Any attractive woman staying at Highclere on her own ( married or single, young or old, frisky or not ) was invariably a target for Porchey's lechery. After dark it was no use just locking the bedroom door as Porchey deviously devised a way of entering a lady's chamber to further his amorous ambitions.

One peeress told the Author " [ Porchey] put into a guest room whoever he fancied. This room had a cupboard which adjoined onto another room so Porchey could enter it easily – whenever he desired. I believe Bert Marlborough had the same arrangement at Blenheim." [822]

The game was on at Highclere  during social gatherings, after race meetings, there was  stiff competition to lure damsels into improper conduct. Chief among the players was Sir Matthew 'Scatters' Wilson, described  by one contemporary as " a funny ebullient bounder, with his blue eyes and hoarse whisper" , an ardent racing man, where he lead Porchey  followed  taking  lessons  in  romancing  several  women simultaneously  this league of dishonourable gentlemen loaned their unfaithful cronies alibis' whenever their long suffering faithful wives smelt a rat.

## Porchester's Acting Career and Dancing With Princess Margaret

Taking  a lead from his mother's acting days when a young woman, Porchester's name appears on the boards for several stage shows in the early 1950s, to raise funds for  charity. With a severely disabled niece, ( Lady Penelope's daughter ) it is of merit that one of the good causes Porchester supported was the  Invalid Children's Association. The charity was  a particular favourite of Princess Margaret, who was also associated with the Porchester stage production. The  Princess  was forbidden by protocol from appearing on stage, but she directed the play. Another  show, from 1954, entitled *The Frog* ( an Edgar Wallace thriller ) was also masterminded by the same dream team of Porchester and Princess Margaret.

Old Porchey graced the performance with his presence too, he occupied a prominent place ( centre stage ) in all the photographs from the newspapers who reported on the show. He was immediately drawn  to woo his old flame Maureen, Marchioness of Dufferin and Ava ( who was one of the actors,  miraculously coaxed into playing  a ladies' lavatory attendant!). To Porchey's dismay Maureen was 'standoffish' with him, one of her chums ( whom she had caught up with in Ireland  at Adele Cavendish's place,   and later dined with in New York ) was Porchey's ex-wife, Tilly Losch. Maureen ( well known for  dealing severely with men on the make ) thought Porchey got exactly what he deserved after buying Tilly's favours and then filling his bed during the war years with Jeanne Stuart. Maureen promptly took delight in emphasizing where her sympathies lay, and in response to his pawing stamped hard on Porchey's foot which cooled his ardour somewhat.

Everyone wanted to party! After the play Porchester and other members of the Margaret Set went to the *Milroy Club*, next to the more famous *Les Ambassadeurs* . One record says " The Princess loved the Milroy and its rather louche clientele." [823] The Princess and Porchester danced together six times to the music of the latest Broadway hits.

Naturally Almina and Catherine, whilst keeping their distance, revelled in glory of seeing their blue eyed boy in such company and on the receiving end of Royal favour.

## 1956

In May, 1956, Porchey was one of the guests at Claridges Hotel for the coming-out dance of Countess Bunny Esterhazy. [824] His eyes drifted across the ballroom like a prospective owner at Tattersall's.

## Tales from New York Crossings: 1947 - 1956

The late 1940s and early-to-mid 1950s saw a flurry of Atlantic crossings by Porchey to America, where he never failed to be a centre of attention on sea and land for any inspiringly nubile next Countess of Carnarvon.

The trip on 11 January 1947 was more to tie up the divorce with Tilly Losch. The other trips over the next few years were simply for pleasure, sports or family matters. These included one trip by Porchey in July 1948 to New York (with his valet, James Spencer) on board the Queen Elizabeth. Spencer was also with Porchey on a trip on the Queen Mary from Southampton to New York on 16 January 1949. By 1955, George Liken had replaced Spencer when Porchey left England on 19 January. Alongside Lord Porchester, Porchey flitted back to New York on board the Queen Mary on 29 December 1955 (with manservant George Liken) and shared the company of the long crossing with Horace Caro, a director of the London Savoy Hotel, and the actor Maurice Denham. This happy trip was for the purposes of attending Lord Porchester's marriage ceremony to his cousin, Jeanie Wallop, in New York City on 7 January 1956.

## Porchester and the Royal Horse Guards

Porchester retired from the Royal Horse Guards in 1947[825] to farm on the Highclere Estate.

Old Porchey had been less and less interested in Estate matters and welcomed his son's input. Like his father, Henry Porchester loved Highclere and all that it meant to the long line of the Herbert family.

## Porchester Falls In Love with his Cousin and Weds in the USA

Henry, Lord Porchester, also served his purpose and pleased his monarch by acting (with others[826]) as escort to protect the wayward Princess Margaret who was threatening to repeat the decision of her uncle (the Duke of Windsor) and seek unofficial exile to be with the person she loved, Group Captain Peter Townsend. With Townsend marooned in Brussels the Princess became embroiled with palace, state and close friends who, one by one, were forced into disarray over her long smouldering romance with Townsend. This turmoil with Margaret and Townsend carried on into 1955, only ending in Margaret renouncing their affair altogether on 31 October 1955.

Before the Townsend affair came to its conclusion Porchester had met an American, Jean Wallop, whilst she was in England during 1954 and 1955 staying with Lord and Lady Rupert Nevill at Uckfield House, Sussex (the same place where Margaret announced her affair with Townsend was over). Jean was a fine horsewoman and a good shot and shared Porchester's interest in farming. She was shy, blonde and pretty, with a good head on her shoulders and was a graduate (in nursing) from the University of Colorado and Garrison Forest in Maryland. Henry made his choice to court the Wallop girl and followed her to America; Jean met him in New York and took him to meet her parents. Jean's father was Oliver Wallop,[827] her mother was deceased but she had a step-mother, Carolyn Towle Wallop.[828]

In November 1955 came the brief announcement that Henry was to marry Jean, an American rancher's daughter from Nether-Wallop Ranch, Big Horn, and Sheridan County, Wyoming. History was almost repeated in Porchester failing to let his family know of the engagement. He only told his father Porchey a few hours before publication of the news in the press.

On 7 January 1956 the tall, handsome, debonair Porchester, dubbed "Princess Margaret's Former Boyfriend" [829] married Jean Wallop in a quiet ceremony at St James Protestant Episcopal Church on Madison Avenue, New York. The groom was aged 31, the bride 20. They were cousins. A small gathering of forty guests included the bridegroom's father, Lord Carnarvon, but his mother, Catherine, was nowhere to be seen. Jean's brother Edward John Wallop[830] acted as best man and her sister Caroline as maid of honour.

After the wedding they went off to Miami *en route* to spending their honeymoon in Cuba. However the couple were so beguiled with Florida that they cancelled the Cuba trip, later visiting friends and relatives, including Jean's parents in Wyoming, before heading back to England. Porchester was keen to get back home to carry on his duties as a local councillor in Hampshire. As well as farming he carved out a place for himself in the years that followed in local government and strategic planning [831]

Back in Britain, Porchester was keen to show off his new bride. On 25 February the Queen and Prince Philip joined the newlyweds to celebrate at a reception at Eridge Castle. The previous night the couple had been the centre of attention at a party at Uckfield House on the estate of the Marquis of Abergavenny. Dozens of cases of champagne and a dance band were brought from London to entertain 120 guests.[832]

## Lake House at Highclere

The new Lady Porchester set up home at the Lake House, within the Highclere Estate. This was more habitable than the Castle itself, which had been without a chatelaine since Catherine left twenty years before (albeit Tilly was there briefly, as were many of Porchey's conquests, but who were never officially asked to act as hostesses). Occasionally Lady Penelope acted as hostess for her father.

A visitor to the Lake House in the 1950s remembers the American accents.[833]

Cynthia, Lady Gladwyn, the wife of a diplomat, records in her diaries for 10 November 1956 that she was staying a Highclere: "We arrived late...but managed to bath and change for dinner. There were staying here just young Porchester and his pregnant wife, and the Blandfords... [old] Porchey is a convivial much-married bounder, but a nice father, and I was quite touched to see him kiss his son goodnight."[834]

## Porchey as a Horseman

Throughout the 1950s and 1960s Porchey remained a top racing man, although he rarely rode again except for charity polo matches (many of which he hosted at Highclere for Lord Mountbatten and Prince Philip). He is credited in racing history as breeding the 1929 Derby winner *Blenheim*, having sold him to the Aga Khan at as a yearling for 4,100 guineas. Porchey had a habit of using half-mocking, almost Eton schoolboy-fashioned, tags for his friends, especially those in the racing world; he referred to the Aga Khan (by whom he was often lavishly entertained at the *Ritz* hotels in London and Paris) as "the dear old fat boy". [835]

There was always an overlap between Porchey and the Aga Khan as both men used Dick Dawson as horse trainer, with input also from Fred Darling who had a knack for turning out Classic winners.

# Chapter 19

## The Last Decades

### Health Scares

In the late 1950s Porchey suffered several serious health scares requiring surgery.[836] To Almina's surprise her son opted for radical surgery in the USA (over a prostate problem). There was a moment during the operation and the long recovery when fears arose that Porchey would not pull through. [837] Porchester went out to New Yorjk and brought the old Earl back safe and sound.

## 1962

In the late 1950s and early 1960s Tilly was on the party scene as one of the old movie stars of a bygone age. She chose to turn out when it suited her and at a party given by Carol Channing Tilly walked away with a $1000 diamond she won in a raffle.

One of Tilly Losch's favourite night spots was the *Colony* in New York. Whilst her appearances there were irregular, her presence was always likely to cause a stir. One hack noticed her looks in 1962: "Tilly Losch was the reason for much table-hopping at the *Colony* when she put in her first appearance in a year. She's still beautiful and elegant." [838]

## 1963

Catherine's brother, Jac Wendell, died in London in February 1963, aged 67. [839] He was survived by Eileen Carr and their son, Major Jac Wendell, and daughter, June Marian Wendell, who was the wife of Major Peter Prescott.

Jac had been involved in business, finance and horse racing; he ultimately became a British subject. June Prescott still survives.

Catherine and Don Momand enjoyed extensive travel during their happy married life. Much of this was to New York where Catherine was reunited with friends and family. With Don's support she escaped from the past pressures that had injured her physical and mental health. She rarely met Porchey again.

# 1964

Tilly was still 'keeping up appearances'. In the *Journals of Leo Lerman*[840] she is listed among the two thousand and more who poured into 1453 Lexington Avenue, New York, for the *Early Twelfth Night Party* on 4 January 1964. The dancers, old and older, arrived together or collided with each other, Tilly with Martha Graham[841] whose influence on dance was legendary. They had both in different ways changed the nature of dance

Tilly's old friend Raimund von Hofmannsthal was also in the company, along with Leonard Bernstein and Rudolf Nureyev.

Tilly loved recalling her very early days before life (and Porchey) had touched her.

The dance critic and historian George Jackson recalls:

"I met Tilly in New York, in the 1960s [at a film screening on *Die Puppenfee*[842]]. She had appeared in this ballet as a child and her first solo as a member of the Vienna company had been the Chinese lady doll's variation. My name had been mentioned to her as someone interested in the Vienna ballet. I introduced myself to her. Her comment on the movie was, yes, "they dance well in Vienna these days but we - we were so beautiful"[843].

Tilly also spoke of her early days to Leo Lerman[844] who records this in his Journals a few weeks before her death:

"Tilly talked about how Richard Strauss had discovered her, a small child at the barre in Vienna, and how she had progressed from helping to carry on the veils (Salome) to Reinhardt's Deutsches Theater and so to Cochran."[845]

Strauss was Tilly's guardian angel. George Jackson reflects on this further:

"Tilly, when in New York, attended New York City Ballet performances often. Lincoln Kirstein had asked her to donate to the company's Stravinsky festival in 1972 but she replied that for a Richard Strauss festival she certainly would. "He meant something to me". Strauss had indeed. It was Strauss, in his capacity as co-director with Schalk of the Vienna Opera in the early 1920s, who had promoted her to soloist. Undoubtedly it was Heinrich Kroeller, the ballet master Strauss enlisted to replace Hassreiter, who had initiated the action and called Strauss's attention to Losch." [846]

## 1966

Debo Devonshire (today the Dowager Duchess of Devonshire and the last survivor of the Mitford girls) remarked after a shooting party at Chatsworth that "Old Porchy was there, he is a one man cabaret."[847]

The marvellous Dowager Debo ( who also said Porchey often reminded her of a bookmaker, which was one of his show off pieces at parties ) reflects further on her own secret method for cooling down Porchey's ardour at dinner by keeping " a loaded water pistol by my place … and if the talk got altogether too much, I threatened his [ Porchey's ] velvet jacket with my short sharp shower."[848]

*Porchey and Porchester on the Turf*

A footnote describes him further as "a brilliant amateur actor".[849] There seems no doubt that Porchey was good company at times and willing to lend a hand in amusing the assembled company, occasionally even venturing into the kitchen to cook up a storm.

Porchey continued to visit the USA where friends like Bert Marlborough (who had a house near Montego Bay) welcomed him with open arms. According to Bert's wife Laura, at one of these visits, "Henry Porchester was overseeing culinary matters.....cooking a suckling pig" for the company.[850]   A romantic link formed in this period between Porchey and Anne Jennings Johnson,[851] a stockbroker, golfer and tennis player, a member of Lyford Cay Club in Nassau, an exclusive establishment that Porchey frequented over several decades.

## Almina's Ninetieth Birthday

On 14 April 1966 Almina was ninety, still in good health and as defiant as ever.  To mark her nine decades of life she had two birthday parties, "one in Bristol for my friends, one for my family in London".[852]  When she was feeling mischievous Almina substituted "enemies" instead of saying her "family".

Porchey organised the celebrations in London, where Almina headed one of the tables at the *Ritz* hotel.

Catherine played a central part in the entire London affair, booking rooms for Almina and her housekeeper, Anne Leadbetter, to stay as guests with her and Don Momand.

Almina's godson, Tony Leadbetter, remembers it well. He was expected to attend and Catherine was happy to provide accommodation but in the end Tony (who was nursing at the time and working inflexible shifts) had to send his apologies.

At the end of the birthday celebrations Catherine invited Almina (with Anne Leadbetter) to stay with her in Switzerland. Whilst this didn't happen because of various health and practical issues, the two women remained in close touch by telephone and letter. Later, the terminal illness of Anne Leadbetter gave rise to much fondness and streams of gifts from all the Carnarvon women, including Lady Evelyn, Jeanne, Lady Porchester and Catherine. Anne was very much loved and respected.

## The Centenary of the Birth of the Fifth Earl

26 June 1966 marked the centenary of the birth of the Fifth Earl of Carnarvon. All family feuds between Porchey and Almina and others were temporarily suspended. A service of dedication "In Memory of the 5th Earl of Carnarvon"[853] was held at Highclere on 21 June 1966 and a memorial raised to his life on his grave on Beacon Hill.

Almina stood as resolute as she had done over forty years before when she had conducted a solitary vigil on the same spot. This was Almina's final act in the midst of her whole family.

## 1969
## Almina's death

Anne Leadbetter, Almina's housekeeper of almost thirty years, died on 28 March 1969 aged fifty-five. Almina lived only a short time afterwards. She choked on a chicken bone at her home at 19, Hampton Road; this required major surgery and she died at the Frenchey Hospital, Bristol, on 8 May 1969.

Almina's death was avoidable, albeit she was aged ninety-three. She did not live long enough to see her beloved grandson, Lord Porchester, become Racing Manager to HM the Queen. He was appointed to that post in the same year.

Among Almina's cherished days was when she was taken by Porchester to the racing.

# 1970-1
## Porchey's Last Stand

In June of 1970, affectionately described as "that avid man of racing"[854] Porchey was in excruciating pain " with an elliptical disc which slipped uncomfortably out of place. " [855] Doctors were treating him. He attributed the cause to standing on the uneven ground at Epsom for the Derby earlier in the year. The specialists diagnosed sciatica, an old problem. Things improved over the next few months but in the early summer of 1970 the seventy-one-year-old Porchey was felled when his sciatica returned again with revenge. His spirits also plummeted when he was told by his latest girlfriend that she was not in favour of marriage.

Aside from romance, Porchey was in good spirits; his stallion *Queen's Hussar* had increased in value after siring *Brigadier Gerald*, the winner of the 2000 Guineas in 1971.

Brighter still was the revival of prospect of marriage to Bunny Esterhazy (who was newly divorced from her husband of eight years, Dominic Elliot,[856] a member of the family of the Earls of Minto).

Bunny was one of Porchey's past girlfriends. He commented: "There is nothing planned, we are just good friends." [857]

Bunny moved back into Highclere soon afterwards, but there was no new Countess.

One informant recalls "Bunny lived at Highclere during old Porchey's declining years and we all thought it very odd." [858]

## Among the Carnarvon Racing Triumphs Take 1974 for Instance

A good racing year for Porchey's heir, Lord Porchester and H.M. Queen's Racing Manager was 1974 when the Queen's filly *Highclere* ( which won the *1000 Guineas* at Newmarket earlier in the same year ) delighted a crowd of 25,000 people at Chantilly to win one of the top races in France the *Prix de Diane*, with Her Majesty cheering on all the way. The honours were shared between Joe Mercer ( jockey), Dick Hern ( trainer) and Henry Porchester ( racing manager). This was a welcome and overdue triumphs as the Royal stables had suffered something of a drought since classic wins, in the Oaks 1957 with *Carrozza* and in 1958 with *Pall Mall* in the 2000 Guineas. [859]

## Tilly's Twilight Years

In the 1970s Tilly Losch was still a sight on the London scene at receptions and parties, especially those organised by her friend, and publicist, Billy Hamilton. She was still playful and mischievous in company. At an exhibition, one memoir writer records a story of once standing before one exhibit and seeing Tilly stick pins into Lady Diana Cooper to get her to move. [860]

Tilly continued to work off and on. She introduced a television show sponsored by General Motors. There were also opportunities to teach dance and make guest appearances at premieres; she still had a loyal following as a queen of the dance.

She never made any more films. It was on the stage that Tilly will be chiefly remembered, her heyday being the 1920s and early 1930s. One commentator records, "the celluloid's loss was the theatre's gain." [861]

On the tricky subject of personal loss, Tilly records in one of her diaries a letter to the playwright Charles McArthur[862] (whose biographer describes her "as graceful as pipe smoke"[863]) "that she had known birth and death". The playwright Joyce Sachs illuminates this further, offering an uplift from an earlier diary entry made by Tilly in which she records that she "lost a son in childbirth after drinking something [Edward] James gave her..." [864]

# 1975
## Tilly's death

On 17 September 1975 Tilly told her friend Leo Lerman, "I'm regressing, not improving...." [865] She was apparently well enough to sip a little borscht.

Lerman records in his Journal for that day, "Tilly dying." He was so deeply overcome and depressed that he turned down an invitation to attend a swell party. He added to his journal entry, "Here was the past, the smell of it, the feel of it, in those huge cat eyes of Tilly's so world famous years ago." [866]

Tilly died of cancer, in New York on Christmas Eve 1975. Leo Lerman records, "Tilly was the last of the really *vie de scandale* ladies". [867]

One biographer of Edward James reflects on the knocks that Tilly took in her life, adding, "If Tilly had ever completed the autobiography she began, perhaps the story could be revised sharply in her favour. Lord Weidenfeld, the publisher and her neighbour in Eaton Place in the sixties, saw a first chapter once." [868]

Apparently it began with the loss of the baby she terminated, whose father was Edward James.

Lord Weidenfeld[869] has graciously provided the author with a memory of Tilly:

"Whereas I only slightly knew 'Porchey' Carnarvon, literally only met him with other people and only vaguely remember how and through whose initiative we [Weidenfeld & Nicolson] published his own book, I knew Tilly Losch very well. I met her after the war in diverse circles e.g. Salzburg Festival immediately after the war, with the son and daughter in law of Max Reinhardt; with Clarissa Churchill (later Mrs. Anthony Eden) and many other British, American and Austrian refugee socialites. She painted, and led a rather solitary life, living in a small flat in Eaton Square, but was still full of life and amusing stories about both her marriage and her very nasty divorce – so nasty that I am told official proceedings had to be greatly toned down when it came to producing evidence of adultery. A friend and loyal defendant of her was Randolph Churchill, who was a good friend of mine. Lady Diana Cooper and Raimund von Hofmannsthal, who knew her well from her *'Miracle* 'days, often spoke to me about her." [870]

## Tilly's Last Farewell

Billy Hamilton[871] (a well-known publicist in London, who died in 1988) was a close friend of Tilly Losch from the late 1950s onward. In 1975 he was charged with organising her memorial service in London (which Porchey attended, with only a handful of others). Hamilton hoped to be involved in attempting to fulfil Tilly's final wish, to have her remains taken back to her native Austria.

Tilly's trustees were at odds with Hamilton; she left an estate of almost £1m[872] but for eight years her remains lay in a casket on a shelf in a New York funeral parlour.

The grounds of Leopoldskron Castle, in Salzburg, the spiritual home of Max Reinhardt, was chosen for a final resting place. However, by the time the bureaucratic bungling had been overcome, Hamilton was still unhappy about the memorial itself.

"It was my idea to produce a profile of Tilly which would be sculptured onto the casket. She was my friend; I wanted to ensure she had a fitting tribute. Instead, the trustees of her estate have produced an appalling likeness of her." [873]

Porchey was another to take no part in her burial in Austria; it all proceeded as no more than a formality, eight years after she died.

Tilly was in her sphere, a legend during her lifetime and remained one in her death. One respected dance teacher linked Tilly's name with the great Nijinsky as someone " whose classical technique had not been ruined by their experiments with the modern". [874]

Tilly's tombstone records :-


TILLY LOSCH

NOVEMBER 15, 1903 – DECEMBER 24, 1975

DANCER   ACTRESS   ARTIST

The wording is in English rather than her native German!

# 1976

## Porchey's Memoirs, America and TV Fame

Porchey became a TV celebrity as a result of his appearances on the Michael Parkinson show. This tied in neatly with his two volumes of memoirs, ghost written by Barry Wynn.

Not surprisingly, the lawyers were alarmed by the earlier versions of the book and the names mentioned. The final print was edited and the ghost writer Wynn paid £10,000 to forget the names of some of Porchey's victims.

*The Daily Express of 17 October 1976 records:*

" The EARL of CARNARVON, 77, is bringing out his memoirs shortly, but I fear they will not be nearly as spicy as the version prepared by writer Barry Wynn. " Porchie" Carnarvon's advisers were so alarmed by his indiscretions on tape to Buckinghamshire-based Mr Wynn that the Earl eventually had to pay him nearly £10,000 to forget the whole thing.

Now Lord Carnarvon, whose life has been concerned largely with race horses and women - he has been married twice- has prepared *No Regrets*, a more subdued memoir which is dedicated to his 70-year-old secretary, Crystal Stubbings. Miss Stubbings has given 40 years of her life to looking after the Earl. Sadly, the book will not contain the story of one of Porchie's most dramatic experiences feature the Wynn Tapes – the night a lady had  fit while having discussions with him in her room. The Sixth Earl.....brought her to her senses with a pitcher of cold water."

The memoirs remain conceited, highly inaccurate and in many cases contrived. But new friendships emerged as Porchey travelled in Britain and USA promoting himself.

Many  past visitors to Highclere in Porchey's last days recall the time with pleasure. The spy journalist, Chapman Pincher  remarks of " the splendid ambience of Highclere Castle…has given my wife and me great pleasure through friendship with the last two Earls [ Porchey and Porchester ]. [875]

Pincher interviewed "young Porchie: The Man who makes the Queen's horses run" in the Daily Express on 23 Januaru 1978.

# 1977
# Catherine's Death

In the closing years of Catherine's life Lord Porchester attended to his mother's affairs. There were always new burdens and staff to recruit, to ease the condition of the old couple living in Switzerland as illness and senility struck and, ultimately, death.

The family intimation in The Times was on 12 April 1977:

"DEATHS: MOMAND: On Sat April 8 1977 Catherine (nee Wendell), beloved wife of Don and adored mother of Porchey and Penelope – peacefully at Lausanne, Switzerland. Funeral Highclere 13 April."

She was buried at Highclere Cemetery.  Don Momand survived her until 1983. His name is recorded with Catherine's on the memorial stone which bears an inscription of *'Blessed Are the Pure In Heart.'*

## 1980s

Throughout the early 1980s, as old Porchey's health failed, Lord Porchester was "waiting for his octogenarian father ... to drop off the perch", as *Private Eye* put it in 1983.  Porchester eventually inherited Highclere Castle and its 6,500 acres in 1987.

*Porchey : Towards the end of his life*

# Silent Service

The Press reported[876] that Porchey was among a number of old buffers who lined up as ever to claim their £80-odd a day expenses for turning up at the House of Lords. After almost fifty years a peer, Porchey had set a remarkable record, since he entered the House of Lords in 1924 – he had yet to make a speech!

In the summer of 1984 the eighty-six-year-old Porchey became seriously ill again requiring major surgery for a stomach complaint.

Reports were mixed about his recovery. But in July it was announced that his Lordship was back at Highclere " calling for his normal diet of salmon and champagne".[877]

One spokesman told reporters " Porchey Carnarvon is a difficult chap to destroy." [878]

# 1987

## Porchey's Death

Porchey lingered for many months in a private nursing home, with crippling Parkinson's disease and age related dementia. He died on 22 September 1987, aged eighty-eight.

One of Porchey's two executors and trustees, Crystal Stubbings, his long devoted ( but retired ) land agent, had moved from living at The Field House on the Highclere Estate to return to her native Norfolk.

## Porchey's Funeral Wishes Snubbed

Porchey requested two things in his Last Will and Testament dated 18 October 1983:

"1. I would ask that a Memorial Service be held for me at St Mark's, North Audley Street, London, W1.

2.   I DIRECT that I would like to be buried three feet on the south side of my father's grave situated on Beacon Hill with my feet facing the stud farm."

The first of these requests was impossible as St Mark's ceased to be a place of worship some years before 1987.

The second of these requests was pointedly not performed by the family. Instead he was buried in Highclere Cemetery on the Estate. Today the flat gravestone is quite unreadable and appears neglected.

## Porchey's Bequests

After several bequests to family members Porchey left a token reminder of his affections to Bunny Esterhazy: "To my dear friend Countess Marianne Esterhazy my favourite picture *The Laughing Philosopher* by Annabel Caracci, currently in my smoking room."

The Right Honourable Henry George Alfred Marius Victor Francis Herbert, Sixth Earl of Carnarvon of Highclere Castle, Newbury, Berkshire left estate valued at £3,102,843 (Gross) £ 2,765,263(Net).

The late Ross Benson recorded a fond farewell to the amorous Earl.

" I cannot allow the Earl of Carnarvon's demise to pass without raising my top hat in memory to a man who brought pleasure and a satyr's love to so many women ( though there is, I acknowledge an army of cuckolded husbands who did not share my affection for the old boy).

Even in his dotage, his eye would still twinkle at the sight of a pretty face, a well-turned ankle – or his own recollection of philanderings past." [879]

# The Last Resting Place of Catherine and Porchey

## At Highclere Cemetery

## The Carnarvon Graves

Far Left : Seventh Earl's gravestone; Catherine and Don Momand ( flat stone ); Reggie Wendell ( Cross); Jac and Eileen Wendell ( flat stone); Marian Fendall Wendell ( Cross) Ellen Mary Hurley ( Nana) (upright gravestone Cross); and Sixth Earl of Carnarvon ( flat stone).

"In Everlasting Memory of Anne Catherine Tredick  Momand born 25 November 1900,  died 8 April, 1977 beloved Mama of Porchey and Penelope and Don Stuart Momand......
Blessed Are The Pure in Heart".  R.I.P.

**Lt. Col The Earl of Carnarvon  Born 7th November 1898, Died 22nd September 1987.**

# GENERAL NAME INDEX
( NB Porchey, Catherine and Tilly are
NOT indexed, follow sub headings in the
text for them.)

---

## END NOTES

[1] The courtesy title of Viscount Porchester was given to the eldest son of the Earl of Carnarvon. Second or third etc sons were termed the 'Honourable'. In 1780 the original title granted was Baron Porchester. Simon Winchester explains in his excellent book "Their Noble Lordships" Random House (1982) that "It became customary ... to give heirs to some of the more celebrated peerages monikers that derived from their courtesy titles."

[2] Henry Howard Molyneux Herbert, (1831-1890). Fourth Earl of Carnarvon.

[3] Before the structural changes made by Sir Charles Barry, begun by the 3rd Earl of Carnarvon ( from 1842) and finished on behalf of the 4th Earl ( after 1849), the building was called Highclere House.

[4] Gosford Park (2001) won Julian Fellowes the Best Original Screenplay Oscar at the Academy Awards.

[5] The Author was told this by a collateral member of the Carnarvon family.

[6] Attributed to the journalist and author, the late Hugh Massingberd (1946-2007) in the Daily Telegraph.

[7] Attributed by the journalist Brian Appleyard in The Sunday Times.

[8] Caxton Hall was built in 1878; it originally served as Westminster Town Hall. It took its name from Caxton Street, renamed from Chapel Street to mark the 500th anniversary of William Caxton's first printing press, which he had installed in the

old Almonry of the Abbey, just to the east. During the Second World War the building was used by the Ministry of Information as a secure venue for Churchill to hold press conferences. After decades of weddings, the Registry Office closed in 1979. It was completely redeveloped and converted into flats in 2006.

[9] Charlie, Mortimer. Dear Lupin: Letters to a Wayward Son. (2012). Constable & Robinson Ltd.

[10] Max Reinhardt (1873-1943). Austrian born American stage and film actor and director.

[11] Sir Charles Blake Cochran (1872-1951). Theatre manager in London in the 1920s onwards.

[12] Edward William Frank James (1907-1984). Wealthy English artist and poet.

[13] George Jackson, the American dance critic writes "There is film of how Tilly Losch danced, not from her initial career in Vienna but from the 1930s and '40s. The earliest footage is her *Hand Dance* (1930 – 1933?). This solo for the hands, arms and upper body was originally co-choreographed with her Vienna colleague Hedy (Hedwig) Pfundmayr. Both rehearsal and performance takes of it are on the Internet [You Tube], the former showing more of her entire body in motion. Tilly's hands in it are expressive but not fussy."

[14] Cartland, Barbara. I search for rainbows. Arrow Books. (1973).

[15] Sidney Franklin directed Tilly in "The Good Earth" (1937); Herbert Wilcox directed Tilly in "Limelight" and King Vidor directed Tilly in "Duel in the Sun" (1947).

[16] Cartland, Barbara. I search for rainbows. Arrow Books. ( 1973).

[17] Jeanne Stuart (1908-2003). British actress, born Ivy Sweet. After the Second World War she moved the USA and in 1952 married Baron Eugene de Rothschild.

[18] There seems to be some conflict over whether the ship was heading for America or Canada or both. The romantic novelist Barbara Cartland says in her "Book of Celebrities" Quartet Books (1982) , which has a few pages devoted to Tilly, that they "travelled to Canada together during the war. There were submarines stalking us, the ship was overrun with children, there weren't enough lifeboats or lifebelts, it was very rough. Tilly lay in bed looking lovely, composed, mysterious and ate caviar."

[19] Sir Bernard Docker (1896-1978). Leading industrialist associated with the Daimler Car Company.

[20] Wyndham, Horace. Chorus to Coronet. British Technical and General Press. London. (1951).

[21] Extracted from articles in Newspaper Archive.com

[22] Ibid.

[23] Ibid.

[24] The quotations mentioned from the London photographer were reported and syndicated in American newspapers, including being repeated in The Helena Daily Independent of April, 1926. See Newspaper Archive.com.

[25] Ibid.

[26] Lady Diana Manners (Cooper) (1892-1986). Prominent Socialite and silent movie star. Born Lady Diana Manners daughter of the 8th Duke of Rutland, she married the diplomat Duff Cooper, later Viscount Norwich.

[27] Diana Manners played the Madonna in the original Broadway production of Karl Vollmoller's "The Miracle" in 1924. Later in 1932 she repeated the role in London at the Lyceum Theatre, for Max Reinhardt. That production also starred Tilly Losch.

[28] Alva Vanderbilt (1853- 1933). Multi-millionaire American socialite.

[29] Consuelo Vanderbilt (1877-1964) 9th Duchess of Marlborough, later Mrs Balsan.

[30] Charles Spencer-Churchill, (1871-1934). 9th Duke of Marlborough. Known as "Sunny". His links (in late life during his last illness) with Almina Carnarvon are outlined in the Author's book "The Life and Secrets of Almina Carnarvon".

[31] In 1895 the diplomat- politician Hon. George Curzon (later a Marquess) married the American heiress Mary Leiter.

[32] The Times of 13 December 1898 records " The baptism of Lord Porchester, infant son and heir of the Earl and Countess of Carnarvon, took place yesterday afternoon in the Chapel Royal, St James's Palace. The Rev Edgar Sheppard, Sub Dean of the Chapels Royal, performed the rite, and used water brought from the River Jordan. The child received the names of Henry George Alfred Marius Victor Francis, and the sponsors were Prince Victor Duleep Singh, Lord Ashburton, Mr. Alfred de Rothschild, Lady Burghclere, and Mrs. Wombwell. "

[33] Horace Wyndham. English writer.

[34] Wyndham, Horace. Chorus to Coronet. British Technical and General Press. London. (1951).

[35] See Rose, Janet R. Historic Sandridge Revisted. St Leonard's Publishing (1999) page 133. "Percival Griffiths obtained a 99 year lease on Sandridgebury in 1902 and completely refurbished it, including the coach house and grounds."

[36] Gertrude uses this name when writer to Lord Porchester (later 7th Earl) during the Second World War.

[37] Two properties Willowbank, Kittery and Frostfields, Newcastle were summer hiomes occupied by the Wendells.

[38] Passenger Lists, in National Archives, Kew.

[39] New York Times, 17 April 1895 and Cincinnati Enquirer 21 April 1895.

[40] See The Sunday Herald, 29 November 1891.

[41] New York Times, 17 April 1895 and Cincinnati Enquirer 21 April 1895.

[42] Evert Jansen Wendell born about 1614-15 sailed from Embden, East Friesland, Holland to New Netherland about 1640, resided for a while in New Amsterdam, ( New York ) and thereafter in Fort Orange, Albany where he lived and died in 1709. Jacob Jnr and his siblings were from the ninth generation after the original Wendell settler. See also James Rindge Stanwood's "The Direct Ancestry of the late Jacob Wendell of Portsmouth, New Hampshire", David Clapp & Son, Boston (1882). Stanwood was a nephew of Jacob Wendell II.

[43] Philip Fendall was a materal kinsman of Catherine. Mehitabel Rindge Rogers ( Mrs J Wendell ) and Jacob Wendell as featured here were great-grandparents of Catherine.

[44] The author recommends William M Emery's "The Salters of Portsmouth, New Hampshire" New Bedford, Mass (1936). Emery describes himself as "a lineal descendant of Captain Titus Salter".

[45] The 1870 US Census for Portsmouth NH (20 July 1870) shows that Marian's parents were living together at the home of Jonathan and Ann Tredick (Marian's maternal grandparents).

[46] Major Philip Richard Fendall (1832-1879) United States Marine Corps. Born in District of Columbia. A member of a notable family caught up on opposite sides in the American Civil War. He made his name as an Indian fighter when based at Portsmouth, New Hampshire, 1856. He died at Portsmouth while still serving with the Marines although is recorded as being on sick leave 1878-9.

[47] Marian's paternal grandparents were Philip Richard Fendall (1794-1868) and Elizabeth Young (1804-1859). General Robert E Lee (1807-1870). One of Philip's son fought for the Confederacy, two sided with the Union.

[48] Anne Catherine Tredick—later Fendall (1836-1889) a grave, with a fine monumental stone, can be located at St Anne's Cemetery, Annapolis, Anne Arundel County, Maryland. Anne is described as a "wife of Major Philip R Fendall of the US MC". One text records her death as " May 12, 1889, at Portsmouth, New Hampshire, Mrs. Anne C. F. Fendall, widow of Major Philip R. Fendall of the United States Marine ... Fell asleep in Jesus"

[49] New York Times, 17 April 1895.

[50] Evert held the intercollegiate record for the 100 and 220 yards dash. He also took part in the quarter mile run.

[51] Ibid.

[52] Marian's paternal [Fendall] grandparents had eight sons and three daughters. The girls were Elizabeth (Bessie), Mary and Florence.

[53] Ibid.

[54] Jacob (known as Jac) Wendell was born on 30 January 1896, he died in 1963. Reginald (known as Reggie) Lee Wendell was born on 19 October 1898, he died in 1928 at Highclere; the death is described in this book.

[55] Jacob Wendell II was born in Portsmouth, NH in 1826. In 1854 he married Mary Bertodi Barrett, daughter of N A Barrett of Boston. Jacob moved to New York in 1863 and was involved in a variety of businesses, he was a director of several banks, insurance and real estate associations and a member of New York's Chamber of Commerce. He died in 1898.

[56] Jacob II knew that his youngest son and daughter in law would need a house for their emerging family and provided them with a Wendell property at 106 East Thirty Fifth Street, New York. On 17 February, 1898, after the birth of their first child, (and another expected), Jacob II added a codicil to his Will that Jacob Jnr should have the right to buy the house for $40,000 to be paid by note, charged against his share of the family estate.

[57] Jacob Wendell (1788-1865). Father of Jacob II. Born and died in Portsmouth, New Hampshire. Jacob was a merchant and importer in the Russian and West Indian trade. He made a fortune as a privateer during the war of 1812. In 1815, Jacob and his brother Isaac Wendell and others established and operated some of

the earlier mills founded in New Hampshire for the manufacture of cotton cloth. The mills earned a handsome profit until the commercial panic of 1827-1828 swept the country and one mercantile crash succeeded another. As a result, Great Falls Manufacturing failed.

[58] Based on a letter in Box 30 in Wendell Papers in the Portsmouth Athenæum. Diana Fitzpatrick's e-mail to the author on 6 August 2013.

[59] Charles W. Wendell, Ph.D. (of Plainfield, NJ) advises the source as follows: "Letters to Evert Jansen Wendell" by A.J.F. van Laer, appear in The Yearbook, 1928 -1929, Volum3 IV, The Dutch Settlers Society of Albany, pp. 1-7. There are three letters. The second one includes the quote: "Further, if it please God, you again sign your name, you must write it thus: Everden Jansen, which is after your blessed grandfather, but Wendell, that is after your blessed grandmother. You can govern yourself accordingly; we write you this for your own sake," p. 6. The letter is signed "Done in Embden, the 27th of December anno 1661, Your brother-in-law Eylert Hommes and my wife Anneke Janssen, your sister, and Jan Ennen and his wife Dedde Janssen, your sister, we together wish you all that is best for you."

[60] The painting of Mary Bertodi Barrett Wendell in 1888, is by John Singer Sargent. Image reproduced by the kind permission of the New York Historical Society. Having a portrait painted by Sargent was a sure sign of wealth.

[61] Self. Robert T. Barrett Wendell. Twayne Publishers (1975).

[62] At Harvard University a Jacob Wendell Scholarship remains to this day "for the highest scholar in the freshman class".

[63] Mary Bertodi Barrett Wendell (1832-1912). Wife and widow of Jacob II.

[64] Barrett Wendell (1855-1921). Assistant Professor of English from 1888 to 1898, Professor of English from 1898 to 1917 at Harvard University.

[65] Self. Robert T. Barrett Wendell. Twayne Publishers (1975).

[66] Ibid.

[67] Ibid.

[68] A detailed obituary of Evert Jansen Wendell is in the Year Book of the Holland Society of New York for 1918. Evert died (from the consequences of diabetes) in France on 28 August, 1917. He had gone there to do war work. The Holland Society year book records "Evert went to France in August, 1917, to aid in founding the American College Union in Paris, which is a general headquarters there for all American college men. He also was to look after the administration of the Aero Club's fund for the welfare of the American airmen in France. When he left home, he was already ill, on this voyage he grew worse. And a week or so after he reached Paris he died in the American Hospital at Neuilly."

[69] Self. Robert T. Barrett Wendell. Twayne Publishers (1975).

[70] Ibid.

[71] Harvard Class of 1882. Secretary's Report. Volume V.

[72] Ibid.

[73] Pedigree of Gordon Wendell ( which equally applies to his niece Catherine ) extracted from the Year Book of The Holland Society of New York for 1910. With thanks to the Society's Archivist Mary Collins.

[74] Charles Wyman Morse (1856-1933) was a notorious businessman and speculator on Wall Street in the early 20th Century. Morse was convicted of violations of federal banking laws. He was sentenced to 15 years in the Atlanta federal penitentiary.

[75] Gordon died at his home 126 East Thirty-Fifth Street on 31 January 1910. His widow was Fannie (Frances Caldwalader Elwyn), daughter of Rev Alfred L Elwyn of Philadelphia. Daughter Frances Gordon Wendell married John Gilbert Marshall Stone in 1920.

[76] Mary Wendell (born 1832) died at her home of   8 East 38th Street, New York on Friday 20 December 1912 aged 80.

[77] The papers of the Club ( from 1795-2011) are in Harvard University Archives. http://oasis.lib.harvard.edu/oasis/deliver/~hua13012

[78] New York Times, 23 April 1911.

[79] Annual Report of the Secretary of State of War. US War Department ( 1897)

[80] There were more rewarding projects. The business between Jacob and Rufus appears to be involved in railways supplies and investment. Rufus highlights ( in a Report for his Harvard Class ) that the business" installed the Gamewell Police Signal System in Havana …as well as being associated in a number of street railway enterprises, including Houghton County Street Railway at Hancock, Mich, and others in New York.

[81] Cambridge Tribune, 28 December 1895.

[82] Ronan Donohoe of Portsmouth Athenaeum, has researched Rufus Leighton MacDuffie to 1921 and comments "he appears quite solvent", which is at odds with a claim that his business partner Jacob Jnr was made bankrupt when he parted company with Rufus in 1909.

[83] Carnarvon, Fiona. [Countess of]. Lady Catherine and the Real Downton Abbey. Hodder and Stoughton. (2013)

[84] The author has asked the Portsmouth Athenaeum to trace any bankruptcy papers on Jacob Jnr, without anything being identified.

[85] New York Sun, 1910.

[86] Ibid

[87] Ibid.

[88] Washington Post, 10 November 1909. Marriage at the Church of Incarnation, New York of Miss Eleanor S Whipple to Francis R Stoddard Jnr.

[89] New York Times, 23 April 1911.

[90] Ibid.

[91] Washington Post, 31 March and 11 May 1911. Mary Lee Fendall [daughter of Philip Richard Fendall and Elizabeth Young, Catherine's paternal grandparents] died at 1319 New Hampshire Avenue, aged 83.

[92] Founded in 1832 and established at the present site in 1842. The Church has long associations with the Roosevelt, Astor and Vanderbilt families. The outcome of some research on the author's behalf by Charles D Wendell on whether Jacob and others are buried there "[reveals] that there are no memorials to the Wendells in the church; the Church has no cemetery of its own; the Church has a columbarium, the beginning of which post-dates the dates of the Wendells sought."

[93] Barrett Wendell Jnr (born 1881). Lived in Chicago.

[94] Ibid.

[95] Mary Wendell, (born 1883). Married Thomas Gorgon Wheelock, she later divorced him and married Reiner Gerrit Anton Van der Woude. Both husbands were international businessmen.

[96] De Wolfe Howe, MA and Milford, Humphrey. Barrett Wendell and his letters. OUP London (1924).

[97] When Mary Wendell died in 1912 she left a large part of her estate to her surviving sisters including her stocks. The residue was left to her sons, however it is unclear whether Marian received her late husband's share.

[98] Mary's estate largely comprised her home. Her capital was greatly reduced over the years. She left $159,023 (of which $ 120,000 was the value of her residence). A surviving sister, Sarah Barrett was left $12,323, with the balance distributed to her two surviving sons, Barrett and Evert and her grandchildren.

[99] Ronan Donohoe of the Portsmouth Athenaeum,  writes in an e-mail to the Author on 19 March 2013 "The exhibit on Catherine Tredick Wendell was a smashing success - focusing mostly on the people and places around here that figure in her early life and mostly before 1911 and the untimely death of her father and the family's removal to England. Childhood photos, exteriors and interiors of family homes - that sort of thing."

[100] Exchange of e-mails between the Author and Ronan Donohoe, 2013.

[101] John George Griffiths (1845- 1922). Sometime President of the Institute of Chartered Accountants. A senior partner in Deloitte and Co, until he retired in 1902.

[102] Gertrude Bailey Tredick (1874-1949).daughter of Titus Salter Tredick and Sarah Bailey.  Gertrude is listed as a crime writer in Allen J Hubin's Crime Fiction IV: A Comprehensive Bibliography 1749-2000. Part 46.

[103] Ibid.

[104] See Cross, William. The Life and Secrets of Almina Carnarvon. (2011).

[105] According to the late Richard Thrale in Thrale, Richard: A Newer Thraliana: A chronicle of the Thrale Family of Hertfordshire. Falconer Press ( 1973) " Back row from left: Sidney French, groom, brother of Hubert; Mr List the butler: Mr Arnold, gardener, "Big" Bert Woolmer, second gardener, later head: probably Sarah French, Hubert's wife: "Little" Bert Slough, gardener: Hubert French, chauffeur: Bert Newman, head gardener, died 1937: Front row : George Beacon, antique repairer, of the three ladies one possibly Isa daughter of Sarah French, and another possibly Macine, Scottish head housemaid. It seems that there was not a housekeeper as such."

[106] The Times of 4 March 1916 records "Deaths: TREDICK: On 2nd March at 11, Upper Grosvenor Street... SARAH B TREDICK, widow of T Salter Tredick of Portsmouth, New Hampshire. Daughter of Rear Admiral Theodores Bailey, USN. American papers please copy."

[107] With thanks to Ronan Donohoe and the proprietors of the  Portsmouth Athenaeum.

[108] A copy of this letter ( in full) has been provided to the Author by Ronan Donohoe of the Portsmouth Athenaeum.

[109] Extract from The Washington Post 13 April, 1913.

[110] Ellen (Nellie) Mary Hurley died in London in 1932, aged 78. She is buried at Highclere Cemetery.

[111] Francis Dudley Leigh, (1855-1938). From 1905 the third Baron Leigh with estates in Warwickshire and Gloucestershire and a house in London's Grosvenor Square.

[112] Rose, Janet R. Historic Sandridge Revisted. St Leonard's Publishing. (1999).

[113] Culled from the Daily Mirror, 9 September 1924.

[114] Carpenter, Louise. An Unlikely Countess. Harper Collins. (2004).

[115] Ladies' Who's Who. Hutchinson. See also Fife, George Buchanan. The passing legions. Macmillan. (1920).

[116] Among the other American women who supported this fund ( raising money and supplies from Britain and USA) were Lady Paget, Viscountess Harcourt, the Duchess of Marlborough, Lady Randolph Churchill and Mrs Whitelaw Reid ( wife of the American Ambassador ).

[117] Culled from the Daily Mirror, 16 November 1917.

[118] Norton-Harjes Ambulance Corps is the historical name given to The American Volunteer Motor Ambulance Corps, which was an organization started in London, England, in the autumn of 1914 by Richard Norton, a noted archeologist and the son of Harvard professor Charles Eliot Norton. Its mission was to assist the movement of wounded Allied troops from the battlefields to hospitals in France during World War I.

[119] d'Oyle Elliott, Ivo [Sir]. The Balliol Register. ( University of Oxford ) ( 1934).

[120] Photograph from the Year Book of The Holland Society of New York for 1918. With thanks to the Society's Archivist Mary Collins.

[121] See The Times 29 June, 1917. This was the wedding at St Albans Cathedral on 28 June 1917 of Captain Horace Frederick Gale (Bedfordshire Regiment) to Helen Frances Anson., daughter of the late Hon. Frederic Anson and Mrs. Anson of Cell Barnes, St Albans. [Catherine is recorded as "Kathleen".]

[122] Long article in The Washington Post, 31 August 1924.

[123] Ibid.

[124] The Times, 17 November 1919.

[125] Hon. Lois Sturt (1900-1937). Youngest daughter of 2nd Lord Alington (died 1919). From 1928 Lois was the Hon. Mrs. Evan Morgan, from 1934 on Evan becoming Viscount Tredegar she became Viscountess.

[126] See Cross, William. Not Behind Lace Curtains. The Hidden World of Evan, Viscount Tredegar. Book Midden. (2013).

[127] In 1928 Reggie Herbert returned to his wife Bee, and Lois married to provide a cover for her and the well matched homosexual Tredegar heir, Evan Frederic Morgan (1893-1949), whose cousins were among the minor Royals, viz the Carnegies of Southesk, whose seat was Kinnaird Castle, Brechin.

[128] The Times, 15 April 1920.

[129] Carnarvon, Fiona [Countess of]. Lady Catherine and the Real Downton Abbey. Hodder and Stoughton. (2013).

[130] Porchey attended Sandhurst Military College and on 27 October 1916 was gazetted as a second Lieutenant in the 7th Hussars and later promoted Lieutenant.

[131] A postal enquiry by the author sent to Fiona D M B Finlay, the granddaughter of Francis Collingwood Drake was unanswered.

[132] The Times, 28 December 1921. Francis was married at St Mark's North Audley Street followed by a quiet reception at Claridges Hotel - owing to mourning in the bride's family.

[133] It is a curiosity that there are very few photographs of Porchey when he was a young man.

[134] See Cross, William. The Life and Secrets of Almina Carnarvon. (2011) and also Cross, William. Lordy! Tutankhamun's Patron as a Young Man. Book Midden. (2012).

[135] Prince Victor Albert Jay Duleep Singh (1866-1918) son of the Maharaja Duleep Singh (1838-1893).

[136] The documentary evidence to support this statement comes from a letter written to Tony Leadbetter (Almina's godson) by a biographer commissioned by the seventh Earl of Carnarvon to write a biography of Almina in the 1990s. The book was suppressed. This letter is on Highclere Castle headed notepaper. The paternity issue is referred to in detail in the book "The Life and Secrets of Almina Carnarvon".

[137] See Cross, William. The Life and Secrets of Almina Carnarvon, (2011) and Carnarvon, Fiona [Countess of]. Lady Almina and the Real Downton Abbey. Hodder and Stoughton. (2011).

[138] Letter to the author dated 23 July, 2013 from Lady CB.

[139] Private Source ( contact Author to verify) commenting on the article "Dark Past of the Real Downton Abbey Duchess" in The Daily Telegraph, 9 August 2011.

[140] http://www.dailymail.co.uk/femail/article-2051649/Downton-Abbey-A-lonely-countess-illicit-love-affair-Egyptian-prince.html

[141] Before her marriage Lady Anne Coventry was summoned by Victor's godmother, Queen Victoria and commanded NOT to have any children with Victor. See Bance, Peter. Sovereign, Squire and Rebel: Maharajah Duleep Singh and the Heirs of a Lost Kingdom. Coronet House Publishing Ltd. (2009).

[142] A remark attributed to contemporaries.

[143] Maharani Bamba Duleep Singh born Bamba Müller (1848-1887).

[144] Author's interview with ML, an octogenarian resident of Newbury, whose family were associated with the Highclere Estate over many generations.

[145] The Times, 13 December 1898.

[146] Aylesbury Census for 1901.

[147] Reading Mercury, 14 April, 1900.

[148] Lady Evelyn Leonora Almina Herbert, born 15 August 1901.

[149] LB comments " Porchey was reared by the strangers on the Carnarvon family's payroll, wet nurses, nursemaids, nannies and servants and when delinquent, or an embarrassment he was beaten by his parents ( whose marriage was a sham ): it is not surprising that as a result he hated their guts."

[150] Sheffield Daily Telegraph, 12 September 1904.

[151] Evening Telegraph, 10 July 1906.

[152] Ibid.

[153] See Balsan Consuelo Vanderbilt. The Glitter & the Gold. George Mann ( 1973).

[154] Letter to the Author dated 30 July, 2013 from CL.

[155] The Duchess of Leeds was Lady Katherine Frances Lambton (1862-1952). Her son was John Francis Godolphin Osborne, (1901-1963), later the three times married 11th Duke, who lived his life on the French Riviera. The Dukedom became extinct in 1964, with the death of the 12th Duke.

[156] Manchester Courier, 18 July, 1908.

[157] Barnet Census for 1911.

[158] Carnarvon, Earl of. No Regrets. Weidenfeld and Nicolson, London. ( 1976).

[159] Ibid.

[160] Elizabeth [Elsie] Catherine Howard (1856-1929), Fourth Countess of Carnarvon from 1878, second wife of Henry Herbert, Fourth Earl.

[161] Captain Frederick Adolphus Wombwell (1869-1912). Brother of Almina, Fifth Countess of Carnarvon.

[162] Lieutenant Henry (Harry) Grace Kerr 9th Lancers was dangerously wounded and taken to 7 Casualty Clearing Station. He later died on 1 July, 1917 from gunshot wounds to the legs (fractured) and thorax. Harry's mother Lady Greville (Olive Grace) was informed at her home at Dean Lodge, Ash Green, Aldershot. Harry was buried at Noeux-les-Mines Cemetery, S of Bethune, in the Lens district of France. Harry was a son by marriage to her late husband, the financier Henry Scanlan Kerr, who died in 1907. Harry was born on Long Island, USA, on 15 August 1896. Before going to Eton Harry was privately tutored, he later went to Cheltenham Cottage and at fourteen transferred to Eton College, where his best friend was Porchey. [Information extracted from National Archives, Kew, file WO 339/66974.]

[163] John Alan Burns (1897-1957). He inherited the title of Lord Inverclyde from his father in 1919.

[164] On the Michael Parkinson TV Show ( in the 1970s) Porchey mentiones " There was a darling girl. She was called Mae, and I met her at Lingfield Races. So I happened to fall madly in love with this girl. Remember I'm at Sandhurst at the time. She was dreamy. " The woman's husband disturbed them in bed and Porchey ended up jumping out of the bedroom twenty feet down into a garden of geraniums.

[165] Carnarvon, Earl of. No Regrets. Weidenfeld and Nicolson. (1976).

[166] National Archives Kew. War Diaries 7th Queen's Own Hussars See WO 95/5084 and WO 95/ 5092.

[167] 2/Lieutenant The Lord Porchester is also included in the "Nominal Roll of officers of the 7th Hussars on 19th November 1917 when the regiment embarked at Karachi for passage to Mesopotamia." See also Evans, Major- General Roger. CB, MC. DL. The Years Between. The Story of the 7th Queen's Own Hussars, 1911-1937. Porchey is not otherwise mentioned in the history of the regiment.

[168] The Daily Mirror of 9 July 1919 records "Lord Porchester had a couple of mounts … although he was unplaced on Sheringham in the Allies Cup, he did better in finishing third on Avezzano in the Dunbridge Welter."

[169] Manchester Courier, 12 April, 1913.

[170] General Sir Horace Dorrien-Smith (1858-1930).

[171] Gibraltar was captured from Spain in 1704 and formally ceded to Britain by the Treaty of Utrecht in 1713. Work began in 1894 to convert Gibraltar into a naval base. Legislative and executive authority was vested in the governor until 1922, when an executive council was appointed. In 1940 the entire civilian population was evacuated to Britain, returning between 1944 and 1951.

[172] National Archives, Kew, UK Passengers Lists, Emigrants.

[173] Tilly Losch's advice cited by Leo Lerman in his Journals [Ed. Stephen Pascal] "The Grand Surprise". Alfred A Knopf. ( 2007)

[174] Carnarvon, Earl of. No Regrets. Weidenfeld & Nicolson. ( 1976).

[175] Ibid.

[176] One informant LB writes "Porchey's time as a soldier, starting as a 2nd Lieutenant at Sandhurst and later serving with the 7th Queen's Own Hussars in Mesopotamia ( Turkey ) was undistinguished, but for the adage of his peer's title to a lowly rank. Service in the Middle East and India turned him into an uncouth polo-playing, pig-sticking snob, a bigot, a bully with a rough edge, a taste for giving subordinates the lash, a cruel and savage streak, akin to the fictional villain, Flashman, [ a character in the Thomas Hughes novel ' Tom Brown's Schooldays' who reappears as Sir Harry Paget Flashman in a series of novels by George Macdonald Fraser ] especially in his attitude to those beneath him or when handing the delicacies of the female of the species. He had no respect for women, they all as bad as his mother at deceiving him, and his blue tongue in their presence was no better than the stable lad's that could the milk sour."

[177] Tommy Frost, an army pal of Porchey and later his financial adviser.

[178] William George Bradley Craven. (1897-1932). From 1921, the Fifth Earl of Craven.

[179] National Archives, Kew, File WO 339/26739.

[180] Ibid.

[181] Cornelia Martin (1876-1961). Fourth Countess of Craven.

[182] Mary Wilhelmina George died 1974. Fifth Countess of Craven

[183] See Ermine Tales. Weidenfeld & Nicolson (1980).

[184] This story is mentioned in Porchey's second volume of Memoirs, Ermine Tales. Weidenfeld & Nicolson (1980). It is also featured in the William Hickey column of the Daily Express, 6 November 1979.

[185] The wife of Jac Wendell (Catherine's brother) was Eileen Carr. She had two brothers, Arthur and Philip Gordon Carr. Arthur was a well known English county cricketer, who briefly captained England. Philip (usually known as Gordon) was a stockbroker with the family firm. But Gordon was a hell raiser. His first marriage in 1924 to Cecelia Lucille Winslow deteriorated in its early days, into a vicious divorce petition, with Cecilia alleging all sorts of abuse and violence by a drunken Gordon. The petition lapsed and the couple separated.

Cecelia (named as Mrs Gordon Carr) accompanied her friend, a vivacious twice married South African, Vera Fraser, Countess Cathcart (an authoress of steamy romantic fiction) on a notorious trip to America in 1926. The trip attracted newspaper headlines when Vera (divorced from her husband, Earl Cathcart, in 1922, on account of her very public affair which was strewn across the British and American newspapers of 1924-25) with the Earl of Craven, including joining him on hunting trip to Africa, which Lady Craven (a famed lover of Porchey ) named Vera in her divorce petition.) Vera (who was in the USA to promote a play) was refused entry as an undesirable alien by the immigration authorities into New York. The exclusion was because she had "admitted committing a crime involving moral turpitude", (namely, running off with Craven to Africa whilst still married). Leaving her shocked friend in custody on Ellis Island (awaiting deportation) Cecilia made her way to Washington to appeal to the authorities on her behalf.

Vera was eventually released after two weeks of backtracking and dogged confusion and diplomatic activities behind the scene between the officials in USA and Britain. Cecilia was waiting to greet her friend and take her for pampering at the Ambassador Hotel, New York. They later returned to Britain, to renewed waves of publicity. Vera later married a third husband, a millionaire baronet, ship owner, Sir John Rowland Hodge. She died in 1993. Cecilia Carr died in 1930 aged only 30, Gordon remarried.

[186] Conversations between the Author and Almina's godson, Tony Leadbetter. Other reports speak of Porchey "dodging the honour of marrying Princess Mary".

[187] See Cross, William. The Life and Secrets of Almina Carnarvon. (2011).

[188] It is credible that Lord Carnarvon was the father his daughter, Lady Evelyn Herbert (1901-1980) since this outcome was the judgment of the biographer of Almina whose book was suppressed by the 7th Earl in the 1990s. The Author has had several conversations with various informants including an octogenarian resident of Newbury who knows the Carnarvon family well over several generations. He raised doubts about the 5th Earl's capacity to father a child.

[189] See Windsor, Edward, Duke of. Letters from a Prince: Edward, Prince of Wales to Mrs. Freda Dudley Ward, March 1918- January 1921. Little, Brown Book Group Ltd. (1998). This book lists the Prince's coterie, starting with Freda Dudley Ward who was the Prince's girlfriend from 1918 -1930s (although both strayed into others' arms). "Freda [Dudley Ward] and the Prince saw the same people over and over again: Shelia Chisholm, the Colin Buists, Poppy Baring, the Eric Dudleys, Hugh Sefton, Esmond Harmsworth ( the future Viscount Rothermere and chairman of the Daily Mail) , Ali Mackintosh, Edwina d'Erlanger " Porchey", [ Lord] Porchester ( the future Earl of Carnarvon), Perry and Kitty Brownlow...."

[190] Murphy, Charles, JV & Bryan, J, III. The Windsor Story. Dell (1981).

[191] Poppy Baring (1901-1979) was the daughter of Sir Godfrey and Lady Baring of Nubia House, Cowes. In 1925 she married William Piers Thursby (died 1977) He was known as Peter.

[192] Fielding, Daphne Vivian. The Duchess of Jermyn Street. Penguin Books (1978).

[193] Poppy Baring and Lois Sturt had known each other from the age of ten as they were bridesmaids together at a large Society wedding in 1910. See the Times 19 March, 1910.

[194] The Guardian 18 December, 1928.

[195] Conversations between the Author and Almina's godson, Tony Leadbetter.

[196] From the Noel Coward song 'Poor Little Rich Girl' "Cocktails and Laughter, but what comes after? Nobody knows." Also the title of a book of Society photographs by Loelia, Duchess of Westminster, edited by Hugo Vickers.

[197] Ibid.

[198] See The Times 26 April 1922. This was the wedding of Lt Commander Gerald M McKenna to Hon. Emily Burns, daughter of the late Lord Inverclyde. Mr. and Mrs. Theodore McKenna were neighbours of Gertrude Griffiths, the Griffiths were sometime at 34, the McKennas at 24 Bryanston Square, London. [Catherine is recorded as "Kathleen"].This link also suggests that Marian kept in with the Inverclydes after the Gibraltar trip of 1921, which led to Cathereine meeting Porchey.

[199] Conversations between the Author and Tony Leadbetter, Almina's godson.

[200] The Times, 14 July 1922

[201] Hon. Mervyn Robert Howard Molyneux Herbert (1882-1929). His wife Mary survived him until 1979. They have three children and there is a surviving Herbert genealogical male line.

[202] See Cross, William. The Life and Secrets of Almina Carnarvon. (2011).

[203] In 2012 the Author, with Tony Leadbetter (who knew Almina from 1942 until her death and whose Aunt Alice Butler and mother Anne Leadbetter were Almina's housekeepers for four decades), visited the village of Bicknoller, Somerset, where Almina lived from 1943-49. An octogenarian resident (whose family worked for Almina) said "Almina always said that Lord Carnarvon died of throat cancer. The rest on insects and curses is bunkum". For source contact Author.

[204] The full line up was Lady Evelyn Herbert, Philippa Wendell, Lady Diana King, Peggy Leigh, Lilian d'Erlanger, Poppy Baring, Margaret Coats, Eileen Carr and Myrtle Farquharson.

[205] The Portsmouth Herald in a retrospective on the Wendells, in the edition of 10 April 1923.

[206] Claude George Bowes-Lyon (1855-1944), 14th Earl of Strathmore and Kinghorne, and Claude Bowes-Lyon, (1824-1904), 13th Earl of Strathmore and Kinghorne.

[207] Prince Albert Victor, Duke of Clarence and Avondale. (1864-1892). Eldest son of King Edward VII (when Prince of Wales) and Princess Alexandra. The subject of many biographies and claims about his sanity, sexuality and bad deeds. His death (which was a convenient one, given his scandalous reputation) is officially recorded as taking place at Sandringham Palace, Norfolk, during a flu pandemic.

[208] This incredible (and somewhat unlikely) claim of Eddy's survival beyond the official record of his death in 1892 (and which requires much further research and appraisal to confirm or reject) was told to the Author by an octogenarian with contacts close to Highclere. There is evidence that Eddy was familiar with the Strathmores when he stayed with his grandmother (Queen Victoria) at Balmoral.

[209] See National Archives, Kew. Tax files relating to the Estate of Alfred de Rothschild. IR 59/519 to IR59/522.

[210] See Cross, William. "Lordy! Tutankhamun's Patron as a Young Man". Book Midden. (2012)

[211] Almina left London by air on 20 March 1923 and arrived in Cairo (says Howard Carter in his diary) on 26 March 1923. The journey was by air, train, boat and finally train.

[212] Letters examined by the Author in Carlisle Archives (Howard Collection) and Somerset Archives (Herbert Collection).

[213] Tony Leadbetter makes clear that *if* morphine was given it was an elaborate process to prepare, and required a doctor to admininister the drug into the patients's bloodstream, gradually increasing doses every 4 hours. Marcus Johnston would have had the means to prescribe this course of action to hasten Carnarvon's death. It was a treatment for terminal pain ( in the absence of anti-biotics).

[214] Interview between the author and ML, an octogenarian resident of Newbury, Berkshire, whose family have worked on the Highclere Estate for several generations.

[215] The Author's book "Lordy! Tutankhamun's Patron as a Young Man". Book Midden. ( 2012) is based on the diaries and letters of the Henry Herbert, 4th Earl of Carnarvon, which are held by the British Library, London and National Archives, Kew.

[216] An account by Lord Carnarvon of the discovery of Tutankhamun's tomb fetched £1,870 at Sotheby's in 1979. The British Library copy is missing from the shelf.

[217] Hoving, Thomas. Tutankhamun: The Untold Story. Hamish Hamilton (1979).

[218] Thomas Hoving (1931-2009). He was a former official at the Metropolitan Museum. He cites seventeen objects at the Metropolitan including ten large pieces originally removed from the tomb by Carnarvon and Carter. Several other pieces were discovered and intercepted by the Egyptian authorities (including a head of Tutankhamun found in a wine case in Carter's office).

[219] Information provided to the Author by a well-placed contact of a collateral branch of the Herbert family who advised, "I suspect you know that the 5th Earl of Carnarvon and Howard Carter were "an item". I was reliability informed of this by a friend of mine whose godfather was intimately involved with that couple." See also Cross, William. "Lordy! Tutankhamun's Patron as a Young Man". Book Midden (2012).

[220] One interesting aside on the curse is the work of the late Dominic Montserrat ( 1964-2002) an Egyptologist, when proposed ( in 2000) that the story of the Pharaoh's curse – said to have killed six people of the Tutankhamun expedition in the decade after the tomb's discovery – actually originated in early 19th century England and was perpetuated by, among others, Louisa May Alcott, the author of Little Women. See The Times, 29 October, 2004.

[221] The Times, 8 January 1919, has details of the Will of Prince Victor Albert Jay Duleep Singh, died June 7, 1918 at Monte Carlo.

[222] LB comments " Despite Victor's love for Lord Carnarvon, Porchey was not loved or given attention or affection in his home life. He was largely ignored by the man he called his father. Frequently Porchey was taunted by his mother especially over the identity of his real father. "

[223] See The Times, May 18, 1923.

[224] Prince Victor Albert Jay Duleep Singh, died June 7, 1918 at Monte Carlo.

[225] Referred to by several newspapers who reported on the contents of the Will of the 5th Earl, published in 1923. See The Times, 18 May, 1923.

[226] When it came down to revealing the existence of a terminal illness in any of her charges , Almina followed the dictate of her mentor Lord Moynihan, which was in effect NEVER to tell a patient they were dying.

[227] This relationship is investigated by the Author is his book "Lordy! Tutankhamun's Patron As a Young Man" Book Midden Publishing ( 2012).

[228] See Cross, William. The Life and Secrets of Almina Carnarvon. ( 2011).

[229] Porchey "declared four pounds over weight for Azimuth in the Hamsey Handicap, and rode an exceptionally well-judged race." See Evening Telegraph, 13 August 1923.

[230] The shadow over the paternity of the Catherine's first child, Lord Porchester, later Seventh Earl of Carnarvon has been mentioned to the Author by Almina's godson ( who was told the story by his Aunt Alice Butler ) and by ML, a long standing Newbury resident. They both suggest further that the later close relationship between Porchester and the Royals stems from this fact.

[231] See Carnarvon, Fiona [Countess of] Lady Catherine and the Real Downton Abbey. Hodder and Stoughton, (2013).

[232] The Times, 31 May 1923.

[233] The Times, 4 July 1923.

[234] The Times 8 February 1924.

[235] Culled from the Daily Express, 24 March 1924

[236] Correspondence between the Author and Andrew Bruce, 11th Earl of Elgin. (Born 1924).

[237] Ronan Donohoe comments: "There are Wendell Family papers at Harvard [University] in the Houghton Library and we have the other half at the Portsmouth Athenaeum. They were split in half for no good reason. Both sets have finding aides available online."

[238] Exchange of e-mails between the Author and Ronan Donohoe (of the Portsmouth Athenaeum), March 2013.

[239] See Washington Post, 17 November, 1921 relating to the Estate of Andrew H Allen.

[240] Papers in the Wendell Archives at Portsmouth Athenaeum ( discovered by Diana Fitzpatrick) suggest that Philippa's brother Reggie Wendell was one of those very surprised to learn that his sister was marrying Galloway.

[241] The Times, 23 August 1923.

[242] Lord Rhidian Crichton-Stuart (1917-1969). Son of the 4th Marquess of Bute.

[243] Randolph Stewart was a member of the infamous Right Club, and Anglo German Fellowship and like his friend Charles Carnegie (later Earl of Southesk) were extreme Conservatives, with pro- German / Hitler sympathies. They both feature in Robin Saika's "The Red Book: The Membership List of the Right Club 1939" Foxley Books. (2010), which also includes William Joyce (Lord Haw Haw).

[244] Almina married Colonel Ian Onslow Dennistoun on 19 December 1923.

[245] She was previously Liliane (Baba) d'Erlanger daughter of Baron Emile d'Erlanger. Catherine's sister Philippa was a bridesmaid at Baba's wedding to Prince Jean Louis Faucigny-Lucinge on 14 November 1923.

[246] The Times, 29 May 1924.

[247] Nottingham Evening Post, 14 July 1924.

[248] Exchange of e-mails between the Author and Charles D Wendell, August-September 2013.

[249] Dundee Courier, 6 January 1936.

[250] What irked Porchey about Almina was that she was a complete waster. She was the rich banker, Baron Alfred de Rothschild's main legatees, in 1918, but spent her legacy foolishly on a roguish second husband, ( who later cost her dearly in a scandalous Court case in 1925), on lavish living, and buying more houses than she ever needed.

[251] Jac and Eileen Wendell lived at 16, Somers Place, London, W

[252] The Hon. Canon Grimston officiated at the christening. As well as the Carnarvons Mr A W Carr, Mr Percival Griffiths and Catherine' sister Philippa.

[253] Evening Telegraph, 28 August 1924.Almina bought Alvie Estate from R B Whitehead.

[254] Ballindalloch Castle is the home of the Macpherson-Grant family One of Ian Dennistoun's aunts Mary Dennistoun married Sir John Macpherson-Grant, the 4th Baronet.

[255] Dundee Courier, 25 August 1924.

[256] £50,000 was raised by Porchey in selling off the prized Carnarvon pearls and other heirlooms. Such was Almina's love of pearls they became one of her fads. She knew the importance of wearing them close to her skin; she was against ever letting the Carnarvon pearls go to sale.

[257] Full details can be gleaned in National Archives, Kew files IR59/519 to IR59/522. A particular curiosity is the Romilly portrait of Lady Hamilton, which Joseph Duveen paid Almina £17,000 on 29 February 1924. According to Tony Leadbetter this portriat ( now the property of an American owner ) was listed in the Eastmore catalogue after Almina sold up on the Isle of Wight in 1938-9. Orginally the property of Alfred de Rothschild, it is known that Alfred had some copies made of his favourite portraits.

[258] Conversations between the Author and Almina's godson, Tony Leadbetter.

[259] Ibid.

[260] See Godfrey. Rupert. Letters to a Prince. Edward, Prince of Wales, to Mrs. Freda Dudley Ward. Little Brown (1998).

[261] Based on conversations between the author and Tony Leadbetter, Almina's godson.

[262] Amy Mary Pauline Cliffe was from a family in County Wexford, Ireland. She married the 11th Earl of Galloway in 1891. He died in 1920, Amy survived until 1942.

[263] Randolph (as Lt Lord Garlies) was among thirty nine British officers who were arrested in Germany in 1915. They were thrown into filthy cells and where the water supply was impure, the food uneatable and the warders brutal. He was

released in January 1918 through the efforts of the Swiss Red Cross at Berne, where his mother went to greet him home.

[264] Lt Hon Keith Anthony Stewart (1894-1915), second son of the 11th Earl of Galloway. Keith died on 8 May 1915, aged 20, killed in action. He was a Lieutenant in the Black Watch.

[265] Notices appear in various newspapers and magazines in the early 1930s offering winter shooting ...At Cumloden- "pheasants, woodcock, snipe, duck etc; splendid woodcock bags..."

[266] The Author's book "The Dustbin Case, an Account of Dennistoun versus Dennistoun" contains a transcript of the Court proceedings.

[267] See Hyde, Harford Montgomery: Norman Burkett: the life of Lord Birkett of Ulverston. Hamish Hamilton (1964).

[268] Time Magazine, Monday 23 March, 1925.

[269] Arthur John Bigge, (1849-1931). 1st Baron Stamfordham.

[270] Also called the Ampthill baby case, involving the paternity of Geoffrey Russell, later 4th Baron Ampthill. The case reverberated for many decades.

[271] Letter from Lord Stamfordham to Viscount Cave from Buckingham Palace 6 March 1925.Copy in files LCO2/775 and WO 374/19236 in National Archives, Kew. [xiv] Interestingly, Sir Ellis Hume-Williams, barrister for Dorothy Dennistoun, opposed any change in the law. See Cabinet Papers ref CAB/24/172 in National Archives, Kew. Clearly Hume-Ellis saw this action as a "gag" on the freedom of the Press.

[272] Dennistoun file WO 374/19236; Cowans file WO 138/52.

[273] C E M Joad's 1926 critique Thrasymacus or the Future of Morals tries to explain this further: "Why should this case [have] attracted so much attention? Why was the wickedness involved considered so shocking? Why did those who would not have looked twice at the six-line paragraph describing a similar occurrence in the remoter suburbs, follow every detail of the case with the most avid curiosity? Because the woman was unusually beautiful, the man unusually powerful and talented. The beauty of the woman aroused the envy of other women; the power and talents of the man excited the envy of other men."

[274] Sir Herbert Creedy (1878-1973), Secretary, War Office, 1929-1924; Permanent Under Secretary of State for War, 1924-1939.

[275] Tony Leadbetter, Almina's godson believes this happened, and Ian and Dorothy only ever wanted to extricate funds from Almina. It begs the question however that Dorothy could have used this to discredit Ian, before, during or after the Court case.

[276] Almina lost no time in consulting lawyers. She was determined to find the Colonel a strong advocate to defend his corner. The story of her telephoning Marshall Hall's chambers in Temple Gardens demanding "a good fighter" is told in H Montgomery Hyde's biography of Norman Birkett.

[277] The Sunday Gleaner, 3 September 1961. "A gallon of coffee helped him to fame."

[278] Marshall Hall acted for Alfred de Rothschild (Almina's benefactor) as Executor to his will. A lighter side to the Dennistoun story is revealed by Almina's godson, Tony Leadbetter. On one of the visits to Marshall Hall's chambers to discuss the case, Almina accompanied the Colonel. They were served tea in what Almina

described as "very common white teacups." As soon as she left Temple Gardens and returned to her Mayfair home, she had ordered a complete set of bone china from a leading London store, and had it sent round to Marshall Hall.

[279] Archibald Edgar Bowker (always known as A E Bowker) who served as clerk (and Judge's clerk) to Marshall Hall and Birkett. The world of Bowker's masters is wonderfully described by him in his memoirs "Behind the Bar" and "A lifetime with the Law". There are several affectionate references therein to Almina Carnarvon.

[280] See National Archives Kew LCO2/961 being an instance of an MP's motion to remove McCardie from the High Court bench.

[281] See ARCHER, Henry: Mr. Hardie. Book Guild Ltd (2003). This book was written by McCardie's illegitimate son.

[282] One commentary in C E M Joad's 1926 critique Thrasymacus Or the Future of Morals declares " For several weeks the Dennistoun case was the chief subject of conversation in trains, 'buses, and bar-parlours, and those whose lips smacked the most greedily over the luscious scandal were the most severe in their condemnation of the vices of society".

[283] Figures like Lady Eveline Miller of Manderston, sister of another legend of the era, George Curzon, who lay at death's door during the end run of the case. One of names of Curzon's cousins, Oscar Pocklington Senhouse, (A member of the Senhouse family of Netherhall, Maryport, Cumbria) who had been killed in the First World War, was dragged through the mire on cross-examinations of Dorothy; he was one of her former lovers.

[284] Sponsors were the Marchioness of Milford Haven, the Countess of Galloway, Mrs Percival Griffiths, Miss Poppy Baring. Sir Brograve Beauchamp, Mr Arthur Portman and Mr Jac Wendell. [Mr and Mrs Arthur Portman were killed in the London Blitz.]

[285] Leatham, PE. The Short Story of a Long Life. Wilton. (2009).

[286] Dundee Courier, 10 April, 1925.

[287] Sunday Times, 28 June 1925. Major Gabriel (Alan) Breitmeyer married Miss AM Parsons. Alan died in 1963.

[288] E-mail exchange between the author and Lord Montagu of Beaulieu 16 August 2013 "My archivist has been unable to find anything other than an entry in my mother's diary for 1925 which says that the Carnarvons were at a lunch party she attended during Cowes Week, but no further details."

[289] The Times, 13 January 1926.

[290] Western Daily Press, 7 December 1926.

[291] Daily Express, 7 December, 1926.

[292] Interviews with Tony Leadbetter, Almina's godson and ML, a longstanding Newbury resident.

[293] Interviews with Almina's godson, Tony Leadbetter and M L, a long standing resident of Newbury whose family knew Almina.

[294] Dundee Courier 15 March, 1927.

[295] Almina sold Alvie to Mr. A Balfour Williamson, a Liverpool shipping magnate, and brother of Lord Forres, who as Sir Archibald Williamson, was sometime MP

for Moray and Nairn. Today (2013) the Williamson family still occupy the Estate which is a popular sporting retreat.

[296] Western Times, 29 July 1927.

[297] The Times, 3 July 1928.

[298] With thanks to Ronan Donohoe of the Portsmouth Athenaeum for extracting this information from the Wendell Archives.

[299] Timothy Walter Boden. (1901-1969). Accomplished English cricketer.

[300] The Highclere version of Reggie's last hours in the book "Lady Catherine and the Real Downton Abbey" is completely at variance with Mary's account.

[301] Gerard Vernon Wallop (1898-1984). Viscount Lymington from 1925 until 1943. Later 9th Earl of Portsmouth, cousin of Porchey.

[302] Hon. Maurice Fox Pitt Lubbock (1900-1957). Son of John Lubbock, 1st Baron Avebury.

[303] Hon. Mary Katherine Adelaide Stanley (1906-1981). Daughter of Sir Arthur Stanley, 5th Baron Sheffield. He was a colonial governor in Victoria, Australia.

[304] Lubbock, Adelaide. People In Glass Houses. Hamish Hamilton. (1978). A photograph reproduced in the book is the wedding party which includes Reggie. The author exchanged letters with Eric Reginald Lubbock (the current Lord Avebury, born 1928) son of Maurice and Adelaide. "I don't remember my father telling me anything about him, though I understood that he was my godfather, and I was named after him." [Eric Lubbock was born a few months after Reggie's death, but his second Christian name was his father's old friend Reginald Wendell.]

[305] See The Times, 18 and 20 July, 1928. On 19 July a memorial service for Reginald was held at Grosvenor Chapel, South Audley Street, Mayfair, the Rev Francis Underhill officiated. Almina's friend, Dr Marcus Johnston, personal physician to the 5th Earl, attended to pay his respects.

[306] The pall bearers were Mr Jac Wendell (Catherine's brother), Porchey Carnarvon, Percival Griffiths, Mr T Boden, Viscount Lymington, Sir Brogrove Beauchamp and the Hon. Maurice Lubbock. See The Times 21 July 1928.

[307] With thanks to Ronan Donohoe of the Portsmouth Athenaeum for extracting this information from the Wendell Archives.

[308] Culled from the Daily Mirror, 21 August 1926

[309] Advertising Campaign – Adverts appeared in the press in the UK, America, and Canada.

[310] Daily Mirror, 7 May 1937.

[311] Daily Mirror, 29 August 1931. Wedding of Inez Cope to William McNamara on 15 September 1931.

[312] This was the point at which Queen Mary found she might turn a blind eye to Almina's public disgrace in the Dennistoun case, a few years earlier. Thereafter from 1928 until 1943, Almina became Queen's Mary provider of nursing services to the Royal Household, with several members of the Royal family entering Alfred House and Almina's later nursing home

[313] See Cross, William. Lady Carnarvon's Nursing Homes. Nursing the Privileged in Wartime and Peace. ( 2011)

[314] Tanis Eva Bulkeley Guinness (1908-1993) Daughter of Benjamin Seymour Guinness. Tanis was married three times. She enjoyed a lucky escape from marriage to Porchey Carnarvon in 1935, in USA.

[315] William Piers (Peter) Thursby (1904-1977).

[316] See various Cricket Archives on the Internet

[317] Lady Helen Cassell (nee Grimston) (1879-1947). Her half sister was Eva Hermione Macintosh, Poppy's mother.

[318] The Times, 20 December 1928.

[319] Arthur R Wendell of Summit, New Jersey was a very successful businessman who owned Wheatena breakfast foods and doted on his English and Scottish cousins.

[320] The Times, 12 June, 1930. Mr and Mrs Arthur Wendell and daughter Eleanor were staying at the Berkeley for the 1930 London season.

[321] National Archives  Passengers Lists show that seventeen- year- old Eleanor Wendell returned to New York ( from London) on 17 October, 1924. Her parents are named as Arthur aged 48 and Grace aged 56. Their address in London was the Savoy Hotel. She made an earlier appearance leaving Britain by boat from Southampton to New York on 26 June 1909.

[322] Dundee Courier, 13 December 1930.

[323] Letter from Mary Van der Woude (nee Wendell) to her mother in Portsmouth Athenaeum.

[324] Passengers Lists, National Archives, Kew.

[325] Dominic Bevan Wyndham Lewis (1891-1969). Wrote the Beachcomber column in The Daily Express.

[326] Rose, Janet R. Historic Sandridge Revisted. St Leonard's Publishing. ( 1999).

[327] Ronan Donohoe, the owner-Curator of the Wendell exhibition at the Portsmouth Athenaeum, New Hampshire in 2012-3 mentions in an e-mail to the Author on 16 July 2013, that "Gertrude is sometimes described as invalid."

[328] The Times, 10 June and 19 July 1933.

[329] The Times, 1 July 1936.

[330] Edward Montagu Cavendish Stanley ( 1894-1938). Porchey mentions in No Regrets that he often stayed at Sansovino, near Cannes with Eddy Stanley and his wife Portia (Sibyl). They were great card players.

[331] Edward Stanley ( 1918-1994). Son of Lord Stanley, notable politician who died in middle age. Edward inherited his grandfather's Earldom.  His mother was  Hon. Sibyl Cadogan, ( always known as Portia ) sister of Mary Blandford later, Duchess of Marlborough.

[332] David Beatty. ( 1905-1972) Second Earl Beatty. Four times married, his mother was one of the Marshall Field family.

[333] The function was held by Mr. and Mrs. Jenkinson. See Winnipeg Tribune, 19 July 1930.

[334] Cocktails & Laughter [ Ed ]Vickers, Hugh. The Albums of Loelia, Duchess of Westminster. Hamish Hamilton ( 1983).

[335] Major Thomas David " Tuddemy" Freeman Mitford died Sagaing, Burma on 30 March 1945.

[336] The Times, 23 January 1931.

[337] Evening Telegraph, 30 December, 1930.

[338] A photograph of Lady Penelope appears in the Daily Express for 2 January 1931 riding on a wolfhound at the Quorn. The Quorn Hunt was one of the oldest fox hunting packs in middle England around Leicestershire and Derbyshire.

[339] Major Hon Lionel Samuel Montagu (1883-1948), DSO, partner Samuel Montagu & Co   married. 4 Oct 1944 Sybil Stanley (former wife of Edward Arthur Vesey Stanley),

[340] National Archives, file HS 9/1052/4

[341] Norman Ross (biographer of Duff Cooper's friend   Harold Nicolson) declares "[Duff's] reputation as a womanizer, given to drink and gambling went before him."

[342] Norwich, John Julius. The Duff Cooper Diaries. Weidenfeld & Nicolson. (2005)

[343] Comment attributed to 'Chips' Channon.

[344] William Brownlow, Third Baron Lurgan (1858-1937).

[345] See Montgomery-Massingberd, Hugh and Watkin, David. The London Ritz. A social and architectural History. Aurum Press. (1980).

[346] Ibid.

[347] The Times 29 May 1931.

[348] Almina's godson, Tony Leadbetter,  had a thirty-year career in nursing, including training at St Cadoc's Mental Hospital, Caerleon,  South Wales. Almina often had discussions about medical matters and procedures with Tony. At Alfred House Almina used the drug paraldehyde. This is a fast acting sedative ( albeit ) primarily used in the treatment of epileptic seizures. It was usually given by injection.

[349] Exeter and Plymouth Gazette, 31 May 1931. In 1931, Priscilla married Cecil George Wilfred Weld Forester (heir to the Barony of Forester of Willey Park), she died 1988. In 1936 Helena married Viscount Maitland, she died in 1999.

[350] The thirty-one -year old Eleanor is with her parents on the Aquitania heading back to New York on 6 July 1938. Seventy- three  year old Arthur turns up on a voyage on the Queen Mary going out of Southampton on 11 May 1949, when he gave his UK address as c/o Earl of Galloway, Cumloden.  Lastly Eleanor appears on the passenger lists for a voyage of the Queen Mary out of Southampton for New York on 9 June 1960.  She is still unmarried. Eleanor  is described as a director of Berkeley St, London, Single, date of birth 16 December, 1906.

[351] Sidney Walter Beer (1899-1971) Racehorse owner and conductor.

[352] See interview with Porchey in James Fox's. White Mischief. Cape (1982).

[353] Furneaux Rupert. The Murder of Lord Erroll.  Stevens & Sons (1961) and Fox, James. White Mischief. Cape (1982).

[354] Obituary in The Times, 2 June 1971.

[355] The Times, 23 July 1932.

[356] Author's interviews with Tony Leadbetter and interview and telephone conversations with ML, a long-standing member of a Newbury-based family with links to the Highclere Estate over several generations.

[357] Sunday Times, 27 March 1932.

[358] National Archives, file J77/3279/196.

[359] National Archives, file J 77/3286/416.

[360] Drogo Montagu was killed in a flying accident in 1940, as a flying instructor with the RAF. Janet Campbell remarried in 1942 a Canadian army officer, she died in 1988, aged 80. She was a notable painter of scenes in Barbados, where she had a home.

[361] Gloucester Citizen 19 December 1932 and Cornishman, 22 December 1932.

[362] Ibid.

[363] Sunday Times, 5 March 1933.

[364] The Times, 21 February 1933.

[365] Sunday Times, 2 April 1933.

[366] Deborah Devonshire ( the Dowager Duchess of Devonshire ) provides an insight into the highs and lows of living with an alcoholic husband ( Andrew Cavendish, 11th Duke of Devonshire ) in her memoirs Wait for Me! John Murray ( 2011). Tony Leadbetter advises ( from his experience of dealing with alcoholics and alcoholism among publicans ( and their wives ) in a health project he was involved in at Bristol in the 1960s and 1970s ) that many alcoholics suffer serious side affects during heavy drinking or afterwards when they return to being sober. This includes slurred speech, shouting-off, vomiting, tremours etc. In Catherine's case she suffered from states of unhappiness, depression and anxiety and went through phases of being elated and then being downcast. The affect on close family was obviously devastating.

[367] Priory Hospital, founded in 1872 at Roehampton, West London, treating mental health issues, including depression.

[368] The Holloway Sanatorium was an institution at Virginia Water ( near Windsor ) from late Victorian times that treated mental health cases, including alcoholics.

[369] The Times, 28 March 1933.

[370] The Times, 30 May, 1933.

[371] Carter, Howard. The Tomb of Tutankhamun. Cassell ( 1933)

[372] This is fully explained in Cross, William. The Life and Secrets of Almina Carnarvon. ( 2011).

[373] Porchey was back on form in July 1933 (and received loud cheering and praise) at Salisbury with Patmos when he won the Bibury Welter. Alex Cottrill rode the second.

[374] The current Baroness Willoughby de Ersby kindly responded to an enquiry. She writes " My father was a keen and rather good amateur jockey along with Anthony Mildnay [ 1909-1950][ who died in a swimming accident], the best man at his marriage. My father as Major Lord Willoughby de Ersby was wounded during the war and after several years in hospital he only ever rode his war horse around the Park at Grimethrope with his stump leg in a bucket. He did visit Lord Carnarvon on occasions in Ireland and he may have dined with him in London."

When in Ireland Porchey could often be found in the company of 'Lump Altmont', who was an old Eton and Sandhurst contemporary, his full name was Ulick de Burgh, 7th Marquess of Sligo ( 1898-1943), ' a cheerful extrovert with a passion for horses". He was the last of the Sligos ' who lived like a lord'.

[375] Western Morning News, 28 July 1933.

[376] The Daily Express of 20 December 1933 records "Ill in older Lady Carnarvon's nursing home, young LADY CARNARVON. Nursing home yesterday refused to confirm or deny report that she had damaged spine.".

[377] Sunday Times 31 December 1933.

[378] Vreda Esther Mary Montagu Douglas Scott (nee Lascelles), (1900-1993). Known as Mollie. From 1921-1935 she was the Countess of Dalkeith, wife of Water Montagu Douglas Scott, heir to the Dukedom of Buccleuch, from 1935 she was Duchess of Buccleuch.

[379] Interviews with Tony Leadbetter, Almina's godson.

[380] Hull Daily Mail, 18 June 1934.

[381] Aberdeen Journal, 18 June 1934.

[382] The Times 22 June, 1934.

[383] See Sunday Times, 1 July 1934.

[384] The Daily Express of 25 September, 1934 has a small photograph of Porchey seeing Lord Porchester off to school at Eton College.

[385] The marriage of Prince George and Princess Marina was announced in August 1934, they were married at Westminster Abbey on 29 November 1934.

[386] See Carnarvon[ Fiona]. Lady Catherine and the Real Downton Abbey. Hodder and Stoughton. (2013)

[387] Maureen Constance Guinness, ( 1907-1998) Marchioness of Dufferin and Ava ( later Buchanan, later Maude ).

[388] Maureen was seen with Porchey at Goodwood races in August 1935 – whilst Catherine was under sedation at Alfred House. Later in October, 1935 they were at a reception, but Maureen was with her husband and Porchey was with 'Chips' Channon.[388] Maureen and Porchey caught up at the various race meetings ( after his return from the USA and the Guinness affair ) as they were also in each other's company at the Epsom Spring meeting in April, 1937. See The Times, 2 August, 1935 and 22 April, 1937.

[389] The character of Ida Sherrington (who ran a nursing home for the most fashionable of London) in A J Cronin's The Citadel, is based on Almina, where this quote has been hacked.

[390] Sir Cecil Walter Hardy Beaton ( 1904-1980). Fashion and Society Photographer and diarist.

[391] Tony Leadbetter recalls on a visit to Highclere Castle that there was a room used by the Fifth Earl as his dark room that was curtained off from the public rooms. At the time of Tony's visit the room was still full of photographic equipment.

[392] Beaton, Cecil and Buckland, Gail. The Magic Image: The Genius of Photography from 1839 to the Present Day. Weidenfeld & Nicolson (1975).

[393] The San Bernardino County Sun, 4 January 1938.

[394] Others were Tallulah Bankhead against a background of balloons and Sheila Milbanke under the glass dome

[395] Emili Otto Hoppe ( 1878-1972). German born British portrait photographer. Another huge rival to both Beaton and Hoppe was Horst P Horst ( 1906-1999).

[396] One assessment concludes " Beaton grasps the starlight quality of Tilly wearing lavish costumes, displaying her elegant hand gestures; in effect what you are seeing is Tilly the actress, the dancer, a glamour queen. Whereas Hoppe captures the opposite, he shows Tilly's deeper,inner character, in one single image, where she looks into the camera in a "mesmeric stare" . Tilly was exotic in looks with a sensual mouth...."

[397] The Times 8 March, 1935. Attended by the Duke and Duchess of York.

[398] The Times, 6 March 1935.

[399] Sunday Times, 9 June 1935.

[400] Kingsport Times, 21 June 1935.

[401] Ibid.

[402] Private source, apply to the Author for details.

[403] The Times, 10 July 1936.

[404] Tony Leadbetter, Almina's godson recalls that letters came in from Switzerland from the Bellevue Sanatorium, Kreuzlingen ran by the psychiatrist Ludwig Binswanger. Among the famous patients were Princess Alice of Battenberg (1885-1969) (mother of the Duke of Edinburgh) and the ballet dancer Vaslav Nijinsky (1890-1950).

[405] Conversations with Tony Leadbetter (born 1938).

[406] William Hogarth (1697-1764) Celebrated painter, engraver and satirist.

[407] Sir Peter Lely (1616-1680). Court Portrait Painter of Dutch origin. Painted Charles II's mistress Nell Gwyn. Percy Griffiths owned Lely's portrait of Lady Elizabeth Wriothesley (1646-1690), who was later Countess of Northumberland and later again, Countess of Montagu.

[408] The National Art Collections Fund reported in 1938 that they had purchased from off the Griffiths Estate "two fine English seventeenth century silver tankards and several pieces of furniture for the Victoria and Albert Museum; portraits of James Gibbs, Sir Walter Scott and John Wilson ("Christopher North") for the Scottish National Portrait Gallery and a Milanese parade helmet of the fifteenth century, for the Fitzwilliam Museum, Cambridge." See The Times 25 May 1938.

[409] After Percy's death the mirrors were sold at Christies in 1939, for £480. They were later sold by Christies in 2012, for £54,050.

[410] The trumpet was by Simon Beale and dated 1677. Beale (who I mentioned twice in Pepys's Diary) was state trumpeter under both Cromwell and Charles II. Philippa Galloway bought the mirrors at Christies from the sale of the Griffith Collection for 240 guineas, she later sold them for 1500 guineas together with a single mirror painting of the eighteenth century, which was sold later for 1000 guineas. See The Times 26 February 1960.

[411] Sunday Times, 28 June, 1931.

[412] The Kingston Daily Freeman 9 November 1936.

[413] Ibid.

[414] Ibid.

[415] Ibid.

[416] The Sunday Times fashion reporter comments on 15 November, 1936 edition " the Countess of Carnarvon [was ] in turquoise blue lace, her sister , the Countess

of Galloway, in pale blue satin, and their aunt, Mrs Percival Griffiths, whose grey satin frock was worn under an ermine and white fox cape."

[417] The Times, 14 November 1936.

[418] Percy Griffiths was the joint Master of the Whadden Chase with Porchey's friends the Earl of Rosebury and Sir Peter Farquhar.

[419] The Sunday Times, 12 December 1937.

[420] The grave stone at Sandridge records " In Loving Memory of Percival Davis Griffiths. Also of Sarah Bailey Tredick and Barbara McKay whose graves are nearby." Adjoining is another gravestone ( with the writing badly faded ) but showing the deceased was originally from New York.

[421] The Author visited Sandridge Church and Churchyard in September 2013.

[422] Percy's collection is well covered in a book by R W Symonds. "English Furniture from Charles II to George II." London (1929). The Foreword (by Percy) explains in detail how he came to collect antique furniture etc. Symonds also includes references to Percy's collection in many articles and journals.

NB The large collection of papers by R W Symonds (1889-1959) can be found in The Winterthur Library, Winterthur, DE 19725, USA. One note records:-

"The collection formed by Percival D. Griffiths, F.S.A (d. 1938) under the wise counsel of R. W. Symonds is considered to be arguably the greatest collection of English Furniture formed in the last century. Indeed, it was Griffiths' collection that provided the content for Symonds' seminal work English Furniture from Charles II to George II, 1929. The interiors at Sandridgebury are happily recalled in 'Sandridgebury: The Country Residence of Percival D. Griffiths', published by Symonds in Antiques, March 1931, pp. 193-196. Symonds later published 'Percival Griffiths, F.S.A.: A Memoir on a Great Collector of English Furniture', The Antique Collector, November-December 1943, pp. 163-169. His collection has come to be recognised as a bench mark of excellence in the arena of collecting early to mid-18th century walnut and mahogany furniture and is discussed by E. Lennox-Boyd, 'Introduction: Collecting in the Symonds Tradition', Lennox-Boyd, Masterpieces of English Furniture, The Gerstenfeld Collection, pp. 12-31."

[423] Rose, Janet R. Historic Sandridge Revisted. St Leonard's Publishing. (1999).

[424] Ronan Donohoe of the Portsmouth Athenaeum advises "Percival Griffiths... collector of important furniture much of which ended up in the Metropolitan Museum in NYC."

[425] The Listener, Volume 103, 1980.

[426] Lt Col Edward Orlando Kellett ( 1902-1943) Known as 'Flash' on account of his dandy style of dress. He was killed in action with the 8th Army. His wife Myrtle was Helen Myrtle Dorothy McGowan ( Atherley) ( 1906-1976).

[427] Osbourne, Frances. The Bolter. Hachette. ( 2009).

[428] Porchey's 'charming friend' Phyllis is mentioned in Ermine Tales, his second book of Memoirs.

[429] Carnarvon [ Earl of ] Ermine Tales. Weidenfeld & Nicolson. ( 1980).

[430] National Archives Kew hold two files on the marriage/divorce of Margot Mills to John Compton Cavendish, 4th Lord Chesham ( who served with Porchey in the Hussars). They were divorced in 1937. Margot later married Francis Lorne and emigrated to Rhodesia, she died in 1985.

[431] Hon Sibyl Cadogan, Lady Stanley, ( 1893-1969). Known as Portia. A Maid of Honour to Queen Mary. She was a early girlfriend of Edward, Prince of Wales.

[432] Carnarvon [ Earl of ] Ermine Tales. Weidenfeld & Nicolson. ( 1980).

[433] According to Ian Zaczek in Dogs Facts, Figures & Fun, AAPPL ( 2006) Charles Munn was the original promoter of greyhound racing in Britain from 1925-6.

[434] Hull Daily Mail, 25 March 1937.

[435] Waugh's first wife was Evelyn Gardner, daughter of the 5th Earl's sister, Winifred, Lady Burghclere. Laura Herbert, Waugh's next bride was a daughter of Hon. Aubrey Herbert, the 5th Earl's half brother.

[436] Sunday Times, 29 August 1937.

[437] Correspondence between the author and David Sealy, (1920-2011), 4th Baron Mottistone.

[438] Cripps (second son of Lord Parmoor) was severely hurt as the result of falling down a lift shaft in a block of flats (where he lived) at Hereford Street, Park Lane, London. He sustained injuries to his legs, shoulders, hands. See The Daily Mail, 4 July 1931.

[439] Mrs Frederick Cripps ( 1891-1983), ( Baroness Paramoor) was born Violet Nelson, she married several times, and was briefly the Duchess of Westminster. She divoreced Frederick Cripps ( 3rd Baron Parmoor) in 1951.

[440] Sir John Charles Peniston Milbanke (1902-1947), his brother Ralph (always known as Toby) inherited the baronetcy. Sir Ralph Mark Milbanke (1907-1949). On Toby's death the baronetcy became extinct. Their father won a Victoria Cross in the Great War. He was killed at Gallipoli in 1915.

[441] Margaret Sheila Mackellar Chisholm (1895-1969). After John Milbanke's death she later married Dimitri Alexandrovitch Romanoff, a Russian prince and a descendant of Tsar Nicholas I. They lived modestly at Belgravia. She died on 13 October 1969 at Westminster, London; she was buried with Episcopal rites in Roslyn chapel, near Edinburgh.

[442] In 1937-8, the "soft voiced" Poppy Baring (when she was Mrs Peter Thursby) went on a world tour with "the lovely" Margaret, Lady Milbanke. After a lavish party given by Lord Dudley (which was attended by the Duke and Duchess of Kent) they flew to Australia and travelled later went to America. Wherever they went they were lavished entertained) as VIPs from London. In 1926 Poppy had been to America with Margaret. They were inseparable friends for many years. See The Guardian 14 October 1937. One commentator in US remarked "Lady Loughborough, later Lady Milbanke, Poppy Baring's best friend, is an Australian. All of them were keenly alive, original and amusing. Amusing— that had become the word. It was the test for everything."

[443] Sunday Times, 12 September 1937.

[444] Geoffrey Seymour Grenfell ( 1898-1940)

[445] National Archives, Kew. File J77/3516/7250.

[446] Sunday Times, 23 January 1938.

[447] The Times, 22 July 1938.

[448] See The Sporting Life, 8 October, 1938.

[449] Georgiana De Ropp was a member of the Pillsbury family and a native of San Francisco. She died on 9 September, 2005, aged 81. A great lover of gardens. She has descendants in the USA and Australia.

[450] Correspondence between the Author and the EL, 2013.

[451] The Observer, 16 July 1939.

[452] The Meopham Air Disaster 21 July 1930, which claimed the lives of several wealthy people returning from a party at Le Touquet, France. These were Lord Dufferin ( Maureen's husband). Lady Rosemary Leveson Gower, who was Viscountess Ednam, Sir Edward Simons Ward and Mrs Henrik Loeffler.

[453] Sir Charles Blake Cochran (1872-1951). Successful English stage manager. He made a musical comedy star out of such cabaret artists as Tilly Losch, Gertrude Lawrence and Jessie Matthews. In his heyday of the late 1920s and early 1930 he produced many of Noel Coward's plays and reviews including Bitter Sweet, Private Lives, Cavalcade and Words and Music. He died in a bath full of scalding water.

[454] Ambrose McEvoy (1878-1927). English artist. Known for his early landscapes and after 1915 became a painter of fashionable Society beauties.

[455] In 1940 Cecil Beaton produced a book entitled "'My Royal Past" which made war-torn London laugh. He later revealed how society women, famous actresses and dancers had helped to create the work of pretentious autobiographies of eminent nonentities. One life story of the Baroness von Bulop was lavishly illustrated with intimate photographs and drawings of the Baroness, her aunt, Maria-Hedwig, Grand Duchess of Hansburg, her boy friends and her relations. Beaton eventually admitted that Tilly Losch had impersonated Maria-Hedwig. The whole thing was a complete hoax.

[456] For "My Royal Past" ....Everybody dressed up! Names mentioned in the cast include Bebe Berard, Lady Bridget Parsons ( always a friend of Tilly), Sir Francis Rose ( with a moustache painted out later ), David Herbert, Osbert Lancaster, Lady Harris, Lord Berners and Michael Duff. Beaton then cut out fashion plates from old editions of La Mode and Figaro, retouched the photographs to produce minute waists and printed the pictures in reverse.

The book was hailed by the critic Trevor Allen as " a souffle of wit and malice" ....Cecil hoped to use the ballet dancer Frederick Aston as the Baroness. Eventually the bisexual drug using diplomat Tony Gandarillas filled the role. Tilly was the beautiful aunt.

Beaton records " When Miss Losch was ill in a Swiss sanatorium I went over there to take some pictures. For some of the illustrations Miss Losch dressed in Edwardian clothes and posed." Beaton always gave Tilly his attentions. After the war she was often alone with him during the summer time in the Reddish House at Broad Chalke.

[457] Richard Strauss (1864-1949). Composer.

[458] Max Reinhardt (1873-1943). Austrian born American stage and film actor and director.

[459] Baron Georg von und zu Franckenstein ( later Sir George Franckenstein) ( 1878-1953). The Baron and his wife Editha were killed in a plane crash, in Germany. The Hofmannsthals were friends of the Baron and his wife. During the Second World War the Baron worked in London tirelessly ( but not always successfully) against the Nazis regime.

[460] Frankenstein, Sir George. Facts and Features Of My Life. Cassell. ( 1939).

[461] Ibid page 275 " At one time or another Tilly Losch, La Jana, Niddy Imperkoven, Pola Nirenska. The Boden-wiesers and the corps de ballet of the Vienna State Opera delighted my guests…"

[462] Curzon, Baroness Mary Irene Ravensdale. In Many Rhythms. An Autobiography. Weidenfeld & Nicolson. ( 1953).

[463] http://www.youtube.com/watch?v=P_dOSfEnKJo

[464] Posner, Bruce Charles. Unseen Cinema : Early American Avant-garde film 1893-1941 : a retrospective. Filmakers Showcase. ( 2001).

[465] The Times has several references to the receptions. Horace Wyndham records in his book Chorus to Coronet: "At times there were private engagements outside the theatre. One such occasion she [Tilly] danced with Anton Dolin [1904-1983] at a fancy press party given by Baron Frankenstein at the Austrian Embassy in London." The latter was the 18th Century Ball held on 13 December 1934, there were over 300 guests. For reports of receptions see The Times, 15 May 1928, 5 November, 1928, 26 June, 1929, 20 April, 1934, and 26 February 1935.

[466] Dolin's Personal Papers are in the Victoria and Albert Museum, London. The catalogue includes "1934 Dolin's appearance at the Foyles Literary Luncheon with Arnold Haskell, Tilly Losch, Agnes de Mille, and Ashley Dukes. 1934 Dolin's performance at the Masked Ball at Austrian Legation December 1934 with Tilly Losch." http://archiveshub.ac.uk/data/gb71-thm/12

[467] See The Dancing Times. 1940. The date of the Gala was 6 August 1940.

[468] Dolin, Anton. Ballet go Round. M Joseph Ltd ( 1938).

[469] Frederick Ashton (1904-1988). Dancer and choreographer. The American dance critic George Jackson advises the author in an email in 2013: "Ashton's biographer David Vaughan told me that Ashton and Tilly had done a duet together on one occasion. It was for a gala. When Vaughan asked them, separately, about it, they could not recall any specifics other than that they had a good time doing it. So Vaughan did not think to mention it in his book on Ashton which goes into much choreographic detail."

[470] Punch. Volume 174, page 387 (1928).

[471] Cochran, Charles Blake. I had almost forgotten. Hutchinson (1932).

[472] Recounted by Douglas Byng in his memoirs " As you were : reminiscences" Duckworth. ( 1970). Byng was openly homosexual.

[473] Georg Hackenschmidt ( 1877-1968) The Russian Lion, A wrestler and strongman. Friend of Harry Houdini. Cockie managed Georg's act with great success throughout the early part of the 20th Century. Thanks to Hackenschmidt

who guaranteeded to pay creditors £15 a week until debts were liquidated Cochran's discharge from bankrupcy was achieved in record time.

[474] See file in National Archives, Kew Ref BT 226/853.

[475] In 1904 Cochran was living at 7 Buckingham Gate Mansions SW.

[476] Cochran . James Harding. Methuen. ( 1988)

[477] Lawrence ( Larry ) Adler ( 1914-2001). American musician.

[478] Adler wrote a long article for the Manchester Guardian, published on 22 February 1969 in which he describes being protected and mollycoddled by Evelyn, including her developing his understanding of several luminaries from the aristocracy coming back stage accompanied by their 'bit' [ i.e their girlfriend ] and that he must not assume the 'bit' was their wife.

[479] Apart from T illy those amongst Cochran's troupe of hand-picked beauties included Anna Neagle, Florence Desmond, Jessie Matthews, Elisabeth Bergner and Evelyn Laye.

[480] Cochran . James Harding. Methuen. ( 1988).

[481] Ibid.

[482] Ibid. Harding refers to Shelia Graham ( under her stage name of Lily Shiel ) as " mistress of the month" and refers to Cockie making a pass by kissing her…and offering more….dinner, cosy suppers …a few nights in Torquay….. Lily didn't take the bait and told him straight that her hours were nine till six. Lily ( like Tilly with Porchey ) played her captive adroitly, allowing him to go no further than kissing…..Lily left the stage changed her name to Sheila Graham, became the consort of Scott Fitzgerald and launched out on her final metamorphosis as a Hollywood gossip writer. See also Graham, Shelia. The Late Lily Shiel. WH Allen. ( 1979).

[483] See Cochran's biography in Oxford Dictionary of National Biography.

[484] Cockie died on 31 January 1951 in Westminster Hospital. See Dr A D Child's evidence to the Coroner at the inquest at Westminster on 2 February 1951. Cockie was cremated at Golders Green. There was a quiet ceremony and no address. Music from Humperdinck's 'Miracle', Schubert's 'Ave Marie' and Beethoven's Fifth Symphony were played.

[485] On his death the newspapers republished Fifty Years, Alan Herbert's tribute to Cockie's half century in the theatre:

Reinhardt and Hackenschmidt were one to you
Carpentier, Bernhardt, Duse did your will
Helen of Troy and Jessie of Revue
Barrie and Pirandello filled a bill

[486] Michael Kilburn advises in his book London's Theatres, New Holland Publishers ( 2002) that the bust is now in a upper circle bar at the Adelphi.

[487] Evelyn A Cochran, death registered Westminster, 1960, aged 80.

[488] The company included Miss Tilly Losch, Holland and Barry, "Snowball", Castleton and Mack, Mr. Leslie Hutchinson, Miss Maisie Gay, Miss Jessie Matthews, Mr. Sonnie hale, Miss Joan Clarkson, Miss Madge Aubrey, Miss Ann

Codrington, Miss Moya Nugent, Miss Shelia Graham, Mr. Douglas Byng, Mr. Lance Lister, Mr. Melville Cooper, Mr. Cecil Stafford and Mr. William Cavanagh.

[489] See Breese, Charlotte. Hutch. Bloomsbury (2012 )

[490] Matthews Jessie and Burgess, Muriel. Over My Shoulder, Ulverscroft Large Print Books. (1990). Michael Thornton records in his biography of Jessie "Backstage at the London Pavilion emotional tension ran high. Jessie found herself having a blazing argument with Tilly Losch – the graceful Viernnese dancer who would later become the Countess of Carnarvon – over nothing more important than the desirability of having the window open or closed in the dressing room which they shared."

[491] The author recommends Sheilah Graham's book "The Late Lily Shiel" (W H Allen, London, 1970) for a delightful write up on the Cochran era and rehearsals for This Year of Grace, and Graham's friendship with Tilly Losch. Sheilah Graham (1904-1988) became a household name as an American gossip columnist and was the lover of F Scott Fitzgerald.

[492] Harold Kreutzberg (1902-1968). Max Reinhart was a patron of Kreutzberg. According to Elizabeth Kendall, in "Where She Danced: The Birth of American Art-dance". University of California Press (1979), the Kreutzberg partnership with Tilly comprised some haunted dance states: "Arabesque, Three Mad Furies, Waltzes (to Richard Strauss), Gothic Dance, Horror, Revolt …"

[493] The London Company comprised Miss Jessie Matthews, Mr Sonnie Hale, Miss Ann Codrington, Mr William Cavanagh, Mr Fred Groves, Mr Douglas Byng, Miss Tilly Losch, Mr Toni Birkmayer, Miss June Roper, and Miss Laurie Devine.

[494] The Bandwagon opened on Broadway at the New Amsterdam Theatre on 3 June 1931 and closed on 16 January 1932, making 260 performances.

[495] Lord Charles Cavendish (1905-1944). Second son of the Ninth Duke of Devonshire. In 1932 he married Adele Astaire. He died of long term acute alcoholism.

[496] Dancing in the Dark was staged by the Albertina Rasch Dancers. The song begins as a solo by a singer whose face is caught by a bright pin spot. As the light expands the resolving stage slowly turns under a play of coloured lights. Eventually Losch appears on high reaching down from the centre of the stage on a series of slanted platforms until she reaches stage level. For the performance Tilly wore a draped gold dress of sparking lame and spiked headdress.

[497] In the Beggar's Waltz, the beggar, Fred Astaire, is seen on the steps of the Vienna Opera House, dreaming about a girl he can only adore from afar – the opera's ballerina, played by Tilly Losch.

[498] Bloom, Ken. Broadway: An encyclopedia. Routledge. ( 2013).

[499] See Billman, Larry. Fred Astaire. Greenwood Press. ( 1997). Cites the influence made on Astaire by partnering Tilly, which led to his classic pieces in films like Limehouse Blues from Ziegfeld Follies.

[500] Tim Satchell mentions in his biography of Fred Astaire " Astaire : The Definitive Biography" Hutchinson ( 1987) that Adele used to defend Tilly on other counts. One being her ethic origins, being quoted as saying in defence of Tilly's Jewish

roots and attacks on her Semitic background in near ' I am Spartacus' mode . " I hope you realise that I, too am a Jew".

[501] Exploring Nebraska Highways. Trip Trivia. ( 2007) makes a meal of it. It is happened more delicately by Diana Souhami and Hugo Vickers on their books on the relationship between Cecil Beaton and Greta Garbo.

[502] See Souhami, Diana. Greta and Cecil. Jonathan Cape. ( 2013) and Vickers, Hugo. Loving Greta. The Story of Greta Garbo, Cecil Beaton and Mercedes de Acosta. Random House. ( 2012)

[503] American Census, 1930.

[504] Manitowoc Herald-Times, 7 July 1933.

[505] A critic said of the portrayal of Salome that " one the most striking performances[ was].. given by Tilly Losch at the Theatre in the Dale, New Milford, Connecticut" ( on 5 August1946).

[506] Reported in Amarillo Daily News. 13 October, 1947. Later in the same rehearsals Monteux went into a Bach selection and remarked to Tilly ' Bach did not play this for me himself. But I have no doubt he would approve.'

[507] Carnarvon [Earl of]. No Regrets. Weidenfeld & Nicolson. (1976).

[508] James, Edward. [Editor: Melly, George]. Swans Reflecting Elephants. My Early Years. Weidenfeld & Nicolson (1982).

[509] Ibid.

[510] In 1980, Porchey was interviewed by James Fox, the author of "White Mischief", Vintage (1982). This book unravels the murder of Josslyn Hay, Earl of Erroll, in Kenya in 1941 and Porchey's friendship with Jock Delves Broughton, who was acquitted of the murder but later committed suicide. Porchey declares that Jock was a poor shot and could not have murdered Erroll. During the interview at Highclere, Porchey describes his fetish for girl's hands and legs and mentions both his wives "My first wife was quite, *quite* beautiful. Then Tilly…was very beautiful. She had a very rare thing. She had green eyes with yellow, amber pupils. Now you only see that once in a lifetime."

[511] In 1939, Tilly's marriage certificate to Porchey gives her father's name is recorded as Emile Adolf Losch (Deceased).

[512] The Tilly Losch Collection, 1907-1975. The archive consists of incoming and outgoing correspondence as well as legal documents, banking records, personal memorabilia, diaries, engagement books, press clippings, photographic portraits, and publicity photos.

[513] Author's e-mails in 2013 with American playwright Joyce Sachs whose father in law [Aarpad Sachs] was a cousin of Tilly. "Her [Tilly's] mother, I think, was a stage mother and her brother Otto took advantage of her success. My father-in-law met up with him [ Otto] in later years in Edinburgh where my husband's family lived after they fled Vienna"

[514] Carnarvon [Earl of]. No Regrets. Weidenfeld & Nicolson. (1976).

[515] See Purser, Philip: Where is he Now? The extraordinary Worlds of Edward James. Quartet Books, London (1978). Pages 38-39.

[516] See Oakland Tribune, 31 January 1937. This contains a promotion of Tilly's film appearance in "Garden of Allah".

[517] American Weekly 1939.

[518] Joyce Sachs advises the author in an e-mail in 2013: "Tilly's mother was Catholic turned Christian Scientist with a big overlay of mysticism – the cards and fortune telling."

[519] Cornelius Vanderbilt "Sonny" Whitney. (1899-1992). Banker, film producer philanthropist. He is cited by Edward James in his autobiography "Swans Reflecting Elephants" as promising to marry Tilly. Whitney's first marriage ended in 1929; he married again in 1931, 1941 and 1958.

[520] The Carnarvon Letters (pages 63-4) [published by the Seventh Earl in 1994] contain reference to Tilly's past that was unearthed by Lord Porchester for his father when Tilly was at her least popular. This insinuates that Tilly "was a low class Jewish girl who through a nobleman got a chance on the stage…she was kept and lived with the nobleman and soon rose to heights with her dancing. She is typical of many others…a b…! [bastard] in some ways."

[521] One of these men was probably John "Jock" Hay Whitney (1904-1982). Diplomat and Newspaper publisher. Mary Tuttle at Binghamton University Libraries writes: "In processing the [Tilly Losch] collection, I've come across a number of romantic letters from a "Chester," spanning 15 years, from 1953-1968. There are some clues in these letters and enclosures that hint at "Chester's" true identity being John Hay Whitney, who was, at the time, married, which explains why they so carefully protected his real identity"

The Author's findings indicate that Whitney was American Ambassador to London in the 1950s. He was also a major player in financing the early colour Hollywood movies ( in the 1930s) and Tilly was one of the actresses/ rising stars caught up in all that, through Whitney's film companies, especially Pioneer Pictures. Tilly was charming the pants off men like Whitney as a matter of course, but that is not to say that later a real romance (and by necessity a secret one etc ) existed between them 20 years later. They knew each other, that's for sure, as very old friends and maybe past lovers. There are a number of other threads to link Whitney to England year on year as a racehorse owner (racing was a passion that Tilly shared with Porchey Carnarvon in the 1930s). Whitney was also an insatiable polo player, an upper-crust sport for the wealthy and Royals. Randolph Churchill's wife, the socialite, the late Pamela Harrison (Churchill) also had an affair with Whitney.

[522] Randolph Frederick Edward Spencer Churchill (1911-1968).

[523] Randolph Churchill lived with Edward James off and on during his marriage to Tilly. Their sexual relationship (which was just above horse play) is referred to in James, Edward. [Editor: Melly, George]. Swans Reflecting Elephants. My Early Years. Weidenfeld & Nicolson. (1982).

[524] See Leslie, Anita. Cousin Randolph. The Life of Randolph Churchill. Hutchinson & Co. (1985).

[525] Tom Mitford (1909-1945), only son of Lord Redesdale. His six sisters were the famous Mitford Girls. Tom was a supporter of Oswald Mosley and a keen member of the British Fascist Union. Tom's sister Diana married Mosley in 1936.

[526] Mosley, Charlotte. The Mitfords: Letters between Six Sisters. HarperCollins UK. (2012).

[527] See De-la-Noy, Michael. Eddy: The Life of Edward Sackville-West. At Eton Tom Mitford had a reputation for his homosexual exploits, but soon changed tack. "Many boys who are far more blatantly homosexual at school …Tom Mitford … was a prime example, become completely heterosexual the minute they leave…"

[528] Edward William Frank James (1907-1984). Art collector and poet.

[529] James, Edward. [Editor: Melly, George]. Swans Reflecting Elephants. My Early Years. Weidenfeld & Nicolson. ( 1982).

[530] Dorothy Wilding (1893-1976). Notable Society and Royal photographer. Her images of the Royals (especially the Queen Mother and the present Queen appeared on postage stamps, from 1937.

[531] James Wedgwood Drawbell (1899-1979). Writer, journalist and editor.

[532] Drawbell, James Wedgwood. A Gallery of Women. Collins (1933).

[533] See Cohen, Selma Jeanne. International encyclopaedia of dance. OUP (1998).

[534] Drawbell, James Wedgwood. A Gallery of Women. Collins ( 1933)

[535] From 1935. The show featured Sir Philip Ben Greet, A. Harding Steerman, Russell Thorndike, Philip Desborough, Laurier Lister, Hazel Terry, Iris Baker, Tilly Losch, Sydney W. Carroll, Robert Atkins, J. Gower Parks

[536] Drawbell, James Wedgwood. A Gallery of Women. Collins ( 1933).

[537] Ibid.

[538] James, Edward. [Editor: Melly, George]. Swans Reflecting Elephants. My Early Years. Weidenfeld & Nicolson. ( 1982).

[539] Drawbell, James Wedgwood. A Gallery of Women. Collins (1933).

[540] The James family migrated from Donegal to America where they grew rich selling timber, investing their profits first in railways and next in copper mines.

[541] Evelyn Elizabeth Forbes, later James, later Brinton (1868-1929). The eldest daughter of Sir Charles Forbes, the 4th Baronet of Newe, Strathdon, Aberdeenshire Scotland; her mother was Helen, "one of the beautiful Moncreiffe sisters". Her mother's sisters all had titles including Georgina, Countess of Dudley, who was a notable Red Cross worker in the Great War and Louisa, Duchess of Athole. Evie's two sisters were Helen Blanche Forbes, later Mrs. John Blundell Leigh and Mabel Susan Forbes, later Lady St Oswald.

[542] William (Willie) Dodge James (1854-1912). Millionaire businessman, the family made its money on the American Railways. Willie's father Daniel married an American.

[543] Cited by the author in his book "Lady Carnarvon's Nursing Homes: Nursing the Privileged in Wartime and Peace." ISBN 978 1905914036.The book is now out of print. The quote is taken from a postcard of the James home at West Dean, Chichester. The great and the good poured into West Dean, including the Devonshires, the Curzons and most notably the Royals.

[545] See Purser, Philip: Where is he Now? The extraordinary Worlds of Edward James. Quartet Books, London (1978). Nancy Astor's biographer Christopher Sykes also reflects on this in Nancy: The Life of Lady Astor. Collins (1972), referring to Evie as "his [Edward VII's] new favourite (and has been conjectured his illegitimate

daughter)." The book (where James is the narrator) continues: "The Forbes [family] had some 20,000 acres of Scottish moorland, one side of their estate running along the Balmoral boundary. Often the King [Edward VII], when he was still Prince of Wales, would come over. Once, on a walk with the headstrong Helen Forbes, [Evie's mother] they had a tumble in the heather — as their grandson Edward James delicately puts it. Effie [Evie's Scottish label] Forbes always knew that she was the King's daughter — and as her son remarks quite forthrightly at one point: "I do not regret Edward VII being my grandfather because it means I have a certain amount of Jewish blood, Prince Albert having been the illegitimate son of a Jewish banker. . ."

[546] Montreal Gazette, 2 May 1925.

[547] Audrey James (1902-1968), later Mrs. Dudley Coats, was a close friend of Edward, Prince of Wales. After divorcing Muir Dudley Coats (who died in 1927) she married Marshall Field III in 1930 (divorced at Reno in 1934); Marshall Field died in 1938. She later married (and divorced) Peter Pleydell- Bouverie.

[548] The author devotes nine pages to Evie James's life in his book "Lady Carnarvon's Nursing Homes: Nursing the Privileged in Wartime and Peace." ISBN 978 1905914036 The book is now out of print but an e-mail ( PDF) version is available (gratis) to anyone who purchases the current book. Please contact the author by e-mail at williecross@aol.com

[549] An attempt to seduce Edward as young boy was made by the notorious sex pest Viscount Lewis (Lulu) Harcourt, a courtier at Windsor. Edward repelled him and told his mother. Evie went public, Harcourt was disgraced and later killed himself, albeit the verdict after he took poison was one of accidental death. The Author discusses the case in his book Not Behind Lace Curtains: The Hidden World of Evan, Viscount Tredegar. ( 2013).

[550] Stern. Keith. Queers in History: The Comprehensive Encyclopedia of Historical Gays. BenBella Books Inc. (2013) see p130 "According to Francine Prose in The Lives of the Muses, James paid off Gala [Dali] with jewellery when she discovered his affair with her husband."

[551] The Guardian, 14 February 1991.

[552] Ibid.

[553] In 1939 James abandoned England as his main home and settled in USA. He stayed with Frieda Lawrence [widow of D H Lawrence] in Taos, and then moved to Los Angeles where he became a follower of Aldous Huxley and the Vedanta movement. He funded various Hollywood ventures. By the late 1940s he became increasingly restless and reclusive, moving aimlessly from one hotel to another. Finally he moved to Northern Mexico where he started a bird sanctuary.

[554] Wyndham, Horace. Chorus to Coronet. British Technical and General Press. (1951).

[555] Graves. Charles. The Cochran Story: A Biography of Sir Charles Cochran. W H Allen. (1951).

[556] Ziegler. Philip. Diana Cooper. Hamish Hamilton. ( 1981)

[557] Ibid. The Miracle later toured outside of London ( without Tilly ).

[558] Wyndham, Horace. Chorus to Coronet. British Technical and General Press. (1951).

[559] Reported in the Courier and Advertiser, 25 May 1932. Tilly told reporters " The Queen talked in German to me" adding " The Queen's accent is excellent".

[560] In the 1934 divorce proceeding a letter was read with this quotation. Tilly denied writing it.

[561] Sir Henry Channon (1897-1958) American born Tory politician and bisexual (known as 'Chips'). Famous for his diaries.

[562] This is referred to in John Lowe's biography of Edward James (Edward James: A Surrealist Life: Collins, 1991) as, "Edward, don't be a fool. Everyone knows you're homosexual. That's why I agreed to marry you."

[563] James, Edward. [Editor: Melly, George]. Swans Reflecting Elephants. My Early Years. Weidenfeld & Nicolson. (1982).

[564] Anna-Anna, "a typically Berlin thirties production concocted by Kurt Weill and Bertolt Brecht on the Seven Deadly Sins…"

[565] Tilly's fellow dancer Tamara Finch advises, "Errante to Schubert's Wanderer Fantasy was Balanchine's creation for Tilly with costumes by Tchelitchew. …… The choreography suited Tilly superbly, as she wrung her hands and threw her body into desperate searching, [and] fighting …."

[566] Menuhin, Diana. "Les Ballets 1933". In Dance Research: The Journal of the Society for Dance Research. Volume 6, No 2, Autumn1988.

[567] See The Times, 4 December 1984.

[568] See Manning, Susan. Balanchine's Two productions of "The Seven Deadly Sins", 1933 and 1958, in Dance Chronicle, Volume 9, No 1, 1986.

[569] See Mordden, Ethan. Love Song: The Lives of Kurt Weill and Lotte Lenya. Macmillan. (2012).

[570] Ibid.

[571] Kater. Michael H. "Composers of the Nazi Era. Eight Portraits". OUP. (1999).

[572] Mordden. Ethan. Anything Goes: A History of American musical Theatre. OUP. (2013)

[573] Spoto, Donald. Blue Angel. The Life of Marlene Dietrich. Rowman & Littlefield (2000)

[574] Ibid.

[575] Farina William. The German Cabaret Legacy in American Popular Music. McFarland. (2013).

[576] Roman Jasinsky (1907-1991). Polish ballet dancer.

[577] One account of Jasinski's life suggests that when Tilly was brought into the company Toumanova was sidelined and " there was no room for Toumanova in the newly created L'Errante". See Roman Jasinski : a gypsy prince from the Ballet Russe by Cheryl Forrest and Georgia Snoke. Tulsa Ballet. ( 2008)

[578] The Times, 5 August 1982.

[579] Arnold Haskell (1903-1980). British dance critic.

[580] Wyndham, Horace. Chorus to Coronet. British Technical and General Press. ( 1951).

[581] National Archives, Kew. File Ref J77/3216.

[582] Ibid.

[583] Ibid.

[584] Purser, Philip. The extraordinary worlds of Edward James. Where Is He Now? Quartet Books (1978).

[585] Ibid.

[586] Weill, Kurt. Speak Low ( When you Speak Love ) : The Letters of Kurt Weill and Lotte Lenya. University of California Press. ( 1997). Letter from Weill in Louveciennes ( after returning from London ) to Lenya ( whereabouts unknown) dated 17 May 1934.

[587] Ibid.

[588] Ava Alice Muriel Astor (1902-1956).One of the richest women in the world, at the age of twenty one she inherited her father's fortune.

[589] Raimund von Hofmannstahl. (1906-1974) Son of an Austrian writer. He married Alice Astor in 1933 (divorced 1939). He later married Lady Elizabeth Hester Mary Paget, daughter of the 6th Marquess of Anglesey.

[590] The Argus [Melbourne] 28 June, 1934. It was alleged that on 22 October 1932, when Tilly discovered she was pregnant, Edward had given her some sal volatile he had fetched from the housekeeper's room. Tilly took one sip and would not take any more saying that she thought Edward was trying to poison her. In evidence Edward thought this absurd and fantastic.

[591] Cited in James, Edward. Swans Reflecting Elephants. Weidenfeld & Nicolson. ( 1982).

[592] Daily Mirror, 27 June, 1934.

[593] Ibid.

[594] Ibid.

[595] Ibid.

[596] Ibid.

[597] Ibid.

[598] According to Philip Purser, Count Freidrich Ledebur "married to [the poet] Iris Tree and later a film actor; most famously as Queequeg in John Huston's Moby Dick."

[599] The incident with Adele and Chips Channon over Tilly and the Prince kissing and hugging was evidence of association, but it was left to the Jury to make up its own mind. This was shear comedy. It was alleged by James side that the kiss had gone on for 50 blocks. One of the longest kisses in history. It had been preceded by Tilly and the Prince making love at the top of the Empire State Building. Adele Cavendish said she had gone up on the lift with the pair and there was no lovemaking.

[600] Adele put her hand up to her nose and wiggled her thumb against it (as did Tilly in response).

[601] After the divorce The Manchester Sunday Chronicle published a series of ( ghost written ) articles about Tilly and her friends called ' My Life'. These were published between October and November 1934.

[602] The Argus [Melbourne] 29 June, 1934.

[603] Tilly's costs were around £10,000. Serge was ordered to pay £4602. 6s.7d in costs (excluding the issue of cruelty).

[604] Mosley, Charlotte. The Mitfords: Letters between Six Sisters. HarperCollins UK. (2012).

[605] Queensland Times, 28 June, 1934.

[606] Morning Avalanche, 26 October 1945.

[607] Obolensky Serge. One Man in His Time. McDowell, Obolensky Inc., New York. (1958).

[608] Daily Mirror, 28 March, 1935.

[609] Short, Ernest Henry. Fifty Years of Vaudeville. Eyre & Spottiswoode. (1946)

[610] Cochran, Charles Blake. Showman Looks on. J M Dent. (1946).

[611] Weill, Kurt. Speak Low ( When you Speak Love ) : The Letters of Kurt Weill and Lotte Lenya. University of California Press. ( 1997). Letter from Weill ( in London ) to Lenya ( in Paris ) 24 January 1935.

[612] Ibid. Letter from Lenya ( in Paris ) to Weill ( in London ) 26 January, 1935.

[613] Ibid. Letter from Weill ( in London ) to Lenya ( in Louveciennes) 24 February, 1935.

[614] Weill, Kurt. Speak Low ( When you Speak Love ) : The Letters of Kurt Weill and Lotte Lenya. University of California Press. ( 1997) Letter from Weill in Salzberg to Lenya in London dated 14 August 1935. " but I'm afraid they won't pay for your trip – Kommer has flatly refused and proved to me that it's never done. Naturally, for the time being I'm sticking firmly to my demands, since the worst that can happen is that we'd have to pay for your trip ourselves. Kommer, who's really repulsive, also seems to be raising a stink about your getting a part ( of course Tilly is behind that …"

[615] Gottfried Reinhardt ( 1911-1994). Film Director and Producer, Son of Max Reinhardt ( 1873-1943).

[616] Reinhardt. Gottfried. The genius : a memoir of Max Reinhardt. Knopf. Distributed by Random House (1979).

[617] Robert Bruce Lockhart.( 1887-1970). Author and sometime spy in Germany in the First World War. In his Diaries of Sir Robert Bruce Lockhart 1915-1938 for Wed 17 July 1935 he records " Lunched at Sibyl Colefax's…Not very exciting. Talked German with Tilly Losch who thinks very little of present Russian ballet at Covent Garden and says that Diaghilev would turn in his grave."

[618] David O Selznick (1902-1965). Film producer famed for "Gone with the Wind".

[619] Louis Golding (1895-1958) British writer and screenwriter. Also worked for Charles Cochran.

[620] Golding, Louis. The world I knew. Hutchinson. (1940).

[621] See Oakland Tribune, 31 January 1937.

[622] A flapper character created by cartoonist Russ Westover which was syndicated across USA from 1921-1959. Tillie was a stylish working girl employed as a stenographer , secretary and part time model.

[623] See Pottstown Mercury, 22 March 1937.

[624] The Times, ( San Mateo, California ) 4 March, 1938.

[625] Sir Michael Duff ( 1907-1980). Socialite, twice married, he divorced his first wife in 1935. His second wife from 1949 was Lady Caroline Paget ( 1913-1973) famous for her nude painting by Rex Whistler at Plas Newydd ( seat of the Pagets – Marquesses of Anglesey). Caroline's sister Elizabeth ( 1916-1980) married Tilly's friend Raimund von Hofmannsthal ( 1906-1974). The Duffs and Pagets were cousins of Porchey. There are a number of letters from Michael Duff to Tilly in the archive at Binghamton University Libraries.

[626] A Welsh estate in Gwynedd, North Wales. Now in private hands, after large scale restorations.

[627] Lady Juliet Duff (later Trevor) ( 1881-1965) Daughter of the 4th Earl of Lonsdale( Lowther).

[628] Sergei Diaghilev ( 1872-1929) Russian patron and ballet impresario. Founder of Ballets Russes. After his death a Society was formed in London to keep his memory alive. Among those lending their name to this was Tilly Losch.

[629] See Souhami, Diana. Greta and Cecil. Quercus. (2013). This books suggests that in New York during the Spring of 1934 " Cecil flirted with the dancer Tilly Losch but found her off hand". He then turned his attentions on Michael Duff.

[630] Wyndham, Horace. Chorus to Coronet. British Technical and General Press. ( 1951).

[631] Ibid.

[632] Ibid.

[633] The American playwright Joyce Sachs advises the Author in an e-mail in 2013: "I was at a dinner held at Highclere Castle, the seat of the Carnarvons, honoring my husband [Professor George Sachs] for his work in the field of ulcer disease. Greeting us were the 8th Earl and his wife and having heard on the bus that Tilly was the wife of the 6th Earl, I asked the two if they knew much about her. Whereupon, they took me to a photo of her residing in a prominent spot and was told she married his grandfather to get out of England because she had a Viennese passport during WWII."

[634] This story is told in Anne De Courcy's The Viceroy's Daughters. Weidenfeld & Nicolson. ( 2000)

[635] Aberdeen Journal, 6 October, 1939.

[636] By December 1939, the school was up and running, and the household staff faced the logistics of providing sufficient food, teachers and medical care for the children. A woman named Nan Stirling oversaw Curzon Crescent Nursery School at Highclere. The children came from a poor area of Willesden, in North London.

[637] The cover story (since Tilly didn't want to be branded a consumptive and passed over for stage/film roles) was that she had had a bad reaction to using slimming aids to help kick start her film career. One report in an Australian newspaper in July 1939 records "Miss Tilly Losch, the famous dancer, arrives back in London this week after a six months' absence that has puzzled all except a few of her intimate friends. The secret of her disappearance was that Miss Losch had been undergoing treatment in a Swiss sanatorium, after nearly losing her life by slimming. "My case should be a warning to all those who have taken up slimming fads,"

[638] Binghamton University Magazine, Summer 2013. http://www.binghamton.edu/magazine/index.php/magazine/feature/a-countess-on-campus

[639] Randolph Churchill married Hon. Pamela Digby at St John's Smith Square, followed by a reception at Admiralty House. The marriage failed in 1945. Pamela ( with a reputation as a man eater one profile says ' she slept her way to the top') later married again twice. As Pamela Harriman she went on to be American Ambassador to Paris under President Clinton. She died in 1997.

[640] Raimund von Hofmannsthal and his wife Elizabeth were a part of the Cecil Beaton crowd and regulars in European holidays haunts with Lady Juliet Duff.

[641] Based on a long article in The Salt Lake City Tribune, 11 August 1940.

[642] Interview between the Author and Tony Leadbetter,Almina's godson.

[643] Passenger Lists, National Archives. Kew.

[644] John Franklin Wharton ( 1894-1977).

[645] Oshkosh Daily Northwestern, 27 July 1940.

[646] Antony Tudor (1908-1987). English choreographer. Teacher and dancer.

[647] Ibid.

[648] Olean Times Herald, 10 January 1941.

[649] Dancille Bee, 24 April, 1941.

[650] Ibid.

[651] Extracted from Binghamton University Magazine, Summer 2013. http://www.binghamton.edu/magazine/index.php/magazine/feature/a-countess-on-campus

[652] Ibid.

[653] Christabel Ivy Stubbings (1906-1991). Land Agent to Porchey on the Highclere Estate for many years.

[654] Extracted from Binghamton University Magazine, Summer 2013. http://www.binghamton.edu/magazine/index.php/magazine/feature/a-countess-on-campus

[655] Papers of Sir Cecil Beaton in St John's Library, University of Cambridge. Ref A1/340. Letter dated 10 December 1944.

[656] Miller, Russell. The House of Getty. Bloomsbury Publishing. ( 2011).

[657] Sir Charles Mendl ( 1871-1958) British Diplomat. and his wife Elsie de Wolfe ( Lady Mendl) ( 1865-1950) Actress and Interior Designer.

[658] The Carnarvon Letters 1943-1944. Compiled by the Earl of Carnarvon. Privately published. ( 1994)

[659] Dr Marcus Beauchamp Johnson (1867-1953). Personal physician to the Fifth Earl and Almina. He delivered both of Almina's children.

[660] James Timothy Stocking (or Stocks) died 1963 aged 64.

[661] Papers of Sir Cecil Beaton in St John's Library, University of Cambridge. Ref A1/340. Letter dated 14 January 1943.

[662] Abilene Reporter-News, 14 May 1944.

[663] Ibid.

[664] Ibid.

[665] Cathleen Mann ( 1896-1959). She was the second wife of the 11th Marquess of Queensberry from 1925 until 1946. She later married John R Follett who died in 1953. Her work comprises mainly portraits, but also some landscapes.

[666] Daily Mirror, 15 November, 1945.

[667] Ibid.

[668] Daily Mirror, 22 November 1945.

[669] The Courier-Mail [Brisbane] 23 November, 1945.

[670] Ibid.

[671] Ibid.

[672] Ibid.

[673] Ogdenburg Journal, 20 August 1946. Frank Gannett ( 1876-1957). Media rival of William Randolph Hearst.

[674] During this trip Porchey witnessed the sale of a horse descended from Whirlaway which was sired by Highclere stud's own stallion Blenheim and mothered by an American mare. The horse sold for $50,000.

[675] This anecdote appears in the Amarillo Daily News, 30 November, 1946.

[676] Cited in Kiernan, Thomas. Olivier : The life of Laurence Olivier. Sidgwick & Jackson ( 1981)

[677] See Garnett, Mark. Alport : A study in loyalty. ( 1999) Arthur Cecil Alport was a British (Tory) politician. The book refers to Alport inviting Tilly and Merle to join him and his son for cocktails whilst on a sea voyage across the Atlantic " Two guests who were too seasick to turn up – the 'two beautiful and famous young ladies from Hollywood, Merle Oberon and Tilly Losch, 'laid low' – as Cecil put it 'by an unchivalrous and angry sea'". .

[678] See Motion Picture. Volumes 71-72 Page 22 ( 1946).

[679] Extracted from Binghamton University Magazine, Summer 2013. http://www.binghamton.edu/magazine/index.php/magazine/feature/a-countess-on-campus

[680] E-mail exchange with the Author 2013.

[681] Wyndham, Horace. Chorus to Coronet. British Technical and General Press. (1951).

[682] Passenger Lists, National Archives. Kew. Dorothy Dyer (aged 39) gave her address as Woodfarls, Langford, Salisbury.

[683] Attributed remark in a gossip column in the Daily Express.

[684] See National Archives, Kew files including several diaries in the Series WO 169, WO 170, and WO 172.

[685] The Claims Commission was set up by Army Order 183 of 1940 to:
a) deal with claims at home made by or against the War Department in respect of personal injury or damage to property arising from the acts of military or civilian personnel for whom the department was responsible, arising out of accidents (including traffic accidents) to persons or property, pillage, looting, theft, explosions of ammunition and shooting, fires and damage to lands and crops caused during training and manoeuvres;
b) advise the Army Council on regulations designed to minimize accidents and damage;

c) supervise and co-ordinate the work of any claims commissions set up to deal with claims in any theatre of war in which British forces were present;

d) keep records of all claims and payments; and

e) where necessary to consult and instruct the Treasury Solicitor, and his equivalents in Scotland and Northern Ireland, regarding claims falling within the jurisdiction of the Commission.

The commission also dealt with claims by the War Department in respect of similar damage to its property. The members of the commission included representatives of outside bodies such as the Accident Offices Association. An assistant director of claims was appointed to each home command to deal with claims other than those concerning damage to land or crops, which were dealt with by compensation officers attached to corps. See National Archives, Kew File Series WO306.

[686] Carnarvon [Seventh Earl of]. The Carnarvon Letters, 1943-1944. Privately printed. (1994).

[687] Catherine received standard letters from the Admiralty on 18th and 19th June 1940. Copies are in file ADM 358/159 in National Archives, Kew.

[688] See Evening Telegraph, 16 August 1940 reporting on the previous day's event.

[689] E-mail exchanges between Ronan Donohoe and the Author August 2013.

[690] Ibid.

[691] The case was widely reported in the newspapers. See Daily Express, 13 December 1940.

[692] Ibid.

[693] The Times, 19 December 1975.

[694] Juniper was a "tree class trawler" an anti submarine vessel. Juniper was launched on 15 December 1939, commissioned on 9 March 1940 and sunk on 8 June 1940.

[695] Extracted from National Archives, Kew, File ADM 358/159.

[696] Ibid.

[697] The Admiralty advised Catherine there were three survivors    CR Batchelor (Ord. Tel, RNVR),   I L Begley (Engineman) and AD Curtis (Seaman Stoker). All three men were prisoners of war. Further details are in National Archive, Kew file ADM 358/159.

[698] Author's conversations with Tony Leadbetter, Almina's godson.

[699] Probate record shows that the executor was Geoffrey's father Riversdale Francis Grenfell. The estate was valued at £37,443. 7s 5d. Geoffrey's father died in 1955.

[700] San Antonio Light, 16 December, 1951. See also Hicks, Pamela. Daughter of Empire: Life as a Mountbatten. Hachette. (2012).

[701] Reiner Gerrit Anton Van Der Woude died at Herondean House, Eastry, near Sandwich in Kent on 5 August 1962.

[702] Elizabeth Winn features in "The Carnarvon Letters".  A postal enquiry by the author sent to Elizabeth Winn (born 1925) went unanswered. Her sister Anne advised that she would probably not be able to reply on account of age and infirmity.

[703] Mlle Huc (Doll) is well remembered by AW, Penelope's best friend, who spoke very kindly to the Author about both Doll and Penelope. As schoolgirls in the late

1930s they were rarely separated. AW remembers visiting Highclere, to stay with Penelope, where the good food was always a highlight.    Doll later went to live in France.

[704] The Sunday Times of 14 December, 1941 comments " ETON : About fifty boys are leaving, including Lord C O E FitzRoy, son of the Duke of Grafton, the Earl of Dalkeith, son of the Duke of Buccleuch, Lord Porchester, son of the Earl of Carnarvon .... and Lord Plunket..." Lord C O E Fitzroy was Lord Charles Oliver Edward Fitzroy (1923-1944), who was killed in action in 1944. He was an officer in the Grenadier Guards.

[705] Patrick Terence William Span Plunket (1923-1975). 7th Baron. Unmarried. He is buried in the Royal Family's private burial ground at Frogmore in Windsor Park.

[706] As five-year- olds Porchester and Patrick Plunket (adorning Raeburn suits, with trousers of red velvet and white shirts) were attendants at Poppy Baring's wedding to W P Thursby in 1928.

[707] Carnarvon [Seventh Earl of]. The Carnarvon Letters, 1943-1944. Privately printed (available on Amazon and Abe Books). ( 1994).

[708] Ibid.

[709] Ibid.

[710] From reports contained in Australian newspapers from April 1942.

[711] Picknell, L, Prine, C & Prior, S. Double Standard: The Rudolf Hess Cover Up. Little Brown & Co. ( 2001).

[712] Gordon Neil Johnson, M.D. practiced surgery in Portland, Maine, prior to serving with the 67th General Hospital in England in the Second World War. He had graduated from Colby College, and then Columbia University College of Physicians and Surgeons. When he returned from the war, he practiced in Houlton, Maine. He was elected to the American College of Surgeons and became Governor. He was recognized and greatly respected for his hand surgery and reconstruction and spoke in various locations around the United States on that topic. His wife was Isa Putnam Johnson.

[713] Carnarvon [Seventh Earl of]. The Carnarvon Letters, 1943-1944. Privately printed. ( 1994).

[714] Louisa Yates Carr died at Hemingford Park in 1946, aged 82. She left estate valued at £41,671.

[715] The Times, 6 October, 1942.

[716] Eric Gordon Steeler, (1899-1972).   MRCS, LRCP. Described in 1972 of 24 Bigwood Court, London NW11 and 14 Devonshire Place, London W1.

[717] Sir Gifford Fox (1903-1959) a Conservative MP and landowner.

[718] Gertrude's second husband, Francis Joliffe Raitt, died at 2, Strathearn Road, Edinburgh, on 29 September, 1944.

[719] Carnarvon [Seventh Earl of]. The Carnarvon Letters, 1943-1944. Privately printed. ( 1994).

[720] Ibid.

[721] Little is known about the order. They are originally from France (foundation date unknown). They fled to Bruges in 1905 to escape a French Law separating the

Church and the State. In 1922 they're in London and formed a convent and nursing home "for chronic invalids and convalescents".

[722] According to the Carnarvon Diaries. The Royal Horse Guards arrived back in Britain ( at Liverpool on the' Monarch of Bermuda') on 21 October , 1944. They then transferred to Beaumont Barracks, Aldershot. The King inspected the Regiment on 7 December , 1944. The Regiment was later sent to North West Europe ( without Lieut Lord Porchester ) where they suffered losses in the last months of the war.

[723] David and Michael Van der Woude, who survive.

[724] Royal biographer, Sarah Bradford, pin points the first meeting as 1944, when Porchester was twenty and Princess Elizabeth was seventeen. There is anecdotal evidence that they had met as children before this.

[725] Almina used this phrase when referring to Porchester's Royal liaisons. The Queen's adviser Patrick Plunket ( previously the King's equerry ) fell into the same category of being allied as the brother Princess Elizabeth never had.

[726] Porchester appears in the Court Circular of 17 June 1946 after returning to Windsor Castle with a number of members of the Royal entourage. Such mention continues at least until the Court Circular of the 14 June, 1954, when again Porchester is listed as part of the Royal Household at Windsor Castle.

[727] Part of the Leadbetter Collection, gifted by Almina to her godson, Tony Leadbetter.

[728] Interviews between the Author and Tony Leadbettter.

[729] Information provided the Author by a Highclere insider. Apply to Author for verification.

[730] Information provided to the Author by CB.

[731] In the later 1950s and early 1960s Prince Philip was a member of a lunchtime group called the Thursday Club, which congregated at a Soho restaurant. The sessions went well into the night with Philip sometimes joining his fellows ( which included Stephen Ward, well known as a pimp, with contacts supplying high level call girls ( prostitutes ) to politicians and Royalty).

[732] The Straits Times, 31 July 1949.

[733] From the mid- 1960s onwards the Queen met Porchester constantly at his mews house in London ( a converted stable block ) where Almina and Anne and Tony Leadbetter stayed for one night in 1966 for a wedding.

[734] Almina told her godson that in 1952 when Princess Elizabeth was in Kenya the unmarried Porchester wrote ( via the Royal diplomatic bag) personal letters to the Princess every day at Treetops Hotel, Kenya. It was nearby, at Sangana Hunting Lodge on the foothills of Mount Kenya and Elizabeth heard of her father's death and that she was Queen. There were also letters sent in March-May 1947 when Princess Elizabeth was in South Africa.

[735] The Author has seen many letters written by Queen Elizabeth, the Queen Mother, ( and holds study copies ) from the Wiltshire Archives ( extracted from the Pembroke Papers, Wilton House ) inviting Sidney Herbert ( 16th Earl of Pembroke and Montgomery) and his wife Mary Hope to shoot at Birkhall.

[736] Attributed to Ian Balding in Willett, Peter. Dick Hern. The Authorised Biography. Hodder and Stoughton. (2000).

[737] In 1988 Dick Hern was controversially sacked from his position as trainer for the Queen by Porchester. At the time Hern was recovering from heart surgery. Later a compromise ( urged by the Queen to save face ) was reached whereby Hern shared the stable with a new incumbent before moving to Kingwood House Stables in Lambourn. Hern died in 2002.

[738] Among the official outings on 20 April 1948 Princess Margaret was with a party of eight including Porchester and Lord Hope at the Victoria Palace Theatre and met the Crazy Gang.

[739] The Author received an invitation ( after a postal enquiry to the present Duke, who was Lord Porchester's contemporary). Although at first invited to Blenheim to discuss the Duke's memories of his father's old friend, the invitation was later withdrawn. The Duke's private secretary wrote as follows, by e-mail " His Grace has asked me to let you know that he has spoken to Lord Carnarvon about your book about Porchey Carnarvon and his wives Catherine Wendell and Tilly Losch, and he is not aware of this book and has not given it his blessing, and therefore His Grace regrets that he is unable to help."

[740] 400 Club was one of Princess Margaret's favourites. It was situated in a cellar and described as "the night time headquarters of society".

[741] This is the term used by Churchill when he went to Ditchley Park, to take a break away from the Blitz in London. It is also the title of Ronald Tree's autobiography See Tree, Ronald. When the Moon Was High: memoirs of peace and war 1897-1942. Macmillan. ( 1975).

[742] Marietta Peabody Tree ( 1917-1991). American socialite and later notable political figure. Mother of the model Penelope Tree.

[743] Princess Margaret fell in love with Peter Townsend who by 1953 was divorced from his wife. He was 16 years older than the Princess and had two children. She declared their wish to marry but it was opposed by her mother, the Queen, the Church and the British cabinet under Winston Churchill on the grounds that he was a divorcee. Later ( under pressure) Margaret issued a statement that she "had decided not to marry Group Captain Peter Townsend." In May 1960 she married society photographer Antony Armstrong-Jones, later Lord Snowden but divorced him in 1978. Princess Margaret died in 2002 only a few weeks before her mother. She once famously remarked 'I have as much privacy as a goldfish in a bowl'.

[744] Reported in The Times, ( San Mateo, California)

[745] Daily Mirror, 24 July 1947.

[746] Gielgud Val Henry. Years of the locust. Nicholson & Watson. (1947).

[747] The Times, 10 February 1948.

[748] John (Eric) Allden, CBE (1886-1949). See The Times, 11 March 1949.

[749] Lubbock Morning Avalanche (Texas) 17 February 1949.

[750] E-mail exchange between the Author and George Jackson, American Dance Critic.

[751] Gertrude died at the Spa Hotel, Bath on 20 July 1949. She left estate valued at £61, 185-7s-5d. Her final London address was at 71, Park Street, London W1.

[752] The Times, 30 July 1949.

[753] See Cross, William. The Life and Secrets of Almina Carnarvon. (2011).

[754] Marian Fendall Wendell left Estate valued at £ 951-11s.

[755] Carpenter. Louise. An Unlikely Countess: Lily Budge and the 13th Earl of Galloway. Harper Perennial.
(2005).

[756] Lady Antonia Marian Amy Isabel Stewart married Sir Charles Mark Dalrymple in 1946. He died in 1971. She was living in a cottage at Newhailes, near Edinburgh (2010) but is now in a nursing home.

[757] Leadbetter Collection.

[758] Ibid.

[759] Alice Butler was discovered by Almina having an affair with JTS. Almina arranged for Alice to leave Orchard Grove and go to work for Ronald Tree and his wife at Ditchley Park, Oxford. Alice went to live with the Trees in America. She returned once a year to see Anne and Tony at Orchard Grove and later in Bristol. Almina dubbed Alice 'the rat'. The full story is in " The Life and Secrets of Almina Carnarvon."

[760] Don Stuart Momand (1891-1983).

[761] Interviews between the Author and Tony Leadbetter.

[762] Leonard C Hanna Jnr ( 1889-1957). Art Collector and Philantropist

[763] Mansfield News Journal, 9 November 1950.

[764] San Antonio Light, 16 December, 1951.

[765] Bruce D McClung. Lady in the Dark: Biography of a Musical. OUP. (2006).

[766] Lubbock Morning Avalanche. 27 September, 1950. Louella Parsons " Tilly Losch is apparently thinking of matrimony again. She'll trade her title of Lady Carnarvon for that of Marquessa."

[767] See The Times Standard, 13 February, 1952. This lists Anglier Biddle Duke ( an American diplomat ), Arch Duke Franz Josef ( cousin of Otta the heir to the Austrian throne ), Sharman Douglas (an American socialite linked to several British peers and with Princess Margaret), the Marquis ( Henry) de la Falaise ( one time husband of Gloria Swanson and Constance Bennett ).

[768] The Spectator, Volume 255. ( 1985).

[769] Duberman, Martin. The Worlds of Lincoln Kirstein. Northwestern University Press. ( 2008).

[770] Higham Charles and Moseley. Princess Merle. The Romantic Life of Merle Oberon. Pocket Books. ( 1985).

[771] The San Bernardino County Sun, 4 January 1938.

[772] George Antheil ( 1900-1959). Musician, composer and author. A friend of Hedy Lamarr. He worked in Hollywood on the musical scores for several films during Tilly's time there. According to Lamarr's biographer, Ruth Barton, Hedy Lamarr : The Most Beautiful Woman in Film. University Press of Kentucky, ( 2010) " Another of Antheil's friends was the Viennese dancer Tilly Losch. He introduced her to Hedy and they seem to have hit it off, both enjoying the easygoing atmosphere of dinner at Antheil's latest home". NB Antheil and Hedy took out a patent together in 1942 for a radio signaling device.

[773] The Scranton Republican, 4 August 1931.

[774] See the Independent Record ( Helena, Montana) 1 September 1940.

[775] See Obituaries for Antheil 1959 including Tuscan Daily Citizen, 13 February, 1959 " Antheil was a respected member of the Gertrude Stein circle of intellectuals [ in Paris].

[776] Duberman, Martin. The Worlds of Lincoln Kirstein. Northwestern University Press. ( 2008).

[777] Balanchine's biographer Richard Buckle makes clear that he liked women, recording he [ Balanchine] " never felt the need for close friendship with another man" and adding " If he took a pretty girl out to dinner, it was unusual if he did not try to make love to her". See Buckle, Richard. George Balanchine. Ballet Master. Hamish Hamilton ( 1988).

[778] Attributed. See Modern Dance: A Quarterly Review V.10/11 ( 1932)

[779] Henry Fitzgerald Heard, known as Gerald Heard ( 1889-1971). Guide and mentor to many well known Americans. Heard used techniques including meditation and voga to help clients deal with stress and drugs and alcohol abuse. A friend of the writer and LSD drug user, Aldous Huxley.

[780] Craft, Robert. An Improbable Life : Memoirs. VANDERBILT University Press. ( 2002).

[781] The odd ball American sculptor Joseph Cornell ( 1903-1972) produced a bizarre image of Tilly ( as a child ) floating suspended on wire of an unseen hot air balloon, above snow covered mountains. Such was the impression the Austrian made on Cornell, described as a man of dreams.
http://onesurrealistaday.com/post/18635445021/untitled-tilly-losch

In his diaries ( for 8 October 1956) Cornell records to Tilly " And I haven't had time to tell you of the ethereal dream I had of you this spring – just a brief scene bathed in an early morning light & a 'sister' dream – tho without you – of a beflowered cyclist riding thru the sky – wondrous visions both & which by the time you return I hope have elaborated."

Cornell ( a reclusive and shy man ) was nervous of exploring any personal affair with Tilly, but she warmed to him as he was about the only man who saw her as the child she still was in her own head. It was through Cornell that Tilly developed an interest in Christian Scientist [ a religion formed around the teachings of Mary Baker Eddy ( 1821-1910)] who believe that the spiritual reality is the only reality and that the material world is an illusion which took hold almost a decade later. In a letter from New York to Cecil Beaton at Christmas 1941 Tilly confides to her old friend of the solace in her new found religion and its fascination. See the Papers of Sir Cecil Beaton in St John's Library, University of Cambridge. Ref A1/340. Letter dated 26 December 1941.

[782] Chartwell ( Kent ) was the principal family home of Winston and Clementine Churchill from 1924 onwards. Tilly's presence at Chartwell is referred by Mary Soames ( daughter of the Churchills ) in Clementine Churchill: The Biography of a Marriage. Houghton Mifflin Harcourt. ( 2003).

[783] John Spencer-Churchill ( 1909-1992). Painter and sculptor. See Roberts, Brian. Randolph : A study of Churchill's son. Hamish Hamilton ( 1984) and Spencer Churchill, John . A Churchill Canvas. Little Brown. ( 1961),

[784] Current biography Year Book. V5. 1945. There are several letters and notes in the Binghamton University Library Collection from Johnnie to Tilly covering the period 1939-1975.

[785] Clarissa Spencer Churchill ( born 1920) Widow of Anthony Eden, British Prime Minister 1955-57.

[786] John Sutro ( 1903-1985). Best known for his films 49th Parallel ( 1949) and The Way Ahead ( 1944). He worked with Roman Polanski on several films and retired to Monte Carlo. To raise money for the war effort in WW2 Sutro and Cecil Beaton produced Bee Herbert ( Countess of Pembroke's ) pantomime 'Heil Cinderella', to much acclaim at London's Fortune Theatre.

[787] Sutro coined the phrase 'Wavian' ( to describe Waugh's style ). He was involved with the likes of Harold Acton, Robert Byron, Bryan Guinness, Hugh Lygon, Brian Howard, Elizabeth Ponsonby and Nancy Mitford. Sutro took part in numerous fancy dress balls in the 1930s ( often as Master of Ceremonies, See Sunday Times report off 11 July 1937, on the 'Anti Dud' Ball at the Dorchester ) and was on friendly terms with all of Cecil Beaton's crowd including Michael Duff, Lady Elizabeth Paget and Rex Whistler.

[788] See Dalley, Jan. Diana Mosley. Knopf ( 2000).

[789] In 1935 Sutro was part of the group ( staying at Ashcombe) with Cecil Beaton, including Lady Caroline Paget, Lady Juliet Duff and John Betjeman who made the amateur film The Sailor's Return. See Pepper Terence and Beaton Cecil. Beaton Portraits. Yale University Press ( 2004).

[790] Obituary The Times, 21 June, 1985. John Sutro's large collection of personal papers are at the Bodleian Library, Oxford. The material on Tilly is dated after her death. There are several letters from Sutro to Tilly in the Binghamton University Libraries Collection.

[791] Sir Harold Acton (1904-1994). British writer and dilettante.

[792] See Acton, Harold, Chaney Edward and Ritchie, Neil. Oxford China and Italy . Writings in honour of Sir Harold Acton on his eightieth birthday. Florence, 5 July 1984. Distribuzione. Passigi Editori. ( 1984).

[793] Patrick Balfour, 3rd Baron Kinross ( 1904-1976). Writer, Journalist and Diplomat. Although married Patrick Kinross was a homosexual.

[794] Ruben Mamoulian ( 1897-1987). Russian born American film director.

[795] The Fresno Bee The Republican, 17 November 1936 reported " Tilly Losch is Ruben Mamoulian's newest girl friend".

[796] Corsicana Daily Sun, 21 June, 1937.

[797] The Fresno Bee The Republican. 18 November, 1936. Louella Parsons column.

[798] Joseph Schenck ( 1878-1961(. Russian born film executive. Some time Chairman of 20th Century Fox.

[799] Harrisburg Telegraph. 7 June, 1937.

[800] Ernst Lubitsch ( 1892-1947). German born American Producer, Film Director and Screenwriter.

[801] Weill, Kurt. Speak Low ( When you Speak Love ) : The Letters of Kurt Weill and Lotte Lenya. University of California Press. ( 1997) Letter of Lenya ( in New York ) to Weill in Hollywood 4 May 1938.

[802] Howe, LeAnne, Markowitz Harvey, Cummings Denise, K. Seeing Red— Holywood's Pixeled Skins. American Indians and Film. MSU Press. ( 2013).

[803] See Tuska, Jon. Encounters with filmmakers. Greenwood Press ( 1991).

[804] John Gunther ( 1901-1970) American writer and journalist. Famous for his 'Inside' books. Gunther's biographer Ken Cuthbertson gives a long string of beautiful women that Gunther dated, including Tilly. His usual haunt was various New York Clubs.

[805] Cuthbertson, Ken. Inside. The Biography of John Gunther. e-book ( 2002).

[806] William Lawrence Shirer (1904-1993). American born writer and historian. Successful author of The Rise and Fall of Third Reich ( 1960). He was a foreign correspondent in Nazi Germany working for the Chicago Tribune in Paris, London and Vienna. He was transferred to Berlin in 1934 by which time he was working for Universal News Service, he later ( when back safely in USA ) published his Berlin diaries. Around the same time he met Tilly and became besotted by her ( having seen her on stage several times in London ). Twice married, his second wife was a Russian émigré. There is a box of 99 letters from Shirer to Tilly in Binghamton University Libraries covering the years 1943-1974.

[807] See Shirer, William Lawrence. 20th century Journey: A native's return, 1945-1988. Simon and Schuster. ( 1990).

[808] Ibid.

[809] Ibid.

[810] There are three pages in Shirer's book "20th century Journey: A native's return, 1945-1988." Simon and Schuster. ( 1990) given to his affair with Tilly, told with affection and love.

[811] John Brahm ( 1893-1982). Actor and Film Director

[812] Carnarvon [ Earl of ] Ermine Tales. Weidenfeld & Nicolson. ( 1980).

[813] According to Hugh Montgomery-Massingberd and David Watkin in " The London Ritz: A Social and Architectural History" Aurum Press ( 1980) Porchey was a close friend of Aly, and advised him about how he could increase his sexual prowess, based on techniques Porchey learned in Egypt.

[814] Ethel Margaret Whigham ( 1912-1993) The Notorious Duchess of Argyll. http://www.nickelinthemachine.com/2008/10/mayfair-the-duchess-of-argyll-and-the-headless-man-polaroids/

[815] The Times, 9 July 1931.

[816] Ross Benson ( 1948-2005). Award winning journalist. He was among the hacks who occupied the exalted position of William Hickey on the Daily Express. He later had his own gossip column.

[817] The 7th Earl did not enjoy being featured in the gossip columns or having his family mocked. In 1994 Ross Benson reported " Carnarvon [ 7th Earl ] ..once threatened to do to me what he does to his horses ( but using a pair of rusty shears)". See Daily Express 8 August 1994.

[818] Logansport Pharos-Tribune) Indiana. 24 March 1954.

[819] Cited by Stephane Groueff (1922-2006) writer and journalist.

[820] Fox. James. White Mischief. Vintage (1998).

[821] Private source – refer to Author. Any child resulting was registered under the name ' Digweed'.

[822] Correspondence between the Author and CL, 2013.

[823] Cited in the London Evening Standard 11 February, 2002.

[824] The Times, 17 May, 1956.

[825] National Archives, Kew contains the War Diaries of the Household Cavalry Regiment in the series WO169 and WO 170. The author has gleaned at WO 170/835 (covering April-September 1944). Lord Porchester is listed as a member of the Regiment.

[826] Princess Margaret's inner circle included Colin Tennant, the Marquis of Blandford, Lord Ogilvy, Mark Bonham-Carter, the Earl of Dalkeith and Billy Wallace.

[827] Oliver Malcolm Wallop (1905-1980) Father of Jean Wallop, 7th Countess of Carnarvon. Oliver's first wife was Jean Moore Wallop (1908-1943), mother of Jean Wallop.

[828] Carolyn Towle Wallop. (1906-1972). Step mother of Jean Wallop, 7th Countess of Carnarvon.

[829] Valley Morning Star, 8 January 1956. Another phrase used was "one of Margaret's beaus".

[830] Edward John Wallop (1930-2000). Committed suicide.

[831] Porchester was a member of Hampshire County Council from 1954 to 1965 and chairman of the new Hampshire County Council from 1974 to 1977. He was also active within the association of county councils. He was chairman of the south east economic planning council from 1971 to 1979 and later a member from 1989 until March 2011. See The Guardian 11 October 2001

[832] Corsicana Daily Sun, 27 February 1956

[833] Correspondence between the Author and CB, a close friend of Lord Porchester, later 7th Earl.

[834] Jebb Miles [Editor]. The Diaries of Cynthia Gladwyn. Constable. (1995).

[835] Montgomery-Massingberd. Great Houses of England and Wales. Laurence King Publishing. (1994)

[836] Almina's godson Tony Leadbetter recalls that Porchey suffered 'retention' and had an inability to pass urine. He was operated on, briefly recovered and suffered a relapse. Lord Porchester kept in touch with the US daily during August 1958.

[837] On 4 September 1958, Lord Porchester left on the Queen Elizabeth liner for New York, to see how his father was progressing. He later accompanied Porchey home to England.

[838] The Oneonta Star (New York), 4 April 1962.

[839] The Times records "On 26 Feb 1963 at his home Jac Wendell, aged 67 beloved husband of Eileen and adored father of Jac and June. Funeral service at St Simon Zeloter, Milner St, SW1 followed by cremation." Eileen died in 1983. The Times records "On 18 Sept 1983 at Westbury House, West Meon peacefully after a long illness Eileen Victoria beloved mother of Jac and June and a dearly loved grandma.

Funeral at Church of the Holy Rood, Holybourne near Alton, Hants." There is a memorial stone to Jac and Eileen at Highclere Cemetery.

[840] The Grand Surprise. The Journals of Leo Lerman. Edited by Stephen Pascal. Alfred A Knopf. (2007).

[841] Martha Graham (1894-1991) American dancer and choreographer.

[842] Jackson says " Tilly had come with a friend, dance historian Parmenia Miguel Eckstrom (1908-1989), to the first American screening of *Die Puppenfee* (presented by Susan Braun's Dance Films Association, it was the Wien Film production, shot prior to the ballet's 1983 authentic restoration). Either the editor of Dance News, Anatole Chujoy (1894 – 1969), or critic Walter Sorell (1905 – 1997) had alerted Losch to the event."

[843] Jackson, George. Conversations with Three Dancers from the Day before Yesterday: DanceView 28 (4), Autumn 2011.

[844] Leo Lerman (1914-1994). American writer and editor.

[845] Grand Surprise. The Journals of Leo Lerman. Edited by Stephen Pascal. Alfred A Knopf. (2007).

[846] Jackson, George. Conversations with Three Dancers from the Day before Yesterday: DanceView 28 (4), Autumn 2011

[847] Mosley, Charlotte. The between Six Sisters. HarperCollins UK. ( 2012)

[848] Devonshire. Deborah. Wait For Me! John Murray. ( 2011).

[849] Mosley, Charlotte. The between Six Sisters. HarperCollins UK. ( 2012)

[850] See Laura, Duchess of Marlborough's" Laughter From A Cloud". Weidenfeld and Nicolson. (1980). NB Six weeks before Bert Marlborough's death he married Laura Charteris, ( 1915-1990). Four times married, her second husband was William Humble Eric Ward, ( 1894-1969) 3rd Earl of Dudley, ( known as Eric, he was the widower of Lady Rosemary Levenson Gower, killed in the Meopham Air Disaster). Eric was a friend of Tilly Losch in England and America. Laura was a sister of James Bond author, Ian Fleming, and a former wife of Tilly's young lover of youth, John Spencer Churchill, as well being the mistress of cousin Randolph.

[851] Anne Jennings Johnston later married William Dawes Miller in 1972.

[852] Interviews between the Author and Tony Leadbetter.

[853] Almina's copy of booklet on the service is held by Tony Leadbetter.

[854] Daily Express, 30 June 1970.

[855] Ibid.

[856] Hon. George Esmond Dominic Elliot-Murray-Kynynmound born 1931.

[857] See Daily Express, 24 May, 1971.

[858] Correspondence between the Author and CB, a close friend of Lord Porchester, later 7th Earl.

[859] As recently as the summer of 2013, The Queen's horse *Estimate* who the Ascot Gold Cup. Her horse *Dunfermline* won the Epsom Oaks and the St Leger in her Jubilee Year, 1977.

[860] Lees- Milne, James and Bloch Michael. Diaries. 1971-1983. John Murray. (2008).

[861] Wyndham, Horace. Chorus to Coronet. British Technical and General Press. ( 1951).

[862] Charles MacArthur (1895-1956). American playwright and husband of the actress Helen Hayes. He worked in Hollywood in the period 1928-1932 and knew Tilly from this time onwards.

[863] Hecht, Ben. Charlie: the improbable life and times of Charles MacArthur. Harper (1957)

[864] E-mail exchanges between the Author and Joyce Sachs, 2013.

[865] The Grand Surprise. The Journals of Leo Lerman. Edited by Stephen Pascal. Alfred A Knopf. (2007).

[866] Ibid.

[867] Ibid.

[868] See Purser, Philip: Where Is he Now? The extraordinary Worlds of Edward James. Quartet Books, London (1978).

[869] George Weidenfeld, Baron Weidenfeld of Chelsea (born 1919). Publisher and philanthropist.

[870] Letter dated 30 July 2013 from Lord Weidenfeld to the Author following his enquiry.

[871] William ( Billy) Keenan Blackburn Hamilton. ( Died 6 July 1988 ). London publicist and close friend of Tilly.

[872] Newspaper sources ( See Daily Mail, 3 December, 1976) indicate that Tilly left behind a considerable amount of jewellery. She left her London flat and contents to her friend Billy Hamilton.

[873] Daily Express, 3 November 1983.

[874] Cited by Irene Vera Young ( 1901-1964) She opened her school of the German Dance in Sydney, New South Wales, in July 1933 after spending seven years in New York studying modern dance.

[875] Pincher, Chapman. Pastoral Symphony. A Bumpkin's Tribute to Country Joys. Swan Hill ( 1993).

[876] Daily Express, 27 October 1983.

[877] Daily Express, 17 July 1983.

[878] Ibid.

[879] Daily Express, 24 September 1987.

## The Research : A Note from the Author

This book aims to add further information to what is already covered in my *four* existing publications on members of the Herbert/ Carnarvon family of Highclere Castle, Hampshire, England.

There is already coverage on Catherine Wendell and Tilly Losch, the two Sixth Countesses of Carnarvon, in *The Life and Secrets of Almina Carnarvon,* my biography of the Fifth Countess, published in 2011.

The latest new title began to emerge as a possible project upon my discovery of a public exhibition about Catherine Wendell held from 5

October 2012  at the Portsmouth Athenaeum, New Hampshire, USA. This museum is one of the main archival centres who hold a good collection of the personal  papers of the Wendell family, and which is supplemented with a further substantial deposit of the same family's records at Harvard University.

I contacted Ronan Donohoe, the curator at the Portsmouth Athenaeum in charge of staging the Catherine Wendell exhibition centred on her early life in *Willowbank*, Kittery and *Frostfields*, near Portsmouth, New Hampshire, USA.  Initially, I  only intended to establish whether there was any material held there on Almina, as I was at the same time working on a revision of my Almina  biography. I was pleased to receive a reply from Ronan  with a reference to Catherine's cousin Arthur Wendell's possible contact with Almina, during the  years of the 20th century when he spent time in London with his wife and daughter,  all of which was new information to further research and appraise.

During the  early  part  of  2012,  I  was  forced  to  bring  some  other research, for a planned book on the dancer Tilly Losch to a close and abandon a working title *The Dancing Countess of Carnarvon: Tilly Losch & Her Husbands.*   This  was  because  I  did  not  consider  it worthwhile proceeding with anything about Tilly  without first drawing on the very substantial archival holdings on her at Binghamton University Library, New York State, USA.

When I became aware that a book was in progress about Catherine Wendell, from Highclere's own publications providing coverage of their chatelaines, I decided to wait until I saw the pre-publicity to follow. When this detail emerged I was confused by the outline sketch, which appeared to be at variance with chronology and facts that had been provided to me by a number of informants about Catherine when I was researching into Almina's life and times.

I tested some points with my earlier informants in letters and personal contact  and  e-mailed  Ronan  Donohoe   again  at  the  Portsmouth Athenaeum. This led to further questions and more research being done.  I concluded that there was scope for a book about Catherine, her early life and an appraisal of her marriage to Henry Herbert, Sixth Earl of Carnarvon, always known as 'Porchey'. I decided that the book could also have a similar approach on Tilly Losch and her time as the Sixth Countess of Carnarvon as well as featuring her life as a whole.

During my previous research on Tilly I was very fortunate to make two important contacts (both in the USA). These were George Jackson, a ballet critic, who met Tilly and had written about her; and Joyce Sachs, an American playwright, who had work of her own in progress about Tilly, and whose husband's family was related to Tilly. Moreover, Joyce had spent time at Binghamton University Library and tapped into Tilly's letters and diaries.

Also during 2013, I exchanged several e-mails with the archivists at Binghamton, as a full scale revamp of the search catalogue on the Tilly Losch Collection was underway. With new advances made on my accumulation of material on Tilly I considered that a reasonable retrospective on her personal life and work could be swept into the new book. I judged that my approach to Tilly ( alongside the Catherine Wendell tale ) would not be too much diminished by the exclusion of material from her collection of papers in Binghamton, especially as she has no published biography.

A work plan was devised and a time frame to produce a book of around 100,000 words, and following a chronological path in the lives of the two Sixth Countesses.

The research and draft have been compiled with considerable help. Ronan Donohoe has been generous with his time and provision of a variety of documents, letters and newspaper items.   My dear friend Diana Fitzpatrick has carried out some painstaking researches of countless boxes at the Portsmouth Athenaeum on my behalf.

Through Ronan I was introduced to Charles W Wendell, a collateral of the Wendell New York-Portsmouth family. Charles  provided me  with insight into the Wendell family origins and   helpful documentation through his links with the Holland Society of New York  together with some outstanding  good will  in making enquiries on my behalf around New York landmarks associated with Catherine's family, including Calvary Church   and   The Players Club, the theatre group, where

Catherine's father Jacob was a member, as was his brother, Evert. Charles also advised me about the John Singer Sargent portrait of Catherine's grandmother, Mary B Wendell.

Concurrently with the researches in the USA  I launched enquiries across a number of people and places, where I hoped some information threads might be held. A number of  members of the British peerage, some of them remarkable  nonagenarians ( and who knew Catherine or Porchey or close family members ) have been very helpful with anecdotes and/ or information and comments by letter and over the telephone.   For the sake of confidentiality  ( and to prevent any embarrassment to the people concerned ) I have *not* identified *all* these informants by name, but the back-up documentation has not been erased, and remains accessible in due course in archival deposit for any verification required.

I note with disappointment that some people approached did not respond or declined to be interviewed.   Those who did respond or agreed to be interviewed in person are generally indicated in the End Notes Section of the book, albeit with only initials. There has been exceptional input by the remarkable Tony Leadbetter, who knew Catherine and Porchey at close quarters, as his aunt and mother were housekeepers of Almina, Countess of Carnarvon over more than thirty years. Tony has been closely involved in the development of the new book. He had allowed me to interview him on several occasions especially to update my knowledge of his still vivid and loving memories of Catherine. Tony has also provided ( as a State Registered Nurse  in the army  and at  St Cadoc's a psychiatric hospital, Caerleon) a professional insight into the use of barbiturate and  sedative drugs and the treatment of  the alcoholism over the course of the 20th century.

Much of the archival and retrieval from  books and documents for the purpose of the citations in the End Notes, has been  carried out at the British Library, London, and at National Archives, Kew.  Site visits have been made to Highclere Cemetery, Sandridge village near St Albans, Sandridgebury,  St Albans and to Sandridge Church, Sandridge, St Albans, the photographs taken at these sites are from the Authors' own collection.

The photographs otherwise used in the book are from the Leadbetter Collection (originally the property of Almina, Countess of Carnarvon, but gifted in her lifetime to Anthony (Tony) Leadbetter). Other images have been uplifted from the albums of Alice Butler (again now a part of the Leadbetter Collection). Other images have been captured from public sources on the Internet.

## Thanks and Acknowledgments

I owe considerable thanks to many people. I am grateful to Monty Dart and Bernard Pearson for their comments and input on reading the early draft manuscript, and Bernard Byrom for the more incisive edit of the final text. I am indebted to Tom Dart for the design of the covers of the book and painstaking work on editing photographs. Monty Dart has tirelessly copied many hundreds of images in National Archives and transcribed from many dozens of books to assist my researches.

I also wish to thank additionally Bernard Byrom (for transport arrangements); Revd. Em Coley ( Sandridge); Mary Collins ( Holland Society of New York); Tom Dart ( Highclere travel and photographs ); Ronan Donohoe and colleagues at the Portsmouth Athenaeum, New Hampshire, USA; Diana Fitzpatrick, Maine, USA; George Jackson, USA; David Lake ( Sandridgebury); Gwent Family History Society ( Kew Trips); Michael Lewis ( for local knowledge of Newbury and Highclere Estate ); Tony Leadbetter ( for interviews, tape recording on Catherine, original photographs and notes on Tilly Losch and Porchey Carnarvon); Newport Hard of Hearing Club ( book launch );New York Historical Society; Christine Nutton ( Sandridge); Richard Ormond; Chris Reynolds ( Genealogy in Herefordshire and for a photograph of Sandridgebury ); Bernard Pearson ( Name Index) Joyce Sachs, USA; Charles W Wendell, USA and Christopher Wilson.

## Author Declaration

The author graciously acknowledges the various authors of material quoted in the text and End Notes and their respective publishers and copyright holders. Such quotes used have been kept modest and incidental. Care has been taken *not* to exceed the spirit of the copyright principles laid down in the respective *"Permissions and Fair Dealing"* guidelines in terms of the limits under the criteria for *"the purposes of criticism or review"*.

Among the public records to acknowledge is the material in Crown Copyright extracted from National Archives, Kew. He also wishes to acknowledge with thanks the use of the following websites: Abe Books; Amazon; Ancestry; Binghamton University Archives and Newsletter; British Library; Find My Past; Holland Society of New York; National Archives, Kew; National Library of Australia; National Library of Wales; New York Historical Society; Newspaper Archive.com; Papers Past; Probate Registry, London; and US Library of Congress.

If the Author has missed out any other person, institution or web site he will be happy to remedy this on any reprint of the book. Any errors in the text etc are the Author's and his alone. He welcomes corrections, with sources and any additional data to include in any future reprints of the book. Finally, he records considerable thanks to his wife Perry and their family and apologies for all the disruption, by necessity, compiling a book creates by day and night.

### *About The Author William Cross*

William Cross (Will) spent 28 years as a Civil Servant, in London. He took early retirement in July 2005 to concentrate on writing and research. His roots are Scottish; his family origins are in Erskine, Renfrewshire and Kilmaronock, Loch Lomondside. Will was brought up in a small coal-mining village in Lanarkshire. After schooldays in Scotland he studied at the Universities of London and Southampton. He now lives in Wales. A Fellow of the Society of Antiquaries of Scotland since 1984, he regularly lectures on Scottish history topics and the Morgan Women of Tredegar House. Will is a Member of the Society of Authors. He is married with two grown up sons and two grandchildren. Contact Will by email: williecross@aol.com

## Copyright William Cross, 2013.
### This book is published by
### William P Cross
### Book Midden Publishing
### 58 Sutton Road
### NewportGwent
### South Wales
### NP19 7JF, United Kingdom

### Other Titles from Book Midden Publishing

*These titles are written by William Cross*

Not Behind Lace Curtains: The Hidden World of Evan, Viscount Tredegar. ISBN 9781985914210

The Life and Secrets of Almina Carnarvon: A Candid Biography of Almina, 5th Countess of Carnarvon. 3rd Edition. ISBN 9781905914081

Lady Carnarvon's Nursing Homes: Nursing the Privileged in Wartime and Peace. ISBN 9781905914036

The Dustbin Case: Dennistoun versus Dennistoun ISBN 9781905914043

Lordy! Tutankhamun's Patron As A Young Man. ISBN 9781905914050

*These titles are written by Monty Dart and William Cross*

A Beautiful Nuisance by Monty Dart and William Cross.
ISBN 9781905914104

Aspects of Evan by Monty Dart and William Cross
ISBN 9781905914159

Other Titles

Daphne's Story: The Long Journey from the Red Brick Building by Daphne Condon. ISBN 9781905914128

Steaming Light: by Bernard Pearson. ISBN 9781905914135

Who Killed Dripping Lewis? By Monty Dart ISBN 9781905914199

Forthcoming Titles from Book Midden Publishing

The Five Lady Tredegars By Monty Dart and William Cross.
ISBN 9781905914203

The Abergavenny Witch Hunt of 1942: A full account of a case of the persecution of over 20 gay men in 1942. By William Cross.
ISBN 9781905914227

To Seanie, With Love. By Greggorie Douglas and William Cross.
ISBN 9781905914166

Contact Book Midden by e-mail williecross@aol.com